TWELVE THOUSAND YEARS

TWELVE THOUSAND YEARS

American Indians in Maine

Bruce J. Bourque

With contributions by Steven L. Cox and Ruth H. Whitehead

UNIVERSITY OF NEBRASKA PRESS

Lincoln and London

Publication of this volume was assisted by a grant from the Libra Foundation.

∞

Library of Congress Cataloging-in-Publication Data

Bourque, Bruce J. (Bruce Joseph)
    Twelve thousand years: American Indians in Maine / Bruce J. Bourque, with contribu-
tions by Steven L. Cox and Ruth H. Whitehead.
        p.   cm.
    Includes bibliographical references and index.
    ISBN 0-8032-1310-7 (cloth: alk. paper)
    1. Indians of North America—Maine—History. 2. Indians of North America—Maine—
Antiquities. 3. Maine—Antiquities. I. Cox, Steven L., 1947– II. Whitehead, Ruth Holmes.
III. Title.

E78.M2 B684 2001
974.1—dc21
                                                                        00-064779

CONTENTS

ILLUSTRATIONS

PREFACE

This book is a product of museum anthropology. It grew out of plans for a comprehensive long-term exhibition on Native history that opened at the Maine State Museum in 1991. Two decades earlier, as I was building the collections of the then new museum and beginning research for the exhibition, it quickly became apparent that our knowledge about the region's Native peoples was both limited and fragmentary. Though archaeologists had gained fascinating insights into specific prehistoric cultures, no coherent cultural history had yet been constructed. Little had been written about sixteenth-century Native peoples in the period following the arrival of Europeans beyond the observation that they had won their first two wars against English colonists, had lost the next three wars, and had ultimately been forced onto reservations in Maine and adjacent parts of Canada as settlers swarmed into their former homelands. Moreover, the history of the French who occupied what is now eastern Maine in the seventeenth and early eighteenth centuries was only beginning to be understood.

This situation has since changed due to a resurgence of archaeological and ethnohistorical research across the Northeast. Recent years have also seen a revival of interest in colonial history among both scholars and members of the public. In general, however, much of what has been written to date about the history of Native peoples in Maine has stressed continuity and tradition. As a result, these narratives have tended to be neither far-reaching nor dynamic in their outlook. Rather, they have been stories of adaptation and survival in which the driving forces of change are presented as largely external to Native communities. Thus, the precontact history of Maine has been understood as a more or less predictable sequence of responses to climatic change and to a challenging natural environment. Events of the historic period have been seen as driven solely by the European world system, with Native people doing their best to survive in an increasingly complex and stressful social climate.

Like other people interested in the Native history of the Maine region, I have learned a great deal from these stories, many of which are based on extensive and meticulous research. Nevertheless, I think these portrayals remain incomplete. In pursuing research for the museum exhibition and eventually for this book, I began to realize that Maine was hardly a culturally conservative backwater as has sometimes been implied. My view of the archaeological record, for example, has often chafed against notions of cultural continuity and the weight of tradition. Instead, to me, the archaeological evidence suggests flashes of rapid population expansion, cultural change, and innovation that strain against explanations based upon passive cultural adaptation. Likewise, Native responses to European arrival in the region make little sense when viewed as the reactions of conservative, tradition-bound tribal cultures. How can we best account for these deviations from expected behavioral constraints? As the chapters of this book will show, the complex and dynamic history of the region appears to be linked to two factors that have yet to be fully appreciated in the scholarship of North American Native culture and history.

In my view, the primary explanation for the cultural dynamism of the Maine region is the long-standing importance of the sea and the rich resources it provided. Certainly, a few Native cultures—such as the Paleo-Indians, the first humans to arrive in Maine some 10,500 years ago—may have made relatively little use of marine resources. Nevertheless, it is clear from the archaeological record that the lives of most Native peoples were strongly influenced by the sea. This was particularly true for groups living on the central and eastern Maine coast beginning about 7,000 years ago, when the near-shore waters of the Gulf of Maine began to attain the high levels of productivity for which they are historically known. Moreover, the sea retained its importance for Native people long after the initial period of European contact, as intrepid Native mariners quickly adopted the use of European sailing vessels to conduct trade and warfare far from their home territories.

A second factor that contributed to Maine's cultural dynamism is its geographic situation. Maine is positioned astride a larger geographic formation known as the Maritime Peninsula—a region stretching northeastward from the Maine–New Hampshire border across southeastern Quebec and the Maritime provinces as far as Cape Breton Island. The Maritime

Peninsula's role in Maine's cultural dynamism is paradoxical. To most archaeologists and historians, it has been regarded mainly as a culture area in the traditional sense of Americanist anthropology—that is, as an isolated geographic region whose ecological uniformity had a similar molding influence upon all Native groups that have occupied it.

On one level, this conventional view is accurate, since there clearly were recognizable cultural patterns shared by contemporaneous peoples throughout the Peninsula during different time periods. However, the following chapters will show that there have also been many instances, during both the prehistoric and historic periods, where the supposedly isolating nature of the mountains and the sea do not appear to have presented obstacles to significant cultural contacts with much larger regions. Actually, the sea and especially its coastlines often seem to have facilitated interaction. The region's several large rivers no doubt also played an important role in this regard for they provided ready access to the Gulf of St. Lawrence and its populations. As a result, powerful cultural influences from the St. Lawrence region are periodically evident in the prehistoric record of Maine. Furthermore, during the early historic period, written accounts mention the presence of Native people from Maine trading and fighting alongside Algonquins in the St. Lawrence River region and far beyond it.

An important theme in much of what follows, therefore, is that populations of the Maritime Peninsula have many times been caught up in faraway events to a much greater extent than has been generally appreciated. The most obvious and generally accepted instance is that of the Paleo-Indians, who are described in Chapter 1. They entered Maine as a result of an explosive expansion of population from western North America that began around 11,500 years ago and reached Nova Scotia less than a millennium later. In more recent times, ties are evident with regions as distant as northern Labrador, the Great Lakes, and the Savannah River in Georgia. Thus, during different time periods, each of these far-flung regions has something important to tell us about Native life on the Maritime Peninsula. For example, Chapter 2 describes beautiful lance tips made of striking translucent quartzite that were buried with the dead in Maine's 4,000-year-old "Red Paint" but that originated 1,500 kilometers to the north on the northern Labrador coast. At the same time, beautifully crafted spear tips from Maine were carried northward, across the Gulf of St. Lawrence, to northern Newfoundland, where they too are buried with the dead.

Chapter 3 presents another example of the far-ranging prehistoric interaction: a small burial mound discovered recently near Halifax, Nova Scotia. The mound contained remarkable artifacts made about 2,400 years ago by people of the Adena culture in Ohio, over 1,500 kilometers to the west. Similar artifacts have been found in Maine as well, although not yet in a burial mound. Finally, there is one incontrovertible piece of evidence that Maine Native people were aware of the Norse who visited Newfoundland and Labrador during the eleventh century: a Norse penny minted between A.D. 1066 and 1085 and recovered archaeologically at a coastal Maine site along with several Native artifacts from the far north.

Connections between the Maritime Peninsula and the larger world are also evident during the historic period, particularly during the seventeenth and eighteenth centuries, when Iroquois-attacks devastated groups living as far west as the Great Lakes region. Recent research has provided sophisticated new understandings of European and Indian conflicts in this region during the colonial era, but, as the final chapters point out, to date no study gives adequate consideration to the role Native peoples of the Maritime Peninsula played there.

This book draws upon the disciplines of archaeology and ethnohistory. The former involves the study of prehistoric cultures mainly through their material remains, while the latter uses written documents to study Native life during the historic or "postcontact" period, which in this case began around A.D. 1600. For the prehistoric period, Steven Cox and I have endeavored wherever possible to include references to the latest archaeological data, some of it as yet unpublished. For the historic period, Ruth Whitehead and I have also consulted numerous sources not previously brought to bear upon matters of regional Native history, including those in several American, Canadian, British, and French archives. These sources have enabled us to clarify certain issues of long-standing interest. Chapters 2 and 3 and 5 through 9 include distillations from some of my earlier published work and from a manuscript now in preparation that focuses exclusively upon Native life during the postcontact era. The latter is coauthored by historian Edwin Churchill, who has helped fill in the English side of that complex story. Nevertheless, both the prehistoric and historic sections are works-in-progress, sure to need revision as research continues.

ACKNOWLEDGMENTS

A great many people provided valuable assistance in producing this book. Chief among them are Robert Lewis, who photographed archaeological materials and organized the other illustrations, and Shirlene Gosline, who volunteered for the complex task of obtaining permission to publish many of the historic images that illustrate these pages. The manuscript benefited greatly from the editorial talents of Judith Terry, the cartography of Richard Kelly, and the design ideas of Donald Bassett.

I would like to thank several colleagues who provided information on archaeological sites and historical events and personalities that were unfamiliar to me, or who read all or parts of the manuscript. These include Robert Funk, George Hammell, Nathan Hamilton, Bruce Jamieson, Laurie LaBar-Kidd, James Leamon, Charles Martijn, Moira McCaffrey, Alvin Morrison, James Petersen, Brian Robinson, David Sanger, and Frank Siebert, whom I wish had lived to see this book published. Arthur Spiess provided numerous faunal analyses, as well as access to several unpublished site reports from the files of the Maine Historic Preservation Commission.

I would also like to thank the Reference Departments of Ladd Library, Bates College, and the Maine State Library, Augusta, for their assistance in tracking down several obscure but informative publications. Harold McGhee graciously provided Ruth Whitehead with hard-to-find source material and encouragement for her ambitious undertaking for this book. Jim Burant introduced both Ruth and me to the wonderful collection of Native images held by the National Archives of Canada. This project was significantly enhanced by generous financial support from the Libra Foundation.

INTRODUCTION:
THE PREHISTORIC PAST

Continuity and Connectedness

AFTER AN EARLY START in the 1860s, Maine archaeology had lapsed into near dormancy by the 1920s. When interest in Maine archaeology revived during the 1970s, a legacy of questions remained: When did humans first arrive in the region? How important was the sea to its inhabitants? What was the relationship between Maine's famous "Red Paint" cemeteries and its ubiquitous shell middens? What was the relationship between Maine's prehistoric people and those elsewhere in North America, and what is the connection between Maine's prehistoric people and Native peoples still living in Maine? Armed with the results of nearly three decades of modern archaeological research, these are among the questions we try to answer in this book.

Archaeologists have now achieved a considerable degree of consensus regarding the broad patterns of regional cultural history in northeastern North America. However, there are still frequent disagreements about how and to what degree these patterns relate to each other in both space and time. Such disagreements are often ostensibly focused on other issues. How important, for example, are long, elegantly shaped lance tips of ground slate versus small-stemmed projectile points in determining cultural connectedness throughout the Northeast forty-five hundred years ago? Does the apparently sudden appearance of a new pottery style signal the arrival of a new population? Does evidence of a long continuum of similar maritime adaptation indicate a stable population or merely the best strategy for any of several successive groups living on the coast? Granting that imprecise data can leave considerable room for differing interpretations of such issues, the actual basis of these disagreements is often more deep-seated, stemming from differing views concerning spatial or temporal continuity versus discontinuity. Explicit recognition of this phenomenon—the tendency to interpret data in light of subjective "hunches" about continuity and discontinuity—will, I feel, increase awareness of the root source of disagreement: that of the potential for cultural dynamism in the prehistoric Northeast.

The endpoints of the spectrum concerning these hunches are widely divergent. On one hand, some regard the apparent spread of a new set of artifact styles from one region to another as merely the spread of new ideas from one resident population to another. They do so in the belief that once prehistoric peoples first moved into the Northeast, they stayed there, one generation leading to the next, slowly changing through the inexorable process of "adaptation." Such arguments are often bolstered by claims that the available archaeological data are insufficient to resolve the matter. On the other hand, some are inclined to regard at least some artifact styles as associated with specific populations, and their spread from one region to another as evidence for population movement. They do so in the belief that human populations around the world have often abandoned their homelands and migrated over long distances to new ones, and therefore that prehistoric population movements in the Northeast are likely to have occurred more than once. They are also inclined to interpret variation in the amount of archaeological evidence over time as perhaps reflecting variability in population size. To them, the extensive archaeological samples now available in the Northeast are good enough in some cases to address such issues of cultural connectedness and discreteness.[1]

The former "conservative" view has been the one favored by most North American archaeologists, especially those working in the Northeast, since the early 1960s. This is not surprising in the light of the many unfounded speculations about migration proposed by earlier generations of researchers who attempted to explain changes in the archaeological record. We have nevertheless argued the latter position in some cases, to challenge what we perceive as complacency regarding this issue and in order to keep hypotheses invoking migration on the table rather than have them peremptorily brushed aside as "old fashioned."[2]

Maine Archaeology Past and Present

This volume reflects a long tradition of archaeological research—one of the longest in the New World, in fact. That archaeology began so early in Maine is a result of the richness of its archaeological record, which, in turn, reflects three principal factors. The first two were touched upon in the preface: the Gulf of Maine and the many rivers that flow into it. For at least the past seven thousand years, the waters and shorelines of the Gulf have provided humans not only with opportunities for widespread cultural contacts but also with a substantial proportion of their subsistence needs, while the rivers—the Saco, Androscoggin, Kennebec, Penobscot, and St. John—have provided not only convenient routes for travel and communication over the entire Gulf of Maine drainage—which reaches almost to the Gulf of St. Lawrence—but also abundant aquatic resources. The third factor, accidents of preservation, have left intact a larger proportion of the archaeological record than in southern New England or the Maritimes. In southern New England, industrial, residential, and transportation development have caused extensive terrain alteration, which has obliterated much of the prehistoric record, while to the northeast, along the Bay of Fundy—the site of some of the world's highest tidal ranges—coastal erosion has taken an extensive toll. It should be added, however, that our understanding of Maritimes prehistory awaits the availability of greater resources for archaeologists working there.

It is not surprising that as modern archaeology began to emerge from speculative antiquarianism around the middle of the nineteenth century, Maine became a focus of intense interest. The initial attractions were Maine's shell heaps, or shell middens as archaeologists now call them. Thousands of these shell-rich accumulations left by prehistoric people dot the shorelines of the world, and hundreds of impressive examples lie along the Maine coast. Early speculation favored the idea that shell middens were formed by unknown natural processes, but by 1839 Maine State geologist Charles T. Jackson was leaning toward the notion that at least some were of human origin. By the 1860s, the issue had been settled in favor of humans.[3] Maine's shell heaps were so impressive and numerous that during the 1860s, with the encouragement of the pioneering Harvard University naturalist Louis Agassiz and Jeffries Wyman—first director of the newly founded Peabody Museum of Archaeology and Ethnology there—began a series of excavations in Frenchman's and Casco Bays. With Agassiz's backing and the help of another of his protégés, Portland native Sylvester S. Morse, Wyman built a collection of artifacts and animal bones that he described before the Boston Society of Natural History and published in the *American Naturalist.*

Comparing Maine's shell heaps to the previously explored Kjoekkenmoeddings (kitchen middens) of Denmark, Wyman concluded incorrectly that "The shell-heaps we have studied yield nothing which indicates as high a degree of antiquity as those of the Old World."[4] Wyman was mistaken about the relative ages of the Maine and Danish shell middens probably because he shared the view common among early anthropologists and archaeologists that Native Americans were fairly recent arrivals from Siberia. Poor health forced Wyman to abandon his Maine research before he realized his error, and his subsequent research focused on the large shell mounds of the Florida coast. Morse also turned his attention elsewhere, eventually exploring shell middens in Japan and in the process earning recognition as the father of Japanese archaeology.[5]

In 1874 Frederick Ward Putnam succeeded Wyman as director at the Peabody and thereafter continued to provide institutional support for research in Maine. In May 1886 Putnam hired local postman Abram T. Garage to organize the excavation of a huge oyster-shell midden in Damariscotta known as "the Whaleback."[6] Then in 1892 Putnam hired Charles C. Willoughby, a commercial artist and talented amateur archaeologist from Augusta, to explore a different kind of site that had recently been discovered on the shores of Lake Alamoosook in Orland. The Lake Alamoosook site included several pits filled with beautifully made tools and large quantities of red ocher, a powdered form of the mineral hematite used for ceremonial purposes by prehistoric people around the world. This was the first of Maine's famed Red Paint cemeteries to receive professional attention, and a few years later Willoughby excavated another on the Union River in Ellsworth.

Willoughby's excavations were brilliantly carried out, and his 1898 monograph describing them remains a model of archaeological reporting. It is in these excavations that we can see the first clear evidence of what Putnam called "the (Peabody) Museum Method," which established the kinds of tight horizontal and vertical controls that characterize current field methodology in North America.[7] Willoughby's experiences with these sites led him to conclude that they were older than the shell middens, an idea generally borne out by later research. Putnam and Willoughby then thrust Maine prehistory into the spotlight at the 1893 World's Columbian Exposition held in Chicago, where Willoughby exhibited his Red Paint cemetery finds along with a marvelously accurate model illustrating the methods used in his Lake Alamoosook excavation.[8]

In 1866 Harvard's Peabody Museum became the first major "private sector" institution to address issues of American archaeology and anthropology. It was followed in 1879 by the creation of the Bureau of Ethnology in Washington, whose first director was John Wesley Powell, noted explorer of the Colorado River and later director of the United States Geological Survey.[9] One of the Bureau's major early accomplishments was determining that the great earth mounds of the Ohio Basin were built not by a vanished race of non-Indians, as was popularly believed, but by ancestors of the Native peoples who inhabited the region in historic times. Other work took Powell and his team across the continent, yet during the 1890s he devoted some effort to exploring Maine's shell heaps, in particular those near his summer home in Brooklin. There, in 1900 his associate Frank H. Cushing, another pioneer in American anthropology, had begun excavations in nearby shell middens, and in April, Powell joined him. Their undertaking ended, however, when Cushing suddenly died.[10]

Professional archaeology in Maine waned after Cushing's death. Willoughby's fieldwork in the area effectively ended when he was appointed director of the Peabody Museum upon Putnam's death in 1915. He continued to think about Maine, however, and in 1935 he published the still-influential *Antiquities of the New England Indians*. Minor efforts continued during the first decade of the century until 1912, when a major new force appeared. In that year, Warren K. Moorehead, director of the recently founded R. S. Peabody Foundation for Archaeology at Phillips Academy in Andover, Massachusetts, began a series of extensive surveys along Maine's rivers. Although he later conducted large excavations in coastal shell middens, most of Moorehead's work focused on Red Paint cemeteries.[11]

These cemeteries came to national attention for a second time in 1913, when Moorehead published his claim that the people responsible for them were a different, more ancient culture than the region's historic Algonquian-speaking peoples. This touched a nerve with many archaeologists who were still not prepared to accept the significant antiquity of any Native population. We now know, of course, that both Willoughby and Moorehead were right in their age estimates, but Moorehead fared poorly at first in the scholarly arguments that followed his publication. After Willoughby joined the debate, however, the profound differences between the Red Paint cemeteries and more recent burial patterns were established as incontrovertible.

Moorehead's interest in Maine declined after he published a report on his surveys in 1922, a period when American archaeologists were turning their attention from local research to more exotic venues. Like archaeologists of many regions of North America, Maine archaeology entered a period of relative inactivity that was to continue for decades. A few researchers persisted, however: during the 1920s, Walter B. Smith, a geologist at the University of Maine conducted research in the Penobscot Valley and Frenchman's Bay, and between the 1930s and the 1950s, occasional surveys and excavations were undertaken, primarily by the Robert Abbe Museum of Stone Age Antiquities, established at Bar Harbor in 1928, and by the R. S. Peabody Foundation.[12]

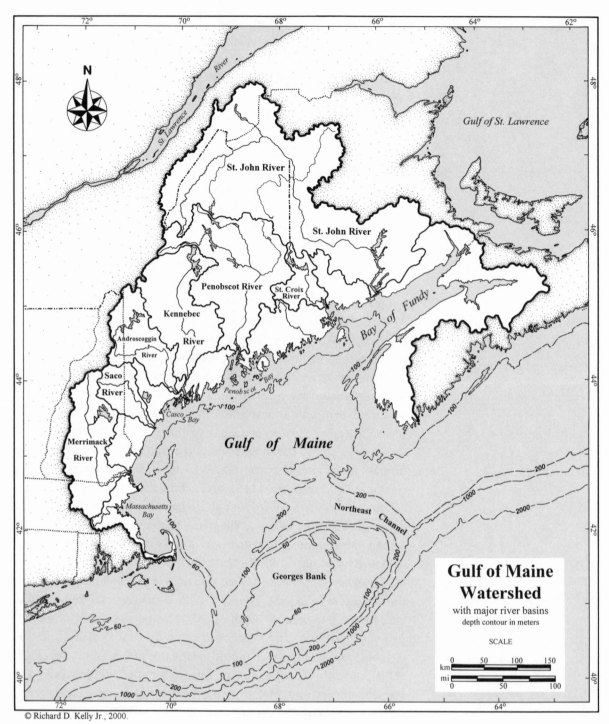

1-1. Gulf of Maine Watershed

The situation began to change in the mid-1960s as local institutions moved to develop Maine-oriented archaeological programs. In 1967 the University of Maine established an active field program, followed by the Maine State Museum in 1972. Added impetus came in the late 1970s and 1980s, as other campuses of the University of Maine system developed research programs. With their different emphases, these programs have made considerable headway in broadening our knowledge of the lives of Maine's ancient inhabitants. Another positive development has been federally mandated cultural resource management, which since the mid-1970s has provided a substantial boost to archaeological field budgets, resulting in a considerable increase in the scope of excavation. Prior to this program, archaeologists often selected sites according to personal preference; after it was introduced, new kinds of terrain had to be explored, and the results have been enlightening. Chief among the new kinds of sites encountered are those on flood plains that have had many successive encampments, each sealed in its own layer of sediment; these stratified sites have been especially helpful in allowing us to sort out cultural remains from different periods, which are often badly intermingled at shallower sites.[13]

Sources and Terminology

A Word about Sources Consulted

Because archaeologists study the material remains of past cultures, this volume relates human history mainly from a materialist perspective. In other words, the artifacts described here, even many from the postcontact era, are not used merely to illustrate a historical narrative based on other sources of information. Rather, they provide the actual foundation for our understanding of prehistory and even for much of history. Of course, archaeologists are also eager to glean insights provided by other sources, such as historic and ethnographic accounts, and we have relied heavily upon such accounts when applicable.

Like most disciplines, archaeology is jargon-laden. We have attempted to avoid using jargon in this book, but some special terms are required for clarity's sake. Starting at the simplest level, most readers understand that to an archaeologist an "artifact" is any object made or modified by humans. Less obvious is the meaning of the term "feature," which is simply an artifact that cannot be conveniently tucked into a bag for transport to the laboratory, such as the remains of a hearth composed of rocks and charcoal or a grave containing skeletal material and artifact offerings. Most

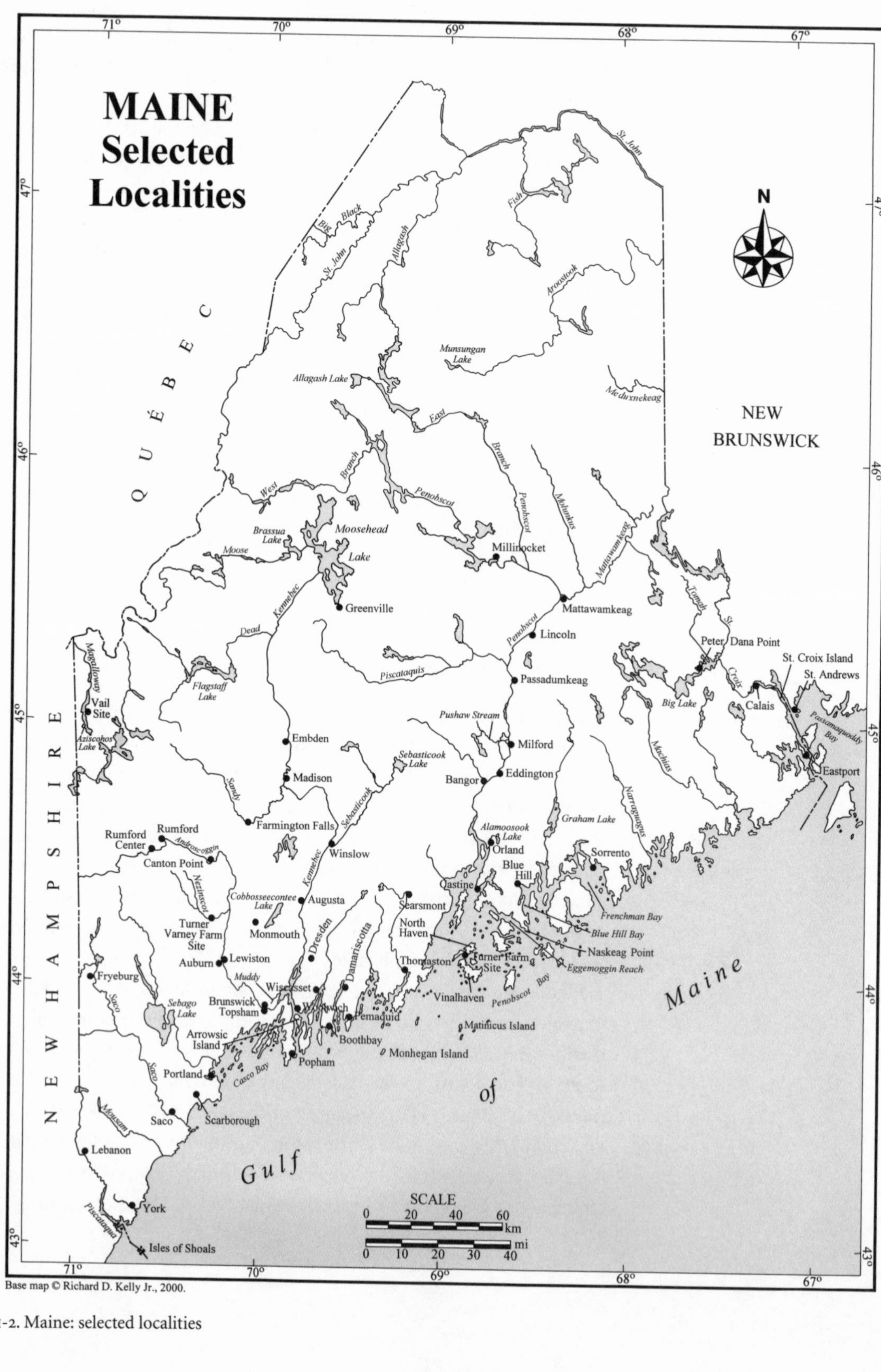
MAINE
Selected
Localities
N
QUÉBEC
NEW BRUNSWICK
NEW HAMPSHIRE
Gulf
of
Maine
71°
70°
69°
68°
67°
47°
46°
45°
44°
43°
St. John
Fish
Big
Black
St. John
Allagash
Aroostook
Munsungan Lake
Allagash Lake
Meduxnekeag
East
Branch
West
Branch
Penobscot
Brassua Lake
Moosehead
Lake
Moose
Millinocket
Penobscot
Molunkus
Mattawamkeag
Mattawamkeag
Greenville
Kennebec
Dead
Tomah
St. Croix
Peter Dana Point
St. Croix Island
St. Andrews
Lincoln
Penobscot
Passadumkeag
Piscataquis
Flagstaff Lake
Magalloway
Vail Site
Big Lake
Calais
Passamaquoddy Bay
Pushaw Stream
Milford
Embden
Sebasticook Lake
Eddington
Bangor
Eastport
Machias
Madison
Sandy
Aziscohos Lake
Farmington Falls
Sebasticook
Narraguagus
Graham Lake
Alamoosook Lake
Orland
Rumford
Rumford Center
Androscoggin
Canton Point
Winslow
Kennebec
Sorrento
Blue Hill
Castine
Nezinscot
Cobbosseecontee Lake
Augusta
Searsmont
Frenchman Bay
Blue Hill Bay
Turner Varney Farm Site
Monmouth
North Haven
Naskeag Point
Turner Farm Site
Eggemoggin Reach
Dresden
Damariscotta
Auburn
Lewiston
Thomaston
Fryeburg
Muddy
Wiscasset
Vinalhaven
Penobscot Bay
Sebago Lake
Saco
Brunswick
Topsham
Woolwich
Pemaquid
Matinicus Island
Arrowsic Island
Boothbay
Monhegan Island
Popham
Portland
Casco Bay
Saco
Mousam
Saco
Scarborough
Lebanon
York
Piscataqua
Isles of Shoals
SCALE
0 20 40 60
km
mi
0 10 20 30 40

Base map © Richard D. Kelly Jr., 2000.

1-2. Maine: selected localities

also understand what an archaeological site is, but when a site was occupied by more than one group, the archaeologist must attempt to sort out what was left by whom; the archaeological remains left by each group are called "components." Thus a site that was occupied by one group around five thousand years ago and by another around three thousand years ago would have two components. At a still higher level, North American archaeologists often employ two concepts to describe the cultures they are trying to reconstruct. The first is the "phase," which usually refers to a culture that occupied a fairly discrete range for a fairly brief period of time. The second is the "tradition," which conveys a sense of change within an ongoing cultural continuum. Thus if one phase gave way to another as a population changed culturally, those two phases would be linked in the same tradition in much the same way in which the modern West is regarded as part of the Judeo-Christian tradition. In practice, however, it must be admitted that archaeologists have not always employed these two concepts consistently, and we will sometimes be confronted with phases that cover large regions and traditions of very brief duration. Finally, dates used in the early chapters on prehistory are given in years before the present (B.P.), which by convention is set at A.D. 1950. This convention arose with the use of radiocarbon dating, which is briefly described below.

Later in this book, as we enter the historic period, we encounter terminological difficulties that should be summarized here in order to explain the choices we have adopted. What's in a name? Sometimes a great deal— for both ethnic groups and the larger society—the parties who, in a sense, negotiate ethnic identity through names.

At the most general level, Native North Americans have been referred to in scholarly publications as Aboriginal People or Native Americans—and, in Canadian contexts, "First Nations." These terms might suffice if it were not for the fact that there is an important distinction to be drawn between two groups: northern peoples of relatively recent arrival in North America and those living in lower latitudes, who probably arrived earlier. These are, respectively, the Eskimos and the Indians of common parlance. Members of the former group living in Canada, however, have adopted "Inuit" in place of Eskimo, while some of the latter group, on both sides of the border, wish to avoid the term Indian because it was imposed upon them by early Europeans who thought they had arrived in Asia rather than on a continent previously unknown to them. In the United States, this avoidance usually takes the form of adopting a "tribal" name specific to each group. But this strategy sometimes breaks down in a scholarly context because specific groups may not have remained stable in their locations, lan-

RADIOCARBON DATING

Central to the discussion of prehistory that follows are the ages of the various archaeological materials mentioned. Dating is a process that may seem mysterious to those not familiar with archaeology. In fact, it was nearly as mysterious to archaeologists until 1950, when a new technique called radiocarbon dating revolutionized the discipline by making it possible to determine the age of animal or plant tissue preserved in archaeological sites. Fortunately, samples of such preserved tissue, mainly in the forms of charcoal and animal bone, are relatively common in sites on the Maritime Peninsula, and our understanding of its prehistory is strongly dependent upon the dates they have produced.

Radiocarbon dating measures the ratio of the radioactive isotope ^{14}C to nonradioactive ^{12}C. This ratio has remained relatively constant in earth's atmosphere for many millennia because, while ^{14}C is constantly being created in the atmosphere, it is also disappearing due to radioactive decay. Because the two isotopes are almost chemically identical, they are incorporated by living organisms in a ratio that matches their ratio in the atmosphere. As long as an organism is alive and exchanging gas with the atmosphere through breathing or transpiration, the ^{14}C:^{12}C ratio remains constant. When the organism dies, gas exchange with the atmosphere effec-

tively ceases. Since ^{12}C is stable while ^{14}C is radioactive, the ^{14}C:^{12}C ratio begins to drop exponentially. It is worth emphasizing that the ratio is independent of the overall amount of carbon remaining in the material. It is for this reason that the ^{14}C:^{12}C ratio in a sample of organic material provides a useful measure of how long ago the organism died.[14]

A common method for determining this measurement is to generate carbon dioxide by burning the fragment and placing a sample of the gas, or one derived from it, into an instrument that can detect its rate of ^{14}C disintegration. For samples with the same number of carbon atoms, one generated from charcoal that is fifty-seven hundred years old will have lost half the ^{14}C it contained when living, and will thus register half the rate of ^{14}C disintegration of one generated from modern wood. A newer, more accurate technique, called accelerator mass spectroscopy (AMS) projects an ionized beam of carbon atoms past a magnet. Because atoms of ^{14}C are slightly more massive than those of ^{12}C, their path will be less deflected by the magnet, which makes it possible to determine the isotope ratios with great precision, even when a very small sample is used.[15] Although somewhat more expensive than conventional radiocarbon dating, AMS dating is rapidly gaining popularity among archaeologists.

guages, or demographic constitution through the period under discussion. The strategy can also founder because of the many meanings evoked by the term "tribe," which can refer to a local group with a unique culture and language, an anthropological construct situated developmentally between a band and a chiefdom, a group formally recognized by the United States Bureau of Indian Affairs (BIA), or a kind of culture less complex than a "civilization." The confusion has been considerably confounded in Canada by the adoption of the formerly anthropological term "band" to refer to officially recognized Native groups and in the United States to some BIA-recognized tribes.

Navigating these terminological riptides can be difficult. The terms we have employed generally reflect the context in which they are used, informed

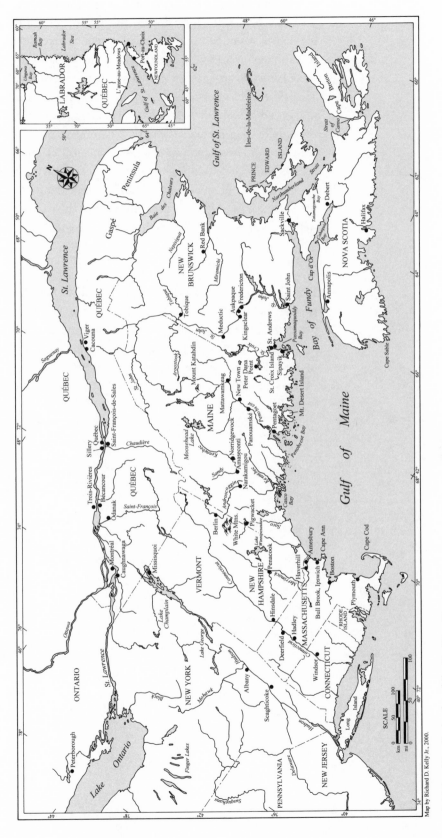

I-3. Maine, New England, and the Maritime Provinces

Map by Richard D. Kelly Jr. 2000.

by our best understanding of the data; generally, for the historic period, they are terms arising from documentary evidence. For the period prior to the French capitulation of Canada in 1760, we have often chosen French terminology over English because it is generally less geographically determined and reflects a greater intimacy with the region's Native populations. Thus the French might refer loosely to a "nation" or a "people" whose identity was not closely linked to place of residence, whereas the English generally employed group names strictly according to place of residence. However, as summarized in the preface to the historic chapters, even the French perspective changed during the seventeenth century as their understanding of ethnicity grew, and as the ethnic composition of Native communities changed. After 1760 we generally shift to the names of "tribes" as they were recognized by English colonial governments.

A Word about Geography

Central to much of what follows is the Gulf of Maine. Because Maine is part of "northern" New England, the Gulf of Maine coast is commonly perceived as trending south-to-north, when in fact, according to compass bearings, the portion of greatest concern to us actually trends more west-to-east. This is the geographical orientation we adopt, reserving the north-south axis mainly to explore distinctions between the coast and the interior.

I THE PALEO-INDIAN PERIOD
Steven L. Cox

The Great Warming

THE FIRST HUMAN inhabitants of the Americas—the ancestors of today's Indians—came to the New World from northeastern Asia many thousands of years ago. The story of their coming is closely tied to events that took place at the end of the last great Ice Age.

At the height of the glacial period, or Pleistocene epoch, northern North America was covered by a very thick layer of ice. In the east, the ice cap extended as far south as Pennsylvania and seaward to the edge of the continental shelf. The area that is now Maine lay beneath ice more than a mile thick. Much of the world's water was tied up in the glaciers, and this lowered global sea levels, causing the shallow bottom of the Bering Strait between Alaska and Siberia to emerge from the sea and form a land bridge between the continents. At its maximum, this bridge was more than 1,500 kilometers wide and provided a natural route for both animals and humans to expand their ranges into the New World.

Beringia—the name given to the vast region made up of northeastern Siberia, the land bridge and Alaska during the Pleistocene—remained largely unglaciated because there was too little precipitation in the region for glaciers to form. However, during the coldest periods of the Pleistocene, when the land bridge was at its most extensive, access from Alaska to the south may have been blocked by the expansion and coalescence of continental glaciers in western Canada. The arrival of humans in the Americas would therefore have depended on the condition of the land bridge, the development of cultural adaptations that would have allowed people to survive in the harsh environment of Beringia, and the existence of ice-free routes south from Alaska.

The Pleistocene lasted almost two million years, ending about ten thousand years ago. During that period the glaciers waxed and waned a number of times, providing numerous opportunities for people to enter the Americas. For years there has been a spirited debate within the archaeological community over the timing of human arrival in the New World. Some evidence from a few archaeological sites suggests that people may have been in the Americas by thirty thousand to twenty thousand years ago, and perhaps considerably earlier. However, none of the evidence for such an early arrival is entirely convincing, and the question of when humans first came to the New World remains open.

Around 18,000 B.P. the final major retreat of the glaciers began, heralding the end of the Pleistocene. By eleven thousand years ago, rising waters of the Bering Strait submerged the land connection between Siberia and Alaska, and retreating continental glaciers made routes south from Alaska accessible. This final glacial retreat seems to have opened up the Americas to a new human population: there is a sudden and unprecedented explosion of archaeological evidence dating to between twelve thousand and ten thousand years ago—our first firm evidence for human presence. Hundreds of archaeological sites dating to this period have been found all over the Americas, most of them characterized by a very distinctive stone-tool technology that varies little from region to region. It is from this period that we have the first evidence for human presence in Maine.

The Deglaciation of Maine

At its late Pleistocene peak, about 21,000 B.P., the continental glacier entirely covered Maine and the Gulf of Maine, reaching out to the edge of the continental shelf at George's Bank. At that time, sea level was about 100 meters lower than at present. Glacial retreat started around 18,000 B.P., and by between 15,000 and 14,000 B.P. the ice had receded to approximately the present coastline of Maine.[1] The great weight of the glacier had depressed the land surface, so that as the ice continued to recede, the sea followed, flooding the lowered land and extending as much as 100 kilometers inland from the present coastline (Fig. 1-1). Fine sediment settling on the seabed created the Presumpscot formation, a clay deposit that covers the coastal lowland areas of Maine below about 120 meters elevation and extends up the Penobscot River Valley as far as East Millinocket and up the Kennebec as far as Bingham. Remains of vertebrate and invertebrate animals from the clay, including walrus (*Odobenus rosmarus*), bearded seal (*Erignathus barbatus*), and cold-water species of shellfish (e.g., *Chlamys islandicus*,

1-1. The retreat of glacial ice in Maine, 14,000–11,000 B.P.

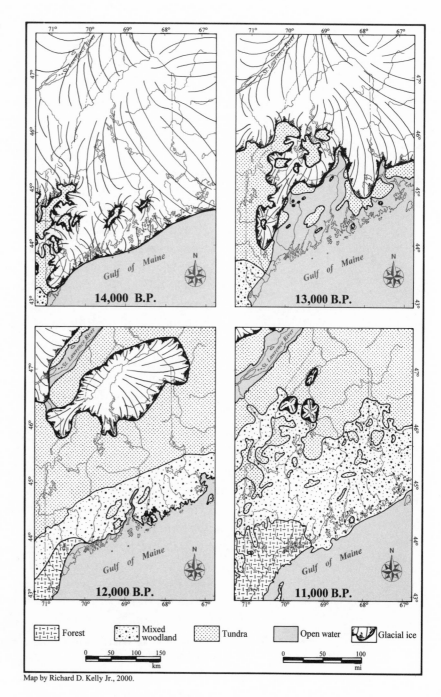

Map by Richard D. Kelly Jr., 2000.

Hiatella arctica, Portlandia arctica, Mya truncata, Mytilus edulis, Serripes groenlandicus) suggest that marine environmental conditions at the time were similar to those that prevail off the southern Labrador coast today.[2]

This marine transgression was relatively short-lived, because as the land was relieved of the weight of the glacier, it began an isostatic rebound upward. The first land form to emerge was George's Bank, which enclosed the waters of the marine transgression, forming a nearly inland body of water called the Degeer Sea. By around 12,000–11,000 the sea had retreated back to the position of the present coastline, and by 10,000–9000 B.P. relative sea level was approximately 60 meters lower and the shore up to 20 kilometers further seaward than it is now.[3] Thereafter, a continually rising sea level caused by the melting of glacial and polar ice gradually overtook the slowing isostatic land rebound, and relative sea level began to rise once again, a process that continues today.

By 11,000 B.P. the glacier had retreated to north of the St. Lawrence Valley, and Maine was essentially ice-free, although remnant ice masses may have persisted for a few centuries longer in northern Maine.[4] Indeed, the next millennium saw a brief reversal of the warming trend, with a return to colder, drier conditions during what is called the Younger Dryas event.[5] The extent and impact of the Younger Dryas in Maine is unclear, although its timing, during a critical period of plant, animal, and human colonization of the region, suggests that it played an important role.

As the land emerged from its burden of ice and water, colonizing plants spread a carpet of life over the raw landscape. The initial immigrants were mosses, lichens, grasses, and sedges—tundra vegetation suited to the cold and to the poor soils of the periglacial land. Later, thickets of willow and alder appeared, followed by stands of the hardier tree species such as poplar (*Populus*) and spruce (*Betula*).

An observer in Maine eleven thousand years ago would have seen a mosaic environment of tundra, shrubs, and trees arranged in patterns determined by latitude, elevation, local soil conditions, drainage, and exposure.[6] Much of northern Maine and the higher elevations of western Maine was still covered by tundra vegetation. A mixed forest of poplar, spruce, pine (*Pinus*), birch (*Betula*), elm (*Ulmus*), larch (*Larix*), ironwood (*Carpinus* or *Ostrya*), fir (*Abies*), and oak (*Quercus*) had penetrated into southern Maine. In central and eastern Maine there was a broad band of woodland—an intermediate condition between tundra and a closed-canopy forest, with a mixture of stands of trees and open areas of tundra—composed primarily of poplar, spruce, and birch.[7]

Although Maine's late Pleistocene woodland and tundra environments generally resembled modern subarctic tiaga (near treeline) or arctic tundra zones, they were probably biologically richer. In all likelihood, Maine, like the rest of the Northeast, supported a large and varied population of late Pleistocene animal species, including mammoth (*Mammuthus primigenius* and *jeffersonii*), mastodon (*Mammut americanum*), horse (*Equus*), muskox (*Ovibos*), bison (*Bison*), and caribou (*Rangifer*). And where these animals wandered, humans—their most dangerous and efficient predators—followed.[8]

Hairy It—The Scarborough Mammoth

In 1959 James and William Littlejohn and Leonard Cash were digging a farm pond in the town of Scarborough when they came upon an elephant tusk preserved in a waterlogged clay deposit about 2 meters down (Fig. 1-2). Their find generated considerable interest, and several scientists visited the site, including geologist D. W. Caldwell of Wellesley College, who recovered three additional rib fragments and examined the geologic context of the find.

After the initial flurry of excitement no further work was done at the site until 1990, when museum personnel, led by natural history curator Gary Hoyle, began an intensive investigation of the remains. Mammoth expert Daniel Fisher of the University of Michigan examined the tusk and determined that it was from a young adult female mammoth.

1-2. Photograph of the 1959 Scarborough Mammoth excavation showing Leonard Cash (*left*) and James Littlejohn with the tusk and ribs. (Courtesy of the *Portland Press Herald.*)

In 1992 and 1993 the museum conducted excavations at the Scarborough site aimed at recovering additional skeletal elements and documenting the geologic context of the find. Geologists Harold Borns of the Institute of Quaternary Studies at the University of Maine, and Woodrow Thompson and Thomas Weddle of the Maine Geological Survey, as well as a large number of volunteer workers all contributed to the effort.

The excavations recovered no additional bones or evidence of human activity, but backdirt from the 1959 excavation yielded several hundred additional bone fragments, including two molars, an atlas vertebra and additional skull, jaw, pelvic, and rib fragments, most from the left side of the animal. Samples from both the tusk and a molar were submitted for dating. The two most extensively purified samples produced AMS radiocarbon dates of 12,200±55 B.P. (molar root) and 12,160±50 (tusk).

Fisher attempted to determine which of the three North American species the mammoth belonged to. Best known is the woolly mammoth (*Mammuthus primigenius*), which was actually a latecomer to North America, having immigrated eastward from Eurasia across Beringia to Alaska at the end of the Pleistocene. Another was the Columbian mammoth (*Mammuthus columbi*), an indigenous species. Finally, many recognize a third species, the Jefferson mammoth (*Mammuthus jeffersonii*), which shows morphological characteristics intermediate between the other two, and may represent convergent evolution from *M. columbi* stock. Evidence from the Scarborough mammoth's molars is equivocal—some traits are more like those of *M. primigenius*, others fall in the *M. columbi* range, and some are intermediate between the two, suggesting the possibility that this was the intermediate species, *Mammuthus jeffersonii*. However, Fisher's examination of the dentin microstructure within the tusk revealed a pattern characteristic of the wooly mammoth and not seen in the Columbian mammoth, leading him to conclude that the Scarborough specimen was indeed *Mammuthus primigenius*.

Geologist Christopher Dorion believes that the mammoth died at a time when the land was rebounding from the marine submergence that followed glacial recession, and that the shoreline was probably not far from the mammoth's resting place. Forests would not yet have moved into Maine, and the land, covered by tundra and grass vegetation, would have been suitable for grazers like the mammoth. It was a harsh environment—glacial ice persisted in northern and western Maine, and frigid sea conditions are evidenced by arctic shellfish species found in the Presumpscot formation clays at the site.

The mammoth died of unknown causes sometime in mid- to late winter. In the spring, during the ice breakup, her partially decomposed carcass was apparently rafted down the proto-Saco River and out its mouth into the sea, finally coming to rest in about 10 meters of water offshore. There the skeleton suffered additional disarticulation as it was gradually buried by sediments in the shallowing sea.

The First Mainers

Snowy Owl next started out to find the camps of human beings to get him a wife. He traveled far to the south, and on the way noticed how the lakes and rivers were drying up. Desiring to learn the cause of the water shrinkage, he ascended the valleys and finally reached a place where he saw what he thought were hillocks covered with brown vegetation moving slowly about. Upon closer scrutiny he learned that these masses were really the backs of great animals with long teeth, animals so huge that when they lay down they could not get up. He saw that they drank for half a day, thus taking up all the water in the basins of the land. Snowy Owl decided that some day he would have to kill them.

Snowy Owl proceeded then to find the monsters which he had seen before. He went to where the animals had their "yards." He cut certain trees where he had observed the monsters were accustomed to lean for rest at night, almost through, so that when the monsters would lean on them they would break. When the creatures went to rest at night leaning against the trees, they fell upon the sharpened stumps when the top bent over and broke and could not get up again, and Snowy Owl shot them all.[9]

This story is the Penobscot Indian version of a widespread northeastern Algonquian myth about a great "stiff-legged bear" said to have once roamed the land.[10] The creature described in the legend bears a fascinating resemblance to reconstructions of mammoths and mastodons. Could this tale be a dimly remembered and myth-laden account of actual elephant hunts by Indians of the distant past, handed down through generations since the end of the Ice Age? It seems unlikely that such an account could have survived thousands of years, and it is quite possible that the mythic animal's resemblance to a mammoth or mastodon occurred by chance, or that the narrative was influenced by descriptions of mammoths or elephants discovered during the historic period. Nevertheless, we know that humans were in Maine shortly after the retreat of the glaciers, we are certain from archaeological evidence that they were hunting mammoths and mastodons elsewhere in North America at about the same time, and we know from fossil finds that such animals did exist in Maine during the late Pleistocene.

Archaeologists, left with the mere traces that constitute the only record of Maine's earliest human inhabitants, often pause as they look out over the remains of a Paleo-Indian camp site to reflect upon Snowy Owl's tale.

Archaeologists use the term Paleo-Indian for the Native inhabitants of the Americas at the end of the Pleistocene and beginning of the present post-glacial period (Holocene), roughly 11,500–8500 B.P. Only a few decades ago, the sole evidence for Paleo-Indians in Maine consisted of a few scattered finds of their distinctive spear points, called fluted points. These finely flaked stone points have a central channel, or flute, running up both faces from the base, which probably facilitated hafting onto a spear or lance shaft. Isolated finds of these points in such diverse localities as Lebanon, Lewiston, Monmouth, Arrowsic, Boothbay, Rumford Center, Graham Lake, Flagstaff Lake, and Brassua Lake clearly indicated that there were Paleo-Indians in Maine, but told us little about their activities or culture.[11] Fortunately, with the discovery and investigation of a series of Paleo-Indian sites over the last two decades, a much more comprehensive picture has emerged.

Some Maine Paleo-Indian Sites and What They Reveal

Our picture of Paleo-Indian life in Maine is under construction; even the most basic issues, such as dating, diet, and geographic range, remain frustratingly unclear. One problem faced by archaeologists who study these issues is the poor preservation of organic tissue in the acid soils of this cool temperate region. Flesh, hide, and wood vanish quickly, and even unburned bone does not last long. All that is left at most sites after a few centuries is wood charcoal and whitened bits of bone that have been calcined by fire. Nevertheless, recent research by numerous scholars is making substantial progress, and new sites are being explored even as this work goes to press. What follows is a summary of information from some of the longer-known, better-understood Paleo-Indian sites in Maine and an explanation of their contributions to our understanding of regional Paleo-Indian culture.

Munsungan Lake

Between 1977 and 1983, Robson Bonnichsen of the University of Maine investigated a series of sites associated with chert outcrops in the vicinity of Munsungan and Chase Lakes, north of Baxter State Park. Two of these sites appear to have been Paleo-Indian workshop and habitation sites where bifacially flaked chert "preforms"—unfinished artifacts probably initially

1-3. Fluted point preforms from Munsungan Lake sites, showing stages of the manufacturing process. (Maine State Museum collection.)

shaped at quarry locations—were flaked into finished tools. These sites are not radiocarbon dated, but their age is suggested by their location along glacial meltwater channels between the two lakes that have probably not been active since the last ice remnants in the region melted.[12]

Artifacts found at the Munsungan Lake sites include preforms, fluted points broken in the process of manufacture, and fluting flakes driven off points to form the central channels. University of Maine graduate student James Payne painstakingly refitted thousands of chert flakes back onto the tools from which they were removed, thus providing a detailed picture of the stone-tool manufacturing processes employed at the sites.[13] In addition to manufacturing debris, these sites produced a variety of other tool types including scrapers and gravers, suggesting that a range of living activities occurred there in addition to stone-tool manufacture.

The Vail Site and the Magalloway Valley Paleo-Indian Complex

While the sites at Munsungan Lake tell us a great deal about Paleo-Indian lithic use and technology, other aspects of Paleo-Indian life have been illuminated by a remarkable series of sites along the Magalloway River in northwestern Maine, where investigations by R. Michael Gramly began in 1979. The largest is the Vail site. Today the site is normally covered by the waters of the artificial Aziscohos Lake, but eleven thousand years ago it lay along the sandy east bank of the Magalloway River. Excavations and surface mapping there revealed eight artifact clusters, called loci by archaeologists, suggesting the locations of dwellings—probably tents—with floors measuring about 4.5 by 6 meters. A hearth or fire pit, perhaps centrally located, would have provided warmth and light as well as a means of cooking. Gramly thinks it unlikely that the loci were occupied at the same time but rather that the site was occupied repeatedly at different loci over the course of several years.[14]

The eight loci produced a total of some four thousand tools, including fluted points, drills, endscrapers and sidescrapers, small stone wedges called *pièces esquillées*, and "cutters"—flakes snapped or retouched to produce sharp edges or tips. The fluted points, which have rather deeply concave bases, closely resemble those from another large northeastern Paleo-Indian site, the Debert site in Nova Scotia.[15] The drills look like small fluted points, but their narrow tips suggest a perforating function, perhaps as bits for bow drills. The various scraper types probably fulfilled a variety of functions, including perhaps the scraping of hides and, along with cutters and wedges, the working of bone, antler, and wood.

Although a suitable source of lithic material lies approximately 25 kilometers north of the site at the headwaters of the Magalloway River, it now appears likely that most of the artifacts were made of material from more distant outcrops in the Champlain lowlands of western Vermont or the Munsungan Lake region, and even from more distant sources in New York and Pennsylvania. Unlike the Munsungan Lake sites, the Vail site contained

1-4. Reconstruction of a hafted fluted point. (Courtesy of Maine State Museum.)

1-5. Plan of the Vail site. (Courtesy of Richard Michael Gramly.)

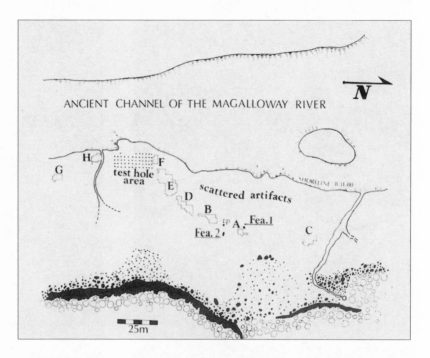

1-6. Aerial view of the Vail site area. (Courtesy of Richard Michael Gramly.)

1-7. (*top left, opposite*) Artifacts from the Vail site: fluted projectile points and drill bits (*top*); point preform (*middle left*); a variety of scraping and graving tools (*middle center and right*); tip of a large fluted point made of lustrous chert from a far-distant source (*bottom left*); three *limace* scrapers (*bottom center*), and two tools with well-defined graving spurs (*bottom right*). (Maine State Museum collection.)

1-8. (*top right, opposite*) Across a fossil river channel from the Vail site lies a small site that produced only whole points and tips. Its limited artifact diversity and situation near a small tributary stream suggest that it was a place where game was ambushed. Archaeologists call such sites "kill sites." The close association of this kill site with the Vail site is demonstrated by these five points, the tips of which were found at the former but the bases of which came from the latter. This pattern almost certainly indicates that hunters damaged their weapons at the kill site and discarded the basal fragments back at the Vail site before attaching new points to their weapons. (Maine State Museum collection.)

1-9. (*bottom, opposite*) Artist's reconstruction of what the scene may have looked like at the Vail kill site between ten and eleven thousand years ago. The Caribou drive is based on hunting practices known from historic arctic and subarctic caribou hunters.

few flakes relative to the number of tools recovered, and most of the flakes that were found appear to result from tool repair and resharpening rather than initial manufacture. Moreover, many of the tools from the site bear evidence of repeated resharpening and reworking. These facts all support the notion that they were made of materials from a nonlocal source.[16]

Radiocarbon dates on samples of charcoal from two pit features within the site ranged from 11,120±180 to 10,300±80 B.P. Three dates cluster at 10,600–10,500 B.P. , a reasonable approximation for the age of the site.[17]

During excavation of the Vail site, a second site, or, perhaps more accurately, a ninth activity locus of the Vail site, was discovered 200 meters to the west, on the opposite side of the ancient Magalloway channel at a point where a stream channel drains a small spring-fed pond. Gramly has argued persuasively that this locus was an animal kill site.[18] It produced only intact and broken fluted points but none of the flaked stone waste and varied tool types found at the habitation loci. Remarkably, five of the point tips found at the kill site could be refitted to bases recovered from the habitation loci, solidly linking the two areas and indicating that projectile points broken during the hunt were discarded and later replaced back in camp.

It seems likely that caribou were the prey of the Paleo-Indian hunters of Vail, but no animal remains survived at the site to confirm this hypothesis. Identifiable bone fragments from two other Paleo-Indian sites in the Northeast suggest that caribou was a staple of the Paleo-Indian economy in the region.[19] The Vail site's location at a constriction of the Magalloway Valley and the kill site's position on a stream between a pond and a river suggest the use of natural terrain features to aid in channeling herd animals toward waiting hunters, a technique still used by caribou hunters in the North.

Since the Vail site excavations, Gramly's continuing surveys in the upper Magalloway Valley have uncovered an additional half-dozen Paleo-Indian sites, all smaller than the Vail site but apparently about the same age. Like the Vail site, most are located on the eastern side of the Magalloway Valley, perhaps because the prevailing northwesterly winds of this region would have wafted the scent of humans away from game animals moving through the valley.[20]

The Adkins site, which lies about a kilometer south of the Vail site, is in some ways typical of the smaller Magalloway sites. Most of the 417 artifacts and flakes recovered there lay in an oval cluster measuring about 2.5 by 3 meters. A smaller cluster of artifacts lay 1.5 meters west of the main cluster, while 11 artifacts lay within a 5-meter-diameter circle partially surrounding the main cluster. To Gramly, these distributions suggest the remains of

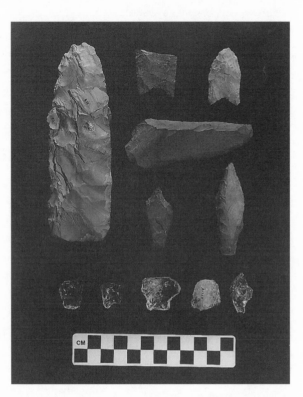

1-10. (*left*) The Adkins site cache. (Courtesy of Richard Michael Gramly.)

1-11. The Adkins site seems to represent a single family encampment. Artifacts from the site include a point preform onto which a number of flakes have been reattached by archaeologists in the lab *(left)*; two fluted points *(top)*, a large scraper *(middle)*; two *limace* scrapers *(next to bottom)*; and scrapers of crystal quartz *(bottom)*. (Maine State Museum collection.)

a one-time single family encampment, with a 5-meter-diameter dwelling and a work area in the front yard.[21]

Artifacts from the Adkins site, including two fluted points, a point preform, scrapers, cutters, and *pièces esquillées*, closely resemble those from the Vail site. The lithic materials, on the other hand, are not so similar. Most striking is the presence of clear crystal quartz, which makes up about a third of the assemblage (by weight). Other lithic types include rhyolite, probably from New Hampshire, and chert, probably from either Munsungan Lake or the Champlain lowlands in Vermont, as well as a few pieces probably from central New York. In sum, the Adkins site and the other sites in the Magalloway complex all closely resemble the Vail site in artifact form but show considerable variation in the lithic raw material composing the artifacts.

A particularly interesting feature of the Adkins site—so far unreported at any other North American Paleo-Indian site—is a ring of boulders surrounding a shallow pit. Just a few meters southwest of the artifact clusters, this feature was recognized only during the last days of fieldwork at the site, when "the crew noticed that the pile of rocks immediately adjacent to the site, that they had been sitting upon to eat lunch, formed a clearly defined ring that must have been the work of humans."[22] The rock ring is oval, about 3 meters across on its long axis, and is made up of boulders weighing more than 100 kilograms apiece. Gaps between the boulders were chinked with smaller rocks, except for a 40-centimeter-wide opening facing north, which may have been the entrance to the structure. The central pit had been dug about 22 centimeters into the underlying sand. The structure closely resembles meat caches constructed during historic times by hunter-gatherer groups in the Arctic and Subarctic to protect surplus meat from scavenging animals and store it for future consumption.

The Vail site and the others of the Magalloway Valley form one of the richest clusters of Paleo-Indian sites known anywhere in the Northeast. The close similarities among their artifact assemblages has led Gramly to suggest that they were nearly contemporaneous, perhaps all dating to a span of no more than a few decades. He has therefore lumped them into a single cultural complex termed the Magalloway Valley Paleo-Indian Complex. This pattern of one large Paleo-Indian site, such as Vail, surrounded by smaller sites of the same age is one we see repeatedly in New England and the Maritimes. We shall return to a discussion of the significance of this pattern in the concluding section of this chapter.

The Michaud Site

The Michaud site lies just to the south of the Auburn-Lewiston airport. It was discovered in 1985 by geologists who came across artifacts on the surface of a proposed new road. Later that year, Arthur Spiess of the Maine Historic Preservation Commission directed excavations at the site in an environmental mitigation project funded by the Maine Department of Transportation.[23]

The site lies on a sandy plain that formed during deglaciation, when meltwater rivers dumped their sediment load into the sea as it regressed from late Pleistocene high stands. Subsequently, winds blew the sand into dunes, and it was amid these dunes that small groups of Paleo-Indian peoples camped. Just to the south of the site, Moose Brook has incised a small valley containing an extensive beaver bog. A peat sample taken more than 6 meters below the surface of the bog, near its bottom, returned a

1-12. Reconstructed cache and mural from the Adkins site exhibit case at the Maine State Museum. The rocks in front are the actual cache rocks, transported from the site by helicopter.

radiocarbon date of 9630±140 B.P., suggesting that the stream valley, and possibly the bog as well, were in existence during the Paleo-Indian occupation and may have been one of the site's attractions.

The Michaud site produced 8 or 9 artifact clusters that were generally smaller and contained fewer artifacts than those at the Vail site, for a total of approximately 150 artifacts and 2,300 flakes. Also, in contrast to the Vail site, some of the clusters produced specialized tool assemblages, suggesting functional differences among the loci. Particularly interesting in this respect were the three from the southwestern portion of the site. All were adjacent and nonoverlapping and all were oriented along an east-west line about 17 meters long. The western-most was dominated by broken fluted points, fluted point preforms, and channel flakes, which suggested that this was an area where projectile point final manufacture and replacement were carried out. This cluster also yielded 3 relatively long and narrow bladelike scrapers sometimes termed *limaces* (the French word for the garden slug, which they resemble), endscrapers, and a concave scraper, all of which may have been used to manufacture and refurbish bone or wood hafts.

At the eastern end of the line, the assemblage from the third cluster was dominated by sidescrapers, relatively large tools with unifacial retouch along one or both of their lateral edges. Studies of use wear (edge modification or damage produced in the course of using the tool) on these tools suggest that the sidescrapers were used to cut and scrape soft materials, such as animal hide. Thus the third cluster appears to represent a game processing area, and, perhaps more specifically, an area for manufacturing clothing, rope, tent coverings, or other animal hide products.

The second cluster, located between and slightly behind the first and third, lacked the functional specificity of the other two. It produced only a small number of tools, no two alike. Spiess and Wilson have suggested that the second cluster represents a tent location, while the first and third were outdoor activity areas on either side of the tent.[24] A feature interpreted as a

1-13. Artifacts from the Michaud *(top three rows)* and Lamoreau *(bottom row)* sites in Auburn, Maine. These points, although fluted like those from Aziscohos, differ in such details as the depth of the basal concavity. Following the three fluted points on the top row are a fluting flake, struck off to produce the characteristic flute channel, and the broken base of a fluted point preform that retains the basal "nipple," a specialized platform used in striking off the flute. (Maine State Museum collection.)

hearth pit, lying just to the southeast of the second cluster, produced a small amount of charcoal that returned radiocarbon dates of 9010±210 and 10,200±620 B.P. The former date is clearly too recent for the Paleo-Indian occupation and may have been contaminated by more recent material, while the latter date covers a time span too broad to be of much use in comparing Michaud with other dated Paleo-Indian sites.

Overall, the Michaud site artifact assemblage resembles that from Vail, although there are some interesting differences. Of the tool types found at Vail, only bifacial drills and *pièces esquillées* were missing at the Michaud site. Michaud fluted points lack the deeply indented bases found at the Magalloway sites, a characteristic that may indicate either a difference in their ages or cultural differences between their occupants. Michaud stone-tool technology is based primarily on four materials: black and gray green chert thought to be from the Champlain lowlands in Vermont, Munsungan chert, a fine-grained rhyolite originally attributed to eastern Massachusetts but now believed to come from Berlin, New Hampshire, and locally derived diabase.[25] Diabase is a granular rock, not suitable for flaking, and was used exclusively for rough tools such as abraders, hammerstones, anvil stones, and choppers.

During the Michaud site investigations a second Paleo-Indian site, named for its discoverer, Henry Lamoreau, was found just across nearby Moose Brook.[26] The Lamoreau site has not been fully investigated, but preliminary testing produced a small fluted point, a point preform, and an endscraper. The artifacts and flakes recovered from the site to date represent the same range of lithic materials as seen at the Michaud site, and it is likely that it was occupied at roughly the same time as Michaud.

The Dam Site

Like the Michaud site, the Dam site in Wayne is located in an area of ancient sand dunes from which the topsoil has been blown away by wind, leaving artifacts exposed on the surface. The site was identified on the basis of several Paleo-Indian artifacts picked up by a hunter within the blown-out area. Subsequent investigations by the Maine State Museum and the Maine Historic Preservation Commission produced a small collection of Paleo-Indian artifacts from what appear to have been three or four loci. They include two fluted points, both with shallowly indented bases, end- and sidescrapers, gravers, and cutters. As we have seen, most Paleo-Indian collections contain a certain amount of nonlocal materials, but the Dam

1-14. Many of the Paleo-Indian sites known from Maine occur on sandy soils. This is the Dam site in North Wayne during excavation. (Maine State Museum collection.)

site collection is remarkably diverse even compared to its larger Paleo-Indian peers. The relatively small assemblage includes cherts believed to come from central New York, western Vermont, Pennsylvania, Nova Scotia, and northern Maine.[27]

Late Paleo-Indian Period

The production of fluted points ceased around ten thousand years ago. In western North America they were replaced by a variety of highly distinctive and beautifully made long, narrow lanceolate point styles. Generally thought to have "evolved" from late fluted point styles, the lanceolate points have often been lumped into what is referred to as the Plano tradition. They have frequently been associated with bison kills, suggesting that during the later part of the period there was a continuation of Paleo-Indian orientation toward hunting large herd animals.

Generally similar points also occur in the Northeast, including the Maritime Peninsula. Unfortunately, we are currently at the same stage in understanding these late Paleo-Indian occupations as we were for the fluted point occupations fifteen years ago. On the Maritime Peninsula, late Paleo-Indian points have generally been found only as isolated specimens or at sites where more recent artifacts predominate—at this writing only one single-component late Paleo-Indian site, located on the Varney Farm in Turner, has been intensively investigated.[28] We therefore know relatively little about the nature and associated lifestyles of late Paleo-Indian culture in Maine.

The Varney Farm site is located on a small sandy knoll between two brooks that flow into the Nezinscot River approximately 100 meters to the south of the site. Excavation there began in 1994 under the direction of James Petersen and Belinda Cox, archaeologists from the University of Maine at Farmington. The artifact assemblage includes fragments of nine broken lanceolate points, two or three drills, scrapers, a flake core, and a hammerstone. A few fragments of unidentifiable calcined bone were also recovered. Charcoal from a pit feature containing flakes and burnt bone produced an initial radiocarbon date of 9410±190 B.P. However, five additional charcoal samples from the same feature subsequently returned AMS dates ranging from 8700 B.P. to 8380 B.P., younger than expected by the investigators but in line with the dating of a late Paleo-Indian component in southern Quebec.[29]

Most late Paleo-Indian points discovered in Maine have been found in sites containing more recent occupations. Often situated along lakes or rivers, the locations of these sites contrasts notably with those of fluted point sites and find spots, which rarely contain more recent components. Thus, it appears that while early Paleo-Indian patterns of settlement and subsistence were obviously different from those of prehistoric cultures during the late Paleo-Indian period, when the region was becoming more forested, we are seeing the emergence of cultural adaptations that characterize the succeeding Archaic period. Additionally, late Paleo-Indian assemblages contain fewer exotic cherts than do the earlier fluted point assemblages, possibly indicating a breakdown of earlier large-scale movement and trade patterns. This shift may have occurred as the landscape became more densely wooded and people became somewhat more sedentary.

Like their western counterparts, late Paleo-Indian lanceolate points from the Northeast often have beautifully executed parallel flaking, but they differ in other respects. They tend to be extremely thin in cross section, with narrow blades and parallel or slightly convex lateral edges, and straight bases. This style of point appears to be distributed from the eastern Great Lakes region, down the Saint Lawrence River to northern New England and Quebec, and into the Maritimes.[30] It may be that once these late Paleo-

Indian sites are better understood, we will see them as evidence of a distinct movement of people eastward from the Great Lakes into northern New England and eastern Canada, perhaps hunting caribou—the last remnants of the Pleistocene game herds in the region.

The Paleo-Indian Occupation of Maine— A Summary of the Evidence

We know a great deal more about the Paleo-Indian occupations of Maine now than we did just a decade ago, but many questions remain to be answered. From the Paleo-Indian sites investigated to date, we have gained a picture of a small, very mobile population that lived in a rapidly changing environment quite different from today's. The abundance of exotic lithic materials found in early Paleo-Indian sites suggests either frequent long-distance movement or very broad-ranging exchange networks, or quite possibly both.

In Maine, as in most areas of North America, it appears that as soon as Paleo-Indians arrived in a region, they immediately sought out, found, and began using most of the available sources of high-quality chert. They must have been remarkably proficient practical geologists to have so quickly discovered these more remote sources such as the chert outcrops around Munsungan Lake. Possibly they kept an eye out for chert cobbles in glacially transported till deposits and once chert had been spotted, followed the glacial boulder train back to the outcrop source.

There are differences in artifact style and content among the various Maine fluted point Paleo-Indian collections that may reflect either differences in time or differing contemporaneous populations. Based largely on typological comparisons to the Great Lakes Paleo-Indian sequence, Wilson and Spiess have suggested a three-phase–Paleo-Indian occupation of Maine.[31] The earliest, pioneering occupation is represented by the Dam site, with its broad range of exotic lithic materials and typologically early fluted points. The next phase is represented by the Michaud site, with its typologically intermediate points, while the final phase is represented by Vail and the other sites of the Magalloway Valley, which are characterized by fluted points with relatively deeply indented bases and a variety of tool types such as drills that are not commonly associated with the earliest known fluted point sites. This scenario is certainly plausible, and it has the added attraction of explaining why the latest sites, those of the Magalloway complex and the closely related Debert site in Nova Scotia, are located in altitudinally higher areas or northern portions of the region, where one might expect to find a tundra- or woodland-adapted culture during a period when forests were expanding in the lowlands and steadily advancing northward. Nevertheless, at present there is little evidence in the form of precisely dated collections to support this proposed sequence, and until there is, it remains largely speculative.

As noted earlier, fluted point Paleo-Indian settlement patterns appear to have been quite different than those of later Maine Indian cultures. Whereas most of the later Archaic- and Ceramic-period interior settlement was along rivers and lakes, this was not true of the Paleo-Indian period, when there

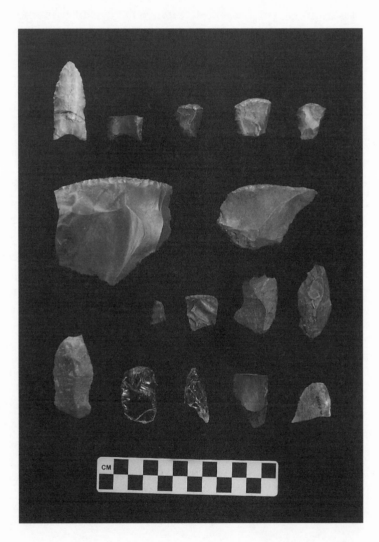

1-15. These artifacts from the Dam site show closer affinities to the Auburn Paleo-Indian sites than to the Aziscohoos group. They are remarkable in the variety of exotic stone materials represented. (Maine State Museum collection.)

1-16. These beautifully flaked points represent a distinctly different and probably later Paleo-Indian culture, traces of which have recently been identified in Maine. They are very similar to those of the late Paleo-Indian Plano tradition on the Great Plains, where they are often associated with bison hunting. There is some evidence to suggest that this culture moved eastward from the Great Lakes region down the St. Lawrence, where several Plano sites have recently been identified in Quebec's eastern townships, and perhaps from there southward into northern New England. (Maine State Museum collection.)

seems to have been a preference for settlement on sandy soils, often in landscapes that had been wind-blown into dunes. Possibly this preference was simply because such soils offered a relatively dry, well-drained land surface in what must have been an otherwise rather wet early post-glacial terrain. It seems more likely, however, that the specific vegetation that developed on sandy soils during this period attracted valued game resources. Moreover, many of the regional Paleo-Indian sites situated on sandy soils are also located near bogs or other wetlands, which may also have provided areas of concentrated resources.

Characteristically, the largest of the Paleo-Indian sites in the New England and Maritimes region are surrounded by a cluster of smaller sites. This is true of the Vail and Debert sites, and the Bull Brook site in Massachusetts. The large sites may represent the seasonal gathering-places of a substantial number of people. Indeed, at Bull Brook there were at least forty-two loci that may represent individual tents, and archaeologists have argued that the distribution of these loci (in a rough semicircle), plus crossmends of broken artifact fragments in different loci, suggest that most or all of the loci were simultaneously occupied.[32] If this was the case, this settlement would have been considerably larger than anything previously envisioned for Paleo-Indians. The smaller sites in the vicinity may be camps occupied during seasons when the population was more dispersed.

As noted above, we have little direct evidence of how Paleo-Indians on the Maritime Peninsula made a living. A few scraps of caribou bone have been found in a couple of northeastern Paleo-Indian sites, and it is very likely that caribou were an important food resource. During certain seasons of the year, particularly the fall, caribou concentrate into herds, a pattern that allows an excellent opportunity to collect a large amount of meat with the expenditure of relatively little time and energy. Mammoths and mastodons, even as individual kills, would have offered a similar opportunity. We do not know if mammoths or mastodons survived long enough to have been hunted in Maine, but both apparently survived on Georges Bank off Massachusetts to around 11,000 B.P.[33]

Paleo-Indians were technologically very well equipped to hunt and butcher the large mammals of the late Pleistocene. The relatively large size of their fluted spear points, scrapers, and knives hints at an orientation toward large mammal hunting, and North American fluted point sites in regions with good bone preservation commonly contain bones from mammoth, bison, and other large prey species. Moreover, modern experiments have demonstrated the efficiency of fluted point–tipped spears in killing animals up to elephant size, particularly when used with a spear thrower or atlatl, which greatly multiplies the force and penetration of the spear.[34]

It would probably be a mistake, however, to think of Paleo-Indians as subsisting on nothing but mammoth and caribou steaks. To date, the only additional species represented at a Paleo-Indian site in the Northeast is beaver (*Castor canidensis*), identified from a single bone found at the Spiller Farm site in Wells.[35] Other species were very likely also hunted when available, however. Native peoples of Canada and Alaska who still hunt caribou today rely heavily on caribou products for a variety of uses as well as sustenance, but in making a living they also invariably exploit a broad range of other resources, including small mammals, fish, birds, and plants, and there is no reason to believe that Paleo-Indians did otherwise. Certainly, the rapid spread of Paleo-Indian culture across a broad range of ecological zones in the Americas suggests a very flexible cultural adaptation.

In the Paleo-Indian sites on the Maritime Peninsula and elsewhere in the Americas, we see evidence of a mobile people whose movements were determined by the seasonal migrations of their prey, the location of necessary resources like lithic raw materials, and perhaps simply by an urge to explore new lands. Skilled in stone and bone technology and consummate hunters, these were the able pioneers of a new land.

II THE ARCHAIC PERIOD

From the Paleo-Indian to the Archaic

PALEO-INDIANS prospered in Maine during a brief period when a fairly open landscape favored the herd animals they depended upon. That environment was not to last, however. Within three thousand years of the ice retreat, most of northeastern North America south of the St. Lawrence River was wooded. By about 10,000 B.P. Maine's forests were undergoing rapid change. Boreal tree species such as spruce, poplar, and birch began to decline and by 9000 B.P., oak (*Quercus*) began to increase, followed by eastern hemlock (*Tsuga*). As woodlands replaced tundra, the animal species that had sustained Paleo-Indian populations diminished and soon disappeared altogether. The extent to which human predation contributed to these faunal extinctions remains a matter of vigorous debate. The new, increasingly diverse forests attracted different fauna from unglaciated areas to the south and west, including moose (*Alces alces*), deer (*Odocioleus virginianus*), bear (*Ursus americanus*), and other smaller mammals. Many of these were among the species that had originally spread to North America from Asia and were thus adapted to survive human predation.[1]

Under these circumstances, Paleo-Indians in the Northeast would have faced three options: if caribou had indeed become their main prey species, they may have followed the herds into northern Canada, where caribou still thrive; if, as seems likely, they had maintained close ties with Paleo-Indian populations in the south, they may have chosen instead to retreat, while also developing new lifestyles based more heavily on vegetable foods; they may also have decided to remain in the region and adapt to its changing environment, developing hunting techniques geared toward the more dispersed game of its forests, and perhaps the fish in its waters as well.

In the Southeast and some of the Midwest, the record is clear: Paleo-Indians adapted to the new conditions there and survived.[2] In the Northeast, however, archaeologists are divided on this issue, for we have few data to help us choose among the three models. No fluted points or other obvious Paleo-Indian artifacts have been found north of the St. Lawrence River, but some possibly derived forms discovered on the Quebec Lower North Shore, the Magdalen Islands (Îles de la Madeleine), and the Maritimes might reflect Paleo-Indian efforts to adapt on the move.[3]

The millennia that followed the Paleo-Indian period, between about 10,000 and 3000 B.P., are referred to as the Archaic period, a term originally employed in 1932 by William A. Ritchie to denote some relatively early archaeological cultures.[4] Today, it is conventionally applied to the long sequence of cultures that flourished prior to the appearance of ceramics. As used by archaeologists, the term "archaic" carries none of the negative connotations of primitiveness that sometimes accompany it in common parlance. In Maine, indeed, some of the most complex and intriguing archaeological cultures date to the Archaic period, and it is perhaps the most interesting and certainly the most intensively studied aspect of the area's prehistory.

The Archaic period spans more than half the time humans have lived in Maine. Consequently, it is subdivided into Early, Middle, and Late subperiods, which are conventionally dated 10,000 to 8000 B.P., 8000 to 6000 B.P., and 6000 to 3500 B.P. respectively.[5] The scarcity of data for the Early Archaic in the Northeast causes much uncertainty about its origins, particularly as we contemplate the recently recognized but still poorly dated and ill-defined late-Paleo-Indian phenomenon discussed in Chapter 1. It remains possible, in fact, that a late Paleo-Indian population was still in the region when new Archaic peoples were entering it from the south.[6] Uncertainty and considerable debate also surrounds the dating of the end of the Archaic, a topic we shall be considering below.

The Early Archaic

Only recently have we found reliable evidence about Early Archaic populations in the Northeast, and the record for the Maritime Peninsula is still extremely sketchy. The paucity of archaeological data from this period in the 1960s led archaeologists to postulate that the low biological productivity of conifer-dominated forests supposed to have existed here during the

EARLY SITES AT RUMFORD

Our understanding of prehistoric life in the interior of the Maritime Peninsula is largely based upon excavations and surface recoveries at sites where soils are thin or where dams have raised water levels, causing destructive bank erosion. These sites have generally failed to produce stratigraphic separations of the cultural remains resulting from sometimes numerous episodes of human occupation (see Fig. 2-1). During the past decade, however, new environmental laws have caused archaeologists to explore promising areas along rivers and streams where flood deposits have deeply buried the remains of prehistoric occupational episodes, sealing them in discrete strata and thus preventing their mixture.[7]

A recent example of this kind of legally mandated research on inland alluvial archaeological sites is the Rumford Archaeological Project, on the upper Androscoggin River in the city of Rumford.[8] The research is being conducted by a team from the University of Southern Maine, led by Nathan Hamilton. The project's goal is to assess the impact on archaeological sites of erosion caused by the continuing operation of dams owned by the Mead Corporation, which runs a paper mill on the river.

Hamilton's team undertook excavations at three stratified sites, numbered 49.24, 49.27, and 49.28. Remarkably, all three preserve evidence of occupation dating to around 9000 b.p. or earlier. What they have learned so far—analysis is ongoing—is that this upland valley was remarkably hospitable to humans even at that

2-1. Stratigraphy at Rumford. (Courtesy of Nathan Hamilton.)

early date. Nut-producing trees—probably used both for food and fuel—are present from the start, and by 7000 b.p. included beech (*Fagus*), hazel (*Corylus*), and oak. The identification of refuse bone suggests heavy reliance upon large mammals, probably including moose, but there is also a curious abundance of turtle.

Research at stratified interior sites is still in too early a stage to allow a detailed understanding of how and why Maine's Archaic populations found these locales so attractive. Nevertheless, these sites have certainly opened archaeologists' eyes to the extent of early occupation in the region, and they have also made it clear that deeply buried sites with great archaeological potential are abundant in a region that was formerly thought to have few stratified sites.

early Holocene epoch (after 10,000 B.P.) severely suppressed human populations. Indeed, some archaeologists have suggested that the region was completely depopulated following the demise of Paleo-Indian culture.[9]

On the other hand, most archaeologists now recognize that many Early (and Middle) Archaic sites are likely to have been destroyed—in larger numbers, in fact, than Paleo-Indian sites—because of their proximity to submerging shorelines. Virtually all Early Archaic coastal sites, for example, must have been completely eroded by sea-level rise and attendant shoreline erosion. Direct evidence for Early Archaic site submersion is

2-2. Projectile points spanning the Archaic period in Maine. (Maine State Museum collection.)

2-3. Projectile points with notched (bifurcated) bases dating between around 8500 and 8000 B.P. (Maine State Museum collection.)

understandably hard to come by, and much of what we do have remains equivocal. Numerous artifacts have been recovered by fishermen all along the Gulf of Maine coast, and some have been interpreted as possible evidence for the occupation of ancient, long-submerged coastlines.[10] Taking into account the whole sample of such recoveries, however, we find that most were probably lost at sea. The majority are of known recent types found at depths that were covered by the sea when such types were in use; surely these must have been lost at sea. The deepest finds, however, are three flaked bifaces found in close proximity to each other in Blue Hill Bay. They do not resemble recent types, but neither are they typical of known Early Archaic types. Continuing uncertainty regarding the timing and maximum extent of sea-level drop leaves open the likelihood that these artifacts, too, fell to the ocean floor from the surface.[11]

Recently, it has become apparent that between about 8500 and 5000 B.P., lake levels may have dropped below modern (pre-dam) levels. The cause was possibly a global rise in temperature, evidence for which has been noted in fluctuations of oxygen and carbon isotope values found in glacial ice cores from Greenland. This mid-Holocene warm period seems to have been accompanied by a drop in precipitation. Scuba divers have recently recovered early-looking Archaic bifaces from what appears to be the submerged prehistoric shoreline of a lake in central Maine. Thus even lakeside sites may have been obliterated from the archaeological record during this period.[12]

At present, however, several Maine sites have produced Early Archaic artifacts, and the great age of some of these sites has been established by radiocarbon dating. These data, together with our growing understanding of how forests changed during the Archaic period, have led to more optimistic assessments regarding the size of human populations that might have lived there following the apparent disappearance of Paleo-Indians.[13]

Like the Paleo-Indians, Early Archaic people made tools by flaking stones, such as chert and rhyolite. They also made many scrapers and other minimally modified unifacial tools from quartz. In fact, an abundance of quartz-flaking debris is one of the hallmarks of Early Archaic sites. Projectile points resemble forms common in the Carolinas, where they may have originated. These include a very small number of the Kirk Corner Notched type and, more commonly, points with a notched or bifurcate base. Tools of bone and antler have also been found in small numbers. Though fragmentary, we can see in them evidence for barbed spears that were to remain in use until they were replaced by items of European manufacture. Early Archaic people also began to manufacture a new range of implements shaped by pecking and grinding less-brittle granular rock types—those not suitable for flaking. Adzes, gouges, and stone rods are most common. The gouges have a groove running their entire length, and their sharp cutting edges were probably maintained by stone rods used as whetstones. As many of these new tool types were meant for woodworking, they apparently reflect an expansion of wood technology, probably to include wooden food vessels, dugout canoes, and fish weirs.[14]

Regarding subsistence, artifacts and small samples of bone refuse from deep, stratified riverine sites indicate that hunters pursued white-tailed deer and black bear, along with beaver (*Castor canidensis*), muskrat (*Ondrata zibethica*), and otter (*Lutra canadensis*); at least some birds and turtles were also taken.[15] That many Early Archaic sites are located along inland waterways suggests that boat travel, if not fishing as well, were important activities. Although numerous bones of anadromous fish were recovered at one Early Archaic site in Massachusetts, direct evidence of freshwater fishing in Maine has been limited, probably at least in part because fragile fish bones are even less likely to survive in early sites than those of mammals and birds.[16] However, most site locations would have provided easy access to anadromous species (i.e., fish that enter streams from the sea to spawn, usually during spring and summer). The most important of these would have been the alewife (*Promolobus pseudoharengus*), shad (*Alosa spadissima*), and probably Atlantic salmon (*Salmo salar*). Early Archaic sites are also relatively numerous along lakeshores, particularly in northwestern Maine, suggesting that nonanadromous species like whitefish (*Coregonus culpeaformis*), brook trout (*Salvelinus frontalis*), and lake trout (*Salvelinus namaycush*) were important resources there.[17] The eel (*Anguilla rostrata*), which is catadromous (i.e., migrates downstream to spawn in the sea), may also have been important by this time.

Coastal resources such as shellfish, fish, and sea mammals may have been exploited, although, as we shall see, there is reason to believe the biological productivity of the Gulf of Maine was still well below levels attained in more recent times. Because of current coastal erosion we have little basis for evaluating how much time Early Archaic people spent on the seacoast; all we have is a small number of isolated projectile-point finds.[18]

Mortuary practices become evident in the archaeological record of the Maritime Peninsula region beginning in the Early Archaic period. Very different from village sites, mortuary sites reflect not merely the interment of human remains but also the ceremonies associated with that activity. Interpreting such sites is a difficult process but one that holds much promise for enhancing our understanding of the cultures involved. Three clear mortuary sites dating to around 8500 b.p. have been found in northern New England. All contained cremation burials situated on prominent elevations adjacent to the river channel, but there the resemblance ends. At the Tableland site on the Merrimack River in Manchester, New Hampshire, the cremations were accompanied by red ocher and grave furnishings, including flaked stone tools and stone rods. At the Morrill's Point site, at the mouth of the Merrimack River in Salisbury, Massachusetts, in addition to ocher and stone rods, there were adzes, gouges, and several projectile points resembling the Kirk Corner Notched type. No furnishings at all were recovered at the Ormsby site on the Androscoggin River in Brunswick, Maine.[19]

The Middle Archaic

Estimates of population size for the Middle Archaic period vary because of uncertainties about unrecognized artifact styles and the likelihood of differential site destruction.[20] The archaeological sample for this period is growing rapidly, however, particularly in southwestern and south-central Maine. While caution is advisable in estimating population size from simple statistics such as artifact or site numbers, these numbers are so much higher for the Middle than for the Early Archaic there that human populations must have grown substantially. To date, however, we have little evidence for occupation on the Maritime Peninsula east of the St. John River prior to 6000 B.P., except for a few probable Middle Archaic artifacts from southwestern Nova Scotia.[21]

Like those of the Early Archaic, Middle Archaic projectile points continue to resemble those of similar age as far south as the Carolinas. Most common are stemmed projectile points of the Neville and Stark types and their variants.[22] Adzes, fully grooved gouges, and stone rods continued to be made, but these heavy woodworking tools were occasionally supplemented by a southern type, the grooved axe. Southern influences can also be seen in finely ground and polished winged spear-thrower weights. By this time, however, styles local to the Northeast had also begun to appear. These include the ground slate point (probably a lance tip) and the "ulu" or semilunar knife which was also usually made of ground slate.[23]

Middle Archaic sites occur both in the interior and on the coast. Most are small and probably represent brief seasonal encampments of between twenty-five and fifty individuals. Our knowledge of other hunter-gatherer societies in this region and throughout the world suggests that larger sites must have existed in Maine, but few have been discovered.[24]

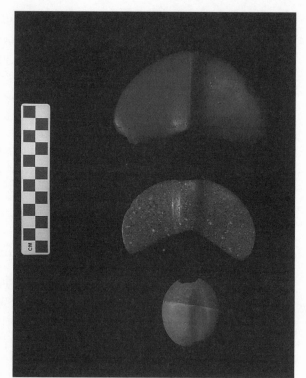

2-4. (*right*) Contracting-stem points of the Neville variant (*bottom*) and slightly younger Stark types (*top*), dating between around 7800 B.P. and a few centuries after 7000 B.P. (Maine State Museum collection.)

2-5. Spear-thrower weights from various southern Maine sites. (Maine State Museum collection.)

Like those of the Early Archaic, Middle Archaic sites in the interior are nearly always situated on or near bodies of water in locations that suggest the continued or growing dietary importance of fish.[25] There is, nevertheless, evidence of the exploitation of a new kind of environment: the relative abundance of turtle and snake bones in a number of sites—remains of animals most likely to be encountered in marshlands. For example, at the Lund site on Lake Cobbosseecontee in Manchester, two clusters of typical Middle Archaic lithic artifacts were found along with small fragments of calcined bone that included the remains of snake and turtle. No clear evidence was recovered that would indicate the season when the site was occupied, but it is nestled at the bottom of a small amphitheater-shaped depression that would have offered shelter from cold northwest winds.[26]

Another possible innovation is that of weir fishing. A recently identified prehistoric weir in Sebasticook Lake at Newport—the oldest known in North America—was first constructed at least six thousand years ago at the beginning of the Late Archaic period and used episodically well into the Ceramic period. What fish species were taken is not known but the weir is well positioned to capture eels.[27]

Marine conditions in the Gulf of Maine were becoming more favorable to biological productivity during Middle Archaic. Lower sea levels and changes in the Gulf Stream and Labrador currents probably caused water temperatures in the Gulf to be warmer and tidal amplitudes lower than today. Paleontological evidence indicates that marine animal communities in the eastern gulf were significantly different from those of modern times, with warm-water species like oysters (*Crassostrea virginica*) and quahogs (*Mercenaria*) more abundant than at present.[28] While biological productivity had not yet attained the high levels of later times, Middle Archaic artifacts have been recovered at a handful of locations along the central Maine coast, suggesting an increase in the exploitation of marine resources. Even islands off the coast were occupied, a clear indication that reliable watercraft were being made.[29]

One such island site was apparently located on Deer Isle, where scallop fishermen recently brought up artifacts that date to the Middle Archaic period. Divers from the Maine State Museum have since recovered additional artifacts at the same locality, which lies nearly 8 meters below mean low tide, within the depth range that would have been dry land during

2-6. Winged spear-thrower weights from various New England sites. The specimen at the bottom left is about 13 cm wide. (Reproduced from Willoughby 1973.)

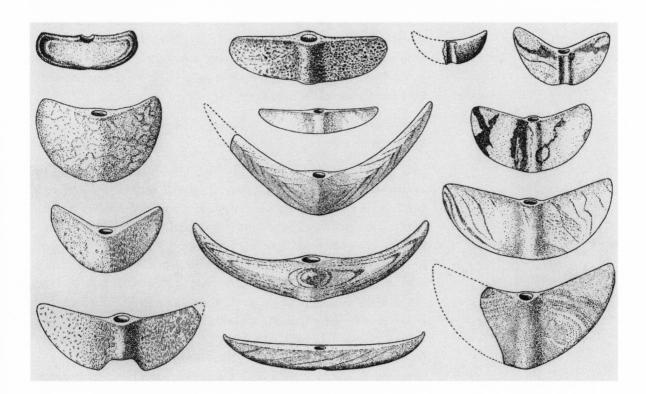

Middle Archaic times. Fishermen have also recovered many large oyster shells nearby, one of which has been radiocarbon dated at 6100±65 B.P. These data suggest a site along the shoreline of an estuary, adjacent to oyster beds.[30]

Evidence for Middle Archaic mortuary behavior is not abundant. To date, only five Middle Archaic burial sites have been found in New England: one in Connecticut, one in Massachusetts, and three in Maine. Moreover, the Maine sites are undated and may actually pertain to the Early Archaic. Red ocher was included in some burials, which are usually located at the summits of prominent rises near rivers. Burial furniture varies from site to site but the range includes projectile points, spear-thrower weights, adzes, gouges, and stone rods.[31]

The Late Archaic

The archaeological record of the Northeast is sparse for the sixth and fifth millennia B.P., and archaeologists have ventured few suggestions regarding the cultural patterns of the period. It seems unlikely that the region was depopulated for so long a period during so recent a time, particularly in light of clear evidence that the Sebasticook Lake fish weir was used periodically beginning about 6000 B.P.[32] The hiatus may thus be largely a matter of our inability to recognize cultural remains from that period. By around 5000 B.P., however, we have much more abundant evidence for human occupation, in the form of two distinct cultures, the Vergennes phase and the Small Stemmed Point tradition.

The Vergennes Phase

One of the patterns that appears by around 5000 B.P. is known as the Vergennes phase, which seems to have been widespread across temperate northeastern North America, ranging primarily eastward from Lake Ontario through northern New England and into western New Brunswick. Archaeological evidence for this culture is rather elusive throughout much its range. It is best known in the Lake Champlain Basin, where it was initially recognized in 1965.[33] Few traces have been found in New Hampshire and very little evidence indeed has been recovered in southern and western Maine. However, small Vergennes sites are fairly common at interior locations between the Kennebec and St. John drainages, and a few typical artifacts have been found as far to the northeast as Nova Scotia.[34] It may be that Vergennes populations also inhabited the coast and that these sites have been destroyed by erosion. This seems unlikely, however, because to date many more Middle Archaic artifacts have been discovered along the coast than have those from the more recent Vergennes phase. The relative scarcity of Vergennes sites in New Hampshire, western Maine and along the coast to the east suggests that this culture's influence on the region came primarily from the St. Lawrence Valley and that it had little impact on either the White Mountains or the New England coastal zone.

We know very little about how Vergennes people lived or why they focused on interior resources. In many ways, their artifacts resemble those of contemporaneous cultures throughout the region. The adze, gouge, plummet, and ulu (all tools found in Vergennes contexts) were probably used for water-related activities like dugout canoe construction and fishing. On

2-7. Fully grooved, ground stone gouges recovered from various sites in Maine. (Private collection.)

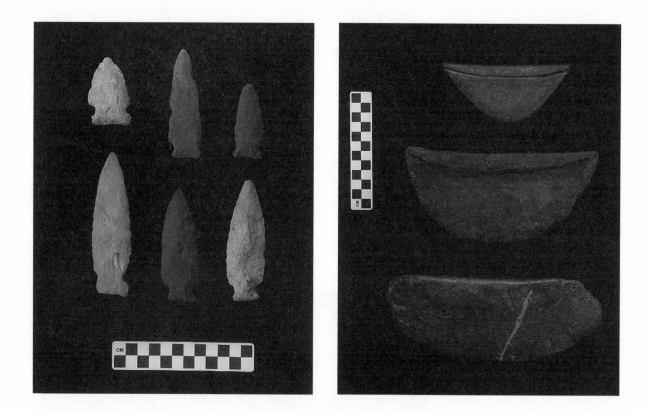

2-8. Otter Creek points dating to around 5000 B.P. (Maine State Museum collection.)

2-9. Ulus from Maine sites. The specimen in the middle was recovered just to the east of Deer Isle, from a submerged archaeological site at a depth of 8 meters. (Maine State Museum collection.)

the other hand, the robust Otter Creek point, which typifies the phase, has generally been regarded as a spear tip, suggesting a reliance upon large terrestrial game.[35] The fact that Vergennes sites are confined to the interior may be further evidence of such a reliance. It may also be significant that by about 5000 B.P. Maine forests were becoming hardwood dominated, much like those to the west where the Vergennes phase appears to have originated.[36]

Recent research by Steven Cox has identified an interesting Vergennes component in southeastern Maine, at a narrows on the lower end of Big Lake in Indian Township.[37] The Narrows site is highly unusual in that it is apparently uncontaminated by the heavy admixture of artifacts from earlier and later occupations that plague so many Vergennes components. Before the lake was dammed, the site probably fronted on a stretch of rapids where anadromous fish and the catadromous eel could be taken easily. Typical Vergennes artifacts found at the site include Otter Creek points, plummets, gouges, ulus, and several of the flat rocks expediently chipped around the edges that archaeologists, unsure of their function, have generally called "choppers."

The importance of the Narrows site is further enhanced by the presence of that rarest of Vergennes site attributes: datable features. Charcoal samples from these features yielded three dates (4965±190, 5070±275, and 5150±160 B.P.), more than doubling the sample then available from only two other sites—one in Vermont and one in southern Ontario.[38] Although all of these dates are in close agreement, many researchers suspect the Vergennes phase is of greater antiquity, extending back into the little understood sixth millennium B.P.[39] The best support for this notion comes from the Lavoie site on the Upper North Shore of the St. Lawrence River near Tadoussac. Here, in stratified contexts, were found typical Vergennes artifacts such as Otter Creek points, ulus and points of polished schist and plummets, all associated with a radiocarbon date of 5550±100 B.P.[40]

The significance of the Vergennes phase and its influence in Maine has been debated for more than twenty years. To some it represents the intrusion into Maine of small, mobile hunting populations whose origins apparently lay in the St. Lawrence River Valley. The less formal tool styles of the Vergennes phase and even its beautifully polished ulus, however, resemble those found in some coastal and near-coastal Middle Archaic sites.[41] Is the Otter Creek point merely a peripatetic style that was adopted by neighboring groups? As it clearly embodies no technological breakthrough this seems doubtful, but time will tell.

The Small Stemmed Point Tradition

Throughout southern New York and New England, archaeological sites have yielded thousands of small, narrow stemmed projectile points, generally made of quartz. They are evidence of what has been called the Small Stemmed Point or narrow point tradition.[42] In southern New England, but less commonly in Maine, these points are often found along with triangular points. Other stone artifacts often found in association are adzes, gouges, plummets, spear-thrower weights, and fully grooved net weights. All these artifact forms suggest that the Small Stemmed Point tradition is derived from the Middle Archaic cultures of the region. The scarcity of archaeological data spanning the sixth millennium B.P., however, leaves the matter of origins unresolved.[43]

In southern New England and New York, this technological tradition dominates the archaeological scene from at least 4500 B.P. to around 3500 B.P.[44] In Maine, east of the Kennebec, dates for the Small Stemmed Point tradition are somewhat earlier, between about 5000 B.P. and 4500 B.P. The earliest dates are from the Turner Farm site on North Haven Island, in

Penobscot Bay, where the deepest component, called Occupation 1, represents at least one visit by a Small Stemmed Point tradition group between 5200 B.P. and 4900 B.P.[45]

Few faunal remains were found in the dated features of Occupation 1, but identified animal species include clam (*Mya arenaria*), cod (*Gadus callarius*), deer (*Odocoileus virginianus*), and swordfish (*Xiphias gladuis*). A second dated component of this tradition, the Davis-Tobie site, lies on the estuary of the Sheepscot River in the village of Sheepscot. This site produced small stemmed points and other quartz tools in association with charcoal dated to 4470±150 B.P., which is slightly later than the Turner Farm dates and more in line with the earliest dates obtained for the tradition in southern New England.[46] Evidence of the Small Stemmed Point tradition has now been identified at several coastal and near coastal sites west of Frenchman's Bay. However, very little evidence of the tradition has been found far above the tidal estuaries of Maine's rivers.

An especially important component of the tradition was discovered at the Seabrook Marsh site, just west of the Maine border in New Hampshire. This site produced small stemmed points, precisely similar to those mentioned above, with human burials dating to about 4700 B.P. A small sample of animal bone was also found that included the remains of a number of species, including deer, cod, and swordfish, the latter represented by a cache of five complete rostra (bills).[47] These are the same species identified in Occupation 1 at the Turner Farm site, where they also dominate the faunal assemblage of the slightly later Occupation 2, which pertains to the Moorehead phase. These Occupation 1 and Seabrook Marsh data are important because they provide good evidence that the maritime-oriented lifestyle of the Moorehead phase had been developed earlier by the Small Stemmed Point tradition.

The available data thus suggest that although peoples of both the Vergennes phase and the Small Stemmed Point tradition were active in the area around 5000 B.P., and perhaps earlier, the former soon disappeared while the latter persisted for about five hundred years. To the extent that these two peoples were contemporaries, the people of the Vergennes phase mainly occupied upland regions and focused upon terrestrial game, while those of the Small Stemmed Point tradition mainly occupied the Gulf of Maine coast, where they practiced a mixed economy that included the pursuit of large fish, particularly cod and swordfish. A similar interior/coastal relationship between these two cultures appears also to have existed in southern New England.[48]

The Moorehead Phase

Between 5000 B.P. and 4500 B.P. there emerged a striking new culture in south-central Maine. It is responsible for the Red Paint cemeteries discussed above and is known as the Moorehead phase, named for the pioneering Maine archaeologist Warren K. Moorehead, who worked extensively on sites of this period.[49] The available evidence suggests that it was a direct descendent of the Small Stemmed Point tradition.

The Moorehead-phase Red Paint cemeteries excavated by C. C. Willoughby in the 1890s, and later by many others, were clearly ceremonial in nature. Most of the grave furnishings were simple utilitarian tools, such as adzes, gouges, and plummets, that are indistinguishable from those subsequently found at village sites. Others, however, are beautiful examples of unparalleled workmanship and fanciful design that were probably intended solely for ceremonial purposes. Among the most striking are the long, delicate, ground-slate "bayonets." Also outstanding are an array of small zoomorphic plummets, plummetlike objects, and effigies of real or imaginary creatures. Projectile points are not particularly common at these sites. The locally manufactured ones are stemmed forms, generally larger than but

2-10. *(bottom left)* Small triangular and stemmed points of the Small Stemmed Point tradition from Maine. (Maine State Museum collection.)

2-11. Fully grooved net weights from Maine sites. (Maine State Museum collection.)

2-12. Moorehead-phase stemmed points. (Maine State Museum collection.)

obviously derived from those of the Small Stemmed Point tradition. More interesting, however, are two types that originated in distant locales. Their significance is discussed below.

Estimates published in 1922 by Moorehead—who had himself overseen the excavation of 440 graves at 12 sites—indicated that by then a total of 23 cemeteries containing 1,440 graves had been excavated, all in the area between the Kennebec and Frenchman's Bay.[50] From these cemeteries had come, according to Moorehead's assessment, 7,200 artifacts—an average of 5 per grave. These impressive figures far exceed the levels attained by any other prehistoric mortuary patterns east of the Adena and Hopewell burial mounds of the Ohio and Mississippi Valleys, which are almost two millennia more recent. However, during the period when Moorehead-phase Red Paint cemeteries were being most avidly exploited, careful excavation was the exception rather than the rule. By 1948, when most such sites had been found and excavated, the site count had risen to 44, from which nearly 2,000 artifacts remained available for study.[51] Since 1948 the extent of Moorehead-phase sites has only slightly expanded westward to the lowermost Androscoggin River and eastward to include the lower St. John River

ISOTOPES AND DIET

The importance of marine hunting by Moorehead-phase people is clearly apparent in the sophisticated bone technology and in the abundance of marine faunal remains of Occupation 2. It is also evident in a newly developed technique for reconstructing diet from human bone chemistry.[52]

Bone is composed mainly of two fractions: apatite, a crystalline substance, and collagen, a protein. It has been demonstrated that bone collagen includes two isotopes of nitrogen, the common ^{14}N and the less common ^{15}N, in ratios that reflect diet, specifically the amount and type of protein consumed. The more meat there is in a person's diet, the more enriched their skeleton will be in ^{15}N. The degree of enrichment is greater if the meat is from a marine organism and if the organism was itself a marine-meat consumer, such as a seal or a large carnivorous fish, enrichment is greater still. The same kind of enrichment occurs with the carbon isotope ^{13}C relative to the more common ^{12}C, but to a lesser degree, making it less useful as a dietary indicator. Another problem with ^{13}C enrichment is that it is proportional to both meat and corn (*Zea mays*) intake. Thus in cases where both marine organisms and corn may have been part of the diet, ^{13}C enrichment cannot distinguish between the two.

The ovals in Figure 2-13 indicate the isotopic ranges (to the first standard deviation) of several coastal Maine populations, one from the Boucher (B) site in interior Vermont and one from Port au Choix (P) in northern Newfoundland. For purposes of comparison, these

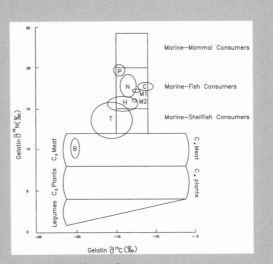

2-13. Isotopes in human bone.

ranges are superimposed upon a series of fields defining the isotopic ranges of vertebrates, including humans, whose diets are known from nonarchaeological information. The isotopic ranges for all the Maine coastal populations indicate a high intake of marine protein (flesh) in their diets. The highest relative values of ^{15}N are for individuals from the Moorehead-phase cemetery at the Nevin site in Blue Hill (N) and are most likely due to the importance of swordfish and cod in their diets, while the lowest values are for the Susquehanna-tradition cemetery (T) at the Turner Farm site.[53]

drainage.[54] The geographic center of their distribution remains the area between the Kennebec and Penobscot Rivers.

While awareness of these spectacular cemeteries spread during the late nineteenth century, understanding of the culture that produced them lagged far behind, mainly because archaeologists were rarely able to identify the habitation sites associated with them. From the late 1930s onward, however, a series of associated habitation sites have been discovered, and many of them have now been investigated. The most extensively studied is the Turner Farm site, where the second component, Occupation 2, has provided a detailed record of subsistence activities during the centuries between about 4500 B.P. and 4000 B.P.

The most striking discovery among the faunal remains from Occupation 2 was the abundance of swordfish. Although we now have evidence of swordfish-hunting during slightly earlier times and have long been aware that swordfish were hunted during the Moorehead phase, the data from Occupation 2 were the first to point to the importance of this formidable fish species.[55] Cod and deer were also major resources, and shellfish—primarily the soft-shell clam but also the now locally extinct quahog—were gathered in huge numbers. Other aquatic resources, such as shallow-water fish species and sea mammals like seals and porpoise, were apparently little used.

Evidence for the seasons when different animal species were taken during Occupation 2 indicates the presence of a year-round population. While the site seems to have been the home base for a substantial group, no doubt some of its population made seasonal visits to other locales, both in the interior and on the coast.

An example of an interior locale that might have been visited seasonally is the Hirundo site, located on Pushaw Stream, a tributary of the Penobscot River. Excavations conducted there by David Sanger of the University of Maine recovered a wide variety of artifacts, including several that closely resemble Moorehead-phase cemetery objects. These artifacts may have been left by the same people who built two hearths dated to about 4300 B.P., which unfortunately contained no artifacts. Little bone refuse is available to shed direct light on subsistence activities, but the site's location next to a set of rapids suggests that anadromous fish were the main attraction.[56]

A coastal site that was probably occupied sporadically is the Stanley site on Monhegan Island, which has been dated to 3700 B.P., close to the end of the Moorehead phase.[57] Swordfish were probably present in the Gulf of Maine mainly during the summer months and then tended to stay mainly in deep water. Thus the Stanley site may have been a convenient base for swordfish-hunting parties who returned portions of their catch, such as fillets and rostra, to village sites like the Turner Farm site. Support for such a scenario comes from the great abundance of postcranial bone from the Stanley site, in comparison to Occupation 2 at the Turner Farm site, which yielded numerous rostrum fragments.

Another probable seasonal site is the Goddard site on Naskeag Point, in Brooklin. Unlike most coastal Maine sites, the Goddard site is not a shell midden, and therefore the bone sample from it is small. The species represented, however, include swordfish and deer. The presence of swordfish and the absence of shellfish, which seem to have been harvested in prehistoric times during late winter and spring, suggest that the Goddard site was a large summer encampment.[58]

To summarize our present understanding of how the Moorehead phase might have developed, it appears that between 6000 B.P. and 4000 B.P., as biological productivity in the Gulf of Maine reached high levels, a local population began to settle on the coast of central and eastern Maine in order to exploit growing stocks of cod and swordfish. Coincidentally, by 4500 B.P. this population had developed a highly distinctive material culture as well as an unprecedented pattern of mortuary ceremonialism.

Relations between the Moorehead Phase and Contemporaneous Cultures

As a highly localized cultural phenomenon, the relationships between Moorehead phase and neighboring populations are of some interest. Evidence for Moorehead-phase occupation of the interior of the Maritime Peninsula is scarce, and there seems to be little competing evidence for a separate population there. Instead, what evidence we have suggests that Moorehead-phase populations made seasonal visits to the interior or merely traversed it en route to destinations farther north.

Archaeological evidence for Late Archaic populations from western Maine southwestward to Massachusetts is not abundant, but what we have suggests that people of the Small Stemmed Point tradition persisted there and farther to the south and west without developing the elaborate ritual patterns apparent in the Moorehead phase.[59] The small stemmed point itself extends still farther southward, occasionally occurring in association with red ocher in simple mortuary features.[60] To the east, artifacts resembling those of the Moorehead phase diminish in frequency beyond the St. John River. Their absence along the Bay of Fundy coast is probably due at least in part to high rates of coastal submersion, but they are also scarce in the interior of New Brunswick.[61]

Artifacts from Moorehead-phase cemeteries reveal important contacts with more distant regions as well. Chert and quartzite Bradley points closely resembling the Normanskill type of eastern New York and dated to about this time, occur frequently in Moorehead-phase cemeteries. It is interesting to note that, aside from an occasional Moorehead-phase slate bayonet, the Lake Champlain region has produced much less evidence for reciprocal Moorehead phase-influence.[62] Evidence for even longer-range contact can be found in projectile points from Moorehead-phase cemeteries that are made of a quartzite found only at Ramah Bay, a fjord on the North Labrador coast.[63]

During the late 1960s and early 1970s, cemeteries similar to those of the Moorehead phase were discovered in northern Newfoundland and southern Labrador, the most interesting being at Port au Choix, Newfoundland.[64] Archaeologists working in that region have classified the culture responsible for these cemeteries as the Maritime Archaic tradition. Like the Moorehead-phase cemeteries, these northern cemeteries were made up of numerous graves furnished with red ocher, slate bayonets, adzes, gouges, marine-mammal effigies, and slate bayonets. Some of the bayonets are virtually identical to forms found in Moorehead-phase cemeteries. Moreover, bone tools from the cemetery at Port au Choix include bone foreshafts, daggers, and harpoons that resemble those found at Moorehead-phase sites in Maine.

Like the Moorehead phase, there is good evidence that people of the Maritime Archaic tradition also focused strongly on maritime hunting. Few faunal remains have been preserved at their sites, but their technology was unmistakably designed for use on large marine prey, probably seals,

2-14. (*left*) Ramah chert points from Moorehead-phase cemeteries. (Maine State Museum collection.)

2-15. Bradley points from Moorehead-phase cemeteries. (Maine State Museum collection.)

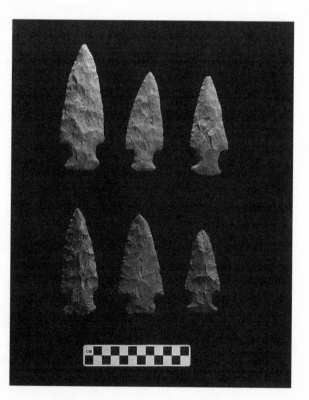

and recent isotopic analysis of skeletons from the Port au Choix cemetery confirms the importance of marine mammals in their diet.[65]

The similarities in technology, subsistence, and ceremonialism between the Moorehead phase and the Maritime Archaic tradition are so strong, particularly in contrast to contemporaneous cultures to the west and south, that some archaeologists saw them as a single cultural entity.[66] As originally conceived in the 1970s, this all-encompassing view of the Maritime Archaic tradition presupposed a common economic base of marine mammals and caribou (*Rangifer tarandus caribou*). Such a notion made sense at the time, for Maine is known to have had a caribou population during historic times and possesses large seal populations today. Subsequent research, however, has made this broad conceptual model untenable.

As we have seen, one important difficulty is the fact that the Moorehead phase clearly appears to have developed locally from the Small Stemmed Point tradition rather than as the result of northern influence. Another problem is that the two groups turn out to have had different prey. There is little evidence for seal hunting during the Archaic period in Maine, and to date only a single specimen caribou bone has been tentatively identified from one late prehistoric Maine faunal collection. The caribou mentioned so frequently in the early sporting literature of Maine were probably from a population that expanded southward recently from the Gaspé Peninsula during a cold period in the seventeenth and eighteenth centuries.[67] In fact, the prehistoric abundance of swordfish in the Gulf of Maine, the presence of quahogs in Occupation 2 deposits at the Turner Farm site, and other environmental indicators mentioned above all show that the region was significantly warmer between about 7000 B.C. and 4000 B.P. than during later prehistory, and it is therefore unlikely that caribou existed in the region at that time.[68]

Another problem with the concept of a broad Maritime Archaic tradition is that the two regions where sites and diagnostic artifacts are most evident are separated by the hiatus of Canada's maritime provinces, where only a few Moorehead phase–like artifacts and no cemeteries have been found.

Finally, the broad Maritime Archaic model was based on the assumption that the cemeteries of Maine were contemporaneous with or slightly later than, and possibly derived from those of Newfoundland and Labrador. Recent redating of sites from both areas, however, suggests that many Maine cemeteries predate 3800 B.P., some by several centuries, while the northern cemeteries date to about that time or slightly later. Instead of regarding the two groups as part of the same cultural phenomenon in an

2-16. Plummets, plummetlike objects, and zoomorphic objects from Moorehead-phase cemeteries. (Maine State Museum collection.)

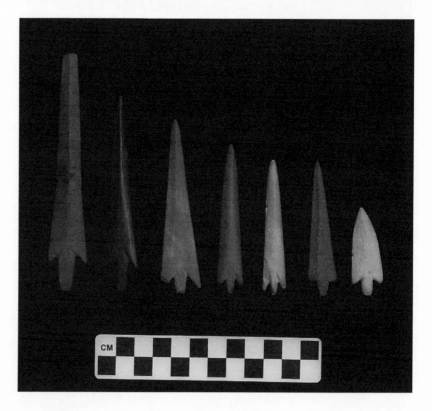

2-17. Ground slate points from the Goddard site. (Maine State Museum collection.)

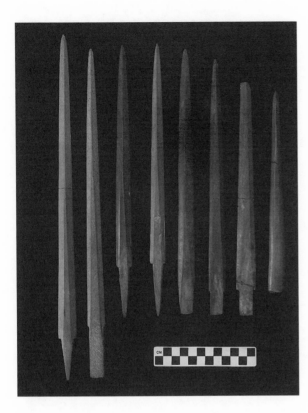

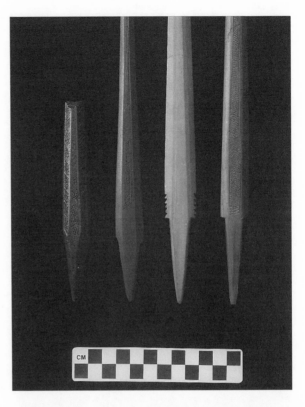

2-18. *(left)* Narrow slate bayonets with hexagonal cross sections, a highly standardized style common found in Moorehead-phase cemeteries. (Maine State Museum collection.)

2-19. *(right)* Elaborate decoration on narrow hexagonal bayonets from the Cow Point cemetery in southwestern New Brunswick. (Collection Canadian Museum of Civilization.)

2-20. *(bottom)* Moorehead-phase bayonets with two facets meeting in a ridge on one side and a simple convex cross section on the other. Similar bayonets have been found in Red Paint cemeteries in Newfoundland. (Maine State Museum collection.)

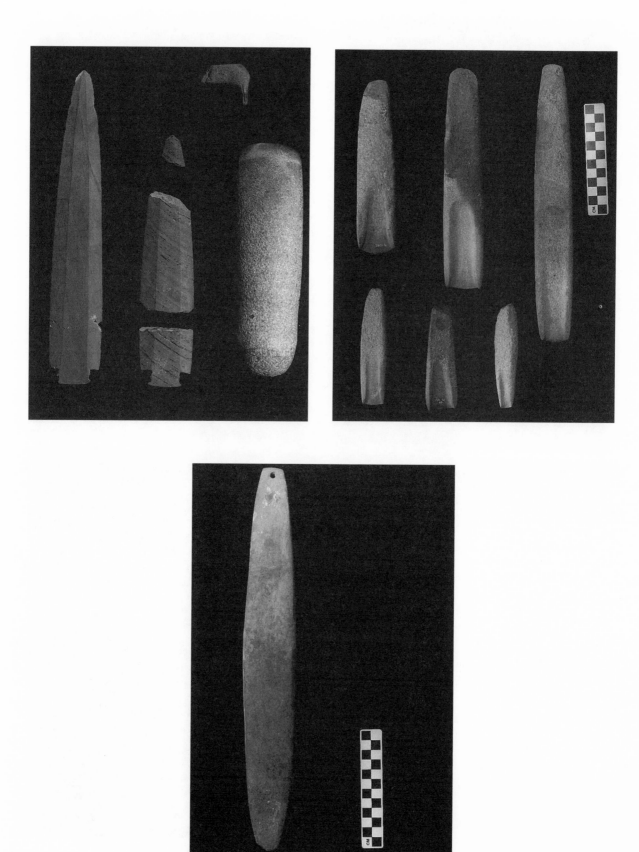

ancestral sense, then, for the present it appears more appropriate to attribute their similarities to their shared focus on maritime pursuits, and to view the evidence for contact between them as the result of the communication one might expect between maritime peoples who normally ranged over long distances.[69]

It remains unclear why both groups developed such unusual mortuary ritualism, which is much more elaborate than anything practiced by their western and southern contemporaries; however, some clues may be found in the anthropological literature. Rituals associated with important prey species are widespread among northern hunting peoples, and there are well-known examples of such groups using rituals for protection when undertaking risky maritime hunting.[70] Elaborate mortuary ritualism is also frequently interpreted as a form of frontier behavior that serves to strengthen group identity in the presence of a culturally dissimilar group. There is reason to believe that both dangerous hunting and culturally different neighbors prevailed during the periods when these two ceremonial patterns flourished.

Finally, there is a very small number of artifacts from Maine that are made of native copper in forms reminiscent of artifacts found far to the west. These include adzes, one gouge, and stemmed and socketed spear points. Unfortunately, only the gouge is from a clear archaeological context: a Moorehead-phase grave on Indian Island, Oldtown. In no way do the other three resemble the small, simple native copper tools of the late Ceramic Period, which are thought to be made from nuggets quarried at Cap d'Or, Nova Scotia. Rather, their forms suggest that, like the gouge, all are Archaic in age and that they are imports from the Lake Superior region, where native copper is abundant. Their relationship to the Moorehead phase so far remains undemonstrated.[71]

The Disappearance of the Moorehead phase

Surprisingly, these highly successful maritime hunting peoples—innovative cultures that prospered by adapting to rich maritime resources—disappeared abruptly around 3800 B.P. and seem to have left no trace in the cultures that succeeded them locally. The Moorehead phase was replaced by a very different archaeological culture known as the Susquehanna tradition; and in Newfoundland and Labrador the Maritime Archaic people were replaced, though not so abruptly as in Maine, by an even more distinct culture known archaeologically as Pre-Dorset or Paleo-Eskimo.[72]

2-21. *(left)* Two broad hexagonal bayonets of banded green slate, a shallow gouge, and a bird's-head effigy found in red ocher in Waldoboro. Similar bayonets have been found in a Red Paint cemetery at Port au Choix. In Maine and the Maritimes, the style has been found in isolated red ocher deposits but not in cemeteries. Specimen on left is 21.2 centimeters long. (Maine State Museum collection.)

2-22. *(right)* Short-grooved gouges like these are the most commonly found artifacts in Moorehead-phase sites. Although probably hafted, most gouges are battered on the poll end, suggesting that they were driven with a mallet. (Maine State Museum collection.)

2-23. *(bottom)* Large tabular whetstone from the Hathaway Moorehead–phase cemetery in Passadumkeag. (Maine State Museum collection.)

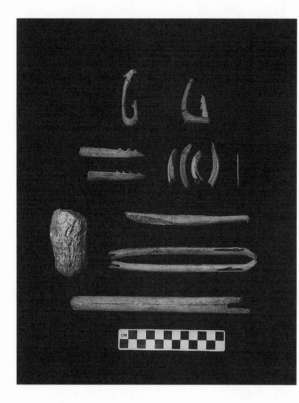

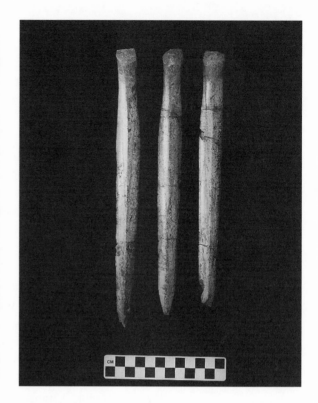

2-24. *(left)* Bone artifacts from Occupation 2 at the Turner Farm site. Shown here, from top to bottom, are bone fishhooks, barbed stone spears (*left*), and beaver-incisor wood-carving tools, a socketed segment of deer antler—probably a knife handle—an effigy of a bird's head (cormorant?), two enigmatic worked Canada goose ulnae, and a harpoon foreshaft of swordfish sword (rostrum). (Maine State Museum collection.)

2-25. Three of several elaborately decorated bone "daggers" from the Nevin Moorehead–phase cemetery in Blue Hill. Lashing impressions are visible on the "handles" of some. Similar daggers were found at the Turner Farm site. (© Robert S. Peabody Museum of Archaeology, Phillips Academy, Andover MA. All rights reserved.)

The Susquehanna Tradition

Between 3600 and 3700 B.P. a new and quite distinct culture known as the Susquehanna tradition suddenly appeared across the Northeast.[73] As its name indicates, it was first recognized by archaeologists working on the Susquehanna River in Pennsylvania and southern New York. Similar manifestations have been identified as far north as the St. Lawrence River, and to the west at least as far as southern Ontario. On the Maritime Peninsula, Susquehanna tradition sites are common as far east as the St. John River, and a few Susquehanna tradition artifacts have recently been recognized across the Bay of Fundy in southern Nova Scotia. Among the numerous Susquehanna tradition components in Maine, by far the largest and richest is Occupation 3 at the Turner Farm site.[74]

In its technology, subsistence practices, and mortuary rituals, the Susquehanna tradition is everywhere strikingly uniform and markedly different from preceding cultures. Indeed, its distinctiveness in so many respects has made it relatively easy to identify in the archaeological record.

Over much of their range, the flaked projectile points, knives, drill bits, and other tools of the Susquehanna tradition represent the largest and most skillfully produced stone artifacts of prehistoric times. In Maine, they include the widest and yet the thinnest bifaces in the prehistoric record, despite the fact that they are generally made of relatively intractable lithic types, such as rhyolite. The much more limited sample of bone tools and ornaments recovered so far—primarily from Occupation 3 at the Turner Farm site—indicates that Susquehanna artisans excelled in this medium as well, but that they worked bone by grinding, rather than scraping with a stone tool, as was the practice during the Moorehead phase. They also produced ground and pecked stone tools such as adzes and gouges, which, although functionally similar to earlier types, were different in detail and made of different lithic materials.[75]

Yet another marked difference between the Susquehanna tradition and the Moorehead phase pertains to diet. The only extensive collection of animal bone from a Susquehanna component comes from Occupation 3 at the Turner Farm site. Occupation 3 deposits include dark, shell-free strata, and extensive shell refuse deposits reaching thicknesses of over 30 centi-

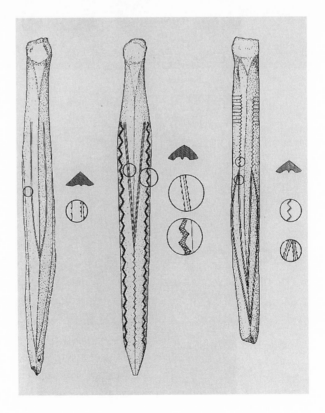

2-26. Line drawings highlighting the decoration on the Nevin daggers shown in Figure 2-25. (Reproduced from Byers 1979; © Robert S. Peabody Museum of Archaeology, Phillips Academy, Andover MA. All rights reserved.)

2-27. View of excavations at the Turner Farm site in 1972. (Maine State Museum.)

meters. There are distinct differences between the animal prey species of Occupation 3 and those of the underlying Occupation 2. Most dramatic is the absence of swordfish in the Occupation 3 diet. Deer bones, on the other hand, while very common throughout the Turner Farm stratigraphic sequence, are most predominant in Occupation 3. Smaller mammals, such as birds and small fish, were evidently taken only in small numbers.[76] The diminished importance of marine resources suggested by these faunal remains is confirmed by the markedly less maritime isotopic signature of the Occupation 3 skeletal population.[77]

Unfortunately, evidence regarding Susquehanna tradition subsistence activities away from the coast are even scarcer than for the Moorehead phase. Interior Susquehanna sites, like those of most other Archaic groups, generally cluster around areas where the seasonal capture of anadromous fish using spears, nets, or weirs would have been relatively easy.

However, two recently investigated early Susquehanna tradition sites in the Merrymeeting Bay area do not conform to this water-oriented pattern. Both are large, exceeding 100 meters in length, and both are in areas that were not heavily occupied by other groups either before or after. The Carey's Garden site lies on a rather featureless stretch of the Muddy River in Topsham, and has a very unusual northern exposure. The Muddy River is actually a small stream within a long-drowned estuary that probably never had a high anadromous fish population. The second is the Hamilton field site in Brunswick, which occupies a large, level sandy plain; the only water nearby is a very small brook that would barely have provided drinking water in a dry year, to say nothing of anadromous fish runs. We do not know why Susquehanna populations chose these unusual locations, but they suggest that some aspects of Susquehanna settlement and subsistence were unique among the Archaic populations of Maine.

It may be more than coincidence that the appearance of the Susquehanna tradition seems to coincide with a slight shift in forest composition toward a more "southern" character, for there is both direct and indirect evidence for the unusual importance of nuts to these people.[78] Butternuts, hickory nuts, and walnuts are ubiquitous in Susquehanna contexts throughout the Northeast.[79] Although only beech nuts were frequently included in Susquehanna burials at the Turner Farm site, acorns could also have been gathered in abundance.

We have direct evidence for acorn processing—most likely by roasting—from a large, charcoal-rich pavementlike Susquehanna feature at a site on the Kennebec River in Waterville, where carbonized remains included acorn shells and meats. At the Turner Farm site, similar features date from Occupation 3 times, suggesting that acorn roasting may have been important there as well. Further evidence for nut processing may be found in stone pestles, which in Maine occur almost exclusively in Susquehanna contexts. In prehistoric North America, pestles occurred most frequently among peoples who heavily exploited nuts or who grew corn. In both cases pestles were used to process the starchy tissue into meal or flour. Finally, even though the abundance of nut trees probably declined with slight climatic cooling after about 3500 B.P., nuts remained an important resource throughout the Northeast, as far north as the Gulf of St. Lawrence, into the historic period, and acorn oil remained an important cosmetic and dietary supplement in Maine into the seventeenth century.[80] It therefore seems reasonable to infer that nuts were at least as important here during the warmer times of the Susquehanna tradition.

Like those of the Moorehead phase, the people of the Susquehanna tradition practiced elaborate mortuary rituals. Once again, however, the differences between the two patterns are dramatic. Cemeteries with twenty or more burials, some furnished with dozens of burned and heat-fractured stone and bone artifacts, have been discovered in several places within the tradition's range. To date, at least six Susquehanna tradition cemeteries have been identified in Maine, all in or near the Penobscot drainage basin.[81] This is a small number compared to the forty-four cemeteries known from the preceding Moorehead phase and in comparison to the very large number of identified Susquehanna tradition habitation components. The difference may be due to two factors. First, the tenure of the Susquehanna tradition in Maine may have been too brief to generate the numbers of cemeteries left by the longer-lived Moorehead phase. It is also possible that, while all members of Moorehead-phase populations may have been buried in Red Paint cemeteries, inclusion in a Susquehanna cemetery was more exclusive. If so, however, inclusion was apparently not based upon age or sex, at least at the Turner Farm cemetery.[82]

Of all Susquehanna tradition cemeteries known from New England, only the one associated with Occupation 3 at the Turner Farm had good bone preservation, because it was overlain by shell midden deposits. A salient feature of this cemetery can best be called "ritualized manipulation of the dead," a practice that takes many forms in numerous archaeological and ethnographic cultures around the world. At the Turner farm cemetery, the process apparently began with the removal of whole or partial skeletons from their place of initial interment for further use in rituals. These remains were apparently combined with the remains of other individuals for inclusion in bundle burials or committed to a cremation pyre along with a rich array of grave furnishings. The use of ocher was rare, but other grave furnishings were sometimes abundant—as many as 144 stone and bone artifacts in the case of one cremation burial. Bone artifacts, although virtually absent from Occupation 3 midden deposits, were fairly abundant in the Turner Farm cemetery.[83] Such rituals may have been occasions for emphasizing group solidarity. Food offerings, which include nuts, berries, and fruits, suggest that the rituals occurred in autumn, perhaps at around the time of the equinox.

Relations between the Susquehanna Tradition and Contemporaneous Cultures

From the early 1960s when it was first described by William A. Ritchie, archaeologists have realized that the Susquehanna tradition was somehow involved with a much broader pattern that occurs over most of eastern

North America. Initially defined mainly by its broad-bladed projectile points, it was soon realized that the tradition included several other artifact types.[84] In 1976 William Turnbaugh offered the hypothesis that these types were brought to the Northeast by immigrants from perhaps as far south as the Savannah River. His suggestion has met with firm resistance from a number of writers who, despite recognizing the novelty of Susquehanna tradition technology in the Northeast, nevertheless prefer to see it as the result of local developments or, at most, as an immigration of people from the Susquehanna Valley area into New England. Others acknowledge the southern origins of Susquehanna tradition technology but remain noncommittal about how it arrived in the Northeast.[85] Resistance to Turnbaugh's migration hypotheses is perhaps the clearest example among archaeologists in the Northeast of a strong, even dogmatic, commitment to the notion that prehistoric migrations were rare or, at best, difficult to prove and that, instead, archaeological change can best be explained as cultural adaptation to environmental change.

The large artifact sample available from Occupation 3 at the Turner Farm site has added several more Susquehanna tradition artifact types—many of them made of bone—to the list shared with contemporaneous cultures of the Southeast, from the Savannah River to the Tennessee Basin in Kentucky. These include flaked stone drill bits, scrapers made on the broken tips of projectile points, flake gravers, flaked stone adzes, pecked and ground grooved axes, long bone pins—some with incised decoration—antler rods (flaking tools?), turtle shell rattles, and socketed antler tines. More specific resemblances can be seen between bone pins from the Occupation 3 and those from various locales in the Southeast. The most specific is between decorative motifs found on a bone comb from the Turner Farm cemetery and those used on bone objects found at the Indian Knoll cemetery in Kentucky. Finally, occipital flattening of some skulls recovered from the Turner farm cemetery and the inclusion of dog remains in one burial echo patterns observed at Indian Knoll.[86] As all of these traits are absent from the Moorehead phase and appear to be slightly older in the Southeast, they offer considerable additional support to Turnbaugh's migration hypothesis, if not to his suggestion that migration was in response to a northward spread of anadromous fish species.[87] In sum, it now appears that the sudden appearance of the relatively nonmarine-adapted Susquehanna tradition in the Northeast is most likely explained by its rather large-scale and long-distance migration northward along the Atlantic slope from some point to the south of Pennsylvania, as suggested by Turnbaugh, or from farther west, as suggested by its resemblances to the Indian Knoll culture of Kentucky.

2-28. Susquehanna-tradition preforms, the starting point for a variety of finished stone tool forms. (Maine State Museum collection.)

2-29. Susquehanna-tradition points. Size range is due mainly to wear and resharpening. (Maine State Museum collection.)

The End of the Susquehanna Tradition in Maine

Sometime after 3600 B.P., artisans of the Susquehanna tradition initiated another innovative technology: the sculpting of bowls from a soft metamorphic stone called steatite, using harder rocks as cutting tools.[88] Steatite bowls are common to the south and west of Maine, as far away as Pennsylvania and Georgia, but to date fewer than ten have been reported between the Saco River in western Maine and the St. John River in New Brunswick, and none at all have been found farther to the northeast. The reason for this scarcity—which contrasts so strongly with the abundance of other Susquehanna tradition artifacts—may be due to the lack of suitable raw material in Maine. A more likely explanation, however, is that the production of steatite bowls did not begin until the Susquehanna tradition occupation of Maine had declined.

Evidence for the Susquehanna tradition is greatly diminished in Maine about four hundred years earlier than to the south, where it persisted until 3000 B.P. or later.[89] It is mainly with these later phases of the tradition that steatite bowls have been associated. We can only speculate about the reasons for the decline in Maine. By 3400 B.P., the southern character of Maine's

2-30. Susquehanna-tradition drill bits from Occupation 3 at the Turner Farm site. Probably mounted on the end of a straight shaft that would have been twisted with a bow and probably used on wood. Length variance is due mainly to wear and resharpening. (Maine State Museum collection.)

2-31. Susquehanna-tradition adzes from Occupation 3 at the Turner Farm site. (Maine State Museum collection.)

2-32. Susquehanna-tradition gouges from Occupation 3 at the Turner Farm site. (Maine State Museum collection.)

2-33. Grooved axes from Occupation 3 at the Turner Farm site. (Maine State Museum collection.)

2-34. Three pendants found in a multiple cremation burial from the Occupation 3 cemetery at the Turner Farm site. They are unique to the Susquehanna tradition. (Maine State Museum collection.)

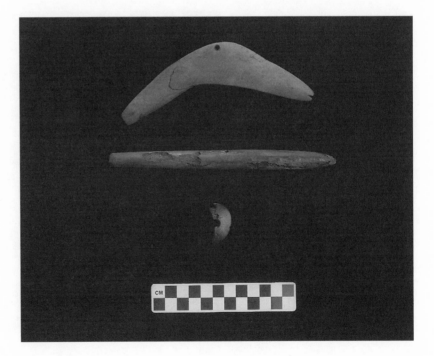

forests had faded, and northern hardwoods and hemlock once again became predominant.[90] While not dramatic, such a shift in vegetation may have had a stronger impact on the Susquehanna tradition than it would have had on a more maritime-oriented culture. Unwilling to turn to the sea—perhaps a relic of the tradition's southern origins—it seems likely that Maine's Susquehanna tradition populations simply underwent a southward territorial contraction.[91]

With the disappearance of the Susquehanna tradition, the prehistoric record in Maine enters a period for which no clear cultural models have been proposed. This is another of those periods whose history varies according to archaeological perspective. Those inclined toward a theory of cultural continuity have pointed to the occasional cobble hearth that dates to later than about 3500 B.P., or to the rare projectile point found in the state that resembles those from the later part of the Susquehanna tradition discovered in southern New England.[92] Others, including myself, comparing these few finds to the evidence of the full-blown Susquehanna tradition, remain unconvinced of this continuity. The point is that whether

2-35. Beads of naturally occurring copper from the Occupation 3 cemetery at the Turner Farm site. These are the only copper beads and nearly the only copper artifacts yet recovered from any Susquehanna-tradition context. (Maine State Museum collection.)

2-36. Turtle-shell parts from the Occupation 3 cemetery at the Turner Farm site. This is the lower shell of a box turtle (*Terrapine carolina*). (Maine State Museum collection.)

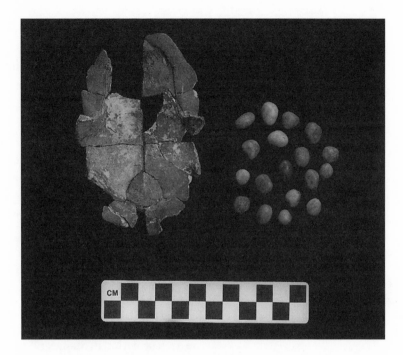

2-37. Decorated bone objects from the Occupation 3 cemetery at the Turner Farm site. (Maine State Museum collection.)

depopulation occurred or not—and negatives are hard to prove—there occurred around 3500 B.P. a collapse, diminishment, or at the least a very substantial alteration of the well-defined Susquehanna pattern that is quite out of step with the continued presence of a recognizable Susquehanna tradition to the south. No clear-cut pattern replaced it for at least another four centuries.[93]

Recently, a few sites dating to the centuries following 3500 B.P. have been identified, and we are beginning to recognize some tool types from the period, including a variety of stemmed point forms, large scrapers, and stone adzes shaped by flaking and grinding.[94] Only a few of these forms might be credibly derived from Susquehanna prototypes, however. Instead, data from the Turner Farm site suggest new technological and subsistence trends beginning sometime around 3000 B.P. and apparently continuing thereafter. On the other hand, pottery, the salient technological feature of the following Ceramic period, does not appear until somewhat later, around 2700 B.P.

The Archaic period in Maine and surrounding areas is emerging as a complex mosaic of cultures whose lifestyles were more varied and external relations more far-flung than archaeologists of previous generations would have thought possible. Although we may grant that there are important threads of continuity running through the fabric of Archaic culture, there are also sharp discontinuities, evidence for the arrival and departure of distinct groups, and important shifts in subsistence behavior, ritual practice, technology, and other aspects of culture that we are only beginning to perceive, much less understand. Although the cultural orientation was generally southward during Early and Middle Archaic times, major influences from the west and north became important in later periods. A final burst of southern influence, most likely caused by a population of immigrants, became the last episode in an era that endured for six thousand years.

The allure that the Archaic period has long held for Maine archaeologists continues undiminished. Recent progress in defining the contours of cultural change during the period has provided some interesting answers and triggered a new and fascinating set of questions. Perhaps the most important lesson to be learned from the past two decades of research is that the answers to these questions must be sought within a larger region than has generally been considered, for it is now clear that Maine was a full participant in the ebb and flow of Archaic cultural change throughout eastern North America.

III THE CERAMIC PERIOD

B Y AROUND 2700 B.P, the archaeological record of Maine begins
to reflect several significant cultural innovations not apparent during the Archaic period; some were episodic, while others were trends
that continued through the rest of the prehistoric period. It is perhaps worth
noting a nonarchaeological change that also occurred in the Northeast at
about this time. This is the appearance of Algonquian languages, thought
by some linguists to have been brought by migrating populations from the
Upper Great Lakes region around 2900 B.P.[1] Given the weakness of the
archaeological record of the Maritime Peninsula for the centuries following 3500 B.P, the near coincidence of this arrival with a revitalized archaeological record at the beginning of the Ceramic period is an interesting one
because it suggests that a substantial migration into the region occurred at
this time.

Ceramics

The most archaeologically obvious innovation of the Ceramic period, and
the one that gives the period its name, is pottery. Peoples of the Northeast
had no doubt used cooking containers for a long time prior to the Ceramic
period. Most likely these were wood or bark vessels to which hot stones
were added to bring the contents to a boil. At some point, however, people
in this region began to fashion pottery vessels that could be placed directly
on the hearth. Humans have long understood the hardening effects of heat
on clay, but making vessels with fired clay is a relatively recent event in
human history. A possible explanation lies in the varying degrees of mobility characteristic of highly mobile nonceramic-using peoples versus more

sedentary ceramic-using ones. The labor involved in making a clay vessel, together with the fragile nature of the final product, renders the technology unsuitable for highly mobile populations. It may be significant in this regard that Maine's coastal and near coastal sites contain a greater relative abundance of pottery than most interior sites. This suggests that life on the coast was more sedentary than in the interior, probably because of the presence of marine resources, which were to become increasingly important to Ceramic-period peoples over time.

North America's earliest ceramics appeared in the Southeast in about 4500 B.P and spread westward to the Mississippi River, arriving there by about 3300 B.P.[2] A variety of regional styles developed throughout this area, one of which spread rapidly across the Northeast as far as eastern Maine by around 2700 B.P.[3]

Known to archaeologists as Vinette 1, after the site in Brewerton, New York, where it was first recognized, this crude pottery was made by building up coils or slabs of clay into vessels with cylindrical bodies and slightly pointed bases. Both the inner and outer surfaces of Vinette 1 ware are generally textured by the impressions of a cord or textile wrapped around a paddle. The face of the paddle was then struck or pressed against the vessel wall to help join its coils and create its shape. Vessel size varied, but most pots would have held about 4 liters of liquid.[4] Vinette 1 and later pottery styles, which retained the basic cylindrical shape and pointed base, were probably used in the manner described much later—at a sixteenth-century Indian village in what is now North Carolina—by the English colonist Thomas Harriot: "After they have set them vppon a heape of erthe to stay them from falling, they putt wood vunder which being kyndled one of them take great care that the fyre burne equally Rounde about."[5]

People began to make Vinette 1–style pottery in Maine at the same time as elsewhere throughout its range. It has been identified at several sites along or near the central Maine coast and at a few sites in New Brunswick and Nova Scotia.[6] Over the next two millennia, pottery in the area underwent a series of changes. The most obvious involved alterations in the decoration of the vessel's outer surface and in the shape of the rim, although changes also occurred in composition and basic mode of construction.[7]

Sometime between 2300 B.P. and 2000 B.P., a new style of pottery embodying substantial technological and aesthetic improvements appeared over the entire Maritime Peninsula.[8] Although there was little alteration in vessel form, the new ware was much thinner and harder, and was often decorated over much of the upper body with impressions made by a narrow-edged tool that was pressed or rocked back and forth into the moist

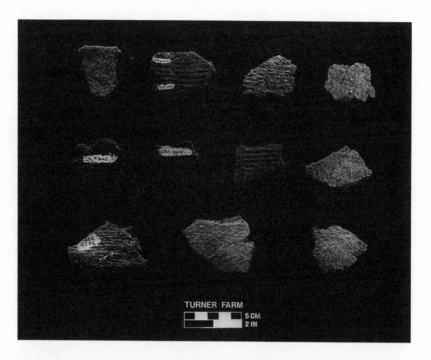

3-1. Vinette 1 pottery from the Turner Farm site. (Maine State Museum collection.)

3-2. Pseudo-scallop-shell-stamped and rocker-stamped pottery sherds, dating between around 2300 and 2000 B.P. (Maine State Museum collection.)

3-3. Drawing of a rocker-stamped pot
from Topsham. This vessel dates to
around 1800 B.P. and is unusual in that
it is somewhat boat-shaped, with
castellated ends about 22 centimeters
apart. (Maine State Museum
collection.)

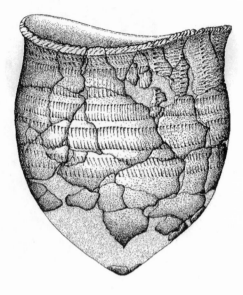

3-4. A rocker-stamped decorated pot
found on an island in Casco Bay.
(Maine State Museum collection.)

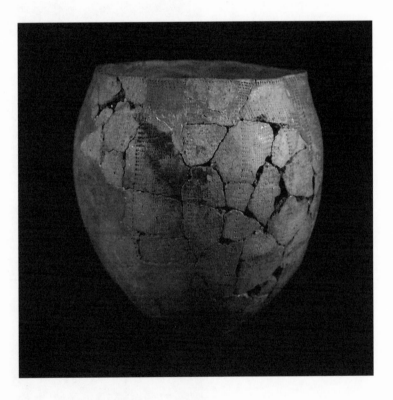

clay. The result is called rocker stamping. The earliest rocker stamping was done with a tool edge that was alternately notched to create so-called pseudo–scallop shell stamping. This style later gave way to dentate (toothed) stamping. Breaks rarely occur along coil or slab junctures, as with Vinette 1, and the abundant coarse grit temper that was mixed with Vinette 1 clay is replaced with smaller amounts of a much finer temper. The rims of these vessels may have multiple peaks (castellations) and complex cross sections (see Fig. 3-5), and other forms of impressed decoration sometimes occur. In general, this second pottery style is among the finest ever made in the region. There is little evidence for its local development from Vinette 1, and, like the earlier form, its origins likely lie far to the west or southwest. Whether this reflects some important cultural or population adjustment is, however, unclear.

This stamped ware underwent changes in construction and decoration over the course of more than a millennium. After about 1800 B.P, much of the change is, technologically speaking, for the worse. Vessel walls became thicker as the quality of the ware declined.[9] Dentate rocker stamping became the predominant decorative motif, rim forms became more elaborate and variable, dentate tooth size increased, and vessels seem to have increased slightly in average size.

3-5. Pottery sherds dating between around 2000 and 1200 B.P., bearing a variety of rocker-stamped decoration. (Maine State Museum collection.)

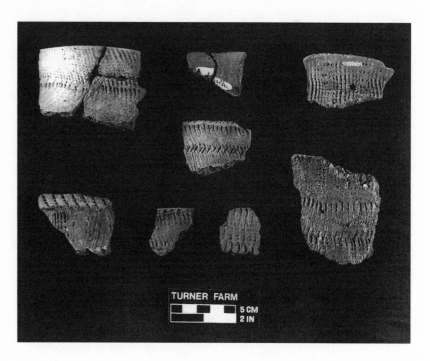

3-6. A cord-wrapped-stick decorated pot from Bradley. (Maine State Museum collection.)

Another marked change in ceramics had occurred throughout much of the Northeast by about 1200 B.P, with the abandonment of dentate stamping and a return to cord-impressed decoration, this time made by wrapping cordage around a stick or thin paddle edge and pressing the tool into the exterior vessel surface.[10] Associated changes include frequent breaks along coils that are once again poorly joined, and the use of crushed shell as temper in some more recent vessels. Like the apparently sudden shift from Vinette 1 to stamped pottery, the shift to cord-wrapped-stick decoration occurred rather quickly, if not suddenly. Only a very few sherds bearing both kinds of decoration have been reported. Most archaeologists nevertheless do not see it as evidence of any major alteration in population composition or lifestyle.

Around 500–600 B.P. (A.D. 1400–1500), the cylindrical vessels with pointed bases of earlier millennia were suddenly replaced by a new vessel form over much of the Northeast, from southern New York to the St. Lawrence Valley and eastward to the coast of New England. The new style featured more spheroidal bodies often surmounted by a cylindrical collar decorated by fields of complex geometric-incised decoration. Once again, this new style appeared suddenly and without clear transitional forms from the earlier style. Collared vessels of this kind were still being made by Iroquoian speakers in the St. Lawrence Valley when Europeans arrived in the sixteenth century and continued to be made by Algonquian speakers in Massachusetts into the 1670s, when they were being replaced with "kettles of brass,

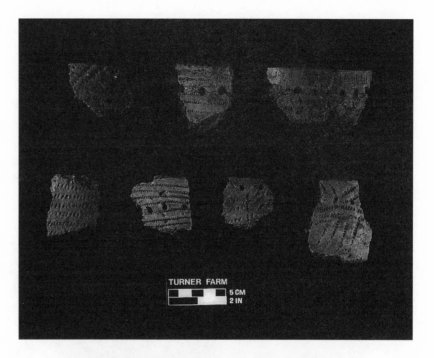

3-7. Pottery sherds dating after around 1000 B.P., bearing a variety of cord-wrapped-stick decorative motifs. (Maine State Museum collection.)

3-8. Late-prehistoric pot with globular body from Fryeburg. (Maine State Museum collection.)

copper or iron."[11] No historic account from Maine or the maritime provinces reports the Native manufacture of pottery. As people in this region had earlier access to European trade goods than did those to the south, they may have been the first to stop making their own fragile wares in favor of trading furs for copper kettles.[12]

Aside from cooking vessels, clay was used throughout the Northeast to make tobacco pipes, and these became important vehicles for symbolism and art among the Iroquoian-speaking populations of the St. Lawrence Valley.[13] In Maine, however, clay pipes are less elaborate than those of the

3-9. Fragment of a crushed collar-incised pot in situ at the Turner Farm site. (Maine State Museum collection.)

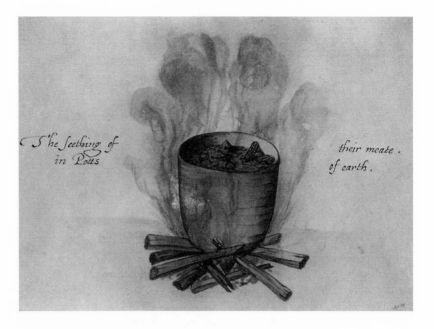

3-10. Watercolor painting by John White showing a pot in use in North Carolina in 1585. (© the British Museum, British Museum Press.)

Iroquois and have been encountered much less frequently. Stone smoking pipes have been recovered occasionally throughout the region; both the forms and materials of the pipes suggest that they were imported, some from as far away as the Ohio Valley.

A final ceramic category of significance in the region is the miniature vessel. Examples of these have been found in late-Ceramic-period sites over the same region as collared vessels, usually in association with them.[14] In Maine miniature vessels have been found at only a few sites and in a datable context only at the Goddard site, where one was present in a grave that also contained European copper. These tiny pots have been regarded by some as simply the toys of young girls, but their frequent occurrence as grave furnishings at the Goddard site and elsewhere in the Northeast suggests that they played a more complex role in adult lives.[15]

Trends and Innovations in Diet

From the time pottery appeared in Maine, the archaeological record suggests substantial if not continuous population growth. This trend can be seen in a variety of indicators, including the number and size of sites and an apparent intensification of faunal exploitation through time.[16] The hunting of large mammals continued during the Ceramic period as before, but on the coast, where human populations concentrated for most of the year, moose became more important. This shift is most evident on the eastern Maine coast, about half as evident in the Penobscot Bay area, and barely detectable around Casco Bay.[17] The reason for the shift is unclear. It coincides with climatic cooling, which can be traced in the pollen record as an increase in spruce pollen, particularly notable during the past millennium.[18] Whether such a climatic shift resulted in a habitat more favorable to moose than deer is, however, uncertain. The picture is complicated by the existence of a parasitic meningeal worm that is endemic among white-tailed deer populations.[19] Deer are not generally harmed by the parasite, but it causes disease and death among moose. Evidence from the Turner Farm site suggests that deer came under increasingly heavy hunting pressure throughout the site's forty-five-hundred-year history: bones from large, mature animals decreased in frequency over the period.[20] An alternative explanation for the apparent rise in moose population may therefore be that fewer deer were available to infect them with the parasite. This is just one more example of the uncertainties that archaeologists struggle with in trying to explain the past.

Faunal remains from coastal sites, as well as isotopic data from human skeletal remains, reflect a strong year-round reliance on marine fish west of Passamaquoddy Bay; around that bay, winter sites located primarily on the mainland lack abundant fish remains—perhaps because of extremely low winter water temperatures—while summer island sites contain more.[21] As this strong maritime focus over much of the Maine coast did not exist during the preceding Susquehanna tradition, it must therefore be regarded as a novel development, despite the fact that the Maine coast supported maritime-adapted cultures earlier in prehistory.

Peoples of the Ceramic period exploited marine resources in very different ways from those of earlier times. Swordfish are entirely absent from Ceramic-period faunal samples and may have been locally extinct due to the cooling of waters in the Gulf of Maine.[22] Cod were still taken, but became relatively insignificant as smaller fish—particularly winter flounder (*Psuedopleuronectes americanus*) and longhorn sculpin (*Myoxocephalus octodecemspinosus*)—took on greater importance. Sturgeon (primarily sea sturgeon, *Acipenser sturio*) and seals, mainly the harbor seal (*Phoca vitulina*) and gray seal (*Halichoerus grypus*), increased in importance at central coastal sites throughout the period. While these are all fairly consistent long-term trends, people suddenly began to focus heavily on seals and flounder toward the end of the prehistoric period.

Among the mollusks, clams remained a significant source of food, along with species of minor importance, such as mussels (*Mytilus edulis*), carnivorous snails and sea urchins (*Strongocentrotus droebachiensis*).[23] Rock crabs (*Cancer irroratus*) and lobsters (*Homarus americanus*) may also have been important, but we cannot be sure because their shells, or "exoskeletons," are made of a protein called chitin, which is not preserved in shell middens. West of Penobscot Bay, quahogs and oysters played a somewhat more significant role in the shellfish diet, although the huge oyster middens on the Damariacotta River must be seen as the result of a highly anomalous situation that allowed a relict oyster population to thrive there between at least 2200 B.P. and 1000 B.P.[24]

Until recently, the preponderance of Ceramic period deposits at the great majority of shell midden sites led Maine archaeologists to overestimate the significance of mollusks in the diet of the period. It now appears, at least at those sites so far analyzed, that shellfish actually declined in relative importance during the period and that most clams were harvested during late winter and early spring, when other resources probably tended to run short.[25] Moreover, at least some of the clams harvested during other seasons may have been used to bait bone fishhooks like those found in Ceramic-period levels at the Turner Farm site.[26] Human bone isotopic data clearly indicate that while mollusks may have been a critical resource during hard times, their overall contribution to the protein diet was minimal.[27]

Two other species exploited by Ceramic-period peoples are of special interest because they are now extinct. The first is the great auk (*Pinguinus impennis*), a flightless, penguinlike relative of the puffin, which once migrated in huge flocks along the Atlantic coast but was hunted to extinction in the nineteenth century.[28] Auks are present in Archaic-period strata at the Turner Farm site, but were apparently little hunted thereafter, until late in the Ceramic period, when their bones once again become suddenly abundant.

The second extinct species is the sea mink (*Mustela macrodon*), a slightly larger relative of the mink (*M. Vison*), which was extirpated in the mid–nineteenth century. Sea mink frequencies increased steadily throughout the Ceramic period according to evidence at the Turner Farm site, but underwent a large increase sometime after 1000 B.P., a change that possibly may reflect a growing interest in their pelts.

Another furbearer, the beaver, also became more popular late in the Ceramic period, although, because this species may have also been important as a food source, the increase may not be due to the value of its pelt alone. It is interesting to note that today, while mink populations are high on Maine's islands and coast, little beaver habitat exists on the islands, and

THE DAMARISCOTTA OYSTER SHELL HEAPS

Located near the head of tide on opposite banks of the Damariscotta River estuary, these two extraordinary middens are composed of oyster (*Crassostrea virginica*) and originally stood as much as 9 meters high. By contrast, few other Maine shell middens exceed 2 meters in depth, and most contain little or no oyster shell, being composed instead mainly of the soft-shell clam (*Mya arenaria*) and the quahog (*Mercenaria mercenaria*).

Although shell middens of comparable magnitude are to be found in Florida and even larger ones in Brazil, the sheer size of these middens in the cold, highly tidal Gulf of Maine caused nineteenth-century researchers to wonder whether they could possibly have been the result of human activity.[29] In 1886 the larger midden, known locally as the "Whaleback" because of its humped profile, was almost totally quarried away for its shell content, which was processed for use in poultry feed.[30] The removal was organized into an archaeological excavation by Abram Gamage. During the excavation, Gamage and his crew recovered shells of great size, some reaching 30 centimeters (1 foot) in length.

Surprisingly, these middens owe their large size not to a very long period of accumulation but to an environmental fluke. Prior to 6000 B.P., when the Gulf of Maine was warmer and less tidal than today, conditions seem to have been hospitable to oysters. Eventually, however, rising sea levels made the Gulf's waters cooler and more saline, forcing oyster populations to retreat up estuaries, where most eventually declined to extinction. They survived into recent times in very few localized estuarine zones.[31] Recent research by David Sanger has demonstrated that, beginning about 2200 B.P., local topography created a zone where fresh- and saltwater mixed, resulting in salinities of ten to twenty parts per thousand, creating conditions that were ideal for oysters. When and why the beds died out is not known with certainty. Sanger has argued that as sea levels continued to rise with time, salinity increased to the point where the predatory oyster drill (*Urosalpinx sp.*) could move into the beds, increasing pressure on the population until it collapsed.[32] A description of the middens written in the early seventeenth century, however, suggests that they may still have been accumulating.[33] If so, then at least some oysters survived into historic times, in which case the beds may have been smothered by sawdust generated by saw mills operating upstream beginning in the mid–eighteenth century.

even on the mainland it is most widespread away from the coast. It therefore seems likely that the residents of coastal villages made regular inland beaver-hunting trips, probably during winter.

Horticulture

The conventional view of agriculture in North America has been that it arrived as a complex including corn, or maize (*Zea mays*), beans (*Phaseolus vulgaris*), and squash (*Curcurbita pepo*), a "holy trinity" of complementary crops thought to have been domesticated in Mexico more than seven thousand years ago. This complex was assumed to have spread to North America and then slowly to the Northeast as the various crops underwent genetic change rendering them suitable for growing in cooler climates with shorter growing seasons. However, this simplistic scenario is currently undergoing radical revision.

In the first place, it has recently been confirmed that Native North Americans domesticated many plant species prior to 3000 B.P., before maize had spread from Mexico. These include sumpweed (*Iva annua*), sunflower (*Helianthus annuus*), chenopod, or lamb's-quarter (*Chenopodium album berlandieri*), and knotweed (*Polygonum erectum*). Maygrass (*Phalaris caroliana*) and little barley (*Hordeum pusillum*) were also cultivated but not demonstrably domesticated. None of these crop plants has yet been archaeologically confirmed in the Northeast, however.[34]

Our understanding of the maize-bean-squash trinity has also changed. Using AMS radiocarbon dating, which can date small plant samples directly, the age of squash domestication in Mexico has been pushed back to 10,000 B.P. Moreover, it now appears that people over a broad region from the Mississippi River to Maine may have cultivated wild squash prior to 5000 B.P. and that those of the Ohio and Mississippi Valleys domesticated it between three thousand and four thousand years ago, independently of the Mexican varieties they later adopted.[35]

Maize domestication, on the other hand, was apparently a more recent event than formerly thought, occurring no earlier than around fifty-five hundred years ago. When people in the Northeast began to grow it remains unclear. It was being grown in the Mississippi River Valley by 2000 B.P.[36] By 1700 B.P. it was grown in the Tennessee Basin, but it increased in importance there only after 1000 B.P., by which time it had reached Ontario and southern New England. Bean and squash cultivation apparently also spread rapidly from the same region at this time. One recently obtained date from a site in western Maine suggests that maize was cultivated there by 1000 B.P., and the full maize-bean-squash complex was present there by about 460 B.P. (A.D. 1490).[37] Samuel de Champlain saw maize growing along the Maine coast no farther east than at Saco, although Indians from the Kennebec River told him that they had grown it formerly but had given it up because raiders—probably Micmacs—stole the harvest. They also told him that it was still being grown farther up the Kennebec.[38] There is no evidence for agriculture farther to the east until the disruptions of warfare during the late seventeenth century sparked an influx of refugees from agricultural regions of New England.[39] It is possible that, as on the Kennebec, maize was grown in the interior farther to the east, particularly prior to a period of cool weather that began around A.D. 1600, although we currently have no evidence that it was.[40]

Housing

Architectural evidence from the Ceramic period is much more abundant than from earlier periods, and indicates that at least two house forms were built; both are forerunners of those known from the historic period, which are discussed in Chapter 4. The simplest is the wigwam, which is the Algonquian version of the basic human shelter found all over the world from earliest antiquity, perhaps even before the appearance of *Homo sapiens*. It consists simply of a pole frame with a wind- and waterproof cover-

3-11. Floor plan of a late-prehistoric longhouse at the Tracy site in Starks. (Courtesy of Ellen R. Cowie and James B. Petersen.)

ing. The wigwam probably had a long history in the region. Indeed, its existence over much of the Northeast has been inferred at several Archaic and later sites from the dark soil-filled post molds left by the poles of their frames.[41]

The existence of wigwams can also be inferred at several Ceramic-period coastal shell middens from the discovery of circular shell-free floors, which are sometimes slightly lower than the main surface and sometimes surrounded with shell-refuse banking similar to the hay bale or spruce-bough banking still seen around the homes of rural Maine in the winter. The fact that both of these construction features would have rendered them relatively free of drafts, together with the type of faunal remains found within them, indicates that these coastal wigwams were probably winter houses.[42] Although similar structures must have been built in the interior by both temporary visitors and permanent residents, none have yet been archaeologically identified.

The largest house form, the longhouse, which is well known to the west of Maine, has recently been recognized at a late-Ceramic-period or early-postcontact-period site on the Kennebec River at Starks.[43] The limits and configuration of the structure are clearly indicated by post molds—dark stains in the soil indicating where posts formerly stood. This longhouse was 5 meters wide—similar to the circumference of a wigwam—but its length was 25 meters, making the overall floor plan similar in proportion to those of the longhouses known archaeologically and historically elsewhere in the Northeast but not, until now, in Maine. Few Maine coastal sites have been excavated extensively enough to determine whether longhouses might have existed there. A 13-meter-long series of post molds discovered at the Goddard site might possibly represent one side of such a structure. It appears likely, however, that the longhouse in Starks was located in the village where Indians told Samuel de Champlain that maize was grown. It is possible, in other words, that longhouses, which probably housed extended kin groups, were only adopted among the relatively dense and stable populations made possible by an horticultural lifestyle.

Bone and Stone Technology

Along the central Maine coast, where most of the research on the Ceramic period has focused, changes in nonceramic technology have been identified that became quite pronounced during late prehistory. The first of these is a rise in the frequencies of bone tools—particularly bone points and beaver incisor tools.[44] The bone points have wear patterns that suggest they

3-12. A variety of projectile points and scrapers, most dating between around 1000 and 500 B.P. Made of exotic lithic materials. (Maine State Museum collection.)

were propelled or thrust against hard objects. A reasonable inference is that they were the tips of arrows or a kind of three-pronged fish spear known as a leister; perhaps they were used for both, and even for other purposes, because they occur by the hundreds at some late sites. Beaver incisor knives were shaped by grinding the tooth's natural occlusal surface into a variety of forms that suggest they were used to work wood.

Regarding flaked stone tools, the early and middle Ceramic periods were apparently marked by episodes when well-defined bifacial types were deposited at several sites, followed by periods for which it is difficult to make any general statement concerning style. In this respect, Maine seems to differ from areas to the south and west, where a fairly consistent progression of definable types has been worked out.[45] During the late Ceramic period, however, distinct styles do emerge. Three bifacial forms in particular, side-notched, corner-notched, and triangular, recur frequently at late Ceramic sites, although their ratios vary significantly from one locale to another. All three are quite small and standardized in shape compared to earlier Ceramic-period points. Many archaeologists suspect that they were used to tip arrows; if so, they may indicate the appearance—or reappearance—of the bow-and-arrow, which had completely replaced the spear-thrower throughout the Northeast by the time of European contact.[46]

The side-notched point is most common in central Maine. When large numbers are found there, they are often accompanied by the corner-notched points of quite similar size and form except for the position of the notches. The corner-notched type becomes more common to the east on the Maritime Peninsula, and variants of it predominate in late prehistoric sites as far north as Newfoundland and Labrador.[47] The third, triangular form becomes more common in western Maine and is the equivalent of the Levanna point of New York and New England. It may be that, in central Maine at least, these styles were popular at slightly different times. The side-notched points, for example, seem to have the longest history in the area. The fact remains, however, that all three came into use very late in the prehistoric period.

Accompanying the appearance of these three point styles is a sharp increase in the use of exotic lithic types—probably due to regional lithic exchange networks—especially for projectile points and scrapers. In Maine, however, the three point styles cannot be sorted out by lithic type; examples of all three appear to have been made of both local and exotic lithic types in comparable ratios. This means that the points themselves were not simply traded from their lithic source area. Thus both exotic lithics and ideas about projectile point form must have been in wide circulation simultaneously.

Water Transport

The first European visitors to North America saw three basic types of boat. Dugout canoes predominated in tropical and southern temperate regions. North of the tree line, a zone occupied mainly by non-Indian Eskimo (Inuit) peoples, cold weather retarded the rotting of hide, making it suitable for boat construction. Between these two zones, across the continent, canoes of birch and other kinds of bark were most common. When Europeans arrived in the Northeast during the early seventeenth century, bark canoes were used as far south as Plymouth, Massachusetts, and were employed universally for interior travel throughout northern New England and the Maritime Peninsula (see Chapter 5). As we shall see, because bark canoes were light and well suited to navigation on interior streams, it is likely that the increased mobility they provided played a role in the development of the expansive exchange networks of the late Ceramic period.

Paper birch (*Betula papyrifera*) has been present in northern North American forests since deglaciation; it is possible that its bark has been used in canoe construction since antiquity.[48] However, certain changes in the archaeological record, particularly during the late Ceramic period, suggest that bark canoes may be of more recent origin. Among the more notable of these changes is a decline in the relative frequency of pecked and ground stone tools, particularly adzes, which many archaeologists believe were used during the Archaic period for dugout canoe construction. It may also be more than coincidence that beaver-incisor tools, presumably used to work wood, became increasingly common as adzes declined. Another marked technological trend is a sharp rise in the relative frequency of small flake scrapers. What they scraped has not been determined but their wear patterns suggest that it was a relatively hard substance, like wood, rather than softer materials like hide or leather. Taken together, these archaeological trends suggest some important change in woodworking patterns; such a change would have been the adoption of a new kind of water craft, and an obvious candidate is the birchbark canoe.

Exchange

With one early exception, noted below, there is little archaeological evidence for long-range exchange with peoples in other regions during the early Ceramic period. By 1000 B.P., however, evidence for the exchange of high quality and visually attractive lithics increases exponentially throughout much of the Northeast.[49] In Maine, this evidence takes the form of arrowheads and scrapers made of chert from Ramah Bay on the north Labrador coast, from northern Quebec, and from the Onondaga escarpment of western New York and Ontario, jasper from Pennsylvania, and chalcedony from Nova Scotia. Chert from Norway Bluff in north central Maine, which had largely gone out of use after Paleo-Indian times, also returned to popularity. Finally, native copper from Cap d'Or in western Nova Scotia has been found in Maine sites, worked into a variety of simple forms. It remains uncertain what other archaeologically invisible commodities may have traveled through this exchange network, but they could have been many; judging from faunal remains at the Turner Farm site, animal furs seem an especially likely commodity.[50]

Although there is evidence of exchange at most late-Ceramic-period sites, the Goddard site on Blue Hill Bay may have played a central role. Here, on a level sandy terrace next to the sea, were deposited several thousand late prehistoric artifacts, over 20 percent of which are of nonlocal lithic types. By far the most exotic of all the artifacts found at the Goddard site, however, site is a small Norse coin. The history of this coin—the only datable Norse artifact among the two dozen or so to have been found in North America—remains a matter of speculation. Enthusiasts of the idea that the Norse explored widely in North America have made incredible claims for expeditions as far as Minnesota and even Oklahoma, where a state park was created in honor of a supposed Norse inscription.[51] In fact, however, the Norse seem to have confined their activities to the Gulf of St. Lawrence, mainly Newfoundland where some Norse people, probably including Leif Ericsson, established a short-lived settlement around A.D. 1000, and to Labrador, which they visited to cut wood and perhaps to trade with Native inhabitants.[52]

Because the coin is of a type minted between A.D. 1065 and 1080, its source was probably not the Norse settlement.[53] Excavations conducted at the Goddard site during the 1970s, plus expert analysis of the several metal artifacts found there, reveal no signs of additional Norse artifacts, so it is also unlikely that some unrecorded Norse group brought the coin with them to Maine. It probably did come from somewhere in the north, however, for the Goddard site excavations also produced numerous tools of Ramah chert and one ground stone tool of a type made by people of a prehistoric Eskimo culture known as the Dorset.[54] The available evidence, then, strongly suggests that the coin was brought to Maine by Indian traders.

Some materials involved in late Prehistoric exchange must have been carried north to south through the Maritime Peninsula via the Kennebec, Penobscot and St. John Rivers. In earlier times, when dugout canoes may have been the only type of water craft available, such travel would have been restricted. Some archaeologists who suspect that the birchbark canoe was available by A.D. 1000 see it as responsible for this movement of trade goods. Indeed, we know that these routes were used in the fur trade by the early seventeenth century and that Maine Indians were active in political and military affairs on the St. Lawrence by then.[55]

The fur trade of the historic period seems to have been modeled upon late-prehistoric exchange patterns in several respects. One characteristic of the trade that comes through strongly in the accounts of early explorers is the violence it engendered. It is perhaps no surprise, then, that a late-Ceramic-period cemetery at the Goddard site contained the remains of two men who were apparently killed with arrows tipped with projectile points of an alien corner-notched style.[56]

Religion: Early-Ceramic-Period Ceremonialism— The Adena Connection

The discovery in 1972 of a burial mound in Red Bank, New Brunswick— the first such feature found on the Maritime Peninsula—brought about the sudden realization that at the very beginning of the Ceramic period this region had participated in one of North America's earliest widespread ceremonial patterns: the Adena complex, named for the Ohio farm where one of the first burial mounds to be excavated was located.[57] Known as the Augustine site, the New Brunswick mound contained twenty burial pits from which the incomplete skeletal remains of an undetermined number of individuals were recovered.

Prehistoric mounds in eastern North America have been known to contain graves since the eighteenth century, when Thomas Jefferson excavated one on his Virginia plantation. These earthen constructions, which could be very large, were initially attributed to an imagined race of non-Indians known as the Mound Builders.[58] After the late nineteenth century, when Cyrus Thomas of the Smithsonian Institution demonstrated that they had actually been built by Indians, archaeologists set about trying to define and delimit the cultures responsible for them.[59]

In the twentieth century, it became apparent that the influence of the Adena complex extended well beyond Ohio and could actually be found throughout much of eastern North America—and, moreover, that in the East it had no single parent culture.[60] It now appears that Adena complex–related cemeteries in the Northeast, whether covered by mounds or not, tend to occur in clusters separated by large areas where no cemeteries, and few Adena artifacts, occur.[61] After the discovery of the Augustine mound, for example, local inquiries by archaeologists turned up a similar collection that had long ago been excavated nearby from another probable cemetery.[62] Other cemetery clusters occur at the north and south ends of Lake Champlain, around the confluence of the Mohawk and Hudson Rivers, along the Connecticut River between Hadley, Massachusetts, and Windsor,

Connecticut, and around Halifax, Nova Scotia. There is also some evidence for additional clusters around Narragansett and Penobscot Bays. I have labeled this series of mortuary sites the Boucher complex, after one especially elaborate cemetery found at the northern end of Lake Champlain. Like the Adena sites of the Midwest and mid-South, the Boucher complex dates between 2500 B.P. and 2300 B.P.[63]

The impressive scale of the Adena burial mounds and associated earthworks, as well as their superficial similarity to the great temple mounds of the later Mississippian tradition, convinced archaeologists that they must have been built by agricultural people, for it was felt that no hunter-gatherer society could have mustered the necessary labor for their construction. After decades of searching for maize in association with Adena sites,

3-13. A variety of pendants dating to the Ceramic period. The bottom four are called gorgets and may have been attached to clothing as ornaments. (Maine State Museum collection.)

Following the brief period of Adena influence in the Northeast, we have little direct evidence of religion, but at some point early in the Ceramic period, people throughout the Northeast, and especially in Maine, began to produce pictorial and ideographic images with clear spiritual significance. Called petroglyphs, these images were made by pecking smooth rock ledge surfaces. The abundance of images at some petroglyph sites suggest that the locations themselves may have had special spiritual importance. Two of the preeminent petroglyph sites of North America occur in Maine, on the coast at Machiasport, where petroglyphs occur on several ledges, and on the Kennebec River at Embden, where they are densely clustered on a single, small ledge outcrop.

Style

Long-term research has allowed Mark Hedden to divide the anthropomorphic images at these two sites into six styles, described here in their presumed order of appearance.[64] Style 1 is rectangular, generally executed with thin lines and often found in pairs. It may be related to a broad spectrum of inactive, frontally oriented anthropomorphs that probably originated in western North America, and by Late Archaic times were produced as far east as the Great Lakes. Style 2, which is apparently derived from style 1, often has doubled legs supporting a single torso. These two have so far been identified only at Machiasport. Style 3 includes a motif in the form of an open-ended hourglass shape with excurved sides. It has been identified at multiple rock-art sites ranging form Pennsylvania to Ontario and resembles a mnemonic sign used into the historic period by the Midewiwin or Medicine Lodge Society of the Ojibwas. Style 4 has broad shoulders and a long torso tapered at the waist and expanded at the base. The only occurrence of this style aside from at Machiasport is on a stone pipe found in Massachusetts, although related forms have been found in New York, on Long Island and Staten Island. Style 5, which is most prevalent at Embden, has a triangular body with various bird attributes. Sexual imagery and canoe forms are commonly associated with this style at Embden. A similar association occurs at Peterborough, Ontario.[65] Like style 3, similar forms were produced by Ojibwa shamans in the nineteenth century. Style 6 often resembles the fifth in body form, birdlike attributes, and sexual imagery but is more angular in configuration. Many examples have the left arm extended, suggesting special powers emanating therefrom. All these characteristics of style 6 evoke the supernatural attributes of the region's historic shamans.

Age

The dating of such petroglyphs is a daunting task, but internal evidence and comparative data from other rock art sites provide clues. Their resemblances to nineteenth-century shamanistic art from the Great Lakes region suggest a common tradition. The Midewiwin has been generally regarded as originating among Algonquian speakers between the Great Lakes and New England during the early eighteenth century, but some of its ritual elements have much deeper prehistoric roots.[66]

however, it has been realized that Adena gardens, if they existed at all, contained only squash, gourds, and a few other cultigens of minor importance. In other words, the mounds had been built by people who lived essentially as hunter-gatherers.[67]

A salient characteristic of the Boucher complex is that its grave furnishings include a much higher proportion of exotic materials than the graves of earlier mortuary patterns. Moreover, a far-smaller proportion of its exotic artifacts occurs outside cemetery contexts. In sum, this burial pattern

The earliest style at Machiasport occurs on ledges now exposed only at low tide, suggesting that they were executed when sea level was lower than at present and glacial till still covered the higher ledges. These low ledges were probably exposed by erosion between 3000 B.P. and 2000 B.P., suggesting that style 1 dated to or shortly after this time.[68] This interpretation accords well with a style 1–like image engraved on a platform pipe from Massachusetts, which probably dates to about 1700 B.P. to 1500 B.P.

Finally, several pieces of evidence suggest that styles 5 and 6 fall in the late prehistoric to early historic range. At Machias, deerlike animal forms associated with earlier styles give way to moose images, paralleling trends in contemporaneous archaeological fauna from coastal sites. At Embden, one petroglyph appears to represent a European-style frame building, while one at Machias represents a sailing ship. At both sites, Christian crosses accompany the later styles, indicating the advent of missionary influence.

Thus ended the aboriginal tradition of petroglyph making in Maine. However, Hedden has described a recently identified site on Grand Lake Stream in eastern Maine that includes strongly naturalistic motifs he associates with mid-nineteenth-century Native American drawings ranging from Nova Scotia to the Great Plains.[69]

Meaning

Even more intractable than the dating issue is the question of what the petroglyphs meant to their makers.

From the Ojibwa association of petroglyphs with shamans—both are designated by the same term—Hedden infers that the Maine petroglyphs pertain to a gradually developing Algonquian shamanistic tradition. In styles 1 to 3, spiritlike glyphs associated with the anthropomorphic forms are of equal size, suggesting spiritual equality. In later styles, however, the anthropomorphs are larger, suggesting to Hedden that a hierarchy was emerging. In the more naturalistic styles 5 and 6 Hedden sees evidence for a change in shamanistic practice to include public performance. He suspects that the explicit sexual imagery associated with these late styles at Embden reflects a concern with enhancing the fertility of newly adopted domestic crops. Such an inference may be supported by the near absence of such imagery among the style 5 and 6 images at Machiasport, which lies beyond the known extent of aboriginal horticulture.

Pictographs in Western Maine

Another form of rock art especially common in arid regions of western North America are images painted on rock surfaces called pictographs. In arid regions some pictographs have survived for millennia. How common they may have been elsewhere is difficult to say, but the recent discovery of painted anthropomorphs at two sites in western Maine suggests that they may once have been widespread in the East as well. Hedden notes that these poorly preserved pictographs probably pertain to his style 5 or 6.

seems to represent both a marked innovation in the behavior of a few specific communities and, simultaneously, a strong directional linkage with the Ohio Valley.

At present, it is difficult to evaluate the significance of these discoveries. In the first place, Boucher-complex cemeteries are so remote from the Adena heartland that we cannot even be sure that the Adena artifacts buried in them served the functions for which they were originally manufactured. Nevertheless, like the Adena sites of the Ohio Valley,

3-14. Various hunting and fishing gear of ivory, bone, and antler from coastal Ceramic-period sites. (Maine State Museum collection.)

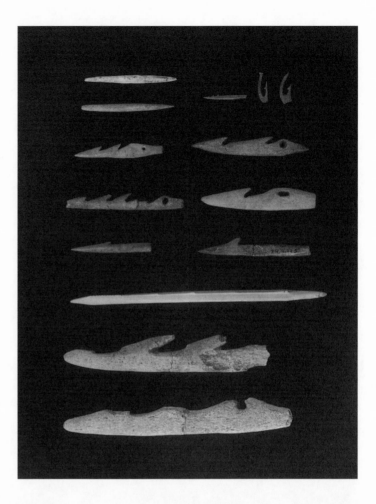

3-15. Canines of various carnivores perforated for suspension on necklaces or to ornament clothing *(top left)*; projectile point (?) made from a shark tooth and a bone comb fragment *(bottom left)*; modified shark vertebrae, possibly for use as jewelry *(top center)*; beaver-incisor knives *(bottom center)*; bone awls and needles *(right)*. (Maine State Museum collection.)

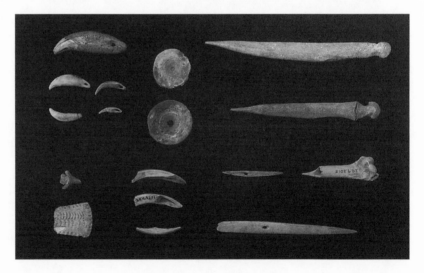

3-16. Artifacts of naturally occurring copper from the Goddard site, Brooklin. At the bottom are partially worked nuggets. (Maine State Museum collection.)

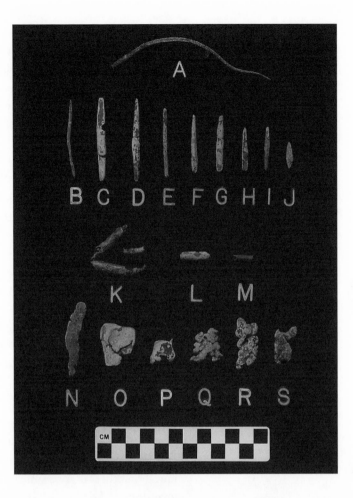

3-17. View of the Whaleback under excavation in 1886.

3-18. Stone pestle for pounding dried corn into meal. Found on the Kennebec River in Vassalboro, it is one of very few pestles known from Maine, probably because of the late arrival of agriculture. Length is 80 cm. (Maine State Museum collection.)

Boucher-complex sites do seem to be burial places for a select few. The ability of these few to garner exotic ritual goods implies that they were probably of higher status than those among whom they lived. A difficulty with this interpretation, however, is that archaeologists are even less inclined to regard hunter-gatherer societies of the Maritime Peninsula as likely to sustain such status differentials than those of the rich American heartland.[70]

It is generally agreed, however, that population was increasing throughout the Northeast at this time. Under such changing conditions, one can imagine numerous scenarios leading to the emergence of a short-lived pattern of elites interacting with each other from their local power bases. But it is presently unclear whether they would have derived power from spiritual sources, the control of economically valuable commodities, or from some combination to the two. Given the nonutilitarian and exotic nature of Boucher complex–grave furnishings, it seems at least possible that their elite owners were perceived as spiritually empowered, perhaps by some special relationship with the larger, more centralized polities of the Midwest.

In the Midwest, Adena was followed by other mound-building cultures, culminating after about A.D. 700 in the Mississippian tradition, a series of complex, hierarchical agrarian societies based on "tributary patron-client relationships" that anthropologists call chiefdoms, which were distributed from the Mississippi Valley eastward to Georgia.[71] In the Northeast, however, it appears that only a single generation of mounds was built, and burial sites thereafter became much simpler and generally lacking in grave furnishings. They are also few in number, suggesting that some other means of disposing of the dead had been adopted.

Postscript

The accounts of Indian life presented by Champlain, Captain John Smith, and their contemporaries have often been interpreted as depicting Natives— "noble savages"—living in a traditional pattern of harmony with their environments. In tracing an archaeological course toward the end of prehistory, however, we have encountered instead a late Ceramic period filled with change, including the arrival of agriculture, a new style of ceramic technology, a widespread pattern of lithic exchange and shared artifact styles, the possible emergence of bark canoe technology, an intensification in the exploitation of marine mammals and an increase in the use of petroglyph imagery as a form of spiritual expression. In many ways, then, the late Ceramic period echoes a pattern not of tradition-bound stability but rather one of dynamism akin to that of an earlier time, during the Late Archaic period, when the Moorehead phase emerged following a long period of cultural stability. As the Moorehead phase suddenly gave way to the Susquehanna tradition, the late Ceramic period also heralds a profound change, as new peoples from across the sea entered the region and gained dominion over it.

IV AN INTRODUCTION
TO THE HISTORIC PAST

Ethnohistory

THE CHAPTERS that follow present a historic account of North eastern Indian societies as they are revealed through documents dating from the late sixteenth century to the present. Chapters 5, 6, 7, and 8 explore the two centuries that followed the arrival of Europeans in the Gulf of Maine, while Chapter 9 briefly summarizes subsequent events. An appendix deals with the region's rich material culture, many aspects of which persisted for a considerable length of time following the introduction of European goods and European ways.

Only recently have scholars made deliberate attempts to write history with the Native perspective as a central focus. Many, both anthropologists and historians, refer to this research as ethnohistory, although some historians prefer the term "new Indian history." The goal of ethnohistory is to piece together fragments of historic information about Native peoples. It thus resembles archaeology to the extent that it ferrets fragments of information out of often obscure deposits—historic documents instead of middens, in this case—and makes them comprehensible through interpretation. This might seem to be a less complex task than archaeology if one assumes that Indian history can simply be read in historical records. In fact, however, contemporary European colonials rarely tried to write the history of these populations. Instead, they wrote mainly about their own concerns, and subsequent historians have also generally focused their research on Europeans, not Indians. Even in historical works where Indians are mentioned extensively, their perspective is rarely the central theme, and what is said about them is often badly distorted by ignorance and cultural bias. Thus the Rev. William Hubbard's account of King Philip's War in Maine describes most of the important military and diplomatic activities of the Indians involved but does so in a way that leaves the English apparently blameless for the war. Similarly, French Jesuit missionaries—who lived and worked much more closely with Maine's Indians than the English—also distorted their accounts in order to aggrandize their own effectiveness as emissaries of their God and their king.[1] And both the English and the French used the same telling term for Indians: "savages."

Nineteenth-century scholars were somewhat more objective but still prone to ethnocentrism—the tendency to place one's own ethnic group above others'. For example, while William D. Williamson's encyclopedic *History of Maine* attempts to deal objectively with the region's Indian population, his New England perspective significantly distorts their story.[2] Francophone scholars, on the other hand, have often been members of religious communities and as such identified closely with the Church's tradition of missionary activity among the Indians. While this perspective placed Native people somewhat closer to the center of interest, the influence over them of the French—and especially the Church—is often exaggerated.

The ethnohistorian must therefore apply the sensitivity of the anthropologist in using a variety of accounts written by people who lived in other places and at other times to construct an accurate and balanced portrayal of Native North Americans during the colonial era. Like the archaeological reconstructions presented earlier, the ethnohistorical hypotheses outlined below must be viewed as works in progress. However, as in archaeology, an encouraging amount of new data has appeared on the scene during the past two decades.

The Historical Record of Maine and the Maritime Peninsula

The historical record of European-Indian contact from the era of "discovery" through the colonial period is different for the Maritime Peninsula than for other parts of North America. This was the arena in which, from earliest times, the English and the French vied for control. This competition generated a wealth of historical data about Native peoples that provides scholars with an English and a French perspective on most important events. One example of how these parallel records can help clarify historical Native positions concerns an event that occurred in 1694, during King William's War. In that year, Massachusetts governor William Phips pressed two beleaguered Indian chiefs, Madockawando and Edgeremet, to cede their lands to him and another Englishman in return for peace. This transaction was recorded in English records as a voluntary sale. The Indians, however, soon "broke" the treaty and resumed hostilities against the English. From the English perspective, the Indians behaved in a perfidious manner.[3] But French sources paint a different picture, pointing out that these two chiefs, who were not native to the lands in question, had no authority to relinquish them, and that their action was actually the trigger that incited an already discontented population to resume the war.[4]

Not only do the two sets of documents provide different perspectives—they also complement each other in various ways. Typically, for example, French accounts of Indian culture and group behavior are more accurate than those of the English, for the French routinely interacted with and married into Indian populations, while the English tended to avoid such intimacies. The English, on the other hand, often recorded individual actions and events in greater detail through documents such as deeds, treaties, and official reports. The dualism is incomplete, however, for during periods of conflict large voids were created in the historical record of one side or the other. Thus the English capture of Acadia in 1652 left a thirty-year gap in the French records that is difficult to compensate for. Likewise, after Indians virtually drove the English out of Maine during King Philip's War, the activities of western Maine Indians are exceedingly difficult to trace. The impact of such irregularities on our perceptions of the past are spelled out in greater detail below.

Natives of the Maritime Peninsula

To set the stage for discussing the Native history of the Maritime Peninsula, we must briefly describe the cultural diversity encountered in the region by early European visitors. All the Native languages spoken on the Maritime Peninsula belong to the eastern branch of the Algonquian-language family, named for the Algonquins of the St. Lawrence Valley with whom the French had many early contacts. Algonquian languages were—and still are—spoken throughout New England, Quebec, Labrador, and Newfoundland. To the west of New England and Quebec, however, lived the Hurons and Iroquois who spoke languages of the Iroquoian family.

Ethnic divisions within the Maritime Peninsula generally followed linguistic ones. The most reliable evidence concerning ethnicity comes from seventeenth-century French sources, particularly those written by people who were associated with a series of early voyages to explore, trade, and settle in Acadia, the portion of the Maritime Peninsula lying to the east of the Penobscot River that effectively remained under French control until the mid–eighteenth century. These voyages began with those of Pierre Du Gua de Monts in 1604 and ended when the English briefly drove the French out of Acadia in 1613. These people maintained close relations with the Natives of their new colony and used them as guides in their explorations of the Gulf of Maine coast.[5] The English seem to have been somewhat less well-informed regarding ethnicity. Nevertheless, since they generally dealt with Indians local to their areas of activity, they were often more perceptive than the French regarding local Native politics.[6]

The early French sources name four ethnic groups on the Maritime Peninsula. As is the case for colonized peoples throughout the world, however, the names used by the French were not generally those these groups used for themselves. Eastward from the Gaspé and St. John River lived the Souriquois, who were apparently named for a river called the Souricoa (possibly the French River of Nova Scotia) that provided access between the Gulf of St. Lawrence at Tatamagouche Bay and Cobequid Bay on the Bay of Fundy. As we shall see in the next chapter, these people seem to have been swift to appreciate both the economic potential of trading furs—some of which they obtained from Indians along the Gulf of Maine coast—for manufactured goods obtained from Europeans in the Gulf of St. Lawrence and the utility of European sailing vessels called shallops in doing so. Most native guides for the de Monts expedition came from this group. In later years, the Souriquois—known to the English as Tarrentines—would come to be called the Micmacs.[7]

West of the Souriquois, between the St. John and Kennebec Rivers, lived the Etchemins who, as it turns out, were actually "so named in their own country."[8] By 1605 members of this group were also engaged in the fur trade and in providing guides to the French. In the late seventeenth century, the Etchemins came to be referred to by the French as the Maliseets (or Malicites) between the St. John and Penobscot Rivers and as the Canibas between the Penobscot and the Kennebec Rivers.[9]

West of the Kennebec and as far to the southwest as Massachusetts lived a third people, whom the Souriquois referred to as Almouchiquois—literally "dog people"—with whom they had been at war. This group's territory began at the Androscoggin River, which John Smith later named the Almouchicoggin.[10] They were linguistically and culturally distinct from their neighbors to the east, wearing different clothing and hairstyles, using some dugouts in addition to birchbark canoes, and practicing horticulture.[11] The French soon abandoned this epithet, and the calamitous epidemics and warfare that broke out during and soon after their initial visit so disrupted the region that it is unclear who, if anyone, remained in former Almouchiquois territory.

Champlain later described a fourth group, the Abenakis, who lived eight days travel south of the newly founded settlement of Quebec at Norridgewock, on the Kennebec River. They lived in "large villages and also houses in the country with many stretches of cleared land, in which they sow much Indian corn."[12] As we shall see, there are indications that during the early seventeenth century, when Europeans began to frequent the Gulf of Maine coast, the Abenakis felt hemmed in by their coastal neighbors and became the first group from the region to eventually establish regular contact with the French in Quebec. In later years, as all the region's coastal populations became increasingly oriented to Quebec, the term Abenaki was extended to all, even the Micmacs at times. The Abenakis proper, however, remained distinct enough to be distinguished from their neighbors until around 1700.[13] To the west of Abenaki territory lay a group associated primarily with the Merrimack Valley and known to the English as the Penacooks. The French of the seventeenth century, however, did not generally distinguish the Penacooks as separate from the Abenakis, referring instead to the Sokokis of the Connecticut Valley as the next named group to the west. This uncertainty probably reflects close early relations among the Native inhabitants of the Merrimack, Saco, and Androscoggin Rivers. Frequent contact among these populations continued into the nineteenth century, by which time most had moved to the St. Lawrence Valley.[14]

Between King Philip's War, which broke out in Maine in 1675, and the capitulation of New France after the Seven Years War in 1763, these Native groups often acted together in war parties and intermingled in other ways, both on the Maritime Peninsula and in mission villages on the St. Lawrence River. It is thus often difficult to identify the ethnicity of specific groups. In the chapters that follow, such ambiguous groups will be referred to using the collective terms appearing in the relevant documents: Eastern Indians in English documents and Abenakis in French ones.

Describing the political and social organization of these groups is more complex than this summary suggests, for the region was undergoing two separate transitions by the time Europeans began to write descriptions of people. If we employ terms commonly used by anthropologists, all groups can be subsumed by the terms "band" and "tribe." Both these terms reflect societies that are generally egalitarian, with interpersonal relationships defined in terms of kinship instead of class or place of residence. The distinction between the two terms is based mainly on the issue of settlement pattern, bands tending to live nomadic lives while tribes tend to have permanent villages. Tribes also tend to have kin groups called clans, between which marriage partners are exchanged, and prominent leaders—often called "big men"—whose authority rests upon consensus rather than inherited authority. Finally, bands tend to have populations numbering in the dozens, tribes in the hundreds.[15]

The two transitions that were affecting the region at the time of contact were the movement eastward of maize-based horticulture, discussed in Chapter 3, and the influence of European traders, who had been operating in the Gulf of St. Lawrence since the mid–sixteenth century, nearly fifty years before Europeans became frequent visitors to the Gulf of Maine. Before these two trends affected the Maritime Peninsula, it is likely that all of its population was organized into numerous bands. By 1600, however, the arrival of horticulture had probably transformed the Abenakis and Almouchiquois into a small number of tribes that lived in settled agricultural villages during much of each year. East of the Kennebec, where agriculture was apparently not practiced, band-level organization may have persisted, but this issue remains in doubt because both the English and French encountered powerful leaders—big men—who engaged in warfare with populations west of the Kennebec all the way to Massachusetts Bay. As we shall see, these big men were involved in the fur trade, especially those belonging to the Souriquois and easternmost Etchemins. It is therefore possible that these peoples, too, had undergone social transformations from bands to larger, more authoritarian tribes.

Sources for the Visual and Material Record

As our account extends into the postcontact era, when the technological influence of Europeans grew rapidly, it becomes clear that European manufactured goods were used creatively and consciously by Native peoples to express lifestyles that were still marginal to the emerging Eurocolonial societies. That so much survives in accounts and images is strong evidence of the creative vigor of Native peoples of all periods—something of which the archaeological record offers only the faintest indication.

Readers may note that many of the artifacts and images discussed below are conserved in Canadian institutions. This is no accident. From the outset, the United States and Canada have had profoundly different political histories. England's original North American territories, which became the United Colonies, were populated by common people who crossed the Atlantic in huge numbers to seek prosperity—or at least an end to persecution—and eventually rebelled against colonial rule. Canada's non-Native populations, on the other hand, never grew large under the French, and Indian populations remained relatively prominent well into the nineteenth century. Around 1760 governance shifted from one European power (the French) to another (the English) and remained imperial in nature. In America the new colonizing populations regarded the Native people as impediments to their economic goals at best and as traditional enemies at worst. Early American settlers struggled to establish themselves in a "wilderness," usually with no help—and sometimes with active harassment—from their local government; they were hardly the kind of people to concern themselves with creating any record of the Native people they encountered. In Canada, however, to both the French and the English, Native people were seen as essential to the economy and as important military allies. During the eighteenth and early nineteenth centuries, an unclear boundary between the United States and Canada meant that officers of the British Army were often stationed near contentious zones. Many took advantage of their colonial posting to acquire fascinating exotic Native artifacts or to make written or visual records of the Native peoples' lifestyles and surroundings.

V EARLY EUROPEAN
AND NATIVE CONTACTS

THE ENCOUNTER between Europeans and Native North Americans that began with Christopher Columbus's 1492 voyage is often portrayed as having broken a barrier that had persisted for some twelve thousand years. This portrayal is inaccurate for two reasons. First, populations on the opposite shores of the Bering Strait had, in all probability, never lost contact at all.[1] Second, between the eleventh and fourteenth centuries, Norse expansion westward across the North Atlantic brought them to North American shores on an indefinite number of occasions.[2] But such contacts as occurred in the pre-Columbian period did not basically alter either the Old or New World populations. It was only during the late sixteenth century, when interaction between Europeans and eastern North Americans became sustained, that profound changes took place.

Among the more important of these differences was the recent advent of horticulture in the New World, particularly in the Northeast. As we have seen in Chapter 3, maize-based horticulture began in the New World only about five thousand years ago and spread to the western portion of the Maritime Peninsula only a few centuries before the contact period, whereas grain crops in the Old World date back ten thousand years. North America also lacked domestic animals except for the dog, whereas animal domestication in the Old World was nearly as ancient as horticulture. These differences meant that Native populations of the Northeast remained small and mobile, whereas those of the Europeans who settled among them became both large and sedentary.

Another outcome of these differences had to do with material culture. Native technology, although artful and impressive in many ways, was designed mainly to serve individuals or small groups in their hunting, war-

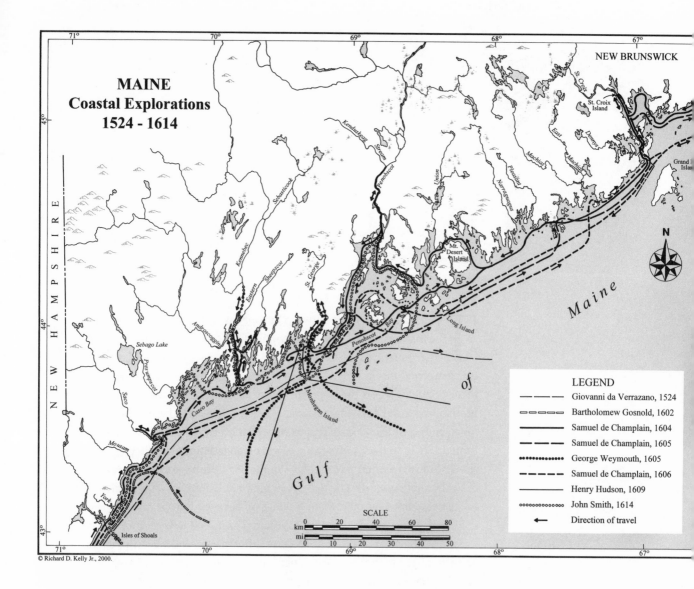

MAINE
Coastal Explorations
1524 - 1614

NEW BRUNSWICK

NEW HAMPSHIRE

Gulf of Maine

LEGEND

— — — — Giovanni da Verrazano, 1524
□ □ □ □ □ □ Bartholomew Gosnold, 1602
————————— Samuel de Champlain, 1604
— — — — Samuel de Champlain, 1605
••••••••••••• George Weymouth, 1605
– – – – – Samuel de Champlain, 1606
————————— Henry Hudson, 1609
∘∘∘∘∘∘∘∘∘∘∘∘ John Smith, 1614
← Direction of travel

SCALE

km 0 20 40 60 80
mi 0 10 20 30 40 50

© Richard D. Kelly Jr., 2000.

5-1. Maine: Coastal Explorations, 1524–1614

fare, water travel, and other activities. European technology, on the other hand, was based on the use of metals and wheeled vehicles. By the sixteenth century, it had become complex, powerful, and mass-produced. Native North Americans recognized immediately that in most contexts their technology was no match for Europe's. The appeal of European trade goods to Native populations across the continent was, therefore, immediate and irreversible.

The most important difference between the Old and New Worlds, however, was in the realm of disease. In the Americas, diseases tended to be chronic and degenerative, affecting only small percentages of any given

5-2a–b. Norwegian penny issued by King Olaf Kyrre between A.D. 1065 and 1080, found at the Goddard site in Brooklin. (Maine State Museum collection.)

community. In the Old World, by contrast, long traditions of close communal living and interaction with livestock had led to the development of acute epidemic diseases, such as chicken pox, the common cold, influenza, measles, mumps, rubella, smallpox, and the plague. Severe as these maladies were, Europeans had become partially immune to many. Lacking such immunity, Native Americans experienced disastrous population loss as a result of germs unknowingly transmitted by Europeans that swept throughout the hemisphere in what are called "virgin-soil epidemics." Such outbreaks often wiped out whole communities, shifting the competitive balance irretrievably in favor of the newcomers.[3]

First Encounters

The timing of Christopher Columbus's 1492 voyage to the New World was no accident. Rather, it was an inevitable outcome of European history. Long a cold, damp, forested backwater compared to the eastern Mediterranean and Asia, during the fifteenth century Europe had been forced to develop sophisticated ships in order to overcome Turkish and Arab control of the major Eurasian overland trade route known as the Silk Road. Completely decked over to shed water and steered with a rudder, these were a new kind of vessel designed for long voyages on the open sea. At the same time, Europe was undergoing political consolidation and economic growth that left it poised for a geopolitical expansion that would reshape the world. The timing of Columbus's voyages was determined by these processes. After several failed attempts to gain support for his intended expedition to Asia, he was finally successful in Spain, but only after a newly unified Spanish crown had freed the necessary financial resources by driving out the Moors, finally completing the Christian reconquest of southern Europe.[4]

From the European point of view, Asia was the desired destination and the "discovery" of the New World was, at first, a decidedly unwelcome one. In fact, Columbus believed he had landed in Asia, as did John Cabot, who crossed the Atlantic in 1497. Other explorers, however, soon realized the problem: the New World was in the way. Their voyages were therefore aimed for the most part not at settling or even systematically exploring this unwelcome new land mass but rather in briefly prospecting it for mineral wealth or in finding a passage through or around it. In 1535 the French explorer Jacques Cartier sailed up the St. Lawrence beyond present-day Montreal where he encountered a major set of rapids, which he believed might lead to a waterway through the continent to the Pacific Ocean. After Cartier's time, in the 1570s and 1580s, English expeditions led by Martin Frobisher and John Davis unsuccessfully sought a more northerly "northwest passage" to the Orient.[5]

Following Cartier's failure to find either wealth or a quick route to the Orient, official European interest in the Northeast declined for several decades. During this period, the principal visitors were privately organized Portuguese, French, and, later, Spanish fishermen off Newfoundland, and Basque whalers in the Gulf of St. Lawrence.[6] Contrary to conventional historical opinion, European-Native encounters in the Gulf of Maine were minimal during the remainder of the sixteenth century. The private companies of fishers and whalers, well organized and focused on maximizing

5-3. Map of Newfoundland, the St. Lawrence River, and the coasts of New France by Marc Lescarbot, 1609. Lescarbot accompanied a French expedition to the Gulf of Maine in 1606. Notice the locations of the Souriquois, Etchemins, and Almouchiquois. (Photo courtesy of Edward E. Ayer Collection, the Newberry Library, Chicago.)

SAGAMORES

Records from the era of European exploration frequently mention leading males called sagamores, a term that occurs in different dialectical variants throughout much of the Algonquian-speaking region, from the Great Lakes eastward to the Atlantic coast. For example, a Massachusett "sachem" was roughly equivalent to an Etchemin sagamore. In central Maine, the sagamore distinguished himself from the common man, called a "sanop."[7]

European observers often imposed their notions of leadership on the role of sagamore. For example, sagamores were often referred to as "kings" and—more commonly—"chiefs." However, even those who used such terms often recognized their failure to adequately translate "sagamore." For example, Christopher Levett, who visited the area of present-day Portland in 1623–24 called a local sagamore a "king" (and his wife a "queen"), but qualified his use of these terms as follows: "Their *Sagamores* are no Kings, as I verilie beleeve, for I can see no Government of Law amongst them but Club Law: and they call all Masters of Shippes *Sagamore*, or any other man, that they see have a command of men."[8] By "Club Law" Levett was referring to the absence of any overarching system of political authority uniting populations over large areas.

While the authority of sagamores he met was local, a few decades earlier leadership patterns were different. The earliest English and French explorers found most of the Maritime Peninsula and Gulf of St. Lawrence under the sway of five superchiefs. Among the Souriquois, Membertou was supreme. To his west lived Bessabez, whose home was between Pemaquid and the Penobscot River but whose authority was said to extend as far westward as Massachusetts. To the west of Casco Bay, at present-day Saco, lived Onamechin, sagamore of a culturally different, horticultural people with ties farther west and south, who apparently lived within a tension zone at the edge of Bessabez's influence. In the interior lived an apparently powerful but shadowy and violent leader named Sassinoa. To the north, on the St. Lawrence, the Algonquin sagamore Anadabijou held sway at Tadoussac where, in 1603, Champlain found him involved in warfare with the Iroquois.[9]

Sagamores generally arose from large families that could provide political and economic support. Their authority, however, was generally noncoercive—that of a chief-among-equals who led by example—although some were also respected and feared as shamans. Relations among sagamores were therefore competitive and fluid, with superiority going to the one who could attract the greatest number of followers. Finally, although their role as military leaders, or "ginap," is readily apparent during the war-torn colonial period, sagamores clearly also played an important role in economic and political affairs. In the hierarchical scheme developed by the anthropologist Morton Fried in 1960, for example, their societies were not egalitarian but ranked. However, although not all its members were equally powerful, the elite did not constitute the kind of lineage group that could sustain its power by the rule of inheritance.[10]

their catch during a short season, were not particularly interested in interacting with the Natives, nor in exploring areas beyond their fisheries in the Gulf of St. Lawrence.[11]

The Fur Trade

European attitudes toward the natives changed dramatically during the last quarter of the sixteenth century, when a new fashion craze swept through Europe: hats of felt made from beaver fur. Europe's beaver popu-

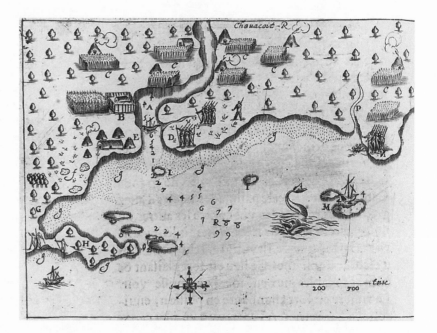

5-4. Map of Saco by Samuel de Champlain, 1613. Note the conical wigwams, longhouses, and cornfields. (Courtesy of the Rare Book Collection, National Library of Canada / Collection de livres rares, Bibliothèque nationale du Canada.)

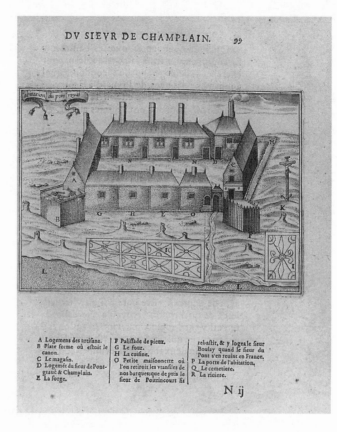

5-5. View of de Monts's habitation at Port Royal, built during the summer of 1605 (Courtesy of the Rare Book Collection, National Library of Canada / Collection de livres rares, Bibliothèque nationale du Canada.)

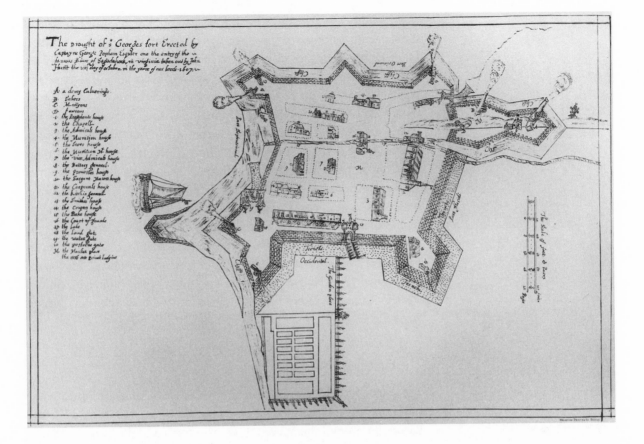

5-6. Plan of St. George Fort, site of the Popham colony, built in 1607 and abandoned a year later. (Collections of the Maine Historical Society.)

lation was far from adequate to sustain the demand, so Europeans turned to the vastness of North America and to its Native peoples.[12] This new fur trade expanded so quickly that by the 1580s those involved in it were communicating in an Indian-Basque pidgin, the kind of made-up language that often develops when groups speaking different languages begin to trade. By 1606 one early French observer actually remarked that "the language of the coastal tribes is half Basque."[13]

This commercial activity in the Gulf of St. Lawrence eventually gave rise to a few more exploratory probes southward into the Gulf of Maine: Simão Fernandez cruised the Maine coast in 1579; a year later, John Walker sailed up the Penobscot and took away three hundred hides from a local wigwam.[14] In 1583 the French merchant Étienne Bellenger sailed from Cape Breton probably as far west as Penobscot Bay. He had hoped to establish a trading post but became discouraged when, on the return voyage along the eastern coast of Nova Scotia, Souriquois killed two of his crew and stole their boat.[15]

As political and religious strife diminished in Europe toward the end of the sixteenth century, resources became available for renewed exploration of the North American Atlantic coast, including the Gulf of Maine. By defeating the Spanish Armada in 1588, England had become a world sea power, ready to expand to the New World.[16] Bartholomew Gosnold's 1602 voyage to the Gulf of Maine sought a site for English Catholics to colonize. He was followed by Martin Pring in 1603, George Waymouth in 1605, and John Smith in 1614.[17] The first English attempt at colonization, at present-day Popham, began in August 1607 but failed only a year later.[18] In 1604 the de Monts expedition, which included Samuel de Champlain, attempted to settle on an island in the St. Croix River—the present-day boundary between Maine and New Brunswick—but lost half of its men to scurvy during the first severe winter; the following spring de Monts moved the company to Port Royal (Nova Scotia), where it continued a fitful existence.[19] In 1609 the Dutchman Henry Hudson also made a voyage of exploration that included a brief visit to Maine, but thereafter Dutch efforts at colonization focused farther to the south.[20]

The First Epidemics

The disparity between European and Indian vulnerability to disease was stark; outbreaks often killed Native people in huge numbers, while the Europeans around them, even those who resided in the same dwellings, remained totally unaffected.[21] As neither the Indians nor the Europeans then understood the biological causes of disease, these epidemics became a source of considerable suspicion among the Native people toward the newcomers.

Regular contact with Europeans by the last quarter of the sixteenth century meant that the Souriquois experienced severe epidemics well before their neighbors to the southwest. In 1610 the early French Jesuit missionary Pierre Biard wrote: "They are astonished and often complain that since the French mingle with and carry on trade with them, they are dying fast and the population is thinning out. . . . [O]ne by one the different coasts according as they have begun to traffic with us, have been more reduced by disease."[22]

The first virgin-soil epidemic west of the St. John River struck seven years later, in 1617.[23] Its source was probably one of several French and English vessels that had recently visited the region. The pathogen has never been identified, but it was highly contagious, and it devastated the population from Massachusetts to the Kennebec. An Englishman who sailed from

BESSABEZ AND THE TARRENTINES

Early English explorers in the Gulf of Maine described a rivalry that reflects the emergence of European influence there during the late sixteenth and early seventeenth centuries. On one side was Bessabez, the supreme Etchemin sagamore whom English sources describe as the preeminent leader of a domain that extended from Frenchman's Bay at least to Saco and possibly as far west as Lac Mégantic in Quebec.[24] On the other side was a group that lived to the east of Bessabez. Known to the English as Tarrentines and to the French as Souriquois, they were mainly the ancestors of those who would later be called Micmacs.[25]

In 1658 Sir Ferdinando Gorges, a prime backer of the 1607 effort to colonize present-day Popham, described the rivalry and its causes as follows:

[Bessabez] had under him many great Subjects . . . some fifteen hundred Bow-Men, some others lesse, these they call *Sagamores.* . . . [He] had many enemies, especially those to the East and North-East, whom they call *Tarrentines.* . . . [H]is owne chief abode was not far from *Pemaquid,* but the Warre growing more and more violent between the *Bashaba* and the *Tarrentines,* who (as it seemed) presumed upon the hopes they had to be favored of the *French* who were seated in *Canada*[.] [T]heir next neighbors, the *Tarrentines*

surprised the *Bashaba* and slew him and all his People near about him.[26]

This passage accurately summarizes information from many other sources. As the first people on the Maritime Peninsula to establish regular contact with the French, the Tarrentines had tried to control the flow of furs toward European traders who visited the Gulf of St. Lawrence annually. Scant data make it difficult to estimate the volume of furs and European goods handled by the Tarrentines but, by all accounts, in 1600 they were experienced sailors of European vessels, and since the 1630s their European contacts had apparently thought highly enough of their carrying trade to include them among those they invited to visit France "in order to better facilitate traffic and friendship."[27]

French and English voyages began arriving in the Gulf of Maine on a regular basis after 1610, forcing the Tarrentines out of their role as middlemen in the fur trade. They subsequently turned to piratical raiding of both Natives and English colonists—as far south as Massachusetts. These attacks, which lasted until at least 1631, terrified New England Indians, who looked to the newly settled English for protection.[28]

Monhegan to Massachusetts in 1619 described a coastline dotted with "ancient Plantations, not long since populous now utterly void; other places a remnant remains but not free of sickness."[29]

The lasting impact of this epidemic is reflected in an account written in 1623 by Christopher Levett, who found at present-day York "good ground and much already cleared, fit for planting of corne and other fruits, having heretofore been planted by the Salvages who are all dead."[30] Even a full decade later, John Winter of Richmond's Island (off Cape Elizabeth) stated that "no Indians lives nearer unto us then 40 or 50 myles, except a few about the River of Salko [Saco]."[31]

The next major epidemic to affect Maine was smallpox, which broke out at Plymouth Colony in 1633 and arrived in Maine in 1634. That August, a letter sent from Richmond's Island stated: "Ther is a great many of the Indyans dead this yeare, both east and west from us, and a great many dyes still to the eastward from us."[32]

European Trade, Settlement, and Conflict

The Abenakis, Etchemins, and Souriquois survived this first cataclysm as definable groups.[33] But even as Maine's Indians were being devastated by epidemics and warfare, Europeans were arriving in ever-increasing numbers. The first resident trader was probably Claude de Saint-Étienne de La Tour, a member of a French company that arrived in Acadia in 1610 to establish Port Royal. La Tour survived the 1613 raids by Samuel Argall of Virginia that swept the French from the coastline of Acadia and destroyed Port Royal. His son Charles also operated a trading business in Acadia, becoming its commander in 1624 and building a strong post called Fort Lomeron at Cape Sable.[34]

Although the English remained active in the fur trade after the failure of the Popham Colony in 1607, they confined their activities mainly to annual summer voyages. After the founding of Plymouth in 1620, however, a major influx of English arrived on Maine's southwest and central coast, conducting fishing operations at Damariscove (1622), Piscataqua (1623), Cape Newagen (1623), Monhegan (1623), and Pemaquid (about 1625–28), and opening trading posts at Cushnoc (1629), Machias (1631), Pejepscot (about 1625–30), Penobscot (1629), and Richmond's Island (1628). Populated mainly by men, these outposts lacked the demographic base to become real settlements.[35]

When the Thirty Years War (1618–48) in Europe brought England and France into conflict in 1627, Scotland asserted a claim to the nascent French colony of Acadia that it acquired from England in 1621. The next year, Claude La Tour nimbly switched allegiance from France to Scotland. In 1629 La Tour and the Scot Sir William Alexander arrived at Port Royal with a small contingent of Scottish settlers. This left Charles and Claude La Tour on opposite sides of the conflict and Fort Lomeron the only viable French settlement in the Acadia.[36] In 1631, encouraged by renewed French interest in Acadia, the younger La Tour set up a new post at the mouth of the St. John River, which was soon raided and sacked by Scots from Port Royal. La Tour responded by raiding the new English post at Machias.[37]

When the Treaty of Saint-Germain-en-Laye returned control of Acadia to France in 1632, the new governor, Isaac de Razilly, expelled the Scots from Port Royal and energetically began to reestablish control over Acadia.

In 1635 Razilly sent one of his lieutenants, Charles de Menou d'Aulnay, to the Penobscot where, with little ceremony, he ordered the Plymouth traders to leave, thus eliminating the last British presence east of the Kennebec.[38] Razilly's death soon thereafter unleashed a decade of intense rivalry between d'Aulnay and Charles La Tour that some have described as a civil war.[39] Meanwhile, during the 1630s and 1640s at least eight permanent English farming and fishing communities sprang up along the coast and riverbanks between the Piscataqua River and present-day North Yarmouth. Factional feuding prevailed there as well but, probably because these were now family-based communities intent upon maintaining social order, rivalries usually remained at the political or legal level, with minimal use of force.[40]

English settlement of central Maine proceeded somewhat differently. In 1629 the Plymouth Colony was granted land allowing it to establish a trading post at Cushnoc, near the head of tide on the Kennebec River in present-day Augusta. In the lower Kennebec and Merrymeeting Bay areas, small settlements then began to spring up that were based on a mixed farming and fishing economy that included small-scale fur trading. Thomas Purchase, a full-time trader, set up a post on the lower Androscoggin River by 1630, and around 1653 the firm of Clark and Lake established a settlement on Arrowsic Island and a truck (trading) house at Taconic in present-day Winslow.[41]

Natives Welcome the Europeans

Early relations between Native people and Europeans throughout the region were generally peaceable, if not always friendly. In 1623, for example, Samoset, a sagamore of some influence who hailed from the Pemaquid area and who is memorialized in New England lore for welcoming the Pilgrims at Plymouth, told Christopher Levett at Casco Bay that the Indians and English should be bound by "*mouchicke legamatch* [friendship]." Levett was also supposedly told, by a group of local sagamores, "that I and my wife and children should be very welcome into that country at any time."[42] To the east, the French also were apparently welcomed. Charles de Biencourt, commander of Port Royal and leader of the small colony there during the 1610s, and his heir and successor Charles La Tour, both claimed the title "grand Sagamo" of the Souriquois and Etchemins. Moreover, Biencourt was said to have spent his last years living among the Souriquois, and La Tour married a Souriquois woman in the early 1620s.[43]

This amity between Native and European peoples was undoubtedly

5-7. Copper kettle from a richly furnished burial at Pictou, Nova Scotia, dating to around 1580. (History Collections, Nova Scotia Museum, Halifax.)

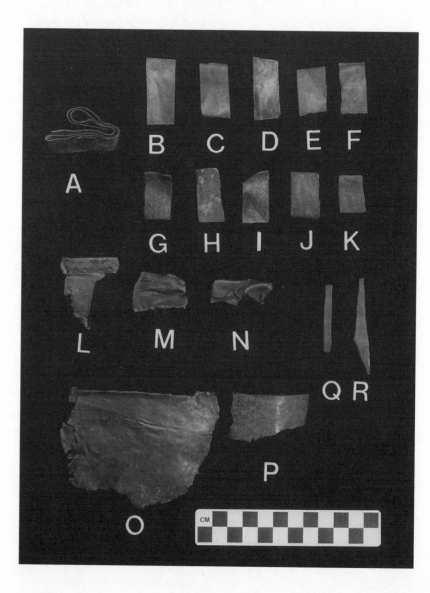

5-8. Cut stock from copper and brass kettles from an early historic Indian site on the St. Croix River. The cut pieces on the upper right are from strips like that on the upper left. The two narrow objects at the center right are brass. All others are copper. (Maine State Museum collection.)

rooted largely in two factors. The first was the desire among aboriginal people for European goods, including cloth, brass kettles, biscuit, liquor, and guns. West of the Penobscot, however, the second factor was fear of the Tarrentines, as many New England Indians called the predatory Souriquois. As Plymouth governor William Bradford put it in 1621: "The People [of Massachusetts Bay] were much afraid of the Tarentines, a people to the eastward which used to come in harvest time and take away their corn, and many times kill their persons." In fact, it was probably in the hope of gaining protection from the English that the Massachusett sachem Chikataubut

5-9. Jew's harp, arrowheads, tinkling cones, and beads made of brass from worn-out kettles and glass trade beads from Norridgewock. (Maine State Museum collection.)

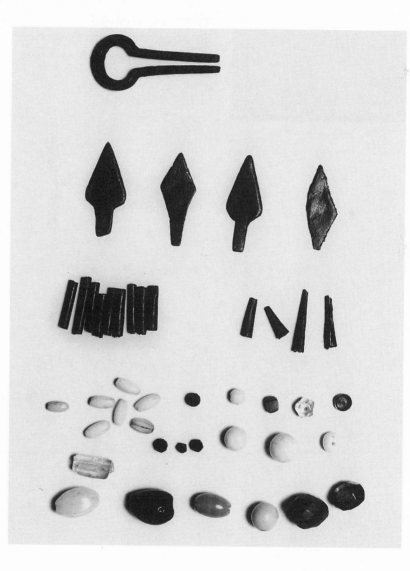

and eight others signed a submission to King James in September of that year, and it was certainly fear of the Tarrentines that motivated Indians of Adawam and Naumkeag, near Salem, to maintain close ties with that new settlement eight years later.[44]

The honeymoon was short-lived, however, as Europeans began to clash over territorial claims and access to furs, often using liquor and firearms to enlist Native support, and resorting to other abusive tactics. According to Bradford, in 1627: "Besides the spoiling of the trade this last year, our boat and men [at Cushnoc] had like to have been cut off by the Indians, after the fishermen were gone, for the wrongs which they did them, in stealing their skins and other abuses offered them . . . and besides they still continues to truck pieces [firearms], powder, and shot with them, which will be the overthrow of all, if it be not looked unto."[45]

So extensive was this trade that a year later, according to Bradford, "the indians are full of pieces all over, both fowling pieces, muskets, pistols, etc.

5-10. Early trade beads from various Maine sites. (Maine State Museum collection.)

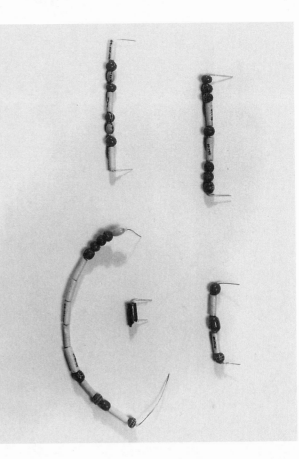

5-11. Felling axes from various Maine sites. (Maine State Museum collection.)

They have also their moulds to make shot of all sorts. . . . Yea, some have seen them have screw-plates to make screw pins [for flint locks] them selves . . . wherewith they are better furnished than the English themselves."[46] And in 1637, Robert Trelawny, proprietor of the Richmond's Island fishing station, complained that his adversary George Cleeve, based at what is now Portland, had "made [the Indians] Ennemys to us and we to them."[47]

Conditions were getting worse in Acadia too. In 1635 Jean Thomas, a French fisherman, reportedly convinced some Souriquois to attack and pillage Razilly's Fort Saint-François at Canso.[48] The next year, Pemaquid trader Abraham Shurt reported: "Here comes natives from [the Penobscot]

TRADING METHODS

In 1672 Nicolas Denys[49] described how Indians conducted the fur trade in Acadia, revealing their considerable skill in manipulating their European counterparts.

At the present time, so soon as the Indians come out of the woods in spring, they hide all their best skins, bringing a few to the establishments in order to obtain their right to something to drink, eat and smoke. They pay a part of that which was lent them in the autumn to support them, without which they would perish of hunger. They insist that this is all their hunting for the winter has produced. As soon as they have departed, they go to recover the skins which they have hidden in the woods, and go to the routes of the fishing ships and keep watch. If they see any vessels, they make great smokes to let it be known that they are there. At the same time the ship nears the land, and the Indians take some skins and embark in their canoes to go to the ship, where they are well received. . . . They promise things first to one then to another, but give nothing. During all the trading, they are promised much if they will go and find [the sailors] at the place where they are going to anchor to make their fishery, and this the women make them hope [they will do]. After that each sailor gives them, secretly from one another, some ship's biscuit; these they always take, assuring them they will go and meet them. But they do not go there at once, but remain on shore, waiting for other ships to come past.

and says that they will remove to some other parts, they are so abused by [d'Aulnay's agents]." Three years later, Indians killed two of d'Aulnay's traders.[50]

Such conflicts not only disrupted the fur trade, they also took much of the European profit out of it. In 1634, for example, Massachusetts Bay governor John Winthrop remarked that the traders were "cutting one another's throats for beaver."[51] Moreover, profit margins were further diminished by the fact that "the Indians are now . . . well seen into our tradinge Commodities" and were willing to buy only first-rate goods: the longest, warmest coats, hats that fit, and coverlets that were "soft and warme." And then only if the price was right; as far as furs were concerned, it was a seller's market.[52]

The English officials made repeated efforts to rectify misdeeds done to Maine Indians and to halt the trade of guns and powder, but governance on the trading frontier during the 1620s and 1630s was not strong enough to halt either.[53] They may have had some effect, however, for during the late 1630s and early 1640s trade-related violence seems to have abated somewhat. By this time land-based English traders shifted their activities eastward and farther inland to posts such as at Pejepscot and Cushnoc. At the mouths of the Penobscot and St. John Rivers, French posts controlled the trade. On the coast, only the fishing port of Pemaquid still remained active in the trade, in part by playing the role of intermediary between French and English traders and by attracting some Indian trade from the west side of the Penobscot and from its own modest hinterland.[54]

Continuing Native Warfare

The disappearance of Iroquoian-speaking populations from the St. Lawrence Valley sometime just prior to 1600 apparently triggered an outburst of internecine warfare throughout the region that lasted for decades. This warfare was no doubt nourished in part by population imbalances caused by virgin-soil epidemics, but there is surprisingly little evidence of major epidemics among the Natives of the Maritime Peninsula during the decades between the 1617 outbreak and the smallpox epidemic of 1634. Instead, the main focus of discord seems to have been access to hunting territory and fur markets.

One of the more persistent patterns of conflict was between the tribes closely allied with the French, who lived to the north of the St. Lawrence, with those who lived south of it. At issue was control of the no-man's-land south of the St. Lawrence River. During the 1630s, Montagnais from north of the St. Lawrence were hunting in Etchemin territory in the upper St. John Valley, and as late as 1652 Etchemins were said to be involved in a "great war" with the Montagnais. Likewise, to the west, the Socoquiois of the Connecticut Valley and Mahicans of the Hudson Valley, along with the Mohawks, fought Montagnais and Algonquins throughout the 1620s, 1630s, and 1640s. Finally, with French intervention, the Socoquiois made peace with the Algonquins in 1653. Thereafter, French sources rarely mention hostilities among Algonquian groups, probably because they and their neighbors were forced to close ranks in the face of a new threat: increasing Iroquois aggression from the west.[55]

VI THE SECOND HALF OF
THE SEVENTEENTH CENTURY

MORE THAN any area to the east of it, life in the Kennebec River region was undergoing rapid change by the mid–seventeenth century, as the English, the French, and the Iroquois all began to affect the lives of the Etchemins and Abenakis. Competition among English trading interests remained intense, and the uncontrolled use of liquor in the trade continued.[1] A steady influx of new settlers added to the competition, and by 1670 there was a glut of unruly traders in the area. The Jesuit Barthelemy Vimont wrote in 1643 that the Norridgewock Abenakis had "no acquaintances or commerce with anyone else, except with some English who are wont to go there; and are much given to drunkenness by means of the liquor that they get in trade with the heretics [English], and with the vessels of the coast."[2] A decade later, the Plymouth Colony admitted that "there hath been great abuses in trading wine and other strong liquors with the Indians . . . [who] in their drunkenness, commit much horrid wickedness, as murdering their nearest relatives &c."[3] Native elders complained that liquor "deprives us of our lives, causes murders among us and makes us lose our wits rendering us like madmen."[4] But Natives depended on trade, for both economic and, increasingly, diplomatic reasons, and liquor was part of that trade.

The disruption brought about by the fur trade, acute though it sometimes was, had mainly local effects. By 1642, however, a broader pattern of ethnic disharmony was emerging. In that year English settlers were reporting "Insufferable . . . Insolencies" from Native people, and there were rumors of a "general conspiracy against the English" not only in Maine but as far away as the Hudson River.[5] The origins of this unrest remain obscure,

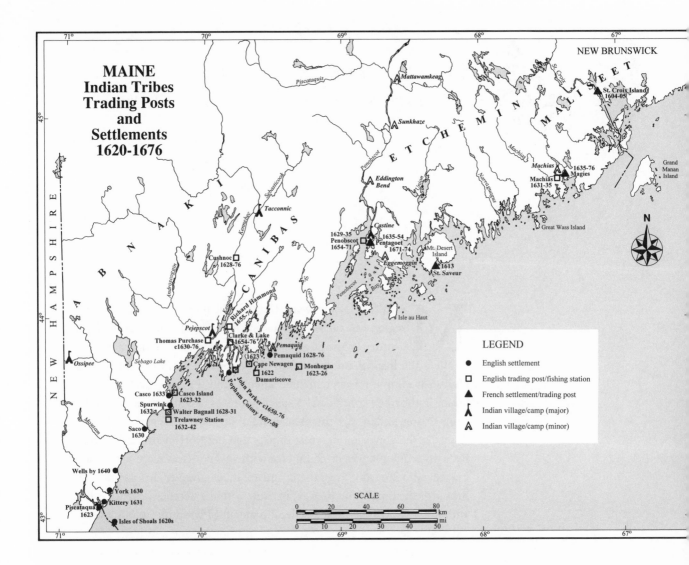

MAINE
Indian Tribes
Trading Posts
and
Settlements
1620-1676

NEW BRUNSWICK

Piscataquis

Mattawamkeag

Sunkhaze

MALISEET

St. Croix Island
1604-05

Machias
1635-76
Magies

Machias
1631-35

Grand
Manan
Island

ETCHEMIN

Eddington
Bend

Great Wass Island

Penobscot

1629-35
Penobscot
1654-71

Castine
1635-54
Pentagoet
1671-74

Mt. Desert
Island

Eggemoggin

1613
St. Saveur

Isle au Haut

Tacconnic

Kennebec

CANIBAS

Cushnoc
1628-76

Richard Hammond
1655-76

Pejepscot

Thomas Purchase
c1630-76

Clarke & Lake
1654-76

Pemaquid

1623
Pemaquid 1628-76

Cape Newagen

Monhegan
1623-26

1622
Damariscove

John Parker c1650-76

Popham Colony 1607-08

Ossipee

Sebago Lake

Casco 1633
Casco Island
1623-32

Spurwink
1632

Walter Bagnall 1628-31
Trelawney Station
1632-42

Saco
1630

Wells by 1640

York 1630

Piscataqua
1623

Kittery 1631

Isles of Shoals 1620s

NEW HAMPSHIRE

ABNAKI

Androscoggin

Saco

Mousam

St. George

Penobscot Bay

Machias

Narraguagus

Union

Sebasticook

LEGEND

● English settlement

□ English trading post/fishing station

▲ French settlement/trading post

⚑ Indian village/camp (major)

⚑ Indian village/camp (minor)

SCALE

0   20   40   60   80
km

0   10   20   30   40   50
mi

N

6-1. Maine: Indian tribes, trading posts, and settlements, 1620–76

but it coincided with the sale to Indians by English traders—particularly on the Connecticut River but apparently along the Maine coast as well—of a "great supply of powder and guns."[6] As English policy was still to keep firearms out of Native hands, tensions on the Kennebec, at least, may have been the result of Massachusetts's seizure of a quantity of powder from Indians in that area.[7] This escalation of the gun trade foreshadowed a far more profound conflict, one that runs like a thread through most of the subsequent history of Native-European interaction: rivalry not among various Native groups but among European colonies.

The St. Lawrence versus the Atlantic Coast

The most profound and persistent colonial cleavage was between the French on the St. Lawrence River and the Dutch and English on or near the Atlantic coast. It must be recalled that Native peoples of the Atlantic coast and the St. Lawrence Valley had been in frequent contact from prehistoric times and that their close contact, both friendly and hostile, continued into the historic period. The obvious routes linking the two areas were the rivers flowing into the Atlantic, which connect by short portages across the height of land to drainages leading to the St. Lawrence River.[8] Thus the natives could, and did, operate in either colonial arena, and Europeans could not take their loyalties for granted.

6-2. Engraving of beavers by Nicholas Giérard as it appeared on a wall map of North and South America by Nicholas de Fer, 1698. It shows supposed similarities between "Des Castors du Canada" and human society, with beavers playing the roles of commander, porters, masons, physicians, etc. Although inaccurate, this allegory indicates the importance of beaver to the European economy. (Courtesy of National Archives of Canada, NMC 26825.)

The French had one important advantage: a huge fur-producing hinterland. But their fur trade was in the hands of a cartel, La Compagnie des Cent-Associés, or "Hundred Associates," which eliminated competition and thus kept fur prices low. This would prove to be a disadvantage in recruiting new settlers from France.[9] A further disadvantage was that the St. Lawrence River froze in the winter, cutting off contact with the mother country. For this and other reasons, trade goods were expensive, hard to get, and often held in lower esteem by Native people than those available from overseas to the Dutch and English.

The Dutch and English, on the other hand, were more remote from the northern beaver country but had year-round access to Europe by sea and thus to better-quality trade goods. After about 1620, first the Dutch and then the English gained another advantage—access to the purple and white shell beads called wampum by the Indians of southern New England and Long Island who manufactured them.[10] This commodity was so popular among northeastern Indians that the Dutch began to manufacture it themselves. The French, on the other hand, found it difficult to obtain and did not learn to make it until the mid–eighteenth century. By 1628 Indians from the St. Lawrence were traveling to the Dutch at Fort Orange [present-day Albany], on the Hudson, in order to obtain it. The popularity of wampum therefore had the effect of siphoning away Canadian furs and redirecting them toward the English and Dutch.[11]

In 1623, fearing competition, the Dutch offered to provide Plymouth traders with wampum, which soon found its way to Plymouth's Cushnoc post on the Kennebec River. Thereafter, there is evidence of numerous trading expeditions to Quebec by Abenakis, sometimes accompanied by Englishmen, and there are even indications that Indians from the St. Lawrence came to trade on the Kennebec. There are, for example, three separate accounts dating from between 1643 and 1649 of Abenakis arriving on the St. Lawrence ostensibly seeking religious instruction but in fact seeking to obtain furs.[12] The Hundred Associates resented this leakage of furs but were unable to stop it. They had a similar problem with the Mohawks, who also had easy access to wampum from Dutch traders on the Hudson.[13]

The Abenakis, the French, and the Iroquois

While the Abenakis clearly wanted to divert furs from the St. Lawrence to the English in Maine, surviving accounts suggest that they were also seeking closer ties to the French and their Algonquian allies, ties that would eventually overpower their economic self-interest. There are two factors that account for this desire. The first was curiosity about French Catholicism. While some Abenakis who traveled to Quebec may have feigned religious curiosity, for others the curiosity was apparently genuine. There were enough of the latter, in fact, to entice Charles Meiaskwat, a Montagnais lay preacher, to visit Norridgewock in 1642. Joining him as an interpreter was a young Abenaki, one of the few who had already taken up residence at the recently founded Jesuit mission village at Sillery, near Quebec. One Abenaki chief went back with Meiaskwat in the spring of 1643, "forsaking his own country in order to dwell [at Sillery] . . . and obtain instruction, so as to be Baptized."[14] After rigorous preparation, he was finally baptized and given the Christian name Jean-Baptiste. By 1646 Jean-Baptiste was back at Quebec, claiming to have made forty potential converts and asking "for a black robe [as Jesuit missionaries were called] to go to the Abnaquiois to instruct them." He promised that "they would no longer come [to Quebec] . . . and would give no offense to Monsieur the governor regarding trade."

Jean-Baptiste's missionary success may have been due in part to the outbreak among the Abenakis of an unidentified but deadly malady that caused the vomiting of blood. As Abenaki territory lay in the interior, it is not clear whether they had suffered from the epidemics that had earlier swept the Gulf of Maine coast. If this was their first exposure to European disease, it may well have shaken their faith in traditional spiritual beliefs and medicine.[15] Whatever the causes, by the late 1640s it seems that Catholicism was taking hold among the Abenakis.

The second reason the Abenakis sought closer relations with the French and their allies was fear of the Mohawks. The Indian scare of 1642 was just the first indication of Iroquois expansionism. Historians customarily refer to Iroquoian military aggression during this period (1638–55) as the Beaver Wars and, to be sure, control of the fur trade was an important dimension of their strategy. But there were other factors of equal importance, all tied together in what Francis Jennings has called a "dream of empire."[16] Feeling hemmed in on all sides by actual and perceived enemies, they tried during the next six decades to ensure their own security through a combination of diplomacy and warfare. Their chosen strategy, which was misunderstood by Europeans—or was at least ambiguous to them—was to create a network of tribute and alliance extending far beyond their homelands. Recent research has made clear that the goal of Iroquois diplomacy was not to dominate their adversaries but rather to "cultivate a landscape of peace"—that is, to maintain a security zone in which the five tribes of the

Iroquoian League, although not imperially ascendant, would be the central players.[17] They certainly tried to forcibly overcome their foes, employing extraordinary violence when they deemed it necessary, but they also adopted captives to replace their dead. The practice of mass adoption was not unique to them, but during the middle decades of the seventeenth century numerous Iroquois villages had adopted so many captives that native-born Iroquois were a minority. In pursuit of these strategies the Iroquois affected the lives of both Natives and Europeans over much of eastern North America.[18]

In the Iroquois League, the Mohawks were "Keepers of the Eastern Door," the door of the metaphorical longhouse inhabited by the league. For all Native groups east of the Hudson River, including those of the Maritime Peninsula, it was the Mohawks who posed the main threat. By 1628 the

6-3. Map titled *Carte pour servir l'eclaircissement du Papier Terrier de la Nouvelle France.* Note the canoe portage routes over which Indians are carrying Micmac-style canoes. (Original map ca. 1678 attributed to J. B. L. Franquelin, H3/900/[1678], in the Bibliothèque National, Paris. Reproduced from a copy in the National Archives of Canada, NMC 17393.)

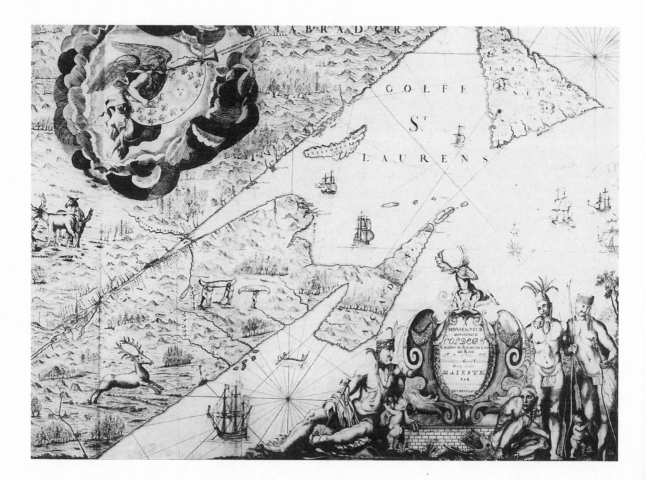

6-4. Musket fitted with a matchlock, an inexpensive firing mechanism widely used during the early colonial period. This German example is similar to those used by the Plymouth colonists. Length: 156 centimeters. (Maine State Museum collection.)

Mohawks had fought and displaced the neighboring Mahicans from the Hudson Valley, thus gaining for themselves primary access to Dutch trade depots on the Hudson. In the following decades they strove to gain comparable ascendancy over the Algonquian groups that were favored by Swedish traders on the Delaware, English traders in New England—particularly on the Connecticut River—and the French on the St. Lawrence and Great Lakes. By 1645 they had gained ready access to Dutch firearms, which they used in their attacks on their Algonquian neighbors. By 1647 they had raided as far as Abenaki territory, probably somewhere west of the Kennebec.[19]

During the 1640s, French attitudes toward the Abenakis warmed considerably, in part because many had converted to Catholicism and in part because they were increasingly seen as useful allies against the Iroquois. The initial French response to Abenaki interest in Catholicism was to send the Jesuit missionary Gabriel Druillettes to the Kennebec in August 1646.[20] There he cared for the ill, studied the Abenaki language, baptized "thirty people prepared for death and for Paradise," joined in an arduous winter hunting expedition, and competed against local shamans. He also visited Capuchin missionaries on the Penobscot as well as the English at Cushnoc and other settlements. Druillettes apparently impressed many Indians, and his visit established a link between the Abenakis and Quebec that would become crucial to both in later years.

When Druillettes returned to Quebec in July 1647, the Abenakis who accompanied him pleaded for his return, and he did go back to the Kennebec twice between 1650 and 1652 but primarily for diplomatic reasons. During his absence, the Iroquois had achieved their first major victory in the Beaver Wars by defeating the Hurons—New France's main fur suppliers—who lived to the west of Quebec, around Lake Huron's Georgian Bay.[21] As the economy of New France depended mainly on the fur trade, Druillettes's charge was to draw the Abenakis and Penacooks into an alliance with the Sokokis and Pocumtucks of the Connecticut Valley against the Iroquois and to negotiate an anti-Iroquois alliance between the English colonies and New France. He succeeded at the former but failed at the latter.[22]

The Struggle for Acadia, 1635–1675

The French regarded the Abenakis as living within the bounds of New England. To the east, in Acadia, lived the Etchemins and Souriquois, with whom they would have closer relations. There, Capuchin friars brought by Razilly in the mid-1630s had begun the task of ministering to the small French populations of the Acadian posts between Port Royal and Pentagoet (Penobscot). Capuchins arrived at Pentagoet with d'Aulnay in 1635, built a small church there in 1648, and conducted missionary activities in the area between 1646 and 1654. One Capuchin in particular, Bernardin de Crépy, learned the local dialect and was credited with numerous Native conversions. In 1646, troubled by the arrival of the Jesuit Gabriel Druillettes on the Kennebec, the Capuchins wrote to Quebec asking that Jesuits stay out of the area, because it was within Capuchin jurisdiction. Two years later, however, apparently realizing that they lacked the personnel to cover so large a region, they reversed their position and invited the Jesuits to resume missionary work on the Kennebec.[23]

Soon after d'Aulnay's death by drowning in 1650, the Capuchins found themselves swept away by political and military events. In the summer of 1654, four English vessels under the command of Major Robert Sedgewick and his son-in-law, Captain John Leverett, both from Massachusetts, at-

6-5. Copper plaque by the Capuchin Leo of Paris, commemorating the construction of a chapel at Pentagoet in 1648. (Reproduced from Wheeler 1875.)

6-6. Costume of the Capuchin order, which provided missionaries to French posts in the Gulf of Maine during the mid-seventeenth century. (Reproduced from Ferrari 1823.)

Laico Cappuccino

tacked Acadia, capturing La Tour's fort on the St. John River and then Port Royal and Pentagoet.[24] Except for a couple of Frenchmen who agreed to run the posts for the English, the inhabitants at Pentagoet and the St. John were sent back to France. At Port Royal, the community's inhabitants were given the choice of staying or returning to France; most stayed, although the Capuchins were expelled.[25] Whatever impact the Capuchins may have had upon the Etchemins apparently soon faded. Two decades later, when the Jesuit Jean Morain established the next mission among the Etchemins, he found them "very averse to Christianity . . . [e]xceedingly addicted to drunkenness, to jugglery [native religious practice], and to polygamy."[26]

Sedgewick's capture of Acadia led to sixteen years of English control, for the most part under the troubled governorship of Thomas Temple.[27] Temple could not evict Charles La Tour, however, because he was heir to the 1630 patent to properties in "Nova Scotia" granted to his father by William Alexander. Temple also had to satisfy William Crowne of England, whose credit helped bankroll the new colony.[28] Ultimately, all of Temple's efforts came to naught when, following a brief war between England and France, the Treaty of Breda returned Nova Scotia to France in 1667.

Temple managed to delay the transfer of Acadia until 1670, when Hector d'Andiqné de Grandfontaine, newly appointed governor of Acadia, arrived at Pentagoet. Grandfontaine quickly restored a semblance of French control, but it was not an easy task, for at that time the population of Acadia stood at a mere four to five hundred.[29] Jacques de Chambly replaced Grandfontaine in 1673, bringing with him a young ensign named Jean-Vincent d'Abbadie de Saint-Castin, who would play a central role in Native life throughout the rest of the seventeenth century. Chambly's regime was brief, however. In July the Dutch mariner Jurriaen Aernoutsz, in league with some Boston merchants, captured Pentagoet and pillaged all French posts along the west shore of the Bay of Fundy. After a month in Acadia, he sailed to Boston, disposed of his pillage and prisoners and, in October, sailed off to Curaçao, never to return.[30]

Soon thereafter, some of Aernoutsz's companions headed back to "New Holland," which they intended to take over. With a zeal wholly inappropriate to their small numbers, they began seizing New England vessels, whereupon Massachusetts threw them into jail in Boston in April 1675, threatening to hang the lot as pirates. They were probably saved by the outbreak of King Philip's War in June. Eventually, all were released and, at worst, banished. The young Saint-Castin was back at Pentagoet by 1676, in time to play a minor role in the war that would permanently alter relations among Natives and Europeans.[31]

The Mohawk Threat at Midcentury

Few details are available regarding relations between the Mohawks and the Algonquians to their east during the 1650s. In 1653 there was a reported gathering of "some thousands of Indians at Piscataque," which caused "great affright of the people in those parts."[32] The English never learned the reason for this gathering, but it was more likely due to hostilities with the Mohawks than animosity toward the English.

During the 1660s Mohawk warfare with Indians to their east reached a debilitating crescendo. In 1661, 400 to 500 Mohawks set out to attack "people of the East" in revenge for an earlier encounter in which "Canada Indians," aided by Kennebec Abenakis, had killed 100 Mohawks. Some of this group went to demand tribute from the Abenakis, for the Kennebec was still considered the richest source of furs in New England. There, all but one were killed.[33] The next April, about 260 set out to take revenge, bound for unknown reasons for the Penobscot River instead of the Kennebec. There they incurred the wrath not only of the Natives but also of the English officials for bullying English traders at the Negew post in present-day Bangor and the fort at Pentagoet, killing some English cattle and capturing 80 "trading Indians"—men, women, and children—who were visiting the fort at the time.[34] The victims were described only as "under the protection" of the English post there, so it is unclear whether they were visitors from the Kennebec and thus "likely targets for revenge" or locally resident Etchemins.[35]

In any case, this was the last major Mohawk incursion onto the Maritime Peninsula, for the Mohawks began to come under attack close to home by Sokokis and their allies. In August 1663, "Northern Indians," mainly Sokokis but including some from as far east as Norridgewock, traveled west to attack the Mohawks, killing several, including a Mohegan. This raid so frightened the Mohegans, who were tributaries to the Mohawks, that they requested permission to build a fort for protection. Less daunted, Mohawks attacked the Sokokis' fortified village at Fort Hill, near Hinsdale, New Hampshire, in November, suffering severe losses.[36] The following spring, the Mohawks, together with the Dutch of Albany, sought peace with the Pocumtucks, neighbors and allies of the Sokokis, but the Mohawk delegates were murdered, probably by Sokokis or Abenakis, before the treaty could be ratified. That summer, a small party of Mohawks raided as far east as the outskirts of Boston, where they were put in jail, and Connecticut Valley Indians retaliated by attacking three of the Mohawks' four villages.[37]

In September 1666, the Carignan-Salières arrived in Quebec, the first regular military regiment ever deployed in North America, for the sole purpose of resolving the Iroquois problem. Under the command of the Marquis de Tracy, the Salières marched into Mohawk country and destroyed all four of their villages.[38] The next summer, Eastern Indians, including Robin Hood, joined Indians from the Connecticut Valley in further attacks on the Mohawks. Then, after a lull in 1668, a force of six or seven thousand New England Indians attacked a Mohawk village during the summer of 1669, with heavy losses to both sides.[39]

All these events took a significant toll on the groups caught up in them, including the Mohawks. One response by Mohawks and other Iroquois was to leave their homelands to take up residence near Montreal at a village called Caughnawaga, the name of the increasingly depopulated easternmost Mohawk village. Although Mohawks attacked and killed Penacooks on the Merrimack in 1670, the Mohawk threat to the Maritime Peninsula had subsided.[40]

The surge in Mohawk warfare may explain one of the more unusual events of the 1660s, one that was to have great long-term significance. In May 1664, Passaconaway, chief sagamore of the Penacooks, submitted to Massachusetts Bay, as several other sagamores from Massachusetts had recently done. Surrendering his sovereignty seems a rash act, even for this leader who had always advised his people to remain on friendly terms with the English. The most likely explanation seems to be that he, like his neighbors to the south, was seeking protection from Mohawk aggression. Whatever the case, the result of that decision was to make the English feel more secure in settling near the Penacooks and their relatives in southwestern Maine, which led to population increases sufficient to ensure the survival of Berwick—alone of all the Maine settlements—during King Philip's War.[41]

English Settlers and Indian Deeds

During the mid–seventeenth century, all along the western Maine coast from Piscataqua to Pemaquid, English communities were growing. By the early 1670s, the Kittery area, Wells, Cape Porpoise, Saco, Winter Harbor, the Scarborough region, Casco Bay, and Sagadahoc all had populations of more than four hundred, for a total of more than three thousand. The economic basis of most of these settlements was agriculture, with fishing in some cases—notably Pemaquid—a close second.[42] The eastern settlements, at Sheepscot, Pemaquid, and in the Sagadahoc region, lacked established governments that could issue land titles. Settlers thus turned to the Native "proprietor," as did colonists in southwestern Maine who sought titles to interior properties beyond the limits of local governments.[43]

As the English of the eighteenth century ultimately used these deeds to dispossess the Natives of their lands, it is tempting to regard this as their original purpose. While such may have been the case for later grants along the western Maine coast, where access to cropland soon became an issue, to the east—where most of the deeds were signed—there is little evidence to support this conclusion. Most deeds simply helped settlers accomplish one of four straightforward goals: to establish a homestead, to establish claims to property already occupied, to enlarge holdings, or to acquire mill sites and stands of timber.[44] The Native grantors continued to reside in the area and to interact peaceably with the English for decades after their sales.[45]

In general, grantors around Sagadahoc, whether Indian or English, showed little anxiety about maintaining access to traditional resources. A few of the Sagadahoc deeds mention the transfer of privileges that seem traditional to Native culture, such as "hawking, hunting, fishing and fowling, &c.," but such phrasing is, in fact, formulaic and derived from conventional English usage, not Native subsistence patterns.[46] It is only west of Sagadahoc, where agriculture was a traditional Native activity, and English population was growing most rapidly, that the wording of some grants reflects the grantor's concern with maintaining an agricultural base. Good illustrations of this concern can be found in the deeds signed by a sagamore from the Newechiwannok (Berwick) and Piscataqua (Kittery) area known as Mr. Rowles. In a 1643 deed, for example, he reserved "a Parcel of Ground called by the Name Comphegan wch he doth keep for himself."[47] And in the early 1670s, in old age and fearing the disenfranchisement of his children, Mr. Rowles asked the settlers to sell or give him one or two hundred acres of land and requested that the transaction be "recorded in the Town Book as a publick Act, that so his children which he left behind, might not be turned out, like Vagabonds, as destitute of a Habitation amongst or near the English."[48]

The deeds generally suggest that the grantors received little compensation beyond "good and valuable consideration" or some paltry amount such as "one peck of Indian corn," "on[e] Bottle of Liquor Yearly," or "One good eare of Indiane Corne." Such apparent inattention to land values, which is also apparent in Native deeds signed elsewhere in the Northeast, has led to a range of explanations focusing on Native credulity or helplessness.[49] In fact, however, such phrasing is merely another instance of formulaic language derived from English deeds of the era; the specified goods were often payable, for example, on "Christmas day" or the "five and Twentieth day of March," the beginning of the new year according to the Julian calendar then in use by the English.[50]

What, then, were the benefits to Native grantors? As the earliest grants were to trading companies, improved or regular access to manufactured goods seems likely to have been perceived as an advantage. The majority of deeds, however, were signed between 1645 and 1667, when ready access to such goods made it a fur seller's market. It may be significant that the frequencies of these later deeds peak during two periods: 1648 to 1654 and 1659 to 1666. As we have seen, these are periods for which there is evidence of Mohawk raids into the region. This being so, these grantors may have been seeking security against the Mohawks from their new English neighbors.

Population and Ethnicity in Seventeenth-Century Maine

There are few data on Native population size in seventeenth-century Maine. For the period around 1610–13, the Jesuit Pierre Biard estimated that there were fifty-five hundred Indians between the St. John and Saco.[51] Conservative as his estimate seems, in 1663 Quebec bishop François de Laval reported a mere 170 families from the St. John to the Penobscot and 200 from the Kennebec area.[52] Reconstructing actual population sizes from such statistics is problematic at best, but taken at face value, these two sources describe a significant reduction in Native population over the first half-century of sustained contact with Europeans. Settlement patterns also seem to have changed: a few data indicate that populations living in areas settled by the English were now concentrating farther up rivers flowing to the coast.

From Casco Bay west, the small population described by John Winter in 1634 had apparently increased, either naturally or through immigration, for in 1651 Druillettes visited "12 or 13 [Indian] settlements or villages" along the Kennebec and "along the coast of Acadia [actually, from Pemaquid west], which the English occupy." Apparently, it was inhabitants of these villages who signed the numerous existing deeds to land in what are now Kittery, Berwick, Cape Porpoise, Wells, Saco, Scarborough, and Falmouth (Portland). Judging from deeds, the small remaining coastal population seems to have been distributed sporadically.[53] The continued existence of interior agricultural communities in the western Maine area can be inferred from records written later in the century that mention Pigwacket (present-day Fryeburg) and Ossippee, New Hampshire.

English activity on the Androscoggin was apparently confined to Pejepscot (present-day Brunswick), and the historic record for the valley's higher regions is correspondingly weaker. Thus, although the Androscoggin valley seems to have supported a substantial population, its range and relationships with populations to the west are not well understood. Its im-

ROBIN HOOD OF MERRYMEETING BAY

Of special interest during the mid–seventeenth century is Mohotoworomet, a man the English called Robin Hood. This eminent figure is known chiefly from the deeds he signed, of which at least twenty-five have been recorded, not counting those he witnessed or cosigned. Although he several times identified himself as residing at Nequasset (present-day Woolwich), Robin Hood signed deeds over an unprecedentedly broad area, covering the region between the Sheepscot and Sagadahoc, where he was occasionally identified as a sagamore, and westward to Casco Bay.[54]

The historic record is ambiguous concerning the source of Robin Hood's prominence. That he was a sagamore seems certain, although we have little evidence of his activities as a leader in warfare or politics. We do know that in 1667 he was cited by Massachusetts authorities as the leader of a group of warriors who stole corn and killed cattle in the Connecticut Valley. This band was assisting Indians from the Connecticut Valley who attacked Mohawk villages that summer.[55] No historic source clearly identifies Robin Hood as a shaman, but there are suggestive clues. For example, the English settlers referred to him—as they did other local men of influence—by unusual names associated with fools of the English May fair, such as Diogenes, Monquine, Jack Pudding, and Dick Swash. He may also be the "Aranbinout" described to the Jesuit Druillettes

by people of Norridgewock as a dangerous shaman. If his position within the Native community was such, this may explain why it was he who volunteered, on the eve of the outbreak of King Philip's War in Maine, to diffuse tensions by performing a special dance in the cause of peace before a group of English settlers.[56]

Robin Hood, however, was unusual among prominent men in his close association with the English and in the absence of references to kinsmen in documents where he is mentioned. In his relations with the English, he seems to have been a favored agent in negotiating land purchases; deeds bearing his signature have similar phrasing, distinct from the many deeds signed by other Natives. This has caused one recent researcher to wonder whether he may have been literate.[57] The kinsmen about whom we have some information include his father and at least one son, but there are no references to the kinds of collateral relatives for whom we have evidence among the Etchemins living just to the north and east of him.

In sum, it seems likely that Robin Hood's authority reflected the changing times in which he lived. Coming of age after the demise of the great sagamores encountered by Samuel de Champlain and John Smith, and after the great plague of 1617–18, he may have been more a skillful cultural interlocutor than a sagamore in the communal tradition of Bessabez.

portant sagamores are associated with Pejepscot, although some apparently had proprietary authority over coastal territories around eastern Casco Bay as well.[58] A fortified village upstream on the Androscoggin at present-day Auburn is first mentioned only later, during King William's War.[59]

On the Kennebec, we know from archaeological and historic data that Norridgewock and Taconic (present-day Winslow) retained agricultural populations, and other settlements probably existed as well, such as Wesserunsett (present-day Skowhegan).[60] Farther east, between the Kennebec and St. John Rivers, where agriculture was not practiced, settlement patterns were probably more seasonally mobile, with at least part of the population moving inland for game and fur hunting during the winter and then back to the coast for marine resources and trade during the warmer months.[61] One map, drawn in 1670, is unique in that it indicates the locations of numerous Native settlements on and around the Penobscot, at Eddington, Milford, and Mattawamkeag and along the coast on Eggemoggin Reach.[62] Unfortunately, there is no indication whether these sites were fairly permanent or merely seasonal.

West of the Kennebec the situation was both different and more complicated. As regards ethnicity, western Maine was formerly the region inhabited by people the French called Almouchiquois; fifty years later, however, Druillettes labeled those living there Abenakis, like the inhabitants of the Norridgewock area. The historic data currently available are not sufficient to establish whether this shift reflects a population replacement in the region.[63] Little is known about the ethnicity of Pigwacket, but its population was probably closely related to the coastal populations of western Maine, the upriver Androscoggin village at present-day Auburn, and Ossippee.[64] During the years of conflict that followed, these interior villages, and another at Canton Point called Naracomigook, were often inhabited by people with strong connections as far west as the upper Merrimack, in central Massachusetts.[65]

English and French sources agree that the Kennebec River represented an important dividing line. Beyond this, however, the English designation of Indians by place of residence forces us to rely on French sources, which continued to apply ethnic names current among their Native associates: Etchemins from the St. John River to the lower Kennebec and Abenakis west of the Kennebec.[66] Norridgewock was still "the highest town of the Abenaquiois."[67]

At the outbreak of King Philip's War in September 1675, however, the Kennebec Etchemins, under the leadership of Madockawando, "forsook their Fort presently and went Eastward and abroad to [the St.] Johns River and to the Sea Side to get all the Indians they could together to come up Penobscot River."[68] There they largely remained after the war, and Madockawando was to become a key figure during the troubled decades of the later seventeenth century.[69] By 1700 the general term "Etchemin" had given way to two more specific ones, apparently of Micmac origin: "Canibas" for those who fled the Kennebec area for the Penobscot in 1675 and "Maliseet" for those who ranged farther to the east to the St. John River. The Souriquois remained from St. John eastward but were now referred to by the French as the Micmacs.[70]

Breaking Point

The aboriginal people who lived in Maine in 1600 had welcomed two groups of quarrelsome Europeans. Having been devastated by their diseases and enthralled by their technology, they were drawn into a world economy that quickly forced them into a series of bloody conflicts with their Indian neighbors—all this within the span of a lifetime. The Native Mainers' struggle with the tumultuous events of the seventeenth century was generally a peaceful one. Until the fall of Pentagoet in 1674, the region's Natives had retained considerable latitude and thus had probably managed to avoid the worst effects of midcentury European squabbling. Whether a post was under the control of the English or the French seems not to have affected commerce.[71] Moreover, the interior, particularly east of Pemaquid, was still free of Europeans—who lived no farther inland than they could navigate; only Port Royal possessed much of a civilian population at this time.[72] With the French gone from Pentagoet, however, the balance of power shifted clearly to the English who, had they perceived the benefits they had derived from six decades of Native forbearance, might have played this monopolistic position to their advantage. Instead, only a year later, when a Native leader known as King Philip rose up against creeping colonial hegemony in southern New England, they panicked and were driven out.

VII THE WAR YEARS

T HE WAR YEARS began in 1675 with a violent June uprising that broke out in Massachusetts and quickly spread to Maine. Known as King Philip's War, it was the first in a long series of conflicts that pitted Indians of the Maritime Peninsula against English colonists. King Philip's War was the result of tensions between a shrinking population of Native peoples and burgeoning colonial ones. In Massachusetts, where the war started, and in Maine, Native peoples had initially welcomed the colonists, but by 1675 they understood what that strategy had bought them—potential dispossession of their homelands.

The war concluded quickly and disastrously for Natives in southern New England, but it apparently ended in favor of those in Maine, who had all but driven out the English. Appearances can be deceptive, however; the "victors"—most of whom actually had not directly participated in the conflict—invited the colonists back, on the condition that they recognize Native sovereignty in the region. Natives were divided in their attitude toward the colonists: all feared further English expansion, but some—mainly those to the east of the Kennebec, where few English had settled—apparently felt they might still keep the English at bay and thus continue to derive the benefits of trade on which they had come to depend.

In the later conflicts of the war years the triggering issues were most often not those that divided Natives and English colonists but those dividing England and France, and it was these that spilled over into North American colonies and entangled Maine's Indians in the process. The older tensions remained a factor in these hostilities, however, and Indians of the Maritime Peninsula overwhelmingly chose the French as allies in these conflicts. Their choice was influenced by differences between these two colonial populations. The numerically superior English, whose lives were mainly based on fishing and agriculture, saw the forest surrounding their tiny dispersed settlements as "a great Chaos, the lair of wild beasts and wilder men"—in other words, a wilderness that was the domain of Indians.[2] There were traders among them who held different opinions of the Natives, but they were a small minority.

French colonial populations, on the other hand, and particularly in Acadia, remained relatively much smaller, more dependent on the fur trade and thus upon the people of the forest who were their suppliers. Religious differences also influenced Native allegiances. The English were Puritans and Calvinists, the kinds of Protestants who believed that we are "slaves to sin, only a few of us to be redeemed at God's caprice" and who thus did not emphasize the conversion of unbelievers such as Indians.[3] The French, on the other hand, were Roman Catholics whose proselytizing clerics often placed the conversion of Natives among their highest priorities. Although Native relations with the French were fraught with their own tensions, on the whole these seemed more manageable in times of trouble than did those with the English.

King Philip's War

The first English casualties in King Philip's War occurred at the newly settled town of Swansea (Massachusetts) on June 24, 1675.[4] Settlers there died at the hands of Pokanoket warriors led by their chief sachem, whom the English called Philip. The son of Massassoit, who had befriended and aided the Pilgrims who landed at Plymouth in 1620, Philip faced a Plymouth Colony encroaching on Pokanoket territory and intent on making him its subject.[5]

Fear that Philip was planning a preemptive strike prompted Plymouth

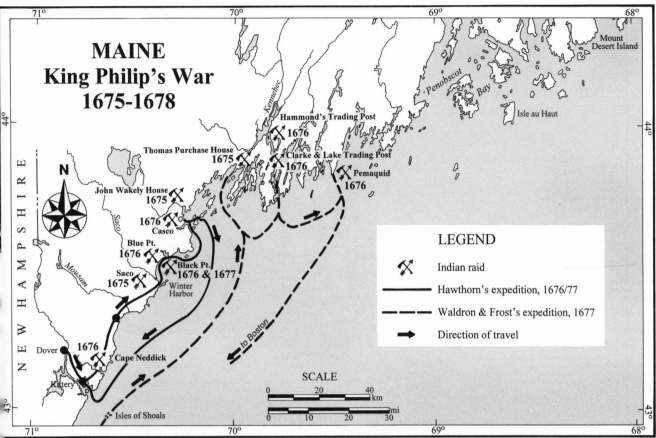

7-1. Maine: King Phillip's War, 1675–78

to establish a garrison near his residence that spring, causing nearby settlers to desert their homes. Soon thereafter, Englishmen caught a party of Indians looting one of these houses and shot one of them. Seven English, including the boy who fired the lethal shot, were killed in revenge; "so the war begun with philop."[6] The war quickly spread into central Massachusetts and the upper Connecticut Valley, as Indians in those areas, also disaffected by English expansion, joined in. In southern New England the war ended with Philip's death in August 1676 at the hands of Major Benjamin Church.[7] It had been a costly victory for the English, and in the words of New York governor Edmund Andros, "the advantages thereby were none."[8]

A significant factor in the outcome was Andros's ability to incite the Mohawks to attack Philip's forces.[9] Following the war, in April 1677, Massachusetts Bay and Connecticut agreed to an alliance with the Iroquoian League of Five Nations and New York's other Indians, which now included some of the combatants in the war who were residing under Andros's pro-

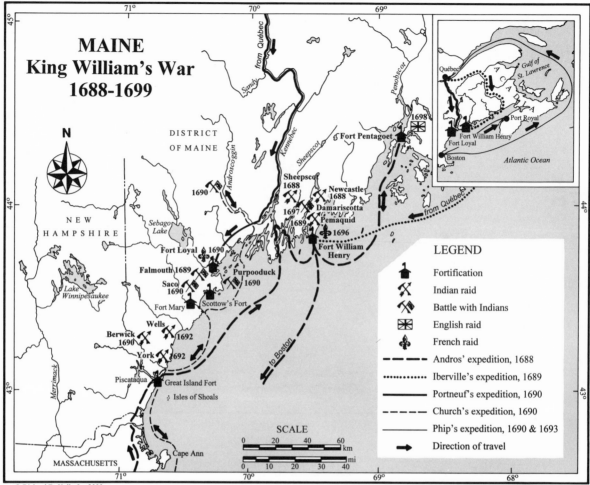

LEGEND

🏠 Fortification

⚔ Indian raid

⚔ Battle with Indians

✠ English raid

⚜ French raid

– – – Andros' expedition, 1688

·········· Iberville's expedition, 1689

——— Portneuf's expedition, 1690

– – – Church's expedition, 1690

——— Phip's expedition, 1690 & 1693

➡ Direction of travel

© Richard D. Kelly Jr., 2000.

7-2. Maine: King William's War, 1688–99

tection at Schaghticoke, near present-day Albany.[10] This treaty, called the Covenant Chain, would have implications for diplomacy among the English and Indians of the Maritime Peninsula into the middle of the eighteenth century.

1675: King Philip's War Spreads to Maine

There has long been debate about whether the Indian attacks against colonists in Maine that began in September 1675 were really part of King Philip's War or part of a separate conflict. Even considering that Maine Indians had their own grievances with the English, the timing of the outbreak, the presence in the raiding parties of refugee warriors from southern New England, and the panic that ensued among the settlers when the war broke out in Massachusetts all suggest that had King Philip not begun the revolt, those in Maine would not have taken the initiative. Indeed, it is worth noting how many in Maine stayed out of the fighting once it began.

Unlike the clustered villages of Massachusetts, the English settlements of Maine were strung out along the coast and estuaries of rivers. Such "ribbon settlements" were difficult to defend. As Yale president Timothy Dwight later put it, "The people were few, scattered and almost defenseless," and when word of Philip's uprising arrived, panic ensued. Diplomatic blunders worsened the situation, compelling many would-be peaceful Natives

7-3. Massachusetts proclamation of a day of thanksgiving for recent successes against King Phillip's forces (misdated 1675). (Courtesy of the Massachusetts Historical Society.)

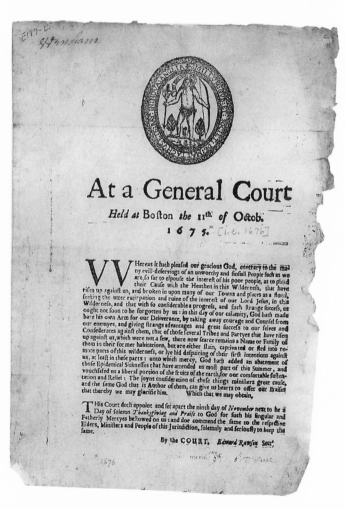

to take up arms. Basically, the Natives demurred when the English demanded that they unilaterally relinquish their arms as proof of peaceful intent. This was an entirely unreasonable demand to make of a sovereign people who lived by hunting and whose only alternative source of supplies—the French post at Pentagoet—had just recently been destroyed with the complicity of Englishmen. Still, the English interpreted their refusal as a sign of enmity. Further contributing to Native hostility was the death in August 1675 of an Indian child at Saco who drowned when the canoe it was in was overturned by English sailors who wondered whether "the Children of the Indians as they had heard, could swim as naturally as any other Creatures." The child's father, the important chief Squando, "was so provoked thereat that he hath ever since set himself to do all the Mischief he can to the English in those Parts."[11]

Native communities from the upper Connecticut Valley to the Penobscot River reacted to the War in various ways. Beginning in the summer of 1675, many fled—some permanently—to take refuge among the French on the St. Lawrence and to Native communities outside the war zone, apparently as far west as the Seneca; others stayed in their homelands, hoping to avoid the hostilities.[12] Between the Androscoggin and Sheepscot Rivers, some even acceded to English demands that they give up their firearms as a show of friendship, a gesture that caused them severe deprivation during the following winter. Throughout Maine, however, many took the warpath, some under the sway of Philip's allies, refugees from the fighting in southern New England.[13]

Hostilities began at Pejepscot on September 4 when Indians ransacked the house of Thomas Purchase, a fur trader of poor repute, along with several others. As in Massachusetts, the first casualty on the Maine front was actually an Indian shot while looting a house—this time at Casco Bay. The first English deaths came on September 9, when Indians killed and captured three generations of the Wakely family at Falmouth (Portland). Raids soon followed from Saco southward to Exeter, New Hampshire, with significant loss of life on both sides. Then, as was generally the case in subsequent wars, hostilities quieted down during the winter. Those active in the raiding were primarily from the Androscoggin River and westward. There is no indication that Indians from the Kennebec and eastward were involved in the raids at that time.[14]

After the September raid at Casco Bay, "divers Indians on the East Side of the Kennebec River repaired to their Fort at Totonnock" (Taconic, present-day Winslow), expecting to obtain supplies for the winter at

Sylvanus Davis's trading post there. Davis, however, had already taken his stock downriver to the fortified Clarke and Lake trading post at Arrowsic, sending a messenger to invite the Indians to meet him there. Instead of inviting them, the messenger ordered them to give up their guns on pain of death. It was this event that caused Madockawando, whom Hubbard referred to as "chief Sagamore of all the Indians about Pemaquid and Penobscot," to withdraw with his followers to the Penobscot, where they remained after the war.[15]

The spring and early summer of 1676 were calm. The winter had been hard on the Indians of the Androscoggin and Kennebec, who may have lost as many of 150 to starvation. In the spring most of the survivors took refuge at Sillery. On August 11, however, one day before Philip was killed in Massachusetts, his comrade-in-arms Simon initiated a second year of hostilities when he led warriors from the Androscoggin region in raids at Casco Bay, killing and capturing 30 settlers. Three days later, a small band of warriors from Taconic destroyed the Clarke and Lake post; only 4 people escaped capture or death. On October 15, after raids too numerous to list, Major Richard Waldron wrote from Portsmouth to Massachusetts governor John Leverett, referring to Maine as "ye deserted and conquered Eastern Country," and telling him that "ye Enemy is Numerous & about those parts having carried all clear before him so far as Wells."[16]

Madockawando Avoids the Conflict

In the spring following Madockawando's departure from the Kennebec, his people were visited by Thomas Gardner, a level-headed Pemaquid trader who wished "to perswade them of the Cuntrys Willingness to continue a Peace with them," at which "They seemed very joyful," bringing "Presents to confirm the Peace, and to that End also delivered up an English captive Boy to those of Kennebeck."[17] Gardner's peace efforts, however, were undercut by the crew of a slave ship owned by Boston merchant Simon Linde (Lynd). Operating under a permit to take captive Indians who had been involved in raids, in July 1676 they instead kidnapped thirty-two noncombatants from the Machias area, Madockawando's original home. The captives were sold into slavery at Faiol in the Azores, and only two ever returned to their homeland.[18] When Madockawando's people learned of this outrage, it became "one of the principal Grounds of their present Quarrel" with the English.[19] But still Madockawando counseled peace. That July the English negotiated a truce with Indians in western Maine and sent a del-

7-4a-4j. Artifacts from the Clark and Lake settlement on Arrowsic Island, destroyed on August 14, 1676. Most of the artifacts were damaged as the settlement burned: (*a*) common colonial "posey ring" or brass ring found with the burned finger bones of a man's hand. It bears the inscription "The Gift of a Frind"; (*b*) fragment of an Oak Tree Shilling minted in Massachusetts between 1660 and 1667; (*c*) nested copper-alloy thimbles, probably meant for trade with local Natives; (*d*) iron trunk key; (*e*) clay pipe bowls of the elbow and belly forms popular in the mid-seventeenth century; (*f*) iron keyhole escutcheon from a piece of furniture; (*g*) small pane of glass, called a quarrel, from a lead-glazed window; (*h*) spoon made of an alloy of copper, zinc, and iron called latten metal; (*i*) felling axe and splitting wedge edge; (*j*) sprig-molded Westerwald mug, a form of Rhenish stoneware. (Maine State Museum collection.)

egation to do likewise with those farther east. Madockawando asked them "Yea, or Nay; whether they should have Powder as formerly or not?"; the English refused.[20] Following this second refusal to provide necessary supplies after overt signs of friendship, at least some of Madockawando's people entered the war.[21]

Those Indians from the Pemaquid and Penobscot areas who did engage in hostilities were aided by French soldiers left behind after the destruction of Pentagoet. One Frenchman wore the uniform of the Carignan-Salières—Saint-Castin, the young ensign who had come to Pentagoet with Grandfontaine in 1670 as second in command and who would become Madockawando's son-in-law.[22] During the three troubled decades to come, Saint-Castin and his sons would do much to further the intertwined interests of the French and the Indians.

English Reactions to the War

Prior to September 1676, English countermeasures were ineffective, even counterproductive. Their first scheme was initiated by Waldron, who arranged a meeting of about four hundred warriors at Oyster River (Dover, New Hampshire) on September 7, 1676, where the main entertainment was to be an elaborate pseudo-combat. Waldron, however, duped the Indians into firing their weapons first, and his men then surrounded them, executing several on the spot; those who had signed the July truce were released, and the rest were sold into slavery.[23]

Next, Massachusetts sent between 170 and 260 militiamen, including 40 "praying Indians"—converts to Protestantism who lived at Natick—to Maine. They arrived around September 20 in time to witness an attack on the settlement at Peakes Island (in Casco Bay) but were unable to help as they had no boats. Having failed in subsequent weeks to make significant contact with their enemy, in November they made an arduous winter march to an Indian fort at Ossippe. Finding it empty, they burned it and returned to the coast.[24]

In February 1677, Massachusetts commissioned Waldron to lead an expedition eastward to ransom English captives and to capture Madockawando and other Native leaders.[25] On February 26, Waldron encountered a large group of Madockawando's people at Pemaquid. Elders in the group asserted that only a few headstrong youths had turned hostile, but Waldron's crew spotted some, including Megunaway, who had fought in Massachusetts. Once the English captives had been redeemed, Waldron attacked, killing eight.[26]

In the spring of 1677, Massachusetts had requested Mohawk aid against the Eastern Indians. As it had been Mohawks who broke the back of Philip's forces the previous year, Massachusetts had similar hopes for Maine. However, it failed to take into account the traditional enmity between Mohawks and nearly all New England Indians. Once in the region Mohawk warriors created havoc by attacking both friendly and hostile Indians, and they were quickly called off.[27]

New York Intercedes

Because Catholic King Charles II of England had granted the area from Pemaquid to the St. Croix River to his brother James, the Duke of York, in 1665, it fell under the authority of New York governor Edmund Andros. Initially, warfare between England and the Netherlands prevented Andros from establishing a government there, but in June 1677 New England's inability to come to grips with the disaster on its eastern frontier provided an opportunity for Andros to intercede. He sent Lieutenant Anthony Brockholtz with the necessary resources and personnel to first fortify Pemaquid and then to negotiate a truce with the belligerents. The truce led to a formal treaty, concluded at Casco Bay the next spring (1678).[28]

Even as Brockholtz was bringing the situation under control, Massachusetts officials undercut his position by mistreating Indian prisoners and imposing unreasonable terms for captive exchange, behaving, in Brockholtz's words, "as if they had no desire to bee concerned in the peace." His success in the face of these difficulties was due, at least in part, to Andros's deployment of Mohawks to Maine, where they persuaded or coerced the Canibas to accept a truce. Although this strategy had been ineffective when attempted by New England, New York officials had much closer diplomatic ties to the Iroquois. Another factor in the rapid resolution of the conflict, however, was apparently the key role played by Madockawando.[29]

An Uneasy Peace: 1678–1688

At the end of King Philip's War the population of New England stood at over fifty thousand and that of New France at around ten thousand. At Pentagoet, near Acadia's boundary with New England, Saint-Castin was building a small economic base, while fewer than a thousand other French were scattered throughout the rest of the province, mainly at Port Royal. By 1677 about fifteen hundred Abenakis and other refugees from King

Philip's War were living at Sillery, near Quebec. In 1680 the Native populations living in the area between the Merrimack and Kennebec Rivers and in Acadia also stood at about fifteen hundred. Their common Iroquois enemy at that time numbered about eight thousand, of whom roughly a thousand were worrisome Mohawks.[30]

About this time, the French stopped referring to Indians between the Kennebec and St. John Rivers as Etchemins and adopted two other terms, apparently of Micmac origin: Canibas for those roughly between the Kennebec and the Penobscot, and Maliseets for those from the Penobscot to the St. John. The Souriquois of Champlain's time, who lived to the east of the Maliseets, had come to be called Micmacs. People of the upper Kennebec and areas west of it were still referred to as Abenakis.[31]

In 1686 Andros was appointed governor of all New England except Connecticut. Although widely resented as the representative of Catholic King Charles, Andros governed decisively, attempting to regulate the fur trade and to maintain garrisons along the coast as far east as Pemaquid. Few settlers returned immediately, however, even though the conditions of the 1678 treaty ending King Philip's War in Maine allowed them to reoccupy their lands. During the 1680s, however, settlers did return to the area between Wells and the St. George River, and tensions once again began to rise. The causes listed by the Puritan divine Cotton Mather included the refusal of settlers to pay the symbolic tribute in corn specified in the 1678 treaty, the stringing of nets across the Saco River that obstructed the passage of anadromous fish, the destruction of Indian crops by wandering livestock, the trading of liquor, and, most importantly, English settlement of new lands beyond the limits occupied prior to King Philip's War.[32]

In 1684 Indians from the Saco area began to verbally threaten English settlers. In response, the Maine Council ordered that garrison houses be constructed in every town, and New Hampshire governor Edward Cranfield wrote New York governor Thomas Dongan requesting the help of Iroquois warriors when the expected raids began. The English suspected that Saint-Castin was behind these troubles, and that August they sent a representative eastward—perhaps to Pejepscot—to assemble "all the Sagamores for nearly a hundred miles round." There they handed out presents and provided food for a sumptuous feast. In return, the Sagamores promised to remain at peace, and they invited the English to rebuild at Pejepscot. Rumors of impending raids persisted, however, and the next May Indians at Saco gathered their corn and left their villages near English settlements, as did the Penacooks on the Merrimack River. When reports that the Iroquois had agreed to Cranfield's request reached them, however, they readily signed a treaty with New Hampshire officials promising not to suddenly withdraw from areas settled by the English in return for English protection from the Mohawks.[33]

Events in New France were also troubling. In 1673 the governor, Louis de Buade, Comte de Frontenac, built Fort Frontenac on Lake Ontario, and by 1680 the rapid proliferation of French traders in the Great Lakes region and south of it—the *pays d'en haut* as the French called it—led to close French ties with Indians as far west as Green Bay on Lake Michigan. Among the Iroquois, the westernmost Senecas, frustrated by their inability to get these western Indians to trade with them, began a series of wars that threatened the flow of furs to Montreal, while the more easterly Iroquois, particularly the Mohawks, threatened to destroy New France itself. To combat the Iroquois threat, the French and their fur-trading allies began to develop an alliance that the historian Richard White has called "the Middle Ground."[34]

Even as this grand alliance was being constructed, however, the French kept a wary eye on New York and New England, whose expanding economies were also beginning to make inroads among their Algonquian fur suppliers. By 1685 Jacques-Réné de Brisay, Marquis de Denonville, the newly appointed governor of New France, wrote prophetically, "We have spoken of the Iroquois as the declared enemy of this Colony.... It is worth considering whether the English are not the same, and to be feared in the future even more than the Iroquois."[35] This realization led the French to solicit the Abenakis to join their alliance. They began in July 1683 by granting the Jesuits land for a new Abenaki mission named in honor of Saint-François de Sales at the falls on the Chaudière River, south of Quebec City. The next year they requested that Saint-Castin provide a few warriors to fight in the *pays d'en haut*. Now married to Madockawando's daughter, Saint-Castin himself stayed to organize a handful of Acadians and his Indian allies in their efforts to oppose English encroachment.[36]

Denonville soon realized that New France was losing its grip on its western alliance to English traders from Albany who, with their Iroquois allies, were beginning to probe the *pays d'en haut*. In order to regain control, in 1687 he attacked the Seneca with a mixed force of thirteen hundred militia and Indians and, to keep them at bay, began to build a new fort at Niagara. Some of the mission-village Abenakis who fought with Denonville in this campaign were embittered by their experience and expressed interest in an alliance with the Iroquois and English. In the war-torn years to come, the English would play on this advantage with a measure of success.[37]

The Coming of King William's War

James II, the former Duke of York, a Catholic and ally of French king Louis XIV, took the English throne in 1685. At the time, Louis's expansionist policies were opposed by a coalition of forces ranging from Rome to Sweden, led by the Dutch William of Orange. In June 1688 the Glorious Revolution began in England, and James was forced to abdicate in December. Parliament then welcomed the Protestant William in his place, setting the stage for war between England and France.[38]

Tensions Rise in Maine

In 1687 Andros was attempting to strengthen the Maine frontier, in part by diminishing the threat posed by Saint-Castin and his Caniba allies at Pentagoet. He began in the spring by distributing gifts to the Canibas and then, in 1688, by personally sailing there and sacking Saint-Castin's residence, holding his property at Pemaquid as ransom for an oath of allegiance to King James. Then, English pirates captured a vessel owned in part by Saint-Castin. It was as a result of these attacks that Saint-Castin abandoned the neutral course he had taken until that time and began to follow orders sent him the previous year to strengthen his defenses and cease trading with the English. Also about this time, the Jesuit Jacques Bigot traveled with a delegation of mission Abenakis to induce those still living close to the English to join him at the mission on the Chaudière. Other Jesuits also began organizing mission villages at Norridgewock, Pentagoet, and Meductic, on the St. John River.[39]

Andros's strategy for defending the eastern frontier once again involved the Iroquois, who, in the winter of 1687 and spring of 1688, sent emissaries to the Penacooks, Abenakis of the St. Lawrence, and the Eastern Indians, probably to offer them membership in the Covenant Chain alliance.[40] This strategy might have succeeded, for as we have seen, sentiment was growing among some Eastern Indians for improved relations with the English and Mohawks. Indeed, as tensions grew in the summer of 1688, Hope Hood, son of Robin Hood, told some English hunters that "the Indians and the Mohawks were all agreed throughout the whole country that they would not fight to kill one another any more."[41] Instead, the events of August and September brought not peace but war.

In August 1688 news came that eleven "French Indians," Penacooks, Nimpucs from central Massachusetts, and possibly Abenakis from the St. Lawrence had killed five Indians near Springfield and six English settlers at Northfield and were reportedly considering attacks against the Mohawks, apparently with the blessing of Denonville in retaliation for recent Mohawk depredations on the St. Lawrence. Simultaneously, Indians in the Saco area, angered by continuing English expansion, began killing cattle and threatening settlers. In reaction to these events, officials at Saco captured several local Indians and imprisoned them, hoping to force the rest into a treaty. To the great annoyance of settlers in Maine, Andros freed the captives, but not in time to avoid reprisals for these "misunderstandings," as Secretary of New England Edward Randolph called them.[42]

Thus began a conflict that once again drove the English from all the settlements east of Wells. By November 1688, attacks had occurred in Maine

7-5. Handbill describing a visit by Mohawk chiefs to Albany at the beginning of King William's War to affirm the Covenant Chain with their English allies. Note is made of diplomatic approaches by some "Eastern Indians" that had reportedly been rebuffed. (Courtesy of the Massachusetts Historical Society.)

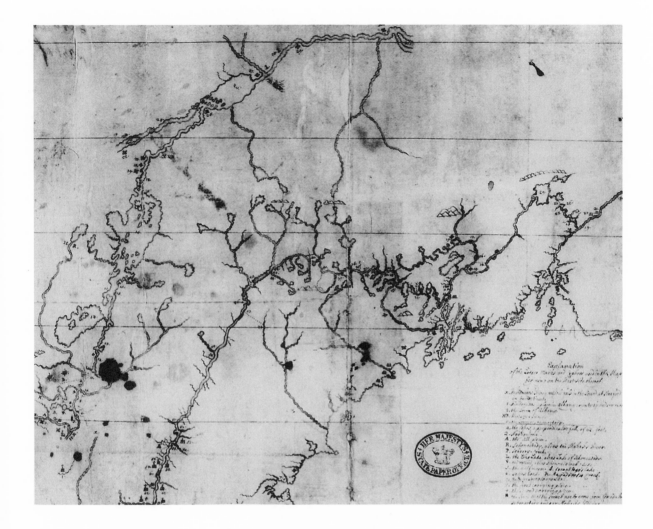

7-6. Detail of an English map drawn about 1688, at the outbreak of King William's War, showing the locations of French, English, and Indian settlements. (Courtesy of the British Public Record Office, Kew, England, co700 New England 2.)

at Cape Porpoise and New Dartmouth (present-day Newcastle). Indians from the Saco were prominent in these attacks, but some from the Kennebec also participated. According to Acadian governor Louis-Alexandre des Friches de Meneval, the Canibas "in the region of Pentagoet" and Abenakis "much more numerous" around the Kennebec were both "as affectionate toward the French as they are hateful of the English," yet the Caniba chief Madockawando of Pentagoet was not involved in the raids.[43]

Andros responded by sending 160 militia out on patrols, including one that went "right up into the country in deep snow and burned two forts." It was at this precise time, however, that Boston learned of the Glorious Revolution, and a revolt against Andros's government ensued.[44] According to Randolph, who, as an official in Andros's administration, wrote from jail

7-7. Wampum belt sent to France about 1699 by Abenakis of the mission of St. Francis de Sales on the Chaudière River near Quebec. It measures six feet long and five inches wide. (Photograph courtesy of Chartres Cathedral and Mary Calvert.)

in Boston, these two raids were so successful that "the Indians could have been reduced to beg for terms, had not Foster and Waterhouse, merchants in Boston and chiefs in the late rebellion, sent a ship in the Governor's absence with forty tons of ammunition and other goods to trade with these Indians and the French between Port Royal and Penobscot. . . . As soon as the soldiers heard of the disturbances they seized their officers and sent them home prisoners, so that forty leagues of seabord is now abandoned to the ravages of the Indians, who have already destroyed many houses and killed many of the people."[45] In March, Indian raiding resumed with an attack at Salmon Falls. In June a much larger force of Caniba and Maliseet raiders, aided by previously peaceful Penacooks, attacked Dover, capturing or killing 54 and singling out for torture Richard Waldron for his unscrupulous trading practices and for violating the 1677 truce at Dover. Further raiding occurred in July at Saco. Massachusetts reacted by organizing militia units, issuing a scalp bounty, and refreshing their covenant with the Mohawks.[46]

It was only after the Abenaki war chief Taxous returned from a visit to Governor Denonville in July or August 1689, that the Eastern Indians, now including Taxous's rival, Madockawando, initiated a purposeful series of raids. A large polyglot force of three to four hundred captured Pemaquid in mid-August, and on September 21 a similar force attacked Falmouth, sustaining several casualties. Part of this group then went on to attack Bluepoint (Scarborough) and Saco. Massachusetts's reaction to these raids was to send militia led by Benjamin Church, the hero of King Philip's War, on offensive patrols.[47]

The state of relations between the Eastern Indians and the Iroquois at this time is ambiguous. Early in 1689, Mohawks told the English at Albany that "there is an old grudge between us and the Onnagongues [Eastern Indians, including those living on the St. Lawrence], who knows how it

will go yet."[48] Nevertheless, in August 1689, just as serious hostilities were beginning to break out, four Eastern Indians met with Mohawks in the vicinity of Lake George, urging them to join in an alliance against all "Christians," English and French alike. In reporting this meeting to the English at Albany, the Mohawks revealed a degree of mutual affection between the two groups because a significant number of Mohawks were adopted captives from among the Eastern Indians. A month later it was clear that none of the Iroquois would "take up the hatchet" against the Eastern Indians until the latter sided with the French.[49]

Frontenac Takes Command in Quebec

After attacking the Seneca in 1687, Denonville had initiated negotiations for a treaty with the Iroquois. Early in 1689, however, the Iroquois learned at Albany that a state of war existed between England and France, and they immediately attacked not Forts Frontenac and Niagara but also rural farming villages near Montreal, all of which, as yet uninformed of the European war, were caught by surprise.[50]

In October, Frontenac returned to Quebec to replace Denonville as gov-

7-8. English flintlock musket typical of the unadorned firearms used by most New Englanders during the late seventeenth century. Length: 228 centimeters. (Private collection.)

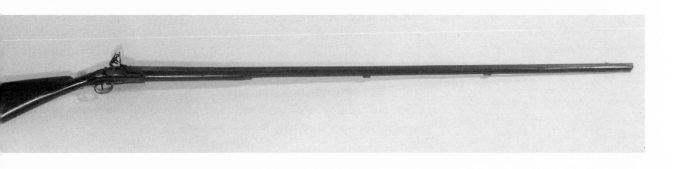

ernor. Finding affairs in New France in disarray because of the Iroquois attacks, he seized the offensive by organizing a series of raids into English territory while making plans for naval and land attacks on Boston and New York. In February 1690, Canadian French and Indians attacked Schenectady, New York, killing around sixty. Another similar party led by Joseph-François Hertel wiped out Salmon Falls in late March and went on to join a third, led by René Robinau de Portneuf and Saint-Castin, in destroying Fort Loyal and Casco.[51]

A major goal of the New England raids was to quell any sentiment among the Eastern Indians for peace negotiations with their English neighbors and the Iroquois. Their success indicates that Frontenac's attention to the Algonquian alliance was beginning to pay off. One important factor in that success was the annual distribution of special supplies—"the King's presents"—sent from France. The French-Algonquian alliance that had begun in the *pays d'en haut* now firmly encompassed Acadia, and a share of the king's presents were regularly delivered there, mainly to the Abenakis and Canibas.[52]

Massachusetts Counterattacks in Acadia

Frontenac's aggressive strategy justifiably frightened Acadian governor Meneval, who anticipated counterattacks against his weak colony.[53] Meneval's fears were fulfilled in May 1690, when Massachusetts major general William Phips, a Maine native who had been driven from his family home in present-day Woolwich during King Philip's War, went on the attack, pillaging his way along the Acadian coast to Port Royal, which surrendered on May 20. Flushed with success, Phips then undertook a ruinously expensive naval expedition against a virtually undefended Quebec, which ended in disaster when his fleet was visited by smallpox, and shipwrecks took the lives of between three and four hundred of his men.[54]

Phips followed up the capture of Port Royal by sending Benjamin Church on a marginally effective search-and-destroy mission in September. Church attacked a fortified village at present-day Auburn, killing and capturing several Indians and recovering some English captives taken in raids earlier that summer. Following these raids, several Abenaki chiefs agreed to a truce, which was signed in November. Commissioners were then appointed to meet with Native war leaders at Wells in May 1691. The meeting resulted in a continuance of the truce, although Native harassment and opportunistic raiding continued throughout the summer.[55]

7-9. Massachusetts's proposal for fortifications and truck houses on the Kennebec, St. George, and Merrimack Rivers and a system for supplying them. (Massachusetts Archives Collection sc1, 45x, vol. 119, p. 162.)

Native Resolve Wavers

Events following the 1691 truce seemed to favor the Indians. In December the potential for Iroquoian intervention in the war was significantly lessened after a force of French and Indians overcame a party of important warriors including twenty Mohawks and eleven Oneidas near Lake Champlain. As a result, the English at Albany reported, "Thus all the principal captains of the Maquas and Oneidas are dead, to the great grief of us all. . . . They recon that the Maquas and Oneidas have lost ninety men in two years . . . most of our praying Indians are now killed, and the fifteen that we most trusted are lost." Then, in January 1692, during a severe winter, a large war party led by Portneuf and Madockawando attacked York, capturing over ninety people and killing forty-eight. Only two garrison houses withstood the attack.[56]

Acadia was also about to be reinforced. In 1690, Portneuf's brother, Joseph Robineau de Villebon, had arrived to take charge of military affairs. Avoiding the damaged Port Royal, Villebon established himself on the St. John River, but before he could unload his cargo New York freebooters captured his ship. Villebon then quickly returned to France, where he was resupplied and promoted to commandant in Acadia, finally returning to the St. John in October 1691. The following April, Canibas and Abenakis visited him at a new fort at Nashwaak, where they received, and gratefully acknowledged, the king's presents, telling Villebon about their raid on York and expressing their desire to continue the war.[57]

Thereafter, however, events took a different course. In the spring of 1992, a force of three hundred warriors under Portneuf and Saint-Castin had failed to capture Wells. Discouraged by this failure, the Indians retreated and refused all exhortations to return to the front that summer.[58] Then, in August, Benjamin Church attacked French and Indian settlements in Penobscot Bay and burned crops at hastily abandoned Taconic. Although a few of the site's residents returned briefly in October, Taconic was never rebuilt and thereafter Norridgewock became the major settlement on the Kennebec.[59] Also that summer, Phips, now governor of Massachusetts, built the massive Fort William Henry at Pemaquid. It was far more formidable than earlier fortifications, and in the fall of 1692 two French supply vessels refused to attack it, to the great disappointment of Saint-Castin and his Caniba allies.[60]

Thus, by 1693 the Canibas and Abenakis were exhausted by war, discouraged at the failure of the French to attack Fort William Henry, and low on supplies.[61] Fearing that the French were abandoning them, some decided to trade their furs at the fort at Pemaquid. Then in August, two Caniba chiefs, Madockawando and Edgeremet, negotiated a treaty of "submission," the humiliating terms of which included giving up important men as hostages.[62] Even worse, it eventually came out that they had in fact ceded much of their people's territory to Phips and to Sylvanus Davis.[63] At this point the French could do little to discourage their Native allies from further capitulating to the English. Not wanting to drive them further toward the English, Governor Frontenac counseled them to strike only if success seemed assured.[64]

In the spring of 1694 came more bad news: Abenaki spies heard rumors that a thousand English militiamen were assembling at Piscataqua, planning to raid their villages. Villebon used this threat to galvanize those still

The following memorandum, dating from 1694, illustrates the type of supplies included in the annual shipments from France known as the "King's presents."

Memorandum or presents to the value of 3640 livres, accorded by His Majesty to the Indians of Acadia, for their warfare against the English.

2000 lbs. of powder
40 kegs of bullets
10 kegs of swan shot
400 lbs. of Brazilian tobacco
200 tomahawks, for which M. de Bonaventure will provide a model.
60 selected muskets like those sent this year.
200 Mulaix [Spain] shirts, averaging 30 sous each.
200 tufts of white feathers to be given to the Indians as a distinguishing mark
    in case of a night attack, which should not cost more than 6 to 7s a piece;
    to be selected in Paris by M. de Bonaventure.

These presents will be distributed among the Indians when they assemble at the appointed rendezvous.[65]

willing to fight. When news got out that Madockawando and Edgeremet "had sold the lands and rivers of their nation to the English," Pierre Thury, the French missionary to the Canibas, and Taxous, a sagamore fiercely hostile to the English, persuaded the Abenakis and the Canibas—even Madockawando—to join in new raids.[66]

Phips's land grab cost more than he had bargained for. Taxous succeeded in amassing a force of more than 200 warriors. Along with at least 14 Frenchmen, they attacked Dover on July 16, 1694, only two days after news of Phips's treaty had convinced the residents that it was safe to work in their fields. The toll was 104 dead, 27 taken captive, 13 houses burned, and the livestock destroyed. Warriors from the Penobscot then went on to attack Groton, Massachusetts, where they killed or captured 47 more English settlers.[67] In the spring of 1695, Villebon convened a large gathering of chiefs to hand out the king's presents and to discuss the issues that had forced them "to make overtures to the English." The chiefs assured Villebon that they would continue to fight in the French interest so long as supplies remained available.[68]

In 1695 a severe epidemic kept Abenaki and Caniba raids to a minimum, and they remained uneasy about their relatives still hostage to the English in Boston. Early in 1696, Pasco Chubb, commander at Fort William Henry, began to entice nearby Canibas to trade, allowing the garrison to go "abrod a gaming" with them and welcoming them to come "frequently & trade for bread tobacco & Rum."[69] In May a group including Taxous, Edgeremet, and one of Edgeremet's kinsmen named Ahenquid approached the fort with their English prisoners under a flag of truce to discuss an exchange of captives. Chubb invited them in but then, in the words of a Caniba, "shot them while they had his bread between their teeth"; only Taxous escaped. Once again, in a single act, the English had turned potentially peaceable Eastern Indians hostile, and once again the French were prepared to use this hostility to their advantage.[70]

Benjamin Church had opposed the building of Fort William Henry, regarding forts in general as "Nests for Destruction." He turned out to be right. On August 15, 1696, three frigates under the command of Pierre LeMoyne D'Iberville sailed into Pemaquid Harbor, while a Native force of three hundred, mainly Canibas and Maliseets, approached by canoe from Pentagoet. The fort, built with poor mortar, began to crumble when its cannon fired, and the garrison, fearful of revenge for the deaths of the sagamores killed there that spring, forced Chubb to surrender. With this major threat removed, the French and Indians allowed King William's War to end with only three further attacks of significant size: at Groton and Haverhill in Massachusetts and one at Wells. Pasco Chubb, dismissed from service for surrendering the fort, was among those singled out for death at Groton. Hostilities between England and France ended in 1697 with the Treaty of Ryswick, and the Maine war officially ended with the signing of a treaty at Casco Bay in January 1699.[71] These treaties would provide a respite from warfare that was welcomed by all but that would last for a mere five years.

Epilogue to an Era

Despite their military successes during King William's War, the inhabitants of the Maritime Peninsula, both Acadian and Indian, realized the need for peaceful relations with the English and their Native allies, the Iroquois. The Canibas invited the English back to Pemaquid, and Governor Villebon hoped that, in exchange for access to Acadia's fishing grounds, New England would provide improved livestock for Acadian farmers and training for Acadian fishermen. For their part, some influential New Englanders saw a need to normalize relations with the Eastern Indians as well, recommending to the recently appointed governor general of New York, Massachusetts, and New Hampshire, Richard Coote, Earl of Bellomont, the "sending of supplies at cheap rates to the Indians at the Eastward . . . Also that strict measures be taken against all private traders, especially in selling any kind of Liquors."[72] These policies would eventually become cornerstones of Massachusetts's Indian policy.

During that brief period before war broke out again, western Acadia saw the disappearance of many who had played important roles during King William's War. Gone from Pentagoet were Madockawando, who had died in 1698; Jean-Vincent d'Abbadie de Saint-Castin, who returned to France in 1701 to fight legal battles; the missionary Pierre Thury, who left to establish a new mission among the Micmacs in 1698; and Villebon, who died on the St. John at Nashwaak in 1700. In Quebec, Frontenac died in 1698 and so did not live to see the policies he initiated bear fruit in a 1701 treaty known as "Great Peace of Montreal," which gave New France the Iroquois neutrality it so badly needed. In New England, Phips was summoned to England in 1694 to answer legal charges and died there of a fever before the investigation was completed.[73]

VIII   THE ERA OF THE MISSION

AT THE END of King William's War, with the fort at Pemaquid destroyed and the coast east of Wells nearly devoid of English, the French asserted that the western boundary of Acadia had effectively been "extended ten or twelve leagues to the Kennebec, which territory should be regarded as the King's, for it is now occupied solely by our allies."[1] Their confidence to make this assertion was due in part to the mission building that had begun during the war. Perhaps it was the diminished strength of the Iroquois that led the French to redeploy assets from the *pays d'en haut* to their borderlands with New England. One such asset was the Jesuit Sébastien Rale, who left the Illinois mission in 1695 and two years later assisted Jacques Bigot in establishing a new one at Norridgewock (within present-day Madison). They selected Old Point on the east side of the Kennebec, opposite the site of Gabriel Druillettes's Norridgewock.

Druillettes regarded the Norridgewock Abenakis as being under New England dominion, and thus Old Point had the advantage of being within the newly declared limits of French territory. Moreover, it was a location considered inaccessible to the English and an important crossroads for Native travel.[2] Their effort was considerable, for by 1705, when English raiders burned the village, it had "a large fort, Meeting house & School-house. . . . [T]he Fort encompassed 3 quarters of an acre of ground built with Pallisado's whearin were 12 Wigwams [probably communal longhouses; see Chapter 4]. . . . The Meeting-house was built of Timber 60 Foot long, 25 Foot wide, & 18 foot studd ceiled with Clapboards."[3] Old Point was one of a series of Native villages straddling the Maritime Peninsula from Penacook (Concord, New Hampshire) to Meductic on the St. John. Between them were Pigwacket (present-day Fryeburg) on the Saco, Narakamigou (present-day Canton Point) on the Androscoggin, Amaseconti (present-day Farmington Falls) on the Sandy River, Norridgewock on the Kennebec, and Panawamské (Indian Island at present-day Old Town) on the Penobscot. Missionaries were in permanent residence only at the easternmost three.[4] During the early eighteenth century, as the region's Native population increasingly avoided close proximity to English settlements, these interior mission villages developed into vital centers for French-Indian interaction. Norridgewock's location on the Kennebec-Chaudière corridor between Quebec and the English settlements of the Maine coast, however, gave it special strategic importance.

Accommodation

From the Native perspective, King William's War had cost much and resolved little. Although they had been joined by some immigrants from the south and west, their populations had been further reduced by disease and warfare. Still dependent on hunting and fishing, they now relied as well on horticulture. While the English had once again been driven from their former settlements, New England's explosive population growth left many Natives with little doubt that it would eventually prevail, and, as we have seen, even before the war had ended there was considerable sentiment among some on the Kennebec and Penobscot for a strategy of accommodation.[5]

On the English side, sobered by the military successes of the Eastern Indians and the costs of the recent war, Massachusetts initiated a policy of proactive conciliation, a strategy that would bear considerable fruit in the coming decades. Soon after arriving in Boston in May 1699, Governor Bellomont ordered a fort built at Casco Bay. By itself, the Natives would have viewed this as a further threat, just as they had at Pemaquid. But this time Bellomont included a truck (trading) house for which he provided supplies. He also sent a ship with supplies to Pemaquid, ordering Cyprian Southack, its captain, to sell them at the lowest prices possible. The next year he even made an offer—unpopular in the Massachusetts House of Representatives—to post a gunsmith at the Casco truck house.[6]

One of Bellomont's failures was his attempt to banish Jesuits from the region and replace them with Protestant missionaries. An earlier Massachusetts law banning Jesuits from its territory had been invalidated when the court and chancery of England annulled its charter in 1684. Bellomont pushed to reinstate this ban based on recently enacted anti-Jesuit laws in England and simultaneously allotted money to send Protestant ministers

ST. LAWRENCE MISSION VILLAGES

Sillery

Founded 2 kilometers from Quebec City for Algonquins in 1637, the population of this settlement had been reduced to a remnant by disease when Abenakis from the Kennebec and Androscoggin Rivers began to move there in the 1640s. Soil exhaustion caused population decline thereafter. Its remaining population moved to Saint-François de Sales de la Chaudière in 1683.[7]

Saint-François de Sales de la Chaudière

Located southeast of Quebec City on the Chaudière River, this settlement was populated by Abenakis and their Caniba and Maliseet neighbors from Acadia in 1683. The mission moved to the St. François River in 1700.[8]

Odanak/Arsigantegok

A series of locations on the St. François River originally occupied by Sokokis from the Connecticut Valley, in 1700 this settlement became a mission for Abenakis from St. François de Sales and later for others from the Kennebec, Androscoggin, Saco, and Merrimack Valleys. Its population went into decline after a 1759 raid by Roger's Rangers, but it survives as an Abenaki reserve.[9]

Bécancour

Located on the Bécancour or Puante River near Trois Rivières, this settlement was occupied by Abenakis from the Lac Mégantic area as early as 1689. In 1700, five hundred inhabitants of Saint-François de Sales moved to Bécancour, and in 1704 Sébastien Rale established the nearby mission of Waweenock for Kennebec Abenakis fleeing Queen Anne's War. It survives as an Abenaki reserve.[10]

Missisquoi

Occupied by Sokokis and Penacooks by 1682, this village was the base for Gray Lock's raids on central New England settlements in 1723. It may have been abandoned for periods between 1730 and 1738. A mission was established there in 1743 and apparently maintained or reestablished after the fall of Quebec in 1759.[11]

Caughnawaga

The second and third locations of a mission village on the south bank of the St. Lawrence River near Montreal originally populated in the 1660s by a mixture of Iroquoian-speaking peoples but later mainly Mohawk in composition and language. It survives as a Mohawk reserve.[12]

eastward. He even considered requesting that the Iroquois arrest the Jesuits among them and deliver them to Albany. The Jesuits, however, remained in place, and Bellomont eventually admitted that his Protestant missionaries had won no Native converts.[13]

The Covenant Chain and *La grand paix de Montréal*

Following the Treaty of Ryswick in 1697, the crowns of England and France directed their governors in North America to compel the Iroquois to stop attacking Indians allied with the French. Thus began a complex series of negotiations that would have ramifications lasting into the nineteenth century. As we have seen, for the Eastern Indians the process of accommodation with the Iroquois began earlier, at the beginning of King William's

War. We have no further evidence of negotiations between the two groups until after the end of the war in 1699, when a party of Penacooks and Eastern Indians, accompanied by some Schaghticokes, visited Mohawks near Albany stating that "since there is now a General Peace, they . . . desire to be linked in the Covenant Chain, to be united with this [New York] Government and to be looked on as Skachkook [Schaghticoke] Indians."[14] Negotiations apparently continued throughout the winter, for early in 1700 "Albany and Eastern Indians" were seen together near Portsmouth, New Hampshire.[15] In September or October, Eastern Indian messengers once again visited the Mohawks, saying that they had broken with their former "father" in Canada and sought welcome into the Covenant Chain as "children under you"—not as "brothers," the normal status of Covenant members. "We take you as fathers," they told the Mohawks, "and desire that the bounds of the Five [Iroquois] Nations may be reconed from the outermost of our five castles [main villages]." The Mohawks accepted their proposal, assuring them that their brother Corlear (their term for the governor of New York) would agree to it.[16]

These Mohawks, however, retained only a shadow of their former prowess. As early as 1680, Jesuit missionaries had won up to fifteen hundred Mohawk converts—a third of their population. Most of the converts, who were called "French" Mohawks, lived at Caughnawaga, near Montreal. One English report explained why, by 1700, that proportion had grown to two-thirds: "The causes of our Indians' desertion are (1) Fear, seeing the French so formidable as to destroy their castles and we not able to protect them. (2) Our neglect of sending ministers among them." The situation of those in Canada, however, was not much better, as by 1692 they had lost half their fighting population. Thus even before official treaties were being negotiated, sentiment for peace had been growing on both sides.[17]

Even as the pro-English Mohawks were accepting Eastern Indians into the Covenant Chain, the rest of the League were surrendering their lands in the *pays d'en haut* to the Ottawas and other groups allied with the French and were simultaneously negotiating a treaty of neutrality with the French governor Louis-Hector de Callières and his allies. Early in 1701, Callières welcomed chiefs of the Five Nations Iroquois and the French alliance with great ceremony at Montreal. There the Iroquois confirmed peace agreements negotiated earlier, promising to remain neutral in any future wars between England and France. Central to the French alliance, and first to sign the treaty, were the Ottawas, followed by the Iroquois. Other signatories included groups that were later "domiciled" in villages near Montreal and Quebec—Abenakis, Algonquins, French Mohawks, Hurons, Nipissings, and Saulteurs. It was these domiciled groups that later came to be known as the "Seven Nations (or Fires) of Canada." Also signing were the Abenakis of Acadia—Canibas, Maliseets, and those Abenakis not domiciled in Canada. These formed their own "Wabanaki Confederacy," which functioned as an extension of the Seven Nations alliance. The last to sign were what the Iroquois called "the Farr Indians," their adversaries from the *pays d'en haut*.[18]

The Montreal treaty was referred to by the French as *La grand paix de Montréal* (Great Peace of Montreal). Simultaneously, the English of Albany were negotiating a similar treaty with the Five Nations. These treaties have collectively been labeled "the Grand Settlement of 1701," but the results were ambiguous in many ways. Bellomont claimed to have saved the loyalty of the Five Nations for England and to have pacified the Eastern Indians. To the French, however, it was their Algonquian alliance, including the Abenakis, that had pacified the Iroquois.[19] Later interpretations of what these treaties meant to the Natives also vary. To some they are seen as a "triumph of the [French-Algonquian] alliance over the Iroquois."[20] Others emphasize instead the significant concessions obtained by the Iroquois, including unfettered access to Montreal, to the French trading posts at Detroit and Niagara, and to hunting territories north of the eastern Great Lakes. As we shall see, for the *Abenakis de lacadie* this ambiguity would have diplomatic implications for the future.[21]

Queen Anne's War

When the War of the Spanish Succession, or Queen Anne's War, began in 1702, the economy of New France was depressed. The costs of the war would eventually be so great that France was no longer willing to provide adequate support for the colony or its Native allies. Even in 1700, just before his return to France, Jean-Vincent d'Abbadie de Saint-Castin noted that the value of the king's presents for Acadia's Indians had been cut from 4,000 to 450 *livres*. For this and other good reasons, most Indians simply wanted to avoid involvement in the coming war. The French committed the costly blunder of misinterpreting this reluctance as a betrayal of traditional loyalties.[22]

Joseph Dudley, who replaced Bellomont as governor of Massachusetts in 1701, continued conciliatory policies, sending ministers and subsidized trade goods eastward and enacting a prohibition of bondage for Indians who could not pay their debts to traders. The Penobscots and other Native groups responded by ratifying a series of neutrality agreements with Mas-

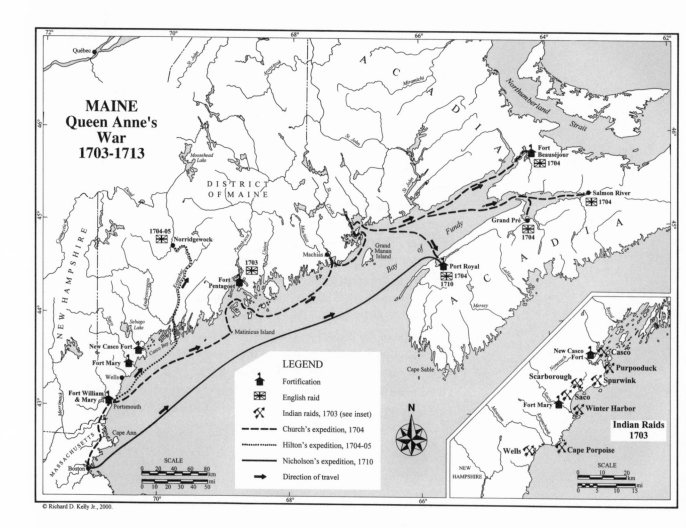

The map contains the following labels:

MAINE
Queen Anne's
War
1703-1713

Québec

ACADIA

Miramichi

Northumberland

Strait

Fort
Beauséjour
1704

Salmon River
1704

Moosehead
Lake

DISTRICT
OF MAINE

St. John

Grand Pré
1704

ACADIA

1704-05
Norridgewock

Machias

Grand
Manan
Island

of

Fundy

Port Royal
1704
1710

1703
Fort
Pentagoet

Bay

NEW HAMPSHIRE

Sebago
Lake

Matinicus Island

Cape Sable

Mersey

N

New Casco Fort

Fort Mary
Wells

Fort William
& Mary
Portsmouth

Casco Bay

ACADIA

LEGEND

Fortification

English raid

Indian raids, 1703 (see inset)

Church's expedition, 1704

Hilton's expedition, 1704-05

Nicholson's expedition, 1710

Direction of travel

Cape Ann

MASSACHUSETTS

Boston

SCALE
0 20 40 60 80
km
0 10 20 30 40 50
mi

New Casco
Fort

Casco

Purpooduck

Scarborough

Spurwink

Saco

Fort Mary

Winter Harbor

Indian Raids
1703

NEW
HAMPSHIRE

Wells

Cape Porpoise

SCALE
0   10   20
km
0   5   10   15
mi

© Richard D. Kelly Jr., 2000.

8-1. Maine: Queen Anne's War, 1703–13

sachusetts in 1701 and 1702. This drift toward neutrality caused the French grave concern, but when war erupted one outrage ensured a degree of Indian hostility toward the English. In March 1703, Samuel Chadwell and the crew of his privateer, the *Flying Horse*, raided the home of Philip Meneer, a French settler at Naskeag Point in present-day Brooklin, killing him and raping his wife, one of Saint-Castin's daughters. In revenge, on May 10, three Frenchmen and three Indians "Came a Perposs from the Eastward to Ballance what Captain Chadwell had committed . . . ," attacking a sloop off Cousin's Island and killing one of the crew.[23]

In the spring of 1703, despite scarce resources, the governor of New France, Philippe de Rigaud, Marquis de Vaudreuil, sent 230 Micmacs and pro-French Mohawks, along with 30 Frenchmen to conduct raids against

English settlements from Casco Bay to Wells. These raids served the dual purpose of preempting English plans to attack Port Royal and, more importantly, of ensuring that "the Abenakis and the English would be irreconcilable enemies."[24] Some Penacooks and Pigwackets had apparently joined in the fighting, forcing Dudley to declare war on them on August 18. In his second goal Vaudreuil was only partially successful, for as soon as Dudley heard about Chadwell's raid he invited all Indians from communities between Penacook and the Penobscot River to meet with him at Casco Bay in order to provide them with compensation. Thus many potential warriors remained neutral, while others withdrew northward at the invitation of Vaudreuil, who hoped they would secure New France's southern border and assure Iroquois neutrality. To aid in this effort, the Jesuit Sébastien

8-2. Handbill announcing the official prices paid for furs and hides by Massachusetts licensed traders at the opening of Queen Anne's War. (Courtesy of the Massachusetts Archives collection, SC1, 45X, vol. 119, 214.)

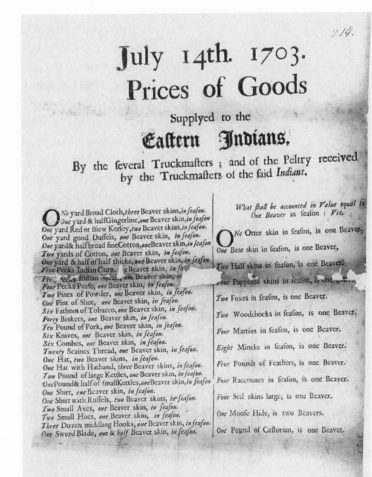

Rale established a new mission village on the St. Lawrence River at Wawenock (Bécancour), principally for the residents of Amaseconti but also for most of the Norridgewock population.[25]

Despite Dudley's efforts at compensation at the Casco conference, minor raids resumed within a few weeks and continued through the winter into 1704. Attacks and ambushes ranged from Casco Bay to Haverhill, Massachusetts. Then on February 29, two hundred Indians and forty-five French militiamen, led by three officers, attacked Deerfield, Massachusetts. The Indian forces included Abenakis and Mohawks from the St. Lawrence missions along with some Penacooks and Pigwackets. The appearance of these warriors from the missions signaled a pattern that would be repeated in subsequent periods of warfare: Indians remaining loyal to the French tended to keep to the missions, while their more neutrally inclined colleagues often stayed behind in Maine and the Maritime Provinces in the hope of maintaining peaceful relations with the English. As we shall see, the populations of the missions would provide warriors not only for operations in New England but also in the *pays d'en haut* and in the Mississippi region.[26]

The Massachusetts government responded to these raids by attacking Indian villages in the interior, including two expeditions to the stockaded village of Pigwacket, "one of their principal Head-quarters." The first found the village abandoned, but the second killed or captured twelve. The next spring, they also sent a party of English and Indian militia to Lake Winnipesaukee and a larger party up the Saco, hoping to encounter Indians at their spring fishing places. In June 1704, Colonel Benjamin Church learned that one hundred French and several hundred Indians were planning to attack Piscataqua, and he countered by pillaging and burning French and Indian settlements from the Penobscot eastward. Militia from Northampton, Massachusetts, also attacked at Cowas, on the upper Connecticut River, killing many Pigwacket and Penacook warriors living there at the time.[27]

Throughout 1704, Indians attacked Amesbury and Haverhill in Massachusetts, Oyster River and Dover in New Hampshire, and York in Maine. In June, following their success at Deerfield, the French sent a force of about seven hundred militiamen from Montreal to raid Northampton, Massachusetts. However, after learning of the strength of English forces there, hundreds of the French troops deserted, leaving only a few to create minor disturbances at Lancaster and Groton, Massachusetts. The impact of this warfare upon the New England frontier was not profound. Throughout Queen Anne's War, the *Boston News Letter* provided coverage of the fighting in Europe but offered few details about local French or Indian activity.

The tide in such warfare had clearly turned in favor of the English. Likewise, domestic affairs in New France seemed little affected; the Iroquois remained neutral, and French forces, aided by the Canibas, Maliseets, and Micmacs, were enjoying considerable success in a series of raids on Newfoundland fishing ports.[28]

For the Indians of Maine, however, the war soon proved to be disastrous. Some remained in their home territories to facilitate raids on the English, but many, perhaps most, chose to withdraw to the St. Lawrence, where Governor Vaudreuil had promised them *"toutes sortes de secours."* He was unable to fulfill his promise, however, because early in 1705 a vital French supply vessel had failed to reach Quebec. And to make the situation worse, the mission villages were suffering from a severe outbreak of measles. In their absence, Lieutenant Colonel Winthrop Hilton, with a force of 250 Englishmen and 20 Indians, marched on snowshoes to a still-abandoned Norridgewock, which they burned. In November 1706 Vaudreuil sent the Jesuits Joseph Aubery and Pierre de La Chasse from Quebec to Maine with their mission populations in an effort to keep these Indians active in the war, despite the fact that, unknown to Vaudreuil, they had already sent a flag of truce to the English and released their captives.[29]

To the west, New York had taken advantage of poor conditions at the St. Lawrence mission villages, and of its growing illicit fur trade with their inhabitants, to woo these Eastern Indians with offers of peace and provisions. In June 1707, fifty Canibas and other Indians (presumably Maliseets) accepted the offer, leaving their homelands to head west and find refuge among the Senecas. Then, a group of pro-French Mohawks from Caughnawaga joined pro-English Mohawks in wars in the *pays d'en haut*. These defections spurred Vaudreuil to increase supplies and urge the Indians to fight on, but as the year drew to a close, Antoine Gaulin, Pierre Thury's replacement as missionary to Pentagoet, reported that Indians all along the Acadian coast were in "very great misery." After a quiet winter, only a single Indian raid occurred, near York in April 1708.[30]

That summer, the French minister of marine, Louis Phélypeaux de Pontchartrain, pressured Vaudreuil into adopting a more active stance regarding the war. As a result, the governor sent two mixed forces of French soldiers and warriors from the St. Lawrence missions to raid Portsmouth, New Hampshire, but desertion and disease took a heavy toll, forcing the French commanders to redirect their efforts against the village of Haverhill. The following spring and summer, Jean-Baptiste Hertel de Rouville led Indian forces in minor raids on Deerfield and other western Massachusetts settlements, but increasingly effective patrols by English troops, now

It is abundantly clear that from the early seventeenth century to the fall of New France, Native people of the Maritime Peninsula generally preferred to remain within or near their traditional homelands. Nevertheless, during times of war, many of them engaged a much wider geopolitical universe.[31] One especially well documented case of an individual who explored options of mobility during the tumultuous years between King William's War and Dummer's War was that of Nescambiouit, whose alias was Tom Sabacaman. Nescambiouit was probably born in the Sebago Lake–Casco Bay area around 1660. His English alias suggests that, like many Indians of southwestern Maine, he had lived in close contact with English settlers during his youth. Nescambiouit is first mentioned during King William's War as a chief at a new fort at Amasocontee (present-day Farmington Falls), later as leader of Caniba war parties, and finally as part of a French naval expedition against Newfoundland. According to Puritan divine Cotton Mather, it was he "that usually heads the Indians when they come to destroy the New Englanders"; Mather credited him with killing or capturing over 150 English during the war.[32] He was active in Queen Anne's War, joining another expedition against Newfoundland at its outbreak in 1703 and performing so well that he was taken to France for an audience with King Louis XIV, who was so impressed with this Abenaki warrior that he presented Nescambiouit with lavish presents and five years later asked Vaudreuil about his welfare. In 1716 he went to live in the *pays d'en haut* among the Fox Indians, a group that was proving troublesome to the French. Why he did so is unclear, but he remained there until at least 1723 when, as ambassador for a Fox faction that wished to make war on their neighbors, he visited Saint-François to invite the Abenakis to join him. He had returned to his homeland by May 1727, when Massachusetts officials hired him as a messenger to Canada. The *New England Weekly Journal* reported his death the following month.[33]

routinely equipped with snowshoes in winter, limited the effectiveness of such attacks.[34]

Throughout the war, the English raids on Indian (and French) villages had resulted in few direct deaths, but this was of little import for, as Massachusetts governor Dudley explained, "this whole War I have kept them [the Indians] from all their Ancient Seats and planting grounds, and driven them to Inaccessible places, and parts, where no Corn will grow for their support."[35] The success of his policy was measured in Native population decline and a definite shift toward neutrality. As a contemporary historian of this war put it, Dudley's scorched-earth strategy "made the Old Men weary of War, and to covet Peace."[36] In October 1709, Vaudreuil acknowledged that he had lost influence over his Indian allies. The next July, a group of delegates from Pigwacket and from the Kennebec and Penobscot Valleys approached the commander of the garrison at Casco Bay to apologize for raiding the settlements. They pleaded "as formerly their desire of Lying still if they could have a Supply, Otherwise they could not live, but must return to yᵉ French."[37]

Ponchartrain's dissatisfaction with Vaudreuil stemmed from the fact that Boston had twice attacked Port Royal in 1707, failing to take it only because of the defense provided by Indians led by Bernard-Anselme d'Abbadie de Saint-Castin, son of Jean-Vincent and Madockawando's grandson. In October 1710, however, General Francis Nicholson's fleet of 26 vessels with a force of 3,400 British regulars and New England militiamen easily captured the port. Leaving the Acadians in place and renaming the settlement Annapolis Royal, the English posted a garrison of 200 royal marines and 250 New England militia, two companies of which were Indians, under the command of the newly appointed governor Samuel Vetch. Emboldened by their victory at Annapolis Royal, the next summer the English again attempted to take Quebec City, but the attack was a failure.[38]

French military action during the rest of the war focused on the English at Annapolis Royal. As Vaudreuil could not afford to mount a naval attack to retake the port, the responsibility for harassing the English there fell to privateers along the coast, and on land to Saint-Castin, who had been appointed military commander of Acadia by Vaudreuil for that purpose. Vetch was hampered by the same rundown fortifications that had aided the British in its capture. He also faced the desertion of marines, many of whom, as it turned out, were Roman Catholic Irishmen. From the start, Vetch was plagued by "sckulking partys of Indians" who were also harassing those few Acadians who obeyed his orders to provide timber for the fort. His situation became more tenuous in June 1711 when a party of 150 led by Saint-Castin and a Penobscot chief named Simhouret ambushed 63 soldiers who were on their way to force reluctant Acadians to resume the delivery of timber.[39]

To counter these threats, Vetch proposed raising a company of Mohawks for "scouring the woods."[40] In early February 1712, 58 Mohawks and their officers were embarked and by June, Vetch reported them "verry well fortified in the most proper place for our defense about a quarter mile from the grand Fort. . . . [W]ee are pretty secure notwithstanding some parties of Indians sent out by the Governor of Canada." Vetch's troubles were not over, however. That summer, a party of 150 to 200 Indians sent by Vaudreuil to learn whether the British planned another attack on Quebec captured some of Vetch's troops. Lacking supplies and faced with increasing rates of desertion by his Irish marines, he was unable to recover his men. He was able to hold on through the winter of 1713, however, and as the end of the war appeared increasingly likely in the spring of 1713, the Mohawks began to desert, and Vetch dismissed the rest from service.[41]

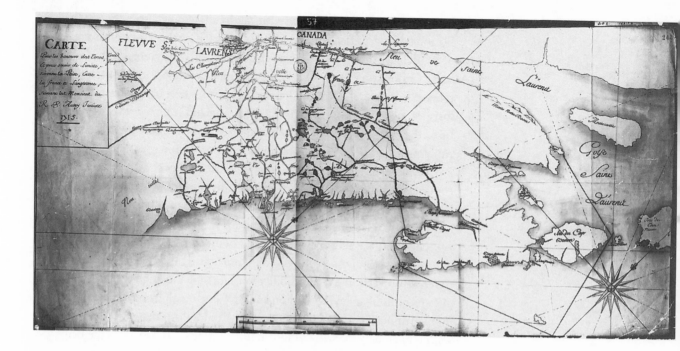

8-3. Map drawn in 1715 by the Jesuit missionary Joseph Aubery, showing Indian villages at Pigwacket, Narakamogou, Amaseconti, Norridgewock, Panawamské, and Meductic. Because most inhabitants of Panouamskee took refuge at St. Lawrence mission villages during Queen Anne's War, it was initially labeled "village abandonné," but "abandonné" was later crossed out, indicating its reoccupation at the end of the war. (Original map, Dépôt des Cartes et Plans de la Service Hydrographique Archives, 124-1-4, Bibliothèque National, Paris. Reproduced from a copy in the National Archives of Canada, NMC 6364.)

After the Treaty of Utrecht

By the time the Treaty of Utrecht was signed on April 11, 1713, ending Queen Anne's War, not only had Saint-Castin failed to drive the English from Annapolis Royal, he had declared himself unable even to hold Pentagoet. The treaty ceded Acadia to England, leaving the French only Île Royale—present-day Cape Breton Island—where they soon began to build the fortified settlement of Louisbourg to protect the approach to Quebec via the St. Lawrence River. Initially, they had high hopes of attracting Acadian farmers and Native allies to Cape Breton, but they were largely unsuccessful in doing so.[42] Thus when the region's Native population, along with Saint-Castin and their missionaries, began soon after the war to return to their homes in Maine, competition for their loyalties was renewed on terms more favorable to the English.[43]

As with earlier treaties, the Treaty of Utrecht made western Maine lands and the Acadian fishing grounds attractive to English settlers and fishermen. By 1717 scattered settlements had been reestablished at present-day Kennebunkport, Biddeford, Scarborough, Cape Elizabeth, Falmouth, North Yarmouth, Brunswick, Topsham, Phippsburg, Arrowsic, Bowdoinham, and Richmond.[44] Despite the initial effectiveness of Massachusetts's Indian policy, however, this rapid repopulation of former English settlements and the reappearance of itinerant traders immediately resulted in complaints from the Native population.

The new English settlers were wary of Native people and hoped to keep them at arm's length if possible. They therefore petitioned for resources to rebuild the fort at Brunswick (formerly Pejepscot), the express purpose of which they candidly admitted was to "dislodge the Indians from their Principal Fishery, keep them from Chief carrying places & be possibly the means of removing them further from us, if another war should happen."[45]

Native resentment at the sheer number of settlers and fishermen arriving on their coast, and at the establishment of a fort at Brunswick, came to the surface at a conference with Massachusetts governor Samuel Shute held at Arrowsic in August of 1717. There Shute told the gathered Indians that they "must Desist from any Pretensions to Lands which the English own."

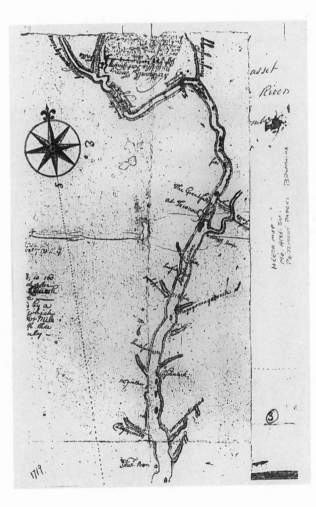

8-4. Detail of a map drawn in 1718 by Captain Joseph Heath of Brunswick, showing the location of "Neridgwalk Town With The Fort Standing Close by y River." Planting fields are indicated on both banks downriver, toward Skowhegan. (Collections of the Maine Historical Society.)

They responded, "We can't understand how our Lands have been purchased, what was Alienated was by our gift," and regarding forts, they said "We should be pleased with King George if there was never a Fort in the Eastern Parts." But the Abenakis' French allies were also causing them problems. During Queen Anne's War, the value of the king's presents to them had been restored to 4,000 *livres*. After the war, however, the allotment dropped to half that amount. Moreover, French goods were excessively expensive. Thus there was strong Native sentiment at the Arrowsic conference favoring accommodation; some chiefs from Androscoggin even requested that a Protestant chapel be built for them near Brunswick. During the next two years, Shute continued a de facto policy of religious tolerance and even allowed Jabez Bradbury, a trader on the Kennebec River, to be hired to build a new Catholic church at Norridgewock, which was subsidized by the French Crown. The same subsidy also provided funds for a church at Meductic, on the St. John River.[46]

Nevertheless, by 1720 a group of land developers known as the Muscongus Company was attempting to settle east of Pemaquid. The Jesuit Rale vehe-

8-5. One of fifteen military commissions issued by Massachusetts governor Jonathan Belcher in November 1734. This, the only one known to survive, was issued to Hanapemawet, awarding him the rank of "Second Captain of the Tribe of St. Johns Indians." (Maine State Museum collection.)

8-6. Woodcut illustrating an account of Captain Johnson Harmon's raid on Norridgewock on August 18, 1724, published in the Boston Courant. (Reproduced by permission of the Huntington Library, San Marino CA, RB 150402.)

mently opposed this expansion into lands he regarded as still Native territory, but Massachusetts's response was to order him to abandon his mission.[47] In protest, the Natives began to kill livestock and threaten settlers in the Casco Bay area. In November, Massachusetts commissioners met with several senior men from the Androscoggin and Saco area who apologized for the unruly behavior of their young men. Massachusetts demanded compensation in the sum of two hundred hides, and the sagamores agreed to give up four men as hostages until they could deliver the hides.[48]

Delivery of the hides, however, did not free the hostages. Up to that time there had been growing support at Norridgewock for continuing the peace.

To counter this trend, in July 1721 Pierre de La Chasse, the Jesuit superior in New France, accompanied by Rale, led a massive body of 250 Indians, in 90 canoes, to a meeting with English officials at Arrowsic. Also in attendance was Joseph d'Abbadie de Saint-Castin, another of Jean-Vincent's sons. The delegation demanded that the English release the hostages and vacate the new settlements within three weeks or be burned out. To convince their opponents of their seriousness, raiding resumed at once.[49] The hostages remained in Boston, along with Saint-Castin, who had been arrested and held six months for interrogation.[50]

Massachusetts also issued an order for Rale's arrest, and in March 1722 Colonel Thomas Westbrook narrowly missed capturing him at Norridgewock. Westbrook did not return empty-handed, however, for among Rale's papers he had found letters from Vaudreuil encouraging Native resistance to English encroachment. This sobering news led to renewed efforts at reconciliation, but, undaunted, the Muscongus Company began establishing a settlement and garrison at St. Georges (present-day Thomaston) at the western entrance of Penobscot Bay. The Reverend Samuel Penhallow, historian of the war that was to follow, questioned the wisdom of this expansion, stating that "many have reflected on the Government for suffering a Fort to be at St. *Georges*, as if that did irritate the *Indians*... [and] that there was too great indulgence at first in the Government in suffering so many Townships at so great a distance to be laid out at once, unless they were more peopled."[51]

Dummer's War Begins

This undeclared war between a threatened Native population and aggressively expanding English colonies is named for William Dummer, the acting governor of Massachusetts and New Hampshire, who helped bring it to an end in 1725. It began in the spring and summer of 1722 after Indians from the Penobscot, Kennebec, and Androscoggin Valleys, aided by 160 warriors from the St. Lawrence missions, resumed raiding from Berwick to St. Georges.[52] To the east, in Nova Scotia, after the end of Queen Anne's War, Micmacs had continued to harass the English to the point where the French, fearing reprisals, felt obliged to compensate the victims of a 1720 raid on the English fishing station at Canso. In 1722 Micmacs increased their sea raids, capturing twenty-two vessels.[53]

The renewed raids in Maine and New Hampshire forced Samuel Shute, the governor of both provinces, to declare war in July and to issue bounties

8-7. Sébastien Rale's writing box, taken in a raid on Norridgewock in 1722, when English militia narrowly missed capturing Rale. In the box was found a letter from the French governor of Quebec, urging Rale's Indians to resist English encroachment. (Collections of the Maine Historical Society.)

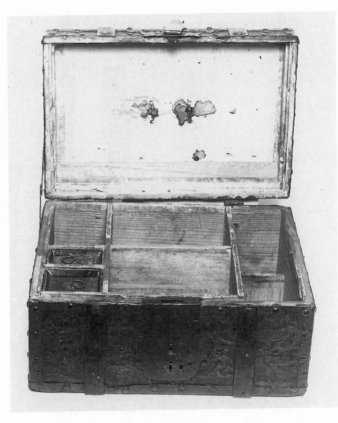

8-8. French flintlock trade musket, made around 1720 to 1730, 167 centimeters long. The French provided arms such as this to Maine Indians as part of the king's presents. (Private collection.)

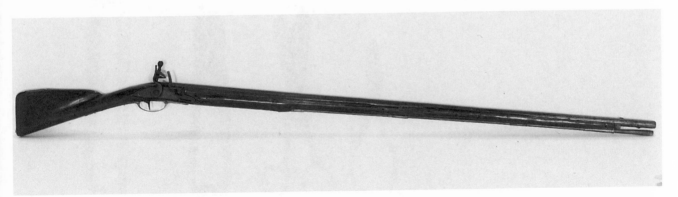

8-9. These tools show that the Norridgewock mission community was well supplied with European technology. Carpenter's hammer, wood rasp, rapier blade, two wood chisels, file, scythe blade (?), knife. (Maine State Museum collection.)

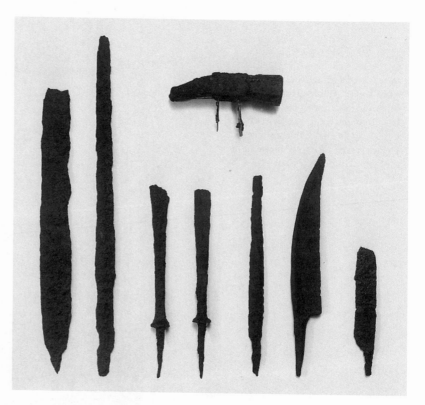

8-10. European tools from the Norridgewock mission community. Duckbill pliers, scissors, metal shears with a copper fragment caught between the blades, pincers. (Maine State Museum collection.)

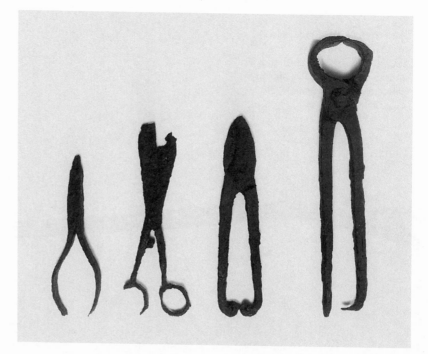

8-11. Barrel from a high-quality French pistol, dating from about 1700 to 1725. This sort of weapon might have been carried by an important man at Norridgewock, some of whom held French military commissions. The barrel has been made useless by blows from a sharp-edged instrument, possibly a sword or tomahawk. The position of the marks suggests that the pistol was used to parry blows in hand-to-hand combat. (Maine State Museum collection.)

8-12. Brass crucifix found at Old Point, the site of the village and mission of Norridgewock. Height: 9 centimeters. (Collections of the Maine Historical Society.)

8-13. Pewter vessels found at Old Point, the site of the mission and village of Norridgewock. They were probably used in religious sacraments. The lidded vessel appears to be an ointment jar. Its lid bears the seal of the Jesuit College of Lyon, where Sébastien Rale taught before coming to North America. Height of second from left: 10 centimeters. (Maine State Museum collection.)

8-14. Church bell from the Norridgewock mission chapel, found near the village site in 1808. Height: 36 centimeters. (Collections of the Maine Historical Society.)

8-15. Proclamation issued by Lieutenant Governor William Dummer in 1724 for a day of thanksgiving following the destruction of Norridgewock. (Courtesy of the Boston Athenæum.)

8-16. Monument erected to the missionary Sébastien Rale on the site of his grave at Old Point by Bishop Benedict J. Fenwick on August 23, 1833 (reproduced from Hanson 1849). The monument was torn down by vandals and the wrought-iron cross eventually found its way to St. Anne's Church on Indian Island in Old Town. The monument, with a new cross, was re-erected on its original site and still stands.

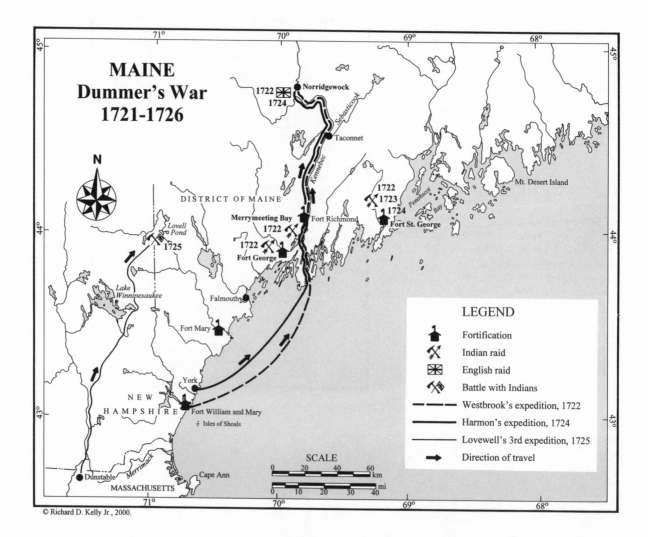

MAINE
Dummer's War
1721-1726

1722 ⊞ ● Norridgewock
1724

● Taconnet

DISTRICT OF MAINE

Mt. Desert Island

1722 ⚔
1723
1724

Merrymeeting Bay ● Fort Richmond
1722 ⚔

Fort St. George

1722 ⚔
Fort George

Falmouth

Lovell
Pond
1725

Lake
Winnipesaukee

Fort Mary

York

N E W
H A M P S H I R E   Fort William and Mary
∴ Isles of Shoals

Dunstable
MASSACHUSETTS   Cape Ann

LEGEND

🏠 Fortification
⚔ Indian raid
⊞ English raid
⚔ Battle with Indians
— — — Westbrook's expedition, 1722
———— Harmon's expedition, 1724
———— Lovewell's 3rd expedition, 1725
➜ Direction of travel

SCALE
0   20   40   60
                    km
0 10   20   30 40
                    mi

© Richard D. Kelly Jr., 2000.

8-17. Maine: Dummer's War, 1721–26

for scalps and captives the next month. In Nova Scotia, Governor Richard Phillips did the same, organizing New Englanders from Canso to attack and disperse the sea raiders. As England and France were then at peace, Vaudreuil's pleas to France for additional support went unanswered. Nevertheless, Indian raids continued throughout the summer, and in Nova Scotia Micmacs continued to capture fishing vessels.[54]

Decisive action by the English did not come until winter, when, in March 1723, Colonel Westbrook's forces burned the recently constructed fort at Panawamské on the Penobscot. By that time, the Penobscots had withdrawn to the St. Lawrence missions, unwilling to face the English without French support. In September, however, an estimated force of over four hundred Micmacs, accompanied by warriors from the St. Lawrence mission villages, attacked Arrowsic, killing one man and fifty cattle and burning twenty-six houses. This was probably the same force that had laid siege to St. Georges in December, narrowly failing to capture it.[55]

As the threat of war increased in 1722, Massachusetts sent an appeal for assistance to its Native allies, the Mohawks, who responded in the fall by sending a party including the Protestant convert Hendrick, to Falmouth. The English misunderstood the Mohawks' purpose, which was not to make war on the Eastern Indians but rather to invite them to a conference in order to remind them of their obligations under the Covenant Chain. The English were reluctant to give the Mohawks diplomatic access to the Abenakis and allowed only one of their number, accompanied by Captain Jabez Bradbury, to visit Norridgewock. They found the village deserted, its population having gone to the mission village of Bécancour for the winter.[56]

While in Falmouth, Hendrick explained to the English what the Mohawks planned to say to the Abenakis:

That in time past the Eastern Indians Earnestly requested of the Five Nations that they might thrust their Arm into the Golden Chain of Amity and Friendship between the Nations and accordingly they were accepted upon their styling themselves Children to those Nations and calling them their parents. . . . You our Sons you have formerly Submitted yourselves to us and thrust your hands into the Covenant Chain between us and thee English and you look upon it to be a great favor to be admitted so to do. But since that time you have Twisted and wrung your Arm cant keep it Still cant hold it still as we do and always have done, if you go on to Act thus much longer you'l get your arm quite out and if so we Dye We will make war upon you to the loss of our Lives. . . . To the young men who are for War our discourse is to you We now bind your hands and desire you to look back to what your fore fathers have Covenanted in their Treaties with the English and see that you fulfill their Treaties.

Hendrick then explained that "it was about Twenty years since the Eastern Indians first submitted themselves to the five Nations." This makes it clear that the events surrounding the Abenakis' entrance into the Covenant Chain were essentially as then–Massachusetts governor Bellomont had reported in 1700.[57]

Throughout the war, Massachusetts repeatedly tried to convince the Mohawks to punish their "disobedient children," but the Mohawks resisted, striving instead to arrange a meeting between the Eastern Indians and the English to make peace. Moreover, Iroquois political unity had continued to unravel since the Great Peace of Montreal, as ever more of them moved to Canada and the *pays d'en haut*.[58] The Mohawks did not wish to break their treaty of neutrality with the French, and in September 1724 they told the Massachusetts commissioners, who were again trying to bully them into warfare, "If we should Take up The Hatchet against The Eastern Indians The Governor of Canada would Look down upon us with Indignation and set The People round about, who are his Children, upon us, and That would Set all The World on Fire."[59] Although a few Mohawks with strong English sympathies did actually join the fighting, they did so independently.[60]

In 1724 rumors that the hostages being held in Boston were dead triggered several small raids across the New England frontier. Penobscots captured fourteen fishing vessels in the Penobscot River and used them to attack St. Georges. Farther east, fifty-six Maliseets and Micmacs attacked Annapolis Royal, killing ten people.[61] The most significant event of 1724, however, was the destruction of Norridgewock on August 18 by a combined force of English, Massachusetts Indians, and three Mohawks, relatives of Hendrick. The victorious troops returned to Boston with twenty-seven scalps, including Rale's. The total number of casualties remains unclear, but it may have been as high as one hundred. The survivors retreated to the St. Lawrence missions. The last major engagement of Dummer's War was the famed Lovewell massacre, which took place in May 1725. A large force of Indians ambushed John Lovewell and his party of bounty hunters near Pigwacket (Fryeburg). Although they killed twelve, including Lovewell, they lost several of their own warriors. At sea during July, a well-outfitted schooner sailed by Indians had driven Massachusetts fishermen from the Maine coast east of Saco.[62]

A Workable Arrangement

With French encouragement, Abenakis domiciled in New France and with their allies of the Seven Nations attempted to continue the war. Those Abenakis still in their homelands, however, could not because the French were unwilling to send them supplies through waters controlled by the English. Drained by the costs of the war and having neutralized Norridgewock, the English sought to negotiate a treaty even as they continued to carry out raids against the Penobscots. After consulting with Governor Vaudreuil in August 1725, the Penobscots agreed to a truce and to a meeting in Boston in November. Their chief spokesman at the conference was Loron (Laurent) Sagouarrab, a Penobscot who claimed to speak for all the "tribes" from St. Francis on the St. Lawrence to Cape Sable in

Nova Scotia. He requested that the English give up their forts at Richmond and St. Georges as a show of peaceful intent. A treaty for which Loron was largely responsible was concluded in December, but the issue of the forts at Richmond and St. Georges remained unresolved. Many Maine Indians spent the following winter on the shores of the St. Lawrence River. Further negotiations took place at a treaty-ratification conference at Falmouth (present-day Portland) during the summer of 1726, when Loron again denied that the English had title to lands above Arrowsic and east of the Kennebec.[63]

Indians from the St. Lawrence mission villages and Norridgewock ratified the treaty with Massachusetts in the summer of 1727, even though some of the key points to which Loron had objected still appeared in the official text. Acting Governor William Dummer, appointed to replace Shute shortly after the war began, released the hostages taken in 1720, dropped the demand that no Jesuits be allowed among those Indians that Massachusetts considered to be within its territories, and agreed to establish a truck house on the Salmon Falls River to serve Pigwacket. Indeed, in 1728 both Dummer and Vaudreuil would support the resettlement of Norridgewock, agreeing to install new altar furnishings to replace those taken in the 1724 raid and to allow Jesuit missionary Jacques Sirême to replace Rale. For their part, the Penobscots kept Dummer informed of threats to the peace via their interpreter, John Gyles. The villages of Amaseconti and Narakamigook apparently were never reoccupied, but a small population remained at Pigwacket and elsewhere on the Saco River, and a small group led by Polan apparently remained in the area between Casco Bay and the lower Androscoggin River until the outbreak of King George's War in 1744.[64]

Massachusetts also responded to Native complaints about trade injustices and acceded to a number of other requests, including permission for Indians to trade with the garrison at St. Georges and even authorizing the garrison to assist in the construction of shelters for use when they visited. Jonathan Belcher, who was appointed governor in 1730, continued Dummer's conciliatory policies, particularly with the Penobscots, who were emerging as the spokesmen for all the region's Native peoples.[65]

Both the Indians and the governor approved of official truck houses but were ambivalent about private traders. On the one hand, the prices offered for furs by these traders were often better that those at the official truck houses. On the other hand, the private traders sold the Indians rum, which was an ongoing source of problems in their communities. As Belcher commented: "I wish we could possibly make out Some proofe upon those that carry on the wicked Trade of cheating and killing the Indians with

Rum. . . . I am clearly of Opinion that it would be better they were wholly debarr'd of it, altho' the Trade with them did not give half the Advantage."[66] By 1734 the governor had decided to prohibit the sale of rum.

Dummer's treaty was an important achievement for both Massachusetts and the Eastern Indians, and it would be reinstated after periods of warfare for the next half-century. In negotiating the treaty, Penobscot leadership considerably enhanced their prestige among both the English and the Indians of New England and Nova Scotia. Their influence can be seen, for example, in their communications with Massachusetts regarding the continuing hostility of Abenaki warriors from the mission villages at St. Francis and Missisquoi, often led by a chief called Gray Lock.[67]

At a series of conferences held in at Boston in 1736, the central theme was inevitably the conduct of the fur trade according to the conditions of the 1726 treaty, and Loron, a stickler for its formalities and protocols, was often the chief spokesman for the Indians. The English seem to have listened attentively during these conferences, and the Indians seem to have expressed their concerns freely. Governor Belcher tried to correct the most severe problems, but it was difficult for him to fulfill all conditions of the treaty. The Indians realized that the beaver population was diminishing and expected the price to increase accordingly. When this did not happen, they found it hard to believe that the truck masters were giving them fair prices. Belcher also had occasion to issue orders that were unpopular among English settlers. In 1739, for example, he ordered Colonel Thomas Westbrook to force the owners of a dam on the Presumpscot River in Casco Bay to allow anadromous fish to pass upstream in the spring, when they were the Indians' main source of food.[68]

Belcher's success in maintaining harmony depended on a few devoted officers at Richmond and St. Georges, veterans of the frontier who were trusted by both sides, such as John Gyles, who had lived among Indians as a captive during King William's War. Maintaining peace also depended upon English forbearance concerning the Jesuits still living among the Indians. Although Belcher, like Bellomont before him, regarded Catholicism as "wicked, ridiculous superstition and idolatry," he too ultimately recognized the failure of his efforts to replace the Jesuits with Protestant ministers. He tried offering auxiliary military commissions to prominent Indian men, but that tactic caused great dissension within Native communities; only three of the commissions were accepted.[69]

Indians in the Penobscot River region had made no complaint about the resettlement of former English settlements during the 1730s, even those as close by as Sheepscot and Damariscotta, for they lay within the former limits of English settlement. However, when settlers began to build a house above the fort at St. Georges, the Penobscots protested, saying "if that Settlement [at the falls] should be allowed it will draw on Warr and blood-shed. It was with great difficulty, that our Old men at several meetings in Council could at last prevail on the younger Sort, to agree to the Settlement of the English on the Main River as high as the falls." Remaining faithful to the terms of the treaty, Belcher ordered the house torn down and awarded the Indians presents worth one hundred pounds. Belcher's defense of Native rights was among the factors that cost him the governorship, for Samuel Waldo, whose patent included the contested land, went to London in 1741 and used his political influence to have Belcher replaced as governor by William Shirley.[70]

King George's War

In 1739 war broke out between England and Spain. French involvement on the Spanish side was inevitable and it came early in 1744. The French had provided king's presents more or less continuously to the Natives of the Maritime Peninsula since the 1680s. Now, however, France was experiencing troubled times, and its navy, purveyor of these presents, was incompetently managed. Moreover, English populations and military strength had increased significantly. Still, as war approached, officials in New France nevertheless expected their traditional Native allies to support them in the war. Thus both England and France were surprised and angered when not only many Indians but their missionaries as well declared their intent to remain neutral and to take refuge in the St. Lawrence River. Forty warriors from Pigwacket actually volunteered to fight for the English, but some others went to live near Boston for the duration of the war.[71]

In Nova Scotia, however, the English were vulnerable, confined as they were to two small outposts at Annapolis Royal, which was surrounded by French Acadians who refused to swear loyalty to King George, and the tiny fishing port of Canso, which was under constant threat from Fortress Louisbourg. News of King George's War did not reach Nova Scotia until May 1744, by which time Micmacs, and possibly Maliseets as well, had captured several Massachusetts vessels that were fishing in Nova Scotia waters. These captures compelled Governor Shirley to declare war on all Indians east of Passamaquoddy Bay. Delayed news of the war also allowed a French naval force to surprise and easily capture Canso. Then, beginning in July, the firebrand missionary Jean-Louis Le Loutre led a force of three hundred Micmacs in unsuccessful raids against Annapolis Royal. Once news of the

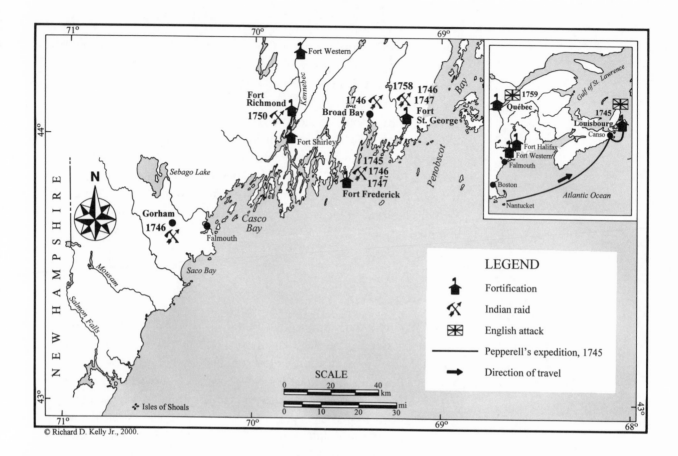

8-18. Maine: French and Indian Wars, 1745–63

war reached New England, Massachusetts heeded the pleas of Paul Mascarene, the fort's commander, for reinforcement. As in Queen Anne's War, the English began by recruiting a company of Mohawks. These, with their commander, Captain John Gorham, arrived in December 1744, in time to scare off Le Loutre and his raiders. They then went on the offensive, killing several Maliseets and Micmacs, whose raids against Annapolis Royal thereafter diminished. Later attempts by the French to capture the fort were hampered by misadventure and by the determination of most French Acadians to remain completely neutral. With further reinforcements from Massachusetts, Mascarene was able to hold on to Annapolis Royal throughout the remainder of the war.[72]

New England merchants and fishermen, however, chaffed under the continuing threat of French vessels sailing out of Louisbourg. In January 1745, William Vaughan, a merchant from present-day Newcastle, Maine, convinced Governor Shirley to undertake a risky attack on Louisbourg in May using only militia forces. Against long odds, the attack succeeded. Although not directed at the Indians, the capture of Louisbourg necessitated a military response. In July, Shirley notified the Eastern Indians of the New Englanders' victory and urged them to remain at peace, but they had already set about attacking English settlements, notably St. Georges.[73] That same summer, Indian raids conducted mainly by warriors from the village of Missisquoi on Lake Champlain and the St. Lawrence missions, created havoc in Vermont, New Hampshire, and Massachusetts. Indians from the Kennebec, Penobscot, and St. John regions, as well as farther east, took some part in these actions.[74] Attacks on English settlements in Maine continued during the summers of 1746 and 1747, but it seems likely that the raiders were mainly from the St. Lawrence missions.[75]

In October 1745, four Penobscots appeared at St. Georges under a flag of truce, hopeful that they and the English might "again Live together as Breatheren." Following this meeting, most Penobscots and other Eastern Indians retreated to the St. Lawrence mission villages, remaining there until the end of the war. Joseph d'Abbadie de Saint-Castin, however, probably remained involved in military activities in Nova Scotia.[76]

King George's War ended in 1748, and Massachusetts reinstated Dummer's treaty in October 1749. At the new Nova Scotian settlement of Halifax, Governor George Cornwallis reached a similar agreement with the Maliseets and some of the Micmacs. Other Micmacs, led by Le Loutre, responded by raiding the English fishing station at Canso, taking their twenty captives to Louisbourg to collect ransom. With the war over, Micmac pleas to the St. Lawrence mission villages for assistance in attacking Halifax and, a year later, to prevent the building of a new English fort, Fort Lawrence, at the head of the Bay of Fundy went unheeded.[77]

Incident at Wiscassett

In December 1749, only two months after the reinstatement of Dummer's treaty, came a harsh test of the Maine Indians' commitment to neutrality. English settler Obadiah Albee, accompanied by a mob of relatives and friends, murdered Saccary Harry and wounded two other Indians—Job and Andrew—near Wiscassett as they were returning from the Falmouth peace conference.[78] Although the Indians expressed their outrage at this act, the government of Massachusetts acted cautiously, fearing reprisals from the murderers' relatives: only one of the culprits, Benjamin Ledite, was convicted, and he was sentenced merely to a lashing. This incident drove many Norridgewocks to seek refuge on the St. Lawrence. In September 1750 a combined force of 110 warriors from Norridgewock, the Penobscot region, and the St. Francis missions planned a retaliatory strike against the fort at Richmond, but conciliatory elements in the Native community warned the fort's occupants and damage was minimal. Failing in their main objective of taking the fort, the raiders separated into small parties and harassed the Kennebec settlements until winter set in. Limited Indian raiding by warriors from Norridgewock and the St. Lawrence missions continued in the spring of 1751. Few, if any, Penobscots were involved; instead, they joined Maliseets in raids on Fort Lawrence and Halifax.[79]

When Massachusetts acting governor Spencer Phips called for a conference of all the Eastern Indians in August 1751, the Norridgewocks were too angry about the Wiscassett murders to attend; only the Penobscots and a handful of Passamaquoddies and Maliseets were willing. Those who participated were anxious to express their concerns about yet another new settlement, called Frankfort (present-day Dresden), on the Kennebec River above Richmond, and the construction by Ebenezer Hall of a house on the important seal-hunting island of Matinicus, in Penobscot Bay. In exchange for reassurances that the conditions of Dummer's treaty would be observed, the delegates were willing to "bury the mischief" of the Wiscassett murder.[80] Although Frankfort was located well within the boundaries of land claimed by Norridgewocks, in October 1752 even they agreed to abide by Dummer's treaty. The Micmacs also reaffirmed the treaty in November.[81]

The Seven Years' War

The Seven Years' War arose over competing British and French claims to the Ohio Valley; competition for Acadia was entirely incidental. Hostilities began at the site of present-day Pittsburgh in May 1754, when French forces clashed with Virginia militia commanded by Lieutenant Colonel George Washington.[82]

As the probability of war increased a year earlier, Massachusetts governor Shirley had returned from diplomatic duties in France. During his absence, settlers at Frankfort had erected a blockhouse and Ebenezer Hall had defiantly returned to Matinicus after the General Court had ordered him to leave. The Norridgewocks and Penobscots considered these matters breaches of Dummer's treaty. Shirley ordered Hall's arrest but responded to the complaint about Frankfort by restating—accurately—that the Indians' forbears had signed deeds relinquishing that area to English settlers.[83]

Shirley then began preparations for war. The people of Massachusetts were in a contentious mood and gave the governor the support he needed.

As one contemporary Massachusetts orator put it, the French and English "must meet at length. . . . The continent is not wide enough for us both."[84] In August 1753 King George instructed the colonial governors to defend English territory but enjoined them "most strictly . . . not to make use of armed force . . . except within the undoubted limits of his Majesty's dominions."[85] In Governor Shirley's view, those limits included Acadia. That winter he began to build up Maine's defenses and formed six "Indian companies"—probably made up of Massachusetts Indian militia—in preparation for attacks by the French and their Native allies. In March 1754, Shirley used rumors of a new French fort on the headwaters of the Kennebec to argue for the construction of a fort and an English settlement on the Kennebec River above Norridgewock.[86]

In the end, Shirley built his northernmost outpost, Fort Halifax, at present-day Winslow on the site of the former Clark and Lake truck house and within the limits of the large land grant made by a local Indian in 1648. Construction of the fort caused minor Indian raiding to resume, and in September 1754 a large force, mostly from the St. Lawrence missions, but including at least one Penobscot, attacked Fort Halifax, killing or capturing five men. It is not clear whether any Norridgewocks were involved in this action, but when the English scout James Cargill led a party up the Kennebec in the summer of 1756 he encountered no Indians at the village, for they had withdrawn to the St. Lawrence, where they were very likely among the many Abenakis who fought with the French on Lake Champlain and elsewhere. Thereafter, although some Norridgewocks moved to the Penobscot region, others returned to the Kennebec, where the Anglican minister Jacob Bailey later reported from Richmond that "a great number of Indians frequent this neighborhood. They are the remains of the ancient Norridgewock Tribe and lead a rambling life."[87]

When raiding resumed in the spring of 1755, the Massachusetts House of Representatives declared war on all Indians east of the Piscataqua, "the Penobscot Tribe only Excepted."[88] Although some accounts indicate Penobscot participation in the raids, Shirley perceived them as still generally committed to Dummer's treaty, and indeed there is evidence that the Penobscots were trying to restrain neighboring groups from engaging in hostilities.[89] The expanding English settlements, however, were becoming more hostile, and in June, Captain Jabez Bradbury, then in command at St. Georges, reported that an armed party "acted directly Contrary to the Gover[ns] Declaration of Warr & his directions to me" by threatening a delegation of Penobscot elders then in conference at the fort. Unsettled by these

developments, this longtime veteran of Indian affairs on the eastern frontier added the postscript: "I intreat your Excellency as I have more than
once already, that I may be dismisd from my Charge here."[90]

The Penobscots' position was a difficult one. Massachusetts insisted that
they take up arms even against fellow Indians who continued to be hostile
to the English. The governor of New France, Ange de Menneville, Marquis
Duquesne, on the other hand, considered them the "mainstay of the colony";
when they did not begin raiding he called them "Englishmen" and threatened to attack them. As a result, many Penobscots tried to avoid conflict by
withdrawing from the St. Georges area, which Massachusetts interpreted
as a preparation for raiding, making it impossible for them to return to the
coast for badly needed supplies.[91]

In July 1755 militiaman James Cargill persuaded members of the garrison at St. Georges to join him in pursuit of hostile Indians. Cargill led the
party to Owls Head, on the west side of Penobscot Bay, where they attacked two unsuspecting camps of peaceful Penobscots, killing twelve and
taking their scalps, for which Cargill requested bounties upon his return to
the fort. Massachusetts expressed outrage, but subsequent raids by warriors from the St. Lawrence mission villages, in which the English suspected
Penobscot participation, tempered their conciliatory sentiments. In November 1755, when other Penobscots refused to join the English in raiding
fellow Indians, Lieutenant Governor Spencer Phips declared war on them—
and on those on the St. John as well—issuing scalp bounties. Cargill was
then released from jail, given the rank of captain of militia and sent back
out on patrols near St. Georges.[92]

A further threat to Maine's Native population was the expulsion of most
of the eighteen thousand French settlers in Acadia ordered by Nova Scotia
governor Charles Lawrence in September 1755. This event, which was memorialized in Longfellow's epic poem *Evangeline*, surely made the English
threat to remaining Indian territories loom large.

Once war was declared on them, the Penobscots had various reactions.
Some continued to occupy their upriver villages, while others moved to
the St. John or even farther east. Those who remained committed to the
war operated out of the St. Lawrence mission villages. Penobscots, for example, were prominent among the "3000 savages from 33 different nations"
who fought with Louis-Joseph, Marquis de Montcalm, during the battle
for the Albany-Montreal corridor.[93] It was there that they took revenge for
Cargill's murders at Owls Head by playing a prominent role in the massacre, memorialized in James Fenimore Cooper's *The Last of the Mohicans*,
of English soldiers and civilians to whom Montcalm had given safe pas-

sage following his capture of Fort William Henry on Lake George in August 1757. To one survivor this massacre was "ye Two Most Sorrowful Day[s] that Ever were known to N[ew] England." In Nova Scotia, Maliseet and Micmac raiders harassed fledgling English settlements throughout the winter of 1755, forcing Governor Lawrence to declare war against them and to offer scalp bounties the next spring.[94]

Those Indians who had remained in Maine during this period initiated peace negotiations in February 1757. Phips responded by renewing an earlier demand that those who wanted peace must move to St. Georges, where they could be distinguished from hostile elements. Refusing to move, these Indians were immediately pursued by English militia. In retaliation, the Indians killed 11 and captured 8 settlers from outlying settlements. In the spring of 1758, war parties from the St. Lawrence mission villages again conducted raids in the Kennebec Valley and St. Georges areas, killing 24 settlers and capturing 36. Then a large force of over 250 Penobscots and Maliseets and 50 French militiamen, which had been operating to the east of the St. John River, turned west to attack St. Georges. Forewarned, the garrison withstood the assault and the attackers turned their attention to surrounding settlements. In February 1759, Penobscots again appeared at St. Georges to petition for peace. Thomas Pownal was now the governor of Massachusetts, having replaced Phips upon his death in 1757. Suspicious that Penobscots had been involved in the raids of the previous year, Pownal continued Phips's policy of offering peace and protection only to those willing to live near the English.[95]

The war wound down during the summer of 1759. As the English defeated French forces around the world, they also pressed toward Quebec City. To neutralize New France's Native allies, Lord Jeffrey Amherst, commander of the British forces in North America, ordered Robert Rogers and his Rangers to destroy Arasagunticook, the main Abenaki village in the St. Lawrence Valley. During the attack the Indians gave as good as they got, losing thirty people but killing forty Rangers. Nevertheless, following the raid the population of the village declined as people returned to their original homes between Lake Champlain and the Penobscot River.[96] As the Seven Years' War drew to a close, the Penobscots had gained the trust of neither the French nor the English. In March 1759 they had written to Pownal: "We have been very ill treated by the French. They have slain four of our People which we sent to Canada last fall to get some supplys. The French say we are English men, and that if we meet with Englishmen, we pass by them so they will give no supplies." When Pownal met with them at St. Georges in May, however, he accused them of being spies for the French, rebuked them for the raids of the previous year, offered them no assistance, and took one messenger hostage. He then formally took possession of what he considered to be captured territory on the Penobscot River as far as the head of tide in present-day Eddington and began laying plans for a new fort at the river's mouth. These actions would provide the basis for Massachusetts's contention following the Revolutionary War that the Penobscots had no claim to aboriginal territory because they had lost it by conquest as allies of the French during the war.[97]

A Flood of Settlers

British forces led by General James Wolfe defeated the French army battalions led by Montcalm at Quebec City on September 3, 1759, and the last French forces surrendered near Montreal a year later. In Maine, as tensions eased, many Natives returned from the St. Lawrence region. In February 1760, Maliseets on the St. John River and at Passamaquoddy Bay agreed to a separate truce with Governor Lawrence of Nova Scotia. Essentially, they once again agreed to reinstate Dummer's treaty but were not forced to move near the settlements. Instead, they agreed to provide three hostages on an ongoing basis in return for a government-sponsored truck house. These events encouraged the Penobscots to approach Brigadier General Jedediah Preble, commander at the newly built Fort Pownal, requesting terms similar to those granted the Maliseets. Preble refused, still insisting on their resettlement near the English. When Francis Bernard became governor of Massachusetts in 1760, the resettlement requirement was lifted and there began a series of negotiations that sought to normalize relations between Massachusetts and the Penobscots. A consistent theme of these negotiations was placing limits on the expansion of English settlements.[98]

The Seven Years' War was concluded by the Treaty of Paris, signed by England and France in 1763. With France's dominion in North America ended, the British Crown issued a proclamation stating that "Nations or Tribes of Indians with whom We are connected and who live under Our Protection should not be molested or disturbed in the Possession of . . . their Hunting Grounds." The proclamation was interpreted as applying only to the newly captured region formerly controlled by the French, which lay to the north and west of the English colonies. As a result, Indians of the Maritime Peninsula had no legal means of stemming the further erosion of their territories by encroaching English settlement.[99]

From 1713, when France lost control of Acadia, until the fall of New France in 1763, the English had claimed control of the entire Maritime Peninsula except for Cape Breton Island, but the proximity of Indians sympathetic to the French had greatly impeded their settlement there. In January 1759, Governor Lawrence issued a proclamation providing generous terms, even stipulating religious freedom for Protestants of all sects, for any who would settle in Nova Scotia. None would, and in 1763 there were still no British settlers in Nova Scotia aside from those at Halifax and a few at the mouth of the St. John River. So tenuous was his control over the province that newly appointed governor Montague Wilmot advocated continuing the French practice of providing annual presents to the Indians.[100]

8-19. Advertisement published in 1754 by the proprietors of the Kennebec Purchase to attract settlers. Frankfurt is modern-day Dresden. (Maine State Museum collection.)

ADVERTISEMENT.

WHEREAS the *Proprietors of the* Kennebeck *Purchase from the late Colony of* Plymouth, *have made and are making divers Settlements on* Kennebeck-River, *particularly at* Frankfort *near* Richmond : *For the Encouragement whereof the said Proprietors have voted to make a Grant of One Hundred Acres of Land to every Family who shall settle there* ; *of which they hereby give publick Notice : And any Person or Persons inclining to settle may apply to the Committee of said Proprietors, who will shew them a Plan of said River and Land, and let them know the Conditions of Settlement :*

And to encourage People hereto, the said Committee hereby inform them, that at the said Town of *Frankfort,* there is a Saw-Mill & a Grist-Mill erected, and about Forty Families settled, who notwithstanding they went there so lately as in the Spring of 1752, have been able the past Year to raise nearly a Sufficiency of every Thing to maintain themselves ; and this present Year will stand in Need of no Assistance, having clear'd a considerable Quantity of Land, and found that it is capable of producing in great Plenty every Thing which this Climate is adapted to : And besides the Advantage of a rich Soil, is situated on a fine Navigable River, which has furnished the said Settlers with a Market for their Wood, by the Sale of which they have been paid considerable for their Labour in clearing the Land.

The Land intended to be granted is no Way inferior either in Respect of it's Quality or Situation to that already settled.

The Subscribers who are the Committee of the said Proprietors, may be treated with in *Boston.*

Boston,
Jan. 2. 1754.

Robert Temple,
Sylvester Gardiner,
Benjamin Hollowell, } Committee.
William Bowdoin,
James Bowdoin.

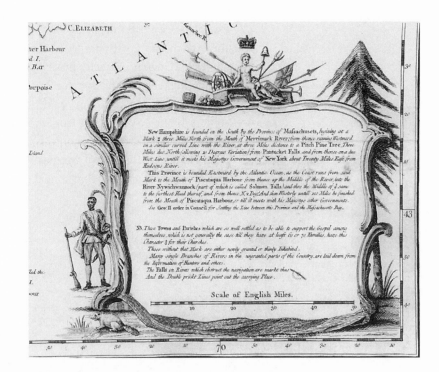

8-20. After the fall of New France, Indians of the Northeast began to be seen in a less threatening light, and images of them began to appear as decorative elements, as on the cartouche of this *Map of the Province of New Hampshire* by Joseph Blanchard and Samuel Langdon, published at Portsmouth in 1761. (Collections of the Maine State Library, NE-761B1001.)

In Maine, however, the flow of settlers that had begun in the 1720s after Queen Anne's War swelled to a flood. Established settlements grew larger, and new ones sprang up eastward along the coast and up river valleys. A small Native population had returned to Norridgewock following King George's War, but by 1764, with English settlement rapidly moving up the Kennebec, they threatened to "stop up the River and block up the fort (Halifax)." That same year Penobscots threatened to "rise against the English" while "The Passamaquoddy indians have also declared that they will not suffer any English to go up their Rivers." The pressure of increased English settlement was felt to some degree as far away as Cape Breton, but clearly the greatest impact was felt by the Penobscots.[101]

Initially, Native concerns were not so much with colonists wanting to settle on their lands as with those wanting to hunt on them. Unlike settlers prior to King Philip's War, who confined their activities to farming and fishing on the coast, marginal male members of newly established settlements began to compete with Native people for game. Massachusetts governor Francis Bernard understood the problem clearly, telling the House of Representatives in 1764: "It seems to me that all the uneasines of the Indians arises from two things, the Settling of the English and their Hunting; which indeed are but one cause, as they fear the one only because it is productive of the other. And indeed they have great reason to be alarmed at the extension of English Hunting; their very existence depends upon its not being permitted; and it is with great justice they complain how hard it is that the English who have many ways of living will interfere with the indians in the only business by which they subsist."[102] One of the worst areas of competition was around Fort Pownal at the mouth of the Penobscot River in present-day Stockton Springs. A year earlier, Penobscots told Bernard: "The Sold^rs of the Gar[rison] hunt & other People, Strangers that we do not know. We have desired Brigr^r Preble to prevent it—He sends them out a hunting instead of preventing them. We desire you would inquire into this matter."[103]

Added to this threat was an even worse one: the intense hostility of the new settlers. The Wiscassett murders of 1749 and the weak governmental response to them are early examples of this menace. Throughout the 1760s and early 1770s this hostility led repeatedly to murders of Indians and to thefts of their property, primarily by hunters. Most of these crimes went unpunished. One outraged one Indian railed: "if ye English is Determined to steel their Lives away by peace meals, for ye sake of Hunting, they say it's better for them to Die lick men, then to be kill'd lick Dogs . . . it would be as easey for them as ye English . . . to Steel as many lives . . . and perhaps maney more."[104]

The government of Massachusetts was not insensitive to these complaints, in part because of pressure from potential settlers wary of moving to the Penobscot so long as the threat of Indian attack remained. In 1763 Governor Bernard prohibited the soldiers at Fort Pownal from hunting beaver, and in February 1764 Massachusetts enacted a law prohibiting settlers east of Saco from hunting outside the towns where they resided. That June Bernard sent the surveyor Joseph Chadwick to map Massachusetts's newly secured territory between Penobscot Bay and Quebec and to place a mark limiting English settlement to the area below the falls at present-day Bangor. At the time, most Penobscots were living at Old Town, but some had taken up residence thirty kilometers upstream at New Town (Passadumkeag).[105]

Governor Bernard's prohibition of further settlement above the head of tide in effect secured the interior for the Penobscots until the end of the Revolutionary War in 1783.[106] Tensions remained, however, and later that year Captain Thomas Goldthwait, commander at Fort Pownal, was forced to respond to a Penobscot complaint that hunters were operating on Quantabacook Pond in present-day Searsmont and Morrill. Goldthwait notified the leader, one Hans Robinson, that "There is a law against english hunting at all but it is hardly yet in force, still I cannot but hope that you are so frindly to the Commonwealth that you won't give the Indians any just cause of complaint the little advantage you may make will be poor compensation to you if by this means you should be the Authors of disturbing the peace and quiet of your Country." Robinson responded, "we would be very glad you would tell the Indians thate would hunt upon the pond that we were upon it first and there was no Signs of any Indians upon it when we came here . . . as we were here first we think it is our Right to hunt here." Hans Robinson was one of James Cargill's companions in the massacre at Owls Head in 1755.[107]

Since Dummer's War, the Penobscot region was a refuge for many Indians who had given up trying to live near the growing English settlements to the south and west. In a 1767 meeting with Governor Bernard in Boston, Espeguent, a Penobscot elder, expressed his people's plight as follows: "We are not acquainted with Husbandry, nor Arts, sufficient to get our living by, and if we have not a sufficiency of Land assigned to us, for our use only, to Hunt in, We and our Wives and our Children must perish." Later in the meeting, another Penobscot stated that "as hunting is daily decreasing we would be glad of a tract of land assigned to us for a Township settled upon us and our posterity for the purposes of husbandry." The fact that the Penobscots were willing to accept the notions of a territory defined by a township and an economy defined by subsistence farming reflects how much autonomy they had lost. In the years leading to the Revolutionary War, they and other Indians of the Maritime Peninsula would see the landscape fill rapidly with European settlers—English, German, Scots, Irish, and French Huguenots—and their place in the emerging new order reduced to marginality.[108]

EPILOGUE

Land, Politics, and Survival to the Present

T HIS BOOK has traced the history of the Native peoples of the Maine region from earliest times to the capitulation of New France, an event that set the stage for a new cultural order in the region. This story should not end, however, without briefly tracing the subsequent history of these peoples, whose descendents still live in their original homelands in Maine, Quebec, and the Maritimes. That history really begins with the American Revolution, and it would require a separate volume. What follows is merely a sketch of that history to the present day.

The American Revolution (1776–1883)

As the American Revolution approached, Indians throughout the Northeast, from Caughnawaga to Cape Breton Island, found themselves courted by both Loyalists and Colonials hopeful of winning their support—or at least their neutrality. Initially, the Continental Congress was more interested in their neutrality, resolving in November 1775 "That the indians of St. Francis, Penobscot, Stockbridge (Massachusetts), and St. John, and other tribes, may be called on in case of real necessity, and that giving them presents is both suitable and proper."[1]

When the Continental Congress approved General George Washington's request to recruit among them in July 1776, Native responses reflected their differing attitudes toward the rebellious Whigs of New England and New York versus the Loyalists to their east and north. On the St. Lawrence River, those formerly allied with the French were unsure about where to place their loyalties, but under the influence of the Caughnawaga Mohawks and the St. Francis Abenakis, most initially resisted the recruiting efforts of the

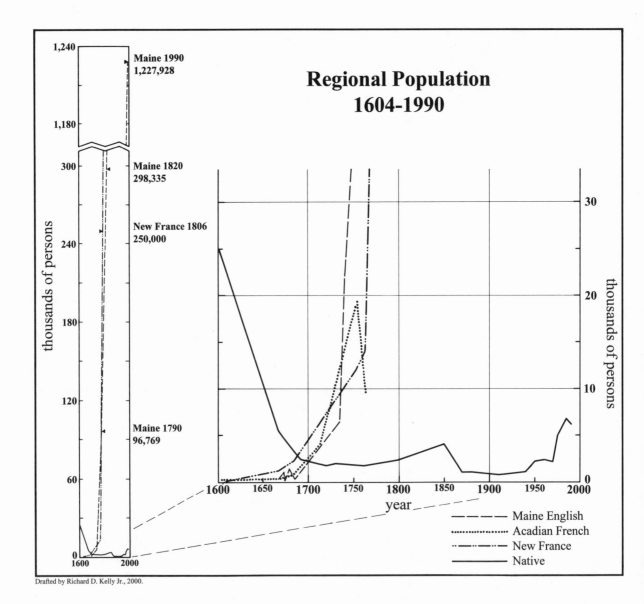

**Regional Population
1604-1990**

Maine 1990
1,227,928

Maine 1820
298,335

New France 1806
250,000

Maine 1790
96,769

thousands of persons

thousands of persons

year

Maine English
Acadian French
New France
Native

Drafted by Richard D. Kelly Jr., 2000.

E-1. Regional population, 1604–1990

British and either remained neutral or volunteered to fight with the Colonials.[2]

While many, perhaps most, of those who had formerly occupied the interior villages between Norridgewock and Pigwacket moved to the St. Lawrence following the Seven Years' War, it is clear that many remained in the area, particularly around Bethel and Fryeburg. One man with a reputation as a leader was Paul Higgins, an English captive who grew up among the Natives. Higgins went to visit Washington in Cambridge, Massachu-

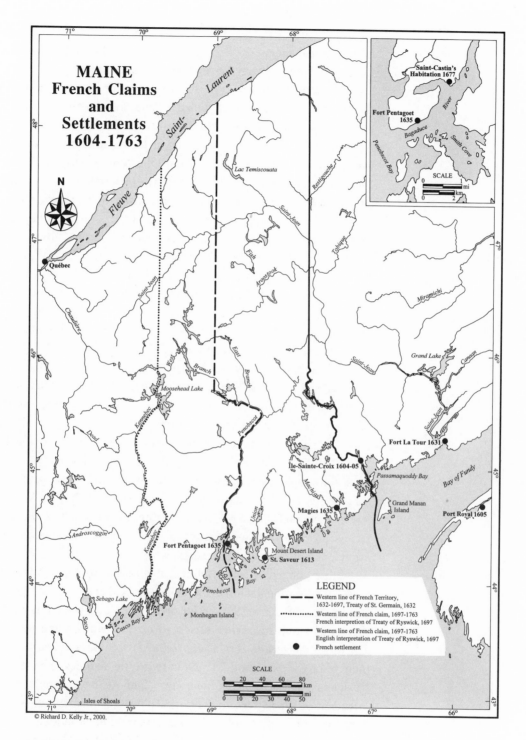

Maine: French claims and settlements, 1604-1763. The following labels appear on the map:

MAINE
French Claims
and
Settlements
1604-1763

N

Québec

Fleuve Saint-Laurent

Lac Temiscouata

Restigouche

Saint-Jean

Fish

Aroostook

Tobique

Miramichi

Chaudière

Saint-Jean

West Branch

East Branch

Moosehead Lake

Penobscot

Grand Lake

Canaan

Saint-Jean

Saint-Jean

Fort La Tour 1631

Île-Sainte-Croix 1604-05

Passamaquoddy Bay

Bay of Fundy

Machias

Grand Manan Island

Magies 1635

Port Royal 1605

Androscoggin

Kennebec

Dead

Fort Pentagoet 1635

Union

Mount Desert Island

St. Saveur 1613

Sebago Lake

Penobscot Bay

Saco

Casco Bay

Monhegan Island

Isles of Shoals

Inset (upper right):

Saint-Castin's Habitation 1677

Fort Pentagoet 1635

Penobscot Bay

Bagaduce River

Smith Cove

SCALE
0   1 mi
0   2 km

LEGEND

- — — Western line of French Territory, 1632-1697, Treaty of St. Germain, 1632
- • • • • • Western line of French claim, 1697-1763 French interpretion of Treaty of Ryswick, 1697
- ——— Western line of French claim, 1697-1763 English interpretation of Treaty of Ryswick, 1697
- ● French settlement

SCALE
0   20   40   60   80 km
0 10 20 30 40 50 mi

© Richard D. Kelly Jr., 2000.

E-2. Maine: French claims and
settlements, 1604–1763

setts, in the summer of 1775 to declare his support for the Colonials against his traditional enemy, the British Crown. Other Abenaki volunteers from the area included Sergeant Lewey from St. Francis and Captains Philip and Swarson from Pigwacket. Others from this group, however, fought with the British, including a chief named Tomhegan, who, in 1781, led a small party of St. Francis Abenakis in raids on Bethel and other upper Androscoggin towns, killing and scalping three and capturing three.[3]

Penobscot chiefs Joseph Orono and John Neptune also visited Massachusetts during the summer of 1775 to declare their support for the Colonials and request relief from settlers who were cutting timber on what they considered to be their land.[4] In return, the Provincial Congress of Massachusetts, meeting west of Boston at Watertown while British forces occupied Boston, promised them a truck house on the Penobscot and passed the Watertown Convention, part of which was intended to "strictly forbid any person or persons whatsoever from trespassing or making waste upon any of the lands and territories or possessions beginning at the head of the tide on Penobscot River, extending six miles on each side of the said river now claimed by our brethren the Indians of the Penobscot Tribe."[5]

In September, Maliseet chiefs Ambroise Saint-Aubin and Pierre Toma wrote to Washington claiming to speak for both the Maliseets and Micmacs, "[We] heartily join with our brethren the Penobscot Indians in everything they have or shall agree with our Brethren of the Colony of Massachusetts." In February 1776, Washington answered their letter, offering them a "chain of Friendship," and Massachusetts responded favorably to their request for supplies, which they asked be sent to the Penobscots on their behalf. They then conducted raids on Loyalists in the St. John Valley. Following these raids, seven Micmacs and three Maliseets paid a visit to Massachusetts, where they reluctantly signed a treaty that called upon them to provide warriors in return for supplies.[6]

A delegation led by Saint-Aubin visited Massachusetts in July, offering to join the Continental forces but emphasizing that their service would be strongly dependent on the receipt of supplies, thus implying that those previously sent eastward had been inadequate. Before leaving, they signed a "Treaty of Alliance and Friendship" with Massachusetts, which called upon them to provide six hundred men in return for supplies to be sent to the truck house at Machias.[7] In January 1777, John Allan was appointed superintendent of the Eastern Indians and colonel of infantry, and sent eastward to recruit Native and settler support on the St. John River. In May he attempted to establish a truck house, but by July he and his Native allies were forced to retreat to Machias by British troops sent from Halifax.[8]

E-3a–b. Silver medal showing George Washington and, on the reverse, an Indian sitting under a stylized Tree of Liberty with thirteen hands representing the thirteen colonies. This medal was one of the presents John Allan gave to the Maliseets in 1778 that they turned over to the British. (Courtesy of the British Museum.)

Allan continued to solicit volunteers among the Maliseets from his base at Machias, and in July 1778 he visited their village near present-day St. Andrew's, New Brunswick, to pass out presents. To each of the "War Captains" he presented a silver medal with an engraved image of George Washington. Thereafter, however, a split developed between Saint-Aubin and Pierre Toma. The Micmacs, too, were of divided loyalties, for they lived closest to the British garrisons. France's entry into the war on the Colonial side in 1778 encouraged some Micmacs to declare their support for the colonies. Others, however, along with Pierre Toma's Maliseets, attended a conference on the St. John in September where they gave to Nova Scotia superintendent of Indian Affairs Michael Francklin their copy of the Watertown treaty and Allan's presents to them and signed a nonaggression treaty with the British.[9]

In the end, Washington did not request that Indians serve *en masse*.[10] In 1782 Allan listed fifty-one Penobscots, forty-six Passamaquoddies, fifty-one Maliseets, and thirty-nine Micmacs as having "Been in the Service of the United States," but few had played an active role in the war, and those who did fight seem to have made the decision on personal grounds.[11] Fifteen Maliseets and four Micmacs fought with Colonel Jonathan Eddy in his attempt to capture British Fort Cumberland near present-day Sackville, New

AN ABENAKI AT VALLEY FORGE

The following excerpt is from a letter written in 1837 by noted French lawyer and intellectual Peter Stephen Du Ponceau, reflecting upon his service as a young man at Valley Forge during the American Revolution. There he served as translator to Freidrich Wilhelm von Steuben, the German who did so much to transform Washington's raw recruits into an effective army.[12] Du Ponceau's letter is notable not only for the glimpse it provides of one Abenaki's musical accomplishments and involvement in the Revolution but also for his insistence upon defining his relationship with Du Ponceau in terms of the old Algonquian-French alliance, fifteen years after the fall of New France.

Another anecdote now strikes my mind, which relates to the first Indian that I saw in the United States. . . . It was at Valley Forge, in the spring of 1778. . . . I was walking one morning before breakfast, in a wood, not far from our quarters, when I heard at a distance a French fashionable opera song, sung by a most powerful voice, which the echoes reverberated. . . .

I cannot describe to you how my feelings were affected by hearing those strains so pleasing and so familiar to me, sung by what seemed to me a supernatural voice, such as I had never heard before, and yet melodious and in perfect good taste. I thought myself for a moment at the Comédé Italiene, and was lost in astonishment, when suddenly I saw appear before me a tall Indian figure in American regimentals and two large epaulettes on his shoulders, my surprise was extreme. I advanced towards him and told him in French *you sing beautifully, Sir*, on this he also appeared astonished, he extended his hand towards me saying *Ah! My father, you are French; I am very happy to see you; We love the French, why did they abandon us?* I was struck with this salutation and particularly with his calling me his father. *It is you*, said I, *who is my father, I am only a young man. Ah!* replied he, *all the French are our fathers, It is thus that we call them, the others are only our brothers.* Then he began to explain to me that the English wanted them also to call them *fathers*, but that the Indians would not consent; the French alone were their fathers. He next asked me a number of questions about the King, the Queen, the royal family and whether they did not mean to reconquer Canada. I thought he [the king of France] never would have done.

The conversation, however, took another turn, and he began to tell me who he was. *I am*, said he, *an Indian of the nation of Abenakis.* . . . He then told me that he had served the United States in the ill-fated invasion of Canada under Montgomery and that when our army retreated he had followed them, and had obtained here the rank of Colonel, "here I am called," said he, "*Colonel Louis; it is the name that I received at baptism, because*," added he, "*I am a good Christian and good Catholic.*" While this conversation was going on we reached the Baron's quarters, who received him cordially and invited him to breakfast. After the repast was over, I again had a long conversation with him, in which he told me that he had been educated by the Jesuits of whom he spoke with great respect. They had taught him reading and writing and many other things which he enumerated. He had some knowledge of vocal music and I am convinced that with a little more teaching, he would have been a valuable acquisition to the French Opera, where I have never heard a voice of such extraordinary power, and at the same time susceptible of modulation. I heard he was in the service of the United States, and had the rank of Colonel. In what manner he was employed, or what became of him afterwards I never knew. All I can say is that I parted with him with much regret, and never saw him since.

Brunswick; sixty Penobscots, Passamaquoddies, and Maliseets helped defend Machias against British attack in August 1777; and Penobscots fought with Captain John Preble in an attempt to dislodge the British from Castine in 1779. Finally, in September 1779 Micmacs began raiding Loyalists living on the Miramichi River in northeastern New Brunswick. The Abenakis of the St. Lawrence and Lake Champlain Valleys also remained divided and indecisive in their loyalties. Many left Canada to seek refuge in their hunting territories in northern New England. However, one estimate is that as many as two hundred had served the British during the war. Others fought with the Continental Army when it attacked Quebec City in December 1775.[13]

After the Revolution

The Abenakis

As many as five hundred Abenakis remained on the upper Androscoggin and Saco Rivers into the late eighteenth century, one of whom was Molliocket (Marie Agathe), an herbalist of some repute among Natives and settlers alike. Despite the land rush that followed the end of the Revolutionary War, some Abenakis continued to live near English settlements in southern and western Maine into the early nineteenth century, particularly around Lake Cobbosseecontee in Winthrop and Manchester and around Lake Androscoggin in Leeds. And as late as the 1840s, a small community of Penobscots, perhaps accompanied by a number of Abenakis, lived near Fryeburg on the Saco River. All these communities maintained close ties to the Abenakis of St. Francis, Quebec, where many of their numbers eventually settled. Some Abenakis returned to Maine in the 1840s to work in the expanding timber industry as it moved into the interior. Two from Greenville served in the Civil War, and the descendents of others still live in Maine.[14]

The Penobscots

The British proclamation of 1763 did not recognize the territorial integrity of Indian communities living within its American colonies, and this policy was continued by Washington when he was inaugurated in 1789. The Penobscots nevertheless hoped that their allegiance to the Colonial cause would protect their remaining lands from seizure by the Americans at the end of the war. This was not to be, however, for Massachusetts did not consider the Watertown Resolve a land grant and began to encourage settlement between the Penobscot and St. Croix Rivers.[15] Although Indian Island Oldtown remained an important Penobscot village throughout the later half of the eighteenth century, as settlers began to move into the lower Penobscot Valley, Penobscots began to move upriver. Recall that at the end of the Seven Years' War, Joseph Chadwick's 1764 survey found them living at Oldtown and Passadumkeag; farther upriver he found Mattawamkeag, formerly their refuge in times of war, nearly abandoned. Occupation was still concentrated between Oldtown and Passadumkeag in 1786, but in 1793 Park Holland's survey found no one living at Passadumkeag, the population having shifted upriver to Mattawamkeag, where he found a "large Indian town, full of inhabitants." At both Oldtown and Mattawamkeag, Penobscots expressed their suspicion of Park Holland's motives and tried to dissuade him from proceeding up the river.[16]

In their dealings with Massachusetts, the Penobscots continued to insist that the Watertown Resolve had indeed granted them title to the six miles on either side of the river above the head of tide, and they repeatedly refused the government's attempts to get them to sign a quitclaim deed to the area. In 1796 the Penobscots did sign a treaty with Massachusetts in

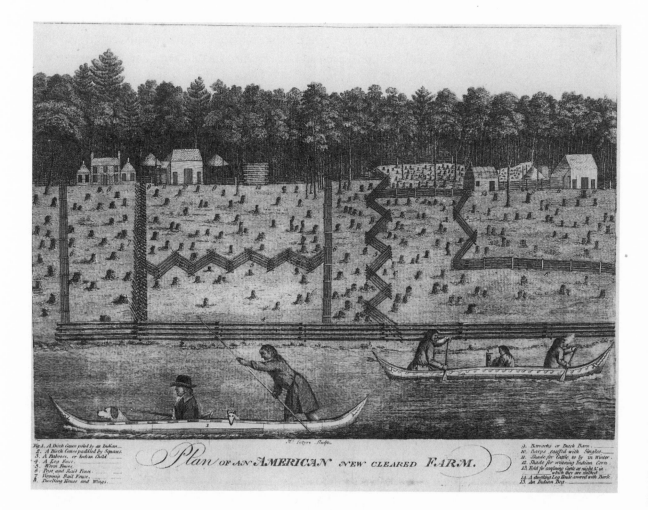

Fig 1. A Birch Canoe poled by an Indian.
2. A Birch Canoe paddled by Squaws.
3. A Papoose, or Indian Child.
4. A Log Fence.
5. Worm Fence.
6. Post and Rail Fence.
7. Virginia Rail Fence.
8. Dwelling House and Wings.

Plan OF AN *AMERICAN* NEW CLEARED *FARM.*

9. Barracks or Dutch Barn.
10. Barns roofed with Singles.
11. Shade for Cattle to ly in Winter.
12. Shade for weaning Indian Corn.
13. Fold for confining Cattle at night &c. at which they are milked.
14. A dwelling Log House covered with Bark.
15. An Indian Dog.

E-5. Penobscots paddling a graceful canoe, 1829. These sketches by Titian Ramsay Peale illustrate his guides on a hunting trip to the Penobscot River. See Peale 1830. (Courtesy of the American Philosophical Society.)

which they were granted title to the islands in the river for thirty miles above Oldtown and an annuity consisting of corn, powder, shot, and cloth. However, they continued to insist that all land from Oldtown northward to Canada was theirs and that they were merely granting permission for others to settle there, not to selling it outright.[17]

Their assertions were of little avail, however, and new settlements continued to appear. By 1807 Massachusetts governor James Sullivan remarked, "their subsistence from hunting is entirely at an end, and subverted by the settlements around and between them and the wilderness toward Canada. Their support from fishing has much decreased, and will continue to decrease in proportion as this country is settled by white people."[18] Under pressure from Massachusetts, in 1818 the Penobscots finally ceded to Massachusetts all but the islands in the river in return for a payment of four hundred dollars, a continuation of the annuity granted in 1796, and four townships, amounting to 216 square miles, between Mattawamkeag and Millinocket.[19] When surveyor Joseph Treat laid out the boundaries of these townships after Maine became a state in 1820, he encountered Penobscots still living far upriver. At Mattawamkeag, however, he made special mention of the prosperous farm of Chief John Attean. A decade later, the painter Titian Ramsey Peale found the upriver islands still well settled.[20]

In 1833 the Penobscots sold their upriver townships to the state, and in 1835 the legislature ordered that their remaining lands between Oldtown and Mattawamkeag be divided into lots and assigned to individual

VILLAGES AND HOUSING DURING THE EARLY NINETEENTH CENTURY

The best description of an early-nineteenth-century Native village in Maine—in this case the Penobscot village at Indian Island—appeared in 1816 in a Boston newspaper:

The village is compact and containing near thirty wigwams all standing on one street and most of them so near together as to have only a narrow passageway between. Each wigwam is constructed according to the Gothic form with gable end towards the street, is one story high, twenty or thirty feet long and half as wide. The plates and ridge pole are supported by notches.

None of the wigwams have any glass windows and the entrance to them is through a narrow aperture without any door hinges. Within is a board or plank platform on each side, next the wall, a foot or more above the ground, three or four feet in width, between these platforms the ground is bare. Here it is the fires are built without any chimney, a hole only being left for the smoke through the roof, four families frequently live in one of these wigwams, one at each corner, a fire serving two of them. On the platform they sit not unlike a tailor on his shop board, there they sleep without any other bedding than a few blankets; there they eat their food in their fingers. They have nothing like a chair or a moveable bench. A few iron and wooden vessels for cooking and a few baskets are all the furniture they have.

This account could equally well have referred to the depiction of Meductic as it is seen in a watercolor by Captain J. Campbell that bears the title "View of the Indian Village (Meductic) on the River St. John above Fredericton 1832" (Fig. E-6). Note the pole-framed houses. It also describes well the view of a Maliseet house interior shown in Figure E-7, probably also at Meductic. It is likely that the early layout and architecture of the Passamaquoddy village of Sipayik, at present-day Pleasant Point in Perry, was also similar.[21]

Penobscot families. This sale was to have important legal implications during the twentieth century, but its immediate impact was to establish a trust fund for the Penobscots, which was to be administered by the state. At about the same time, the state also established a trust fund for the Passamaquoddies that was funded by proceeds from the sale of hay and timber from their lands. The proceeds from these sales, however, were largely consumed by the expense of supporting the state's Indian agent on the Penobscot reservation at Oldtown.[22]

Around 1826 the Penobscots split into two parties—the Old Party and the New Party—over a political rivalry between John Attean, the Mattawamkeag farmer and tribal governor, and the charismatic lieutenant governor, John Neptune. Neptune and his followers left Oldtown in 1832, moved downriver to Brewer, and did not return until about 1850. During their self-imposed exile, a different, cross-cutting conflict arose over Penobscot relations with the Anglo community that led to the formation of two political parties. One contentious issue was education. The New Party adhered to the policy of the Catholic missionaries among them, who, at the time, did not favor formal education of the sort provided by the

E-6. Watercolor by Captain J. Campbell that bears the title "View of the Indian Village (Meductic) on the River St. John above Fredericton 1832." (Courtesy of the National Archives of Canada, C-11-79.)

E-7. Interior of a pole-framed house. (Courtesy of the New Brunswick Museum, St. John NB.)

area's public schools, while the Old Party did. Strife between the parties had become so intense by 1839 that the Maine legislature intervened, initiating—with Penobscot approval—an electoral system whereby governors would hold office not for life (as formerly) but for two-year terms. Conflict continued, however, and in 1866 the legislature again intervened, establishing alternating terms of office for the two parties.[23]

By the 1840s industrial development in the Bangor area was burgeoning. Henry David Thoreau, writing of his travels in the Maine woods beginning in 1847, commented that even a decade earlier there were 250 sawmills between Bangor and Oldtown. The growing timber industry provided employment opportunities for the Penobscots, who began to concentrate near Oldtown. In 1836 Governor Attean moved to Lincoln from Mattawamkeag, which, when Thoreau visited it in 1847, had been taken over by white settlers.[24] Lincoln, however, where Thoreau hired a guide, still had a sizeable Penobscot population. During his last trip to the Penobscot in 1857, Thoreau noted isolated Penobscot houses on several islands below Lincoln, but he also commented that the population was

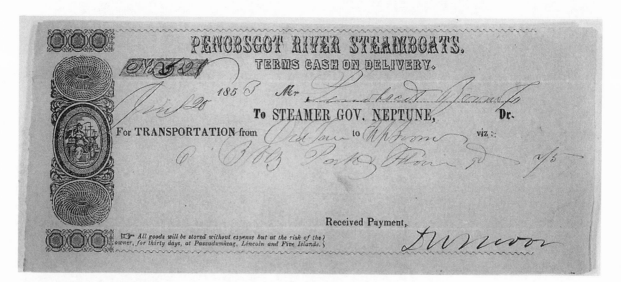

E-8. Ticket purchased on April 20, 1853, by the Penobscot Boom Company, a log driving operation, for transportation on the steamer John Neptune, then in service on the Penobscot River. The vessel was named after the controversial Penobscot lieutenant governor. (Maine State Museum collection.)

E-9a–c. *From top to bottom*, village scenes at Sipayik, Peter Dana Point (then called Lewis Island), and Indian Island. (Reproduced from Vetromile 1866.)

increasingly clustered at Oldtown. By the 1860s the Penobscots were well integrated into the timber industry, and one observer commented in 1863 that "Some very good river-drivers are found among them." The population increase noted by Thoreau, however, was also due in part to the immigration of Passamaquoddies and Maliseets, a trend that continued well into the twentieth century.[25]

Changing housing styles during the mid–nineteenth century reflected increasing Penobscot involvement in the larger community. In 1847 Thoreau described the village at Indian Island as reflecting the mobile lifestyle of a hunting people, but a decade later he noted several frame houses—in fact, by 1863 the entire population was living in frame houses. Thoreau made particular mention of one house that looked "as good as an average one on a New England street . . . surrounded by fruit-trees, single cornstalks standing thinly amid the beans." This was the house owned by Thoreau's guide, Joe Polis, who attended the Protestant church in Oldtown along with several other Penobscots and told Thoreau that his son was the best scholar at the local public school.[26]

An important factor driving these changes was the passage of Maine's early game laws. In 1850 large numbers of Abenaki hunters from Odanak

E-10. Penobscot silver brooches. The specimen to the left bears the mark of Jacob Bennett, who worked in Philadelphia between 1825 and 1850. The specimen to the right bears the mark of Jonathan Tyler, who was working in Montreal in 1817. (Maine State Museum collection.)

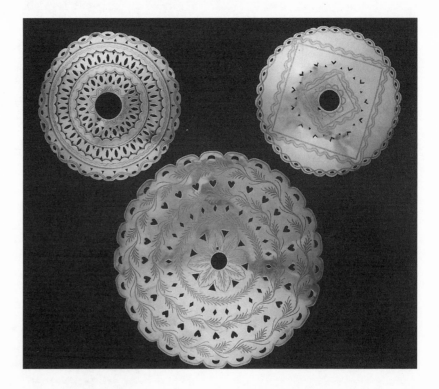

E-11. Early- to mid-nineteenth-century trade silver cuffs and a hat band or coronet. (Courtesy of the Bangor Historical Society.)

made "a great slaughter of moose" in northern Maine. To make matters worse, they took only the hides, leaving the carcasses. Penobscot hunters protested this massive waste of resources to the Maine legislature, which responded in 1852 by passing an act prohibiting "All foreign citizens and Indians belonging in the British provinces" from hunting deer or moose in Maine. Fearing that the herds were being depleted, however, in 1853 the legislature went on to prohibit hunting between April and October, thus establishing Maine's first hunting season. No exception was made for Indian hunters. These laws began a trend toward ever stricter limits on hunting and fishing, further curtailing traditional subsistence activities that had already been in decline since the beginning of the nineteenth century.[27]

One alternative to hunting that was encouraged by the Maine legislature was farming. Between 1839 and 1887 the state's budget consistently included funds to subsidize farming, and by 1863 one observer reported the "considerable success" of the Penobscots in this activity.[28] Thoreau described Polis, for example, as a man of substance who owned farmland and employed whites to tend his crops.[29] However, farming in the Oldtown area declined in general during the late nineteenth century.

In addition to increasing employment in the rapidly growing timber and sporting industries, the Penobscots were also engaged in the commercial production of wood and leather products such as canoes, paddles, snowshoes, moccasins, birchbark containers, and especially ash-splint baskets. Initially, these products were made for sale locally to the timber industry, sportsmen, and farmers. By the 1830s, however, throughout much of northeastern North America, commercial production of many utilitarian items began to decline as men became involved in other occupations. Women, on the other hand, became increasingly involved in making baskets, particularly "fancy baskets" of ash splints in a wide variety of ornate styles to

a

b

c

E-12a–c. Three early portraits of Native women. All are wearing beaver hats with broad silver headbands, silver brooches, and wampum necklaces: (a) Mary Balassee Nicola, known as Molly Molasses, a Penobscot, is shown here in a print dating from the mid–nineteenth century (Courtesy of the Old Town Museum); (b) Sarah Nicola, Mary's daughter, painted by Jeremiah Hardy in 1835 (Courtesy of the Tarratine Club); (c) Mary Mitchell Sopiel, a Passamaquoddy from Sipayik, photographed in the 1880s (Courtesy of the National Anthropological Archives, Smithsonian Institution, photo no. 74-8344.)

satisfy Victorian tastes. In Maine and the Maritime Provinces, utilitarian items such as snowshoes continued to be made, but the rise of Victorian summer resorts along lakeshores and the seacoast was creating a large new tourist-driven market for fancy baskets.[30] Of the 266 Penobscots listed in the federal census of 1910, women were almost exclusively basketmakers, while men were chiefly employed in the timber industry. With the rise of automotive travel, the large Victorian summer resorts declined in popularity. Nevertheless, women continued to make baskets for sale to vacationers passing through Oldtown. By 1942, however, basketmaking was in decline as other sources of income became more important and as changing tastes decreased the demand for fancy baskets.[31]

A brief account of the Penobscots, written by amateur ornithologist Montague Chamberlain in 1899, describes the main Penobscot village at Indian Island as made up of frame houses, including "the two-story dwelling of the modern American type," a dignified church, a "substantial and well-planned schoolhouse," and a home for the nuns who taught there. Economic activities still included guiding sportsmen, making baskets, snowshoes, and other wooden products and working in the timber industry.[32]

It is likely that at least some Penobscots fought in the Civil War, and certainly many were conscripted during World War I. During the depression many worked on the reservations for the Works Progress Administration, a federal job-creation program. Many also fought in World War II. By the 1940s several additional factors were increasing Penobscot interactions with the larger society. For example, after the war most able-bodied men held jobs off the reservations, though they tended to return to the reservations when work ran out. Most children attended public high school in Oldtown. As a result of these various factors, intermarriage with non-Indians, which had been discouraged during the early twentieth century, became more common, as did residence off the reservations.[33] The construction of a bridge linking Indian Island to the mainland in 1951 further opened the way for Penobscot integration with the non-Native population of Maine. One outcome of all this change was that the Penobscots increasingly adopted English in preference to their native language. The last Penobscot-speaker died in 1993; Passamaquoddy, however, is still spoken there by older people.[34]

The Passamaquoddies and Maliseets

The Maliseets, living astride the as-yet-undefined boundary between the western portion of Nova Scotia (New Brunswick after 1784) and Massachusetts, had split into pro-British and pro-Colonial factions during the

Revolutionary War. By that time those living near Passamaquoddy Bay were known as Passamaquoddies. Following the war, the pro-British faction, led by Pierre Toma, remained on the St. John River and continued to be referred to as Maliseets. The pro-Colonial faction, led by Ambroise Saint-Aubin, occupied the St. Croix River drainage in what was presumed to be American territory. Most Passamaquoddies lived at St. Andrews, New Brunswick, until 1784, when loyalists fleeing the United States occupied the area. Many then moved to Deer Island in Passamaquoddy Bay but left when the island was assigned to the British, moving westward into American territory. Most lived by hunting and fishing along the St. Croix River and among the islands of Passamaquoddy Bay. In the same area, however, lived other hunting peoples who intermingled and intermarried with them, so extensively in fact that John Allan commented in 1793: "A correspondence & intercourse have been open'd a long time, thro' the several tribes, Viz, from Penobscot St Francis in Canada & the whole of the Mickmac Country as far as [the Bay of] Chaleurs. . . . Thus connected there appears no distinction in the right of the several hunting grounds, for all by some tie or other have an equal claim, are fully domesticated as if natives of the district."[35]

By a 1794 treaty with Massachusetts, the Passamaquoddies ceded lands in the eastern part of Maine in return for title to a twenty-three-thousand-acre tract on the St. Croix River, which included a newly built village located on Lewis Island (Peter Dana Point) and a small plot at Sipayik. Despite their continuing preference for a mobile, hunting lifestyle, after the erection of a church at Sipayik in 1804 a settled, partially agricultural community began to coalesce around it. The village had become a substantial one by 1821, when the tribe's population stood at 379. By 1850 all the village's residents lived in frame houses.[36]

During the 1820s, Passamaquoddy politics were rent by a division mainly between the villagers at Sipayik and those who still lived a hunting life. As with the Penobscots, major issues included formal schooling—in this case provided by a Protestant missionary at Sipayik who was paid by the state—and economic engagement with the community of Eastport, principally concerning the sale of hay and timber on tribal lands. During the 1830s this split led to the formation of a traditional Old Party and the more village-oriented New Party.

As among the Penobscot, Passamaquoddy political leadership had been vested in a governor with life tenure. John Francis, son of previous governor Francis Joseph Neptune, held the office after his father's death in 1836. During the 1840s, however, the New Party attempted to change this system by proposing annual elections and electing a different governor. The Old Party boycotted the election, further dividing the tribe. The split became permanent in 1848. At Sipayik, John Francis remained governor for life, while the New Party moved to Peter Dana Point. In 1849 the Maine legislature approved the first of what would become annual expenditures from the tribe's trust fund of one hundred dollars for plowing and harrowing at this new community. A small group soon split off from it to form another at Calais, which survived into the early twentieth century when most of its residents moved to Sipayik. The Calais settlement is noteworthy mainly because it was there, in 1890, that Jesse Walter Fewkes of the Bureau of Indian Affairs made the first sound recordings of Native North American music.[37]

E-13. Ambrotype of an Indian river driver, probably a Penobscot, with caulked boots, which provided sure footing on floating logs as they were floated downriver to saw mills. 1860s. (Maine State Museum collection.)

E-14. Engraving of Passamaquoddy governor John Francis as he appeared in the *London Illustrated News* on September 5, 1863. He is wearing a military-style coat, traditional wool leggings, and a sash with the ends cut out in the shape of animal legs and a tail. His unusual-looking firearm is an under-hammer percussion rifle.

JOHN FRANCIS, CHIEF OF THE PASSAMAQUODDY INDIANS.

The economic activities of the Passamaquoddies from the mid–nineteenth century on resembled those of the Penobscots except for the persistence of traditional activities owing to the lack of industrial development in eastern Maine. As hunting declined during the mid–nineteenth century, the Passamaquoddies turned increasingly to the manufacture of wood products, including splint baskets. Situated near the fishing communities of Eastport and St. Andrews, New Brunswick, the Passamaquoddies of Sipayik also produced birchbark torches and herring sticks for herring fishermen. A rare set of statistics for 1884 tells us that those at Peter Dana Point earned $3,000 selling baskets wholesale to a local dealer, in addition to $600 for furs and $1,500 for ash hoop poles (to be split and bent to form hoops for splint-basket rims).[38] Like the Micmacs and Penobscots, some Passamaquoddies earned cash by hunting porpoise for the high-quality oil their blubber yielded. Around the turn of the century, however, cheaper petroleum-based lubricants took over the market for porpoise oil.[39] The state's subsidies for agriculture were less successful among the Passamaquoddies than they had been among the Penobscots. Of the 386 Passamaquoddies listed in the 1910 federal census, most men were basketmakers or timber workers, while women were exclusively basketmakers.

Another rare statistic tells us that fourteen Passamaquoddies fought in the Civil War. Many more served in World War I.[40] During the Depression Works Progress Administration jobs brought in significant income. Public high school attendance increased throughout the early twentieth century. Many Passamaquoddies participated in World War II, and after the war Passamaquoddy men generally worked off-reservation most of the time, although traditional economic pursuits like basketmaking, by men as well as women, continue to the present day. As among the Penobscots, off-reservation activities led to more frequent marriages with non-Indians.[41]

On the St. John River, a Maliseet village existed at Meductic, twelve miles below present-day Woodstock, New Brunswick, from at least 1686. It was located on the west bank of the river near the popular Eel River canoe portage that connected the St. John to the Penobscot River at Mattawamkeag. Before the fall of New France, Meductic was one of the series of "mission villages" stretching westward as far as Pigwacket that the French had supported as a line of defense against English attack. As at Norridgewock, a church had been constructed there with funds provided by King Louis XIV following Queen Anne's War.[42] It was completed by 1717, at which time the village's population stood at between 300 and 400 people. Population declined in the following decades, reaching a low point after the fall of New France. Following the Revolutionary War, when Loyalist settlers entered the area in 1783, Meductic was abandoned, its church was burned on the orders of its missionary, and its inhabitants apparently moved up the Saint John to Madawaska. But many must have returned, for a Loyalist-run school opened at Meductic in 1788. The school closed in 1794, to be replaced by a consolidated Indian college at Sussex, New Brunswick, that continued in operation until around 1835. The population of Meductic in 1792 was about 150 families in residence with another 100 visiting occasionally. An 1822 report stated that the Maliseets of Meductic "live mingled with about two hundred French families, in a village of about thirty wigwams, or lodges." By 1841, however, the village had once again declined to a few families, most of its residents having moved downriver to Aukpaque, at Springhill, near present-day Fredericton, New Brunswick, where there had been a Maliseet village since at least 1721.[43]

In the late eighteenth century, Aukpaque became the largest settlement until the area was taken over by Loyalists in 1794, whereupon much of its population moved to nearby Kingsclear, an area that the province later recognized as a reserve (similar to a U.S. reservation). During the second half of the nineteenth century the province of New Brunswick created several other reserves along the St. John and its tributary, the Tobique, to accommodate Maliseets spreading out to seek their livelihood, when possible by

E-15. Peter Mitchell, a Passamaquoddy veteran of the Civil War, wears his Grand Army of the Republic uniform, in this photograph from the late nineteenth century. Beside him is his wife, Alice. (Courtesy of the National Anthropological Archives, Smithsonian Institution, photo no. 74-8345.)

E-16a–b. Passamaquoddy porpoise hunters. (Reproduced from *Scribner's Monthly, October 1880.*)

their traditional means of hunting and trapping.[44] Likewise, Maliseet reserves were created at Viger (1827–70) and Cacouna (1891) near the St. Lawrence River in Quebec. Populations remain on most of these reserves today. By the early twentieth century several Maliseet families were established in northern Maine. Among the 148 Maliseets from northern Maine who were listed in the 1910 census, most men were farm laborers, while women were basketmakers. Their descendents were granted tribal recognition by the Maine Indian Claims Settlement in 1980.[45]

The Micmacs

As the English east of Passamaquoddy Bay had not joined the Revolution, and neither the Continental Congress nor Massachusetts had the resources to control the region, the Micmacs were able to avoid some of the stresses that had befallen their western neighbors. Nevertheless, by the 1760s they were beginning to feel pressure on their lands as new English, German, and other European settlers took up residence in territories emptied by the expulsion of the French Acadians. The pressure increased after 1784, when Loyalist New Englanders began to arrive in the area.[46]

Although some Micmacs of Quebec and Nova Scotia had adopted village life and agriculture early in the nineteenth century, most continued to favor their traditional trapping and hunting well past midcentury. This kept them active over a broad region that included Maine, where they had

E-18. Passamaquoddies at Sipayik in 1901, wearing special outfits possibly linked to ceremonies or performances. (Maine State Museum collection.)

traded regularly prior to the Revolution, and Quebec, where they had hunted and traded since the seventeenth century. By 1870, however, most had learned English, lived in frame houses, and were discarding traditional forms of clothing. Agricultural development on the upper St. John continued to bring them into Maine and New Brunswick during the late nineteenth century and thereafter. But the Micmacs, too, were drawn into the emerging industrial economy, to which they contributed as woodsmen, sawmill workers, guides, and craft workers. At least one Maine-based Micmac fought in the Civil War.[47] The 1910 federal census listed only twenty-three Micmacs as residing in Maine.

During the 1960s, work in high-steel construction attracted many Micmacs away from seasonal agricultural work to urban areas, particularly Boston, but the large majority of Micmacs live on or near twenty-

E-19. Maliseet guides with their "sports" on the St. John River. (Reproduced from *Picturesque Canada, vol. 2, 1882.*)

seven reserves in eastern New Brunswick, Nova Scotia, Prince Edward Island, and Quebec. Since the eighteenth century, and perhaps earlier, Micmacs were established on Newfoundland as well, and their descendents presently occupy a nonreserve community at Conne River in the center of that province.[48]

Politics

The Wabanaki Confederacy

As we have seen, from the mid–seventeenth century onward the Native groups of the Maritime Peninsula had a history of close, generally cooperative relations. Since the late nineteenth century, anthropologist Frank G. Speck and others have attributed this tradition of cooperation to an alliance Speck labeled the Wabanaki Confederacy, composed of the Penobscots, Passamaquoddies, Maliseets, and Micmacs, which had ceased to exist during the mid–nineteenth century. A salient feature of the confederacy was that it maintained regular diplomatic ties with a larger group whose central council fire was among the Mohawks of Caughnawaga. There the larger group met every three years to discuss political matters. Although the Micmacs were considered members of the confederacy, Speck thought

E-20. Penobscot basketmakers, photographed at Indian Island in 1896. (Peabody Museum, Harvard University.)

E-21. Maliseets spearfishing for salmon by torchlight on the Restogouche River in Quebec, 1882. (Reproduced from *Picturesque Canada, vol. 2, 1882.*)

E-22. Maliseet guides preparing birchbark torches for use in night fishing. Note the upswept ends of their canoes, a form typical of the region between the Penobscot and St. John Rivers. (Reproduced from *Picturesque Canada*, vol. 2, 1882.)

their status within it was "somewhat apart." Yet even the Micmacs of New-foundland apparently once made visits to the Caughnawaga council.[49] Being the closest to Caughnawaga, the Penobscots were regarded as the eldest "brothers," a status they must have attained after the abandonment of Norridgewock, on the Kennebec, in the 1760s. This geographic logic meant that the Micmacs were the youngest brothers. Preeminent in the larger alliance were the Ottawas, who "were held in the highest esteem by the tribes of the [Wabanaki] Confederacy."[50]

Since the time of Speck's research the Wabanaki Confederacy has been mentioned frequently, but little additional information about it has come to light aside from accounts of its use of wampum protocols and some information about cooperative behavior exhibited by its four constituent members, such as the communal "raising up" of new chiefs for individual tribes.[51] Recently, however, some long-ignored documents and a better un-

E-25. Late-nineteenth-century Penobscot camp in Bar Harbor. Bar Harbor, on Mount Desert Island, was a popular shore resort and a good place to sell baskets to summer visitors. (Courtesy of Earle Shettleworth.)

E-26. Early-twentieth-century Penobscot baskets. The manufacture of baskets and other craft items became highly organized. This photograph shows more than thirty craft items, numbered for ordering purposes. (Maine State Museum collection.)

derstanding of Native-European relations in the seventeenth century have confirmed the main points of Speck's description and thrown considerable new light on the origins of the confederacy, its continuation throughout the eighteenth century, and its eventual decline in the nineteenth.

While it had been the pro-English faction of the Mohawks that had initiated the original Covenant Chain alliance with the English in 1677, by that time many, perhaps most, Mohawks were living at Caughnawaga as allies of the French and converts to Catholicism. After 1701, when the Great Peace of Montreal was signed, these "French" Mohawks, together with other Native groups that were settling in the region around Montreal and Quebec, and would eventually form an alliance referred to in contemporary documents as the Seven Nations of Canada, whose council fire burned at

Caughnawaga.[52] With the Ottawas, these had been the key players in the French-Algonquian alliance that brought about the Great Peace of Montreal. This alliance conforms well with Speck's description of the Caughnawaga alliance. Indeed, Gilles Havard, historian of the Great Peace of Montreal, has argued that the Great Peace was the founding event of the Wabanaki Confederacy, and Jean-Pierre Sawaya, historian of the Seven Nations of Canada, has argued that the Wabanaki Confederacy's linkage to the French-Algonquian alliance was through the Seven Nations confederacy.[53]

Prior to the Seven Years' War, the Penacooks and Abenakis of the Androscoggin and Kennebec had been accepted into the Covenant Chain, but it is not clear that Indians east of the Kennebec were included. In any case, the nature of Native-European diplomacy changed after the Seven Years' War. Although the Seven Nations alliance had been born of the French-Algonquian alliance to resist the Iroquois and English, in 1760 the British nevertheless confirmed its rights and territories, even granting it neutrality and freedom of religion. Moreover, when the Covenant Chain between the British and the League of (now) Six Nations was renewed after the fall of Quebec, its council fire was joined with that of the Seven Nations alliance. The center of Native diplomatic contact with the British remained the council fire of the league among the Onondagas, to which the Caughnawaga council was subordinate. Nevertheless, Caughnawaga was designated as the principal intermediary between the British and all Indians of the *pays d'en haut*. It assumed even greater importance when the Revolutionary War broke out, for the Six Nations could not agree upon what course to follow. This greatly diminished the authority of their council fire and they agreed to extinguish it for the time being. Then, with the defeat of the British and the further dispersion of the Six Nations Iroquois at the end of the Revolutionary War, the Covenant Chain passed into history, while the Seven Nations alliance assumed paramount importance in British-Native diplomacy.[54]

Among the functions of the Seven Nations alliance, acting through its council fire at Caughnawaga, were affirming certain political decisions taken by its constituent nations and approving the elections of their chiefs. It remains unclear whether the council played an equally central role in Wabanaki political affairs, but there is evidence that during the late eighteenth and early nineteenth centuries it did play such a role, one that was recognized by governmental authorities in Maine and New Brunswick. Thus when the Passamaquoddies negotiated their 1794 treaty with Massachusetts, the latter acknowledged that it was confirmed at "a large Council of the several Tribes . . . at a distant Village . . . which proceedings were com-

E-27. Penobscot basketmaker Philomene Nelson in 1953. (Maine State Museum collection.)

municated accompanied with strings of Wampum."[55] The distance of the village, the presence of several tribes at the council, and the prominence of wampum all leave little doubt that these proceedings took place at Caughnawaga. Thereafter, until 1865, numerous accounts mention Wabanaki trips to Caughnawaga, many with the active support of officials in Maine and New Brunswick. Most were for the stated purpose of renewing their treaty of peace and friendship with the Seven Nations, but two accounts from the nineteenth century indicate Caughnawaga's continued involvement in Wabanaki political affairs. The first refers to an effort by some Maliseets, Passamaquoddies, and Penobscots to form a political union in 1839. The Royal Gazette of Fredericton, New Brunswick, reported "That this application for a union of the Tribes could not be complied with until authority was received from their head chief at Caughnawaga, to whom the matter was referred; that upon such reference authority was given to them, and at a Council lately held at Penobscot, at which were present the Chiefs of the respective Tribes, it was decided that they should be united as one tribe." Another from 1848 describes a meeting of the Maliseet and Penobscot governors at Sipayik where "all parties agreed not to choose a new [Passamaquoddy] Governor for one year or until they could hear from the King of the Indians in Canada."[56]

Historical documents suggest that the power of the Caughnawaga council declined during the nineteenth century but that the relative importance of the Mohawk in it was growing. In 1838, for example, continuing political

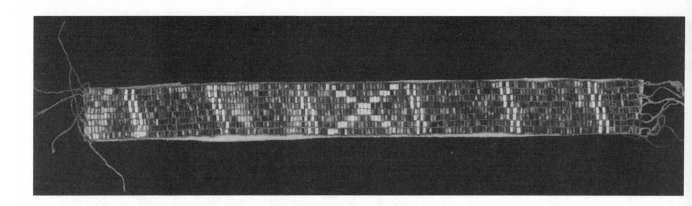

e-28. Wampum belt reputedly from Indian Island, intended as a summons to the Wanabaki Confederacy to attend the council at Caughnawaga (Speck 1919: 37). (Reproduced from Clarke 1931: 111.)

strife among the Penobscots required the intervention of the Maliseets and Passamaquoddies and was apparently the stimulus for a Wabanaki trip to the Caughnawaga council that was scheduled for the summer of 1839. Strains on the traditional protocols of the council are evident in a letter written in August of that year by the council chiefs to the three tribes:

We send you these our words in writing as frequently heretofore some of your people with evil intentions have come here to the Great Fire to ask advice of us concerning certain affairs that exist among you. We at all times to the best of our knowledge gave them good council and advice. It is with sorrow that we now learn that these said people on their return home to you related to you quite the contrary to what we had told them. We are therefore absolutely obliged to abandon our ancient custom of sending our words to our brethren by Wampum Belts. We now send our words in writing.[57]

The council's conservative position on the Wabanakis' political troubles was clearly conveyed in the rest of the letter: "strictly follow the Roman Catholic Religion . . . obey your chiefs. Listen attentively to the good advice of your Missionarys. Be very careful of your Lands do not sell or dispose of them." This message was probably not accurately passed on because it was at odds with the political sentiments of the messengers.[58]

The last meeting of the confederacy for which we have a specific historical account took place in July 1855, "the due time of appointment." It was in response to a visit by Passamaquoddy delegates, who, in the traditional manner, "delivered their speeches with the talking pearl, or beads, unto our said council fire at Caughnawaga." It seems clear that such councils had become rare by then and that memories of their protocol had faded, for the Caughnawaga chiefs commented that:

[A]s we are destitute of ancient men, we managed it as we possible could in translating the right meaning of our ancient Language [wampum protocol].

We Caughnawagas are desirous of holding the aforsaid Council Fire, in order to reassemble our Indian Brethren and remind you of the Chain of Friendship, of which the links of said Chain will never sever.[59]

It is worth noting the use of the chain metaphor in this letter, which suggests that the Caughnawaga council, as the mediator of diplomacy between the British authorities and the Eastern Indian tribes, felt that it was carrying on the traditions of the Covenant Chain.

Speck's main informant regarding the Wabanaki Confederacy was a Penobscot named Newell Lyon, who had witnessed its operations as a child. According to Lyon, the Penobscots withdrew from the Caughnawaga council in 1862 when the issue of their subordinate status vis-à-vis the Mohawks, and possibly of the costs of sending delegates to Caughnawaga, came to the fore. When the council wampum was brought back that year, one tribal council member angrily threw it to the ground and no one in the Penobscot leadership reclaimed it.[60] Joseph Nicolar, another Penobscot, placed the end of the confederacy at 1840 but also felt that the break came because some Penobscots thought the Mohawks "wanted to be the commander ... boss." Significantly, Nicolar stated that it was the Ottawas, preeminent in Canadian Native diplomacy since the seventeenth century, who had actually initiated the break, suggesting that the departure of the Wabanaki was part of some larger fragmentation of the Seven Nations confederacy.[61]

The last known document referring to Passamaquoddy participation in the Caughnawaga council is dated July 31, 1865. In it the Caughnawaga chiefs once again offer advice to the Passamaquoddies:

Be very careful in not letting white people taking possession of your lands, and also as far as you can to prevent the sale of wood, which if continued will ultimately ruin you, as if your lands, and wood were bought out of your hands through cunning craftiness, you would be left entirely destitute, and no one to care for you.

The Iroquois speak from experience, and as a burnt child dreading the fire, we are now adopting measures to prevent white settlers coming into our place, and the sale of wood, which has been a great bane here.[62]

There is one last reference to a Passamaquoddy delegation attending the Caughnawaga council in 1870. It comes in a letter from the council chiefs to the Passamaquoddies that mentions a political change that may have contributed to the end of the Wabanaki Confederacy and the larger Caughnawaga council: the confederation of Upper and Lower Canada into the Dominion of Canada, thus creating an international boundary separating the Wabanakis from the rest of the Seven Nations alliance. In the letter, council chiefs express a concern that the terms of an earlier treaty be maintained so that "No Boundary line should exist between us Indians Brothers Not any Duties or taxed be levied upon us." The letter also states that the League of Six Nations, which resided in Upper Canada, had proposed a meeting with the Seven Nations of Lower Canada and with the Wabanakis three years hence to consider these matters, but no available evidence indicates that the Wabanakis ever attended such a meeting.[63]

Speck is silent regarding when the Maliseets stopped sending representatives to Caughnawaga or when they left the confederacy. Oral tradition maintains that the Micmacs continued their visits until 1872, although those of Newfoundland had stopped making visits to the grand council fire prior to 1839.[64]

To summarize, it seems that ambivalence regarding the Wabanaki Confederacy's status in the Caughnawaga council during the mid–nineteenth century contributed to its rejection of the council and thus to its dissolution. An influencing factor, however, may have been the issue of Native freedom to cross international borders following the confederation of Canada—an issue that remains contentious to this day. Finally, in the mid–nineteenth century, growing economic involvement of Wabanakis with the larger society probably made continuing participation in the great council at Caughnawaga increasingly burdensome.

Although the political activities of the Penobscots, Passamaquoddies, Maliseets, and Micmacs are now autonomous, in other respects intertribal cooperation continues. Particularly since federal recognition in 1980, there are references to a Wabanaki confederacy as Native people of the Maritime Peninsula begin to explore cooperative ventures to advance their interests.

Governmental Relations

When the United States emerged as a new nation at the end of the eighteenth century, the attitudes of Massachusetts and, after 1820, of the newly independent state of Maine toward the Indians who lived within its borders underwent a shift from hostility to indifference to paternalism. As elsewhere in North America, the view of the dominant society became that Native populations would likely dwindle and disappear if protective measures were not undertaken, and this was especially the case for the

Penobscots and Passamaquoddies, who had not been given recognition by the federal government. The sentiment expressed by the early Maine historian William D. Williamson in 1822 is typical: "In the gradual diminution, and final extinction, of these tribes, who were the terror of the early settlers, we have a melancholy specimen of what has happened in like manner to all the Indian tribes, who once inhabited the territory of New-England. . . . And such will be the inevitable destiny of all Indians now mingled with our white population, if a radical change in our treatment of them be not adopted." The first concrete measure of assistance was taken in 1831, when the small trust funds of proceeds from the sale of timber and hay from tribal lands were established and played a role in allowing the Penobscot and Passamaquoddy communities to remain intact, as did later state subsidies for the support of the poor.[65]

After Maine became a separate state in 1820, it gave little political voice to the Passamaquoddies and Penobscots beyond subsidizing visits by their representatives to the legislature, where they were allowed to express their concerns. The state dealt with the Penobscots and Passamaquoddies as separate tribes whose governors took counsel from male heads of families. As we have seen, however, the continued operation of the Wabanaki Confederacy meant that the Passamaquoddies, Penobscots, and Maliseets continued to act collectively in many matters. Thus during the first half of the nineteenth century, elections and installations of governors were conducted in the presence of the other two tribes. Later in the century, however, three factors combined to threaten this tradition and indeed the very integrity of the tribes. First, the decline of their connections to the Seven Nations of Canada diminished their ability to act cooperatively with respect to outside pressures. At the same time, growing involvement with the cash economies of Maine and New Brunswick created political tensions that decreased unity in what had traditionally been close-knit communities. Finally, paternalistic governmental policies became increasingly autocratic, to the point where, during the 1930s, the legislature began to define the degree of Native ancestry required to qualify as Indian.[66]

In 1941 the Maine legislature took two steps that further eroded the legal status of the Passamaquoddies and Penobscots. First, it removed seating and speaking privileges of the tribes' legislative representatives, reducing them to the status of observers. It then authorized a study of the state's fiduciary relationship with the tribes. Among the central issues considered were determining who qualified as Indian, whether Indians should vote, and whether the state-recognized reservation system should be abolished. All three issues clearly indicated that, so far as the Maine legislature was concerned, the tribes' legal futures were in doubt. They remained so throughout the 1950s, as sentiment for terminating the tribes was encouraged by a similar policy then in practice at the federal level. The voting issue, at least, was resolved in the Indians' favor at the national level, but in Maine their voting places were located in adjacent municipalities, not on the reservations, and their right to vote in state elections was not granted until 1967.[67]

Political Reemergence

During the 1960s two factors combined to reverse the state's drift toward tribal termination. First, the emergence of a national civil rights movement drew attention to the tribes' political and economic marginality and to their lack of control over even their reservations' resources. It was in this environment that Passamaquoddy and Penobscot activists advocated maintaining, even strengthening, their tribal status. At about the same time, the

Maliseets and Micmacs of New Brunswick formed the Union of New Brunswick Indians to publicize their civil rights issues. These events were accompanied by a decline in sentiment at the federal level for a policy of encouraging Native assimilation by terminating tribes. As a result, in 1965 the Maine legislature reaffirmed its recognition of the tribes by creating a Bureau of Indian Affairs.[68]

Among the claims made by Passamaquoddy and Penobscot activists was that their tribal lands had been illegally seized or purchased by Massachusetts and, later, by Maine. Picking up on this contention, a 1971 article in the Maine Law Review questioned the legal basis for these land transfers as well as the state's authority over the Passamaquoddies and Penobscots. Thus began a series of political and legal proceedings that by 1980 led to passage of the Maine Indian Claims Settlement Act, which granted federal recognition and a federal payment of $81.5 million to the two newly recognized tribes. The act also provided federal recognition to approximately five hundred Maliseets of northern Maine, who received an award of $900,000 for land acquisition. The approximately four hundred Micmacs of Aroostook County were passed over during this first round of settlements, but they finally received federal recognition, along with $900,000 for land acquisition, in 1991.[69]

Today, not all tribal members view the Maine Indian Claims Settlement Act as an unqualified blessing. Some resent the loss of traditional ways the act seems to have accelerated, while others feel that the tribes relinquished too much potential sovereignty by agreeing to the enforcement of state laws on their reservations. Nevertheless, the federal funds provided by the act have created new opportunities for economic and cultural development, and many economic indicators are positive. The Maliseets and Micmacs have established reservations, and housing and public utilities have improved greatly on the Passamaquoddy and Penobscot reservations. While most of the approximately twelve hundred Passamaquoddies and five hundred Penobscots commute to off-reservation jobs, both also run a variety of reservation-based business operations. The Penobscots operate a plant that manufactures tape cassettes on their Indian Island reservation. The Passamaquoddies recently purchased, rehabilitated, and sold at a profit a large cement-manufacturing plant, retaining rights to an innovative air pollution scrubber technology developed while the plant was under their ownership. They also own and operate a large blueberry-growing enterprise and operate a rapidly growing garment manufacturing business. Both tribes also earn income from the management of tribally owned timberlands and from high-stakes bingo, offered in community halls. Cultural education is now part of the curriculum in their schools. The Penobscots have also developed a vocational education training program, and the Passamaquoddies have instituted a program for teaching their native language in the schools.[70]

Like many other newly recognized tribes, the Passamaquoddies, Penobscots, Maliseets, and Micmacs of Maine have begun to evolve complex new identities within the larger society. On the one hand, the transfer of fiduciary responsibility from the state of Maine to the federal government reaffirmed their status as communities separate in important ways from the rest of Maine. On the other hand, those cultural and economic influences that, since the nineteenth century, have drawn them in the opposite direction will likely grow stronger with time. It is unclear how these two influences will affect the tribes in the future. What is clear, however, is that predictions of their disappearance, so widely announced during the nineteenth century, show no signs of coming to pass as we enter a new millennium.

APPENDIX

The Traditional Material Culture of the Native Peoples of Maine

Ruth Holmes Whitehead

> Every Indian tribe has its peculiar form and pattern for every thing they
> make and wear—their canoes, wigwams, or snowshoes; their embroidery
> on birchbark, cloth or leather; in moosehair, wampum, or porcupine quills.
> The Indian instantly knows, by its fashion, to what tribe the slightest
> ornament or utensil belongs.
>
> R. G. A. Levinge, *Echoes From the Backwoods*

T HE MATERIAL culture of the Native peoples of Maine—literally "everything" they made and made use of—is a fascinating subject, but also a difficult one to study, for a number of reasons. First, very few items in materials other than stone remain after centuries of burial. The arrowhead survives, but what about the arrow shaft, its fletching, the hafting necessary? What did the bow look like, or the bowstring, or the quiver? What of the tools and materials needed to make all the above? Only a few fragments are left to speak to us.

Second, there is no recorded history that predates European contact. The first early records, moreover, if they mention the Native peoples at all, give us brief generalizations with very little technical detail. An example is an Englishman's report of the voyage by Frenchman Étienne Bellenger in 1583 along the coast of Cape Breton Island, Nova Scotia, down into Maine and back again:

In many places he had traffique with the people which are of very good disposition and stature of Bodie. They weare their hayre hanging downe long before and behynde as lowe as their Navells which they cutt short only overthwart their browes. They all go naked saving their privities which they cover with an Apron of some Beastes skynn, and tye it unto them with a long buff gerdle that comes three times about them beeing made fast behynde and at boath the endes it is cutt into little thynn thonges, which thonges they tye rownde about them with slender quils of birdes feathers [porcupine quills] whereof some are as red as if they had byn dyed in cuchanillo [cochineal] Their girdells have also before a little Codd or Pursse of Buff [soft leather] wherein they putt divers thinges but especiallie their tinder to keepe fire in, which is of a dry roote and somewhat like a hard sponge and will quicklie take fyer and is hardlie put out. Their weapons whereof he brought hoame store to the Cardinall [of Rouen] are Bowes of two yardes long and arrowes of one yarde hedded with indented bones three or fower ynches long, and are tyed into a nocke at the end with a thong of Lether. In divers places they are gentle and tractable.[1]

Wonderful stuff, but which "divers places" did Bellenger visit? If we could tie his information to specific areas, specific peoples, we could make better use of it. The account also mentions, for instance, collecting skins "painted on the innerside with excellent colors as redd, tawnye, yellowe, and vermillyon."[2] We know this technique was practiced in Nova Scotia, but was it common in Maine as well? Without a definite statement, we are left only with probabilities. The seventeenth-century English explorers also tend toward the general, speaking merely of "the natives"; and though the French did subdivide the Native peoples they encountered into Etchemins and Almouchiquois and though they recorded the occasional Souriquois trading or raiding party, no comprehensive studies of these peoples were written until the twentieth century.

Finally, in examining this material culture we are dealing with a lengthy time period, even if we restrict ourselves to the span from European contact to the present. Although the adaptation of the Native peoples of the Northeast had resulted in a working technology that was extremely well suited to their environment, and consequently one that was slow to change, it was not static. Before European contact, Native peoples traded with outside groups, invented tools, and altered their ways of living. Such change, however, was radically accelerated by exposure to European goods and techniques. By 1700, for example, lithic technology and the bow had been superseded by metal and the gun, and leather had been almost completely replaced by cloth. As the lifestyle of the peoples altered, the older ways were lost or restructured.

We will attempt here to build a picture of the material culture of Native

Mainers as seen by the first Europeans to reach the area. We will also flesh out our view a little with comparisons to other closely related Native groups, by references to archaeological evidence, and by examinations of techniques and items from the postcontact period that survive today. While the available data might seem fairly sparse, we do have a base from which to start a reconstruction. We know which raw materials were accessible, and we understand the basic techniques by which these materials were worked. So when we come across an early reference to mats made of reed (*Scirpus lacustrus*), for example, we can make quite accurate assumptions about how and when the reeds were gathered, as well as how they were dyed and woven.

It is true that the lack of data and artifacts means we cannot always put our finger on that individual group stamp, that "form and pattern" specific to a particular people—whether Etchemins, Souriquois, Almouchiquois, or their descendents—that marked the "slightest ornament" as theirs alone. But tribal differences were not quite as dramatic for an area the size of the Maritime Peninsula as the romantic statement by Levinge at the beginning of this chapter might lead us to believe. The group stamp is reflected more often in a variation on a theme than a change in the basic structure, engineering, or raw materials of comparable objects. We will look first at these traditional objects and then examine how Native material culture was modified and techniques adopted, adapted, or lost over the succeeding centuries. Through these changes, as one Canadian observer said in 1847, "you may apparently see that necessity was at first the mother of all inventions."[3] The inventions of the Native peoples of Maine have been marvelous indeed.

Clothing, Accessories, Decorative Techniques

Prior to the introduction of European goods, clothing was made largely from leather and furs. Skins of moose, deer, bear, seal, and beaver were tanned using a mixture of animal brains, bird livers, and fish oil. Smoking the skins kept them soft even when wet, and by altering the length of the smoking process or the type of wood used, they could be colored a variety of shades. The resulting leather was soft, supple, and easy to work. All preparation of the skins and the fabrication and decoration of the clothing was done by women.

The basic costume, for both men and women, was much the same throughout the Maritime Peninsula: men wore moccasins, leggings, and a

BASIC CLOTHING

We are fortunate to have available several early descriptions of clothing from the eastern Gulf of Maine region. Those quoted here convey a general picture of costume there.

Penobscot Bay, 1604–1605

All these peoples of Norumbega [Penobscot Bay and River area] are very swarthy, and are clothed in beaverskins and other furs like the Canadian Indians and the Souriquois; and they have the same manner of life. . . . In winter they clothe themselves with good furs of beaver and moose. The women make all the clothes, but not neatly enough to prevent one seeing the skin under the armpits [this is the separate sleeve, purposely not sewn to the robe].[4]

Pemaquid Area, 1605

Their clothing is Beavers skins, or Deares skins, cast over them like a mantle, and hanging downe to their knees, made fast together upon the shoulder with leather; some of them [the men] had sleeves most had none; some had buskins [leggings] of leather tewed [fringed]: they have besides a peece of Beavers skin betweene their legs, made fast about their waste. . . . [The women] being covered with thin leather buskins tewed, fastened with strops to a girdle about their wastes.[5]

Maine and the Bay of Fundy, 1606

[The Souriquois and Etchemin] cover these parts with a skin tied in front to a leathern strap, which, passing between their buttocks, join at the back the other end of the said strap; and for other garments, they have on their backs a cloak made of many skins, if these be of otters or of beavers, and of a single skin, it be of moose, bear, or lynx, which cloak is tied near the shoulder with a leather strap, usually with one arm out; but when indoors they put it off, unless it be too cold. . . . Notwithstanding they have more civility, in that they cover their privy-members. As for the women, they differ only in this one thing, that they have a girdle over the skin they have on. . . . But in winter, both sexes

A-1. Snowshoe boots made from the hide of the upper hind leg of a moose. These were made in the early 1900s by Eunice Nelson, a Penobscot. (Maine State Museum collection.)

make good beaver sleeves, tied behind, which keep them fine and warm. . . . As for the Armouchiquois . . . they have no furs, but only chamois; indeed they have very often only a piece of mat upon their back large enough to swear by, yet with their privy members covered with a piece of leather or foliage. . . . [I]n the winter, going to sea, or a-hunting, [they] put on great and high stockings, like our boot-hose, which they tie to their girdles, and on the outer edge are a great number of points without tags [fringe]. . . . Besides these . . . [they] wear shoes, which they call *mekezin*.[6]

Western Maine, 1671

Their Apparel before the *English* came amongst them was the skins of wild Beasts with the hair on, Buskins of *Deers*-skin or *Moose* drest and drawn with lines into several works, the lines being coloured with yellow, blew or red. Pumps too they have, made of tough skins without soles . . . under their belly they wear a square piece of leather and the like upon their posteriors, both fastened to a string tyed about them to hide their secrets; on their heads they ware nothing.[7]

A-2. Early-nineteenth-century
Penobscot moccasins of leather and
wool, ornamented with beads and
ribbon. (Maine State Museum
collection.)

A-3. Maliseet, Passamaquoddy, or
Penobscot moccasins of leather and
wool, ornamented with beads and
ribbon, about 1860. (Maine State
Museum collection.)

A-4. Maliseet, Passamaquoddy, or
Penobscot child's moccasins of leather
and wool, ornamented with beads and
ribbon, mid–nineteenth century.
(Maine State Museum collection.)

loincloth attached to a belt at the waist, with a robe of hide or fur over one or both shoulders, which fell to the knee. Women also wore moccasins, leggings, and a loincloth and belt, although their body robes could be draped in a variety of ways. Both sexes wore garments described as "sleeves." These seem to have consisted of two separate pieces—each covering an arm and a shoulder—tied together in the front and back, or the whole skins of animals, such as lynx, through which a single arm would be thrust. Tobacco pouches and accessories completed the costume. Babies were swaddled in soft furs or skins; when they could walk they appear to have worn smaller versions of the adult costume.

Moccasins were cut from thick hide, seal or moose being favored. The extended piece that formed the sole was folded up around the foot and gathered to a vamp in tiny tucks. A high moccasin, used in winter for snowshoeing, was made from the skin of a moose foreleg that had been stripped whole from the animal. The bend at the moose's knee formed the heel of the moccasin, and the only stitching necessary was across the toe.

Loincloths, made of the softer skins, were sometimes worn rather like a codpiece; others had a flap in front and/or back, or were wrapped around the waist. Leggings were tubes of leather tapered to fit and sewn up on the outside of the leg, with the selvages fringed. Pouches were long drawstring bags made of either leather or the uncut skin of an entire small fur-bearing mammal whose body had been removed through a slit in the throat and the cleaned skull reinserted into the head.

Women's body robes could be worn draped over one shoulder, or wrapped like a bath towel under the arms. In what is now Nova Scotia and New Brunswick, Micmac women sometimes wore dresses of two complete hides, one in front, the other down the back, and the two laced together at the shoulders and sides. Robes were not usually tailored, because they were removed at bedtime to serve as coverings. In emergencies they could be used as shelters, sacks, canoe covers, or even boiled and eaten. (Sewing was accomplished with bone awls, and an excellent thread was prepared from the fibrous muscle-sheathing, often called sinew, that runs up both sides of the spine of moose, deer, and caribou. When dried, this sheathing separates into long threads ideal for sewing.) The robe most favored by both men and women seems to have been sewn from the furs of beaver or otter (*Lutra canidensis*).

Costume was not rigidly fixed; garments were removed or added as the weather and the occasion demanded, and there were variations in style. The variations were on a central theme that prevailed throughout much of northeastern North America, for the basic costume was eminently practical: leggings protected the legs in the brush, robes doubled as bedclothes, soft moccasins were necessary for snowshoeing.

It was in the decoration, rather than the cut, that the differentiation between groups was more apparent. Ornamentation—sometimes visually stunning—made each costume unique, and often group-recognizable. Clothing, especially ceremonial clothing, was highly ornamented. We tend to think of this type of work as purely decorative, but to the people who wore these clothes it served a functional purpose as well by conferring strength and status. The personal or tribal designs and symbols employed, the form of an ornament, and even the raw materials used in fabrication carried specific meanings and were seen as sources of real power—power that aided and protected the wearer. Many complex "decorative" techniques might be involved in the manufacture of a single item.[8]

As one account makes clear (see p. 252), leather could be painted—that is, "drawn with lines into several works." There is little more than this in the early sources about painted clothing from Maine, but we do have descriptions from the Maritimes of painted borders on robes, on moccasin cuffs and vamps, and across the bottoms and up the sides of leggings. These decorations consisted of similar parallel bands of lines, realistic and geometric motifs, and a lacelike pattern, possibly the double-curve motif common to many Algonquian groups.[9] Paints were made from red and yellow ochers, from charcoal, lignite, and manganese, and from ground white shell. These pigments were mixed with fish roe or bird egg yolk and applied with bone painting tools. No such tools have survived, but some may have been tined like a fork to permit the painting of parallel lines.

"They have excellent colours," wrote James Rosier in 1605, "and having seen our Indico, they make shew of it, or of some other like thing which maketh as good a blew."[10] This "thing," probably a vegetable dye like indigo, is now unknown. Other plant sources such as bloodroot (*Sanguinaria canadensis*), red bedstraw (*Galium tinctorium*), and the barks of alder (*Alnus rubra*) and spruce (mainly black spruce, *Picea mariana*) were used to dye the "glistering quills taken from the *Porcupine* . . . some black, others red . . . the white are natural."[11]

Porcupine quills were used in a variety of ways to decorate clothing. They could be woven into strips that looked almost like woven beadwork. It is possible that such strips, attached to a leather backing, were used to create the "bags of porcupine quills woven and dyed" noted by Josselyn.[12] These strips were apparently made using a bow loom: sinew-thread warps were strung on a bent length of wood, like a bow, and passed through evenly spaced holes in birchbark dividers at either end. A weft string, also of sinew,

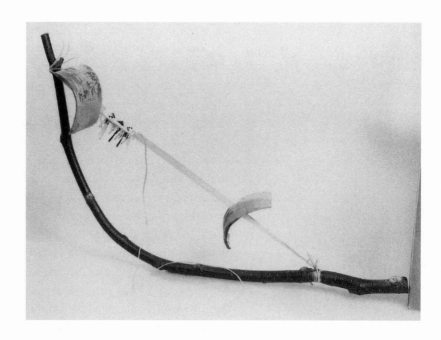

A-5. Reconstruction of a bow loom used to weave porcupine quills. (History Collections, Nova Scotia Museum, Halifax.)

was then woven over and under both the warp *and* the wet flattened porcupine quills, which were placed between each warp string as an additional warp element. New quills were added as required, and designs in different colors could thus be produced. The warp and weft strings were completely hidden on the finished piece, and the quills curving over the weft strings resembled cylindrical beads. The final product could be backed with leather and fashioned into a belt, collar, moccasin cuff, or appliquéd decoration. Micmac bow looms were used in the early seventeenth century to produce strips at least one-third of a meter long and 20 centimeters wide, and the work of Etchemin women must have been similar.

Quill embroidery on leather was created by folding wet flattened quills over and under a single or double line of stitches. The quills did not penetrate the leather but were laid flat on the surface, stitched over, folded up over the stitch (or down over it), then stitched over again. A variety of folds produced different effects, and as one account points out (see p. 252) leather fringe could also be wrapped with individual quills, the ends tucked under the body of the wrap that stiffened as the quills dried.[13]

Early European visitors observed an astonishing number of materials incorporated into personal ornaments. These included shells, paint, leather, furs, quills, beaks, feathers, bone, antler, teeth, claws, and other animal parts as well as wood and stone, but chief among them was copper in a wide variety of forms. At Pemaquid in 1604, Rosier saw children's belts that were

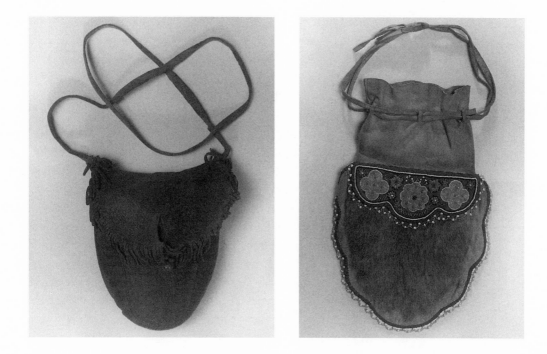

A-6. Mid-nineteenth-century Penobscot pouch made from a moose-hide moccasin. (Maine State Museum collection.)

A-7. Elaborately decorated pouches were often made for sale. This one, with fur of bobcat or lynx, probably dates to the mid–nineteenth century and is probably Maliseet or Passamaquoddy. (Maine State Museum collection.)

"decked round about with little round peeces of red Copper."[14] And in 1606 the French noted that the Almouchiquois men "have a fashion of wearing on their wrists, and above the ankles, plates of copper, formed like fetters, and about their haunches girdles fashioned of copper quills as long as one's middle-finger, strung together to the length of a girdle."[15] In 1603 at Provincetown, Massachusetts, English explorer Martin Pring reported that a few members of what was probably a Massachusett party had "plates of Brasse a foote long, and half a foote broad before their breasts."[16] A year earlier, among a probably Nauset group, Gabriel Archer had seen "a plate of rich Copper, in length a foot, in breadth halfe a foot for a brest-plate" and noted in "the Eares of all the rest Pendants of Copper."[17] His companion, John Brereton, described the tobacco pipes they saw as follows: "the necks of their pipes are made of clay hard dried . . . the other part is a piece of hollow copper, very finely closed and semented together."[18] Finally, Brereton recorded the presence of copper even south of Cape Cod, far from its presumed source in the Maritime Provinces:

They haue also great store of Copper, some very redde, and some of a paler colour [brass]; none of them but haue chaines, earrings or collars of this mettall: they head some of their arrows herewith much like our broad arrow heads, very workmanly made. Their chaines are many hollow pieces semented together, each piece of the bignesse of one of our reeds, a finger in length, ten or twelve of them together on a string which they weare about their bodies like bandelieres a handfull broad, all hollow pieces, like the other, but somewhat shorter, foure hundred pieces in a collar, very fine and evenly set together.[19]

Certainly, Native peoples of the Northeast had learned to work native copper into a wide variety of forms thousands of years before European contact. On the Maritime Peninsula the main sources of native copper were at Cap d'Or, and nearby Isle Haute, Nova Scotia.[20] However, the amounts of the metal seen by early observers and the artifact forms into which it was made suggest that these descriptions refer instead to European smelted copper.[21] In any event, smelted European sheet stock, often in the form of cooking pots derived from Europeans in the Gulf of Saint Lawrence, replaced native sources in the Maritimes during the sixteenth century, and some of this imported metal reached Maine before 1600.[22] The techniques for working native copper—cold hammering and annealing—were easily

A-8. Beaded shirt panels such as this were used on ceremonial occasions by Penobscots, Passamaquoddies, and Maliseets during the late eighteenth and early nineteenth centuries. This example is decorated with double curve motifs in a style typical of the mid–nineteenth century. (Maine State Museum collection.)

A-9. Maliseet, Passamaquoddy, or Penobscot pouch of wool broadcloth, decorated with beads and ribbon. (Maine State Museum collection.)

adapted to the European metal. During the seventeenth century, Europeans and Natives alike recycled worn-out pots into a wide variety of products.

The most prevalent form of jewelry was shell beads. Initially these were manufactured by numerous coastal groups south of the Saint Lawrence, including those in Maine, as the following quote from Lescarbot indicates. "The . . . Armouchiquois do make carkanets [carcenets or gorgets] and bracelets . . . of the shells of those great sea-cockles, called *vignols* [whelks], like snails, which they break into a thousand pieces, and polish them upon a sandstone till they make them very small; then they pierce them and make them into rosaries, of which the beads are black and white, and very pretty they are. . . . [T]hese collars, scarves, and braceletts, made of vignol or porcelain, are richer than pearls."[23] Lescarbot seems to be describing the production of discoidal beads, which are ubiquitous in northeastern archaeological sites that have good shell preservation. He goes on to indicate how valuable these could be in trade with people who lived in rich fur-bearing country north of the range of mollusks suitable for beadmaking: "[I]n Port Royal and its confines, and towards Newfoundland, and at Tadoussac [on the Upper North Shore of the Saint Lawrence], where they have neither pearls nor vignols, the maids and women make *matachias* [jewelry] with quills or bristles of the porcupine . . . but they esteem more

A PASSAMAQUODDY FEMALE'S COSTUME

Figure A-10 shows a painting, probably by a Lieutenant Villars, labeled "Denn—daughter of Francis Joseph [Neptune]—Governor of Passamaquoddy, Eastport Sept. 18th, 1817." The subject's costume fits Levinge's description perfectly. She has a conical cap, probably of wool, which is so heavily appliquéd with ribbons—red, yellow, blue (two shades) and striped (two kinds)—that it is difficult to see the blue material of the cap itself. Two pairs of ribbon bows and an odd black object adorn the cap's somewhat blunted peak. The earrings consist of two metal loops with a pendant hanging from the smaller lower loop. Around her neck she wears a crucifix on a necklace of small round beads. Her white belt, or girdle, is decorated with yellow, red, and blue dots—possibly representing wampum or beadwork—and fastens with a gold metal buckle. The jacket is held closed by two silver brooches, which seem to bear a design in the shape of a star. Her blue cloth leggings have unfringed selvages with blue-and-white ribbon appliqué, while her moccasins have blue cloth vamps with white beading. Her upper garment, a jacket, is red with appliqué in yellow, red, and green, and there are red and white stripes on the sleeves. The bodice appliqué is in two shades of gray, with a wide outside edging of yellow with red dots. This last ribbon edging continues down the skirt front and around the hem.

A-10. Passamaquoddy woman's costume. (Courtesy of Nina Fletcher Little.)

highly the *matachias* which come from the Armouchiquois country, and these they buy very dear."[24] Discoidal beads, popular as they were, were largely displaced early in the seventeenth century by a tremendously popular cylindrical form called wampumpeag, wampum, or peag, which could be strung, woven, or sewn individually onto a backing. As noted, wampum came in two colors: "of these there are two sorts, blew Beads and white Beads, the first is their Gold, the last their Silver, these they work out of certain shells ... [T]hey dril them and string them, and make many curious works with them to adorn the persons of the *Sagamours* [sagamores, or elders] and principal men and young women, as Belts, Girdles, Tablets, Borders for their womens hair, Bracelets, Necklaces and links to hang in their ears."[25] White wampum was made from the inner columns of the shell of the whelk (*Busycon sp.*). The outer curl of the shell was broken away and the core smoothed into a cylinder, then cut and drilled. The more valued purple wampum was cut from the shell of the quahog, or hard-shell clam (*Mercenaria mercenaria*).

Although the manufacture of wampum was a Native tradition, its popularity seems to have been the result of its use by Europeans as currency in the fur trade—especially the Dutch on the Hudson River. It later spread to the English and became a currency among the specie-poor Colonials as well as natives.[26] Writing in 1646, Plymouth governor William Bradford gives its concise history among the English.

But that which turned most to their profit, in time, was an entrance into the trade of wampampeag. For they now bought about £50 worth of it of them [the Dutch], and they told them how they would find it so at Kennebec. And so it came to pass in time, though at first it stuck, and it was two years before they could put off this small quantity, till the inland people knew of it; and afterwards they could scarce ever gett enough for them for many years together. . . . And strange it was to see the great alteration it made in a few years among the Indians them selves; for all the Indians of these parts and the Massachusetts had none or very little of it, but ye sachems [leaders] and some special persons that wore a little of it for ornament. Only it was made and kept among the Narragansetts and Pequots, which grew rich and potent by it, and these people were poor and beggarly and had no use of it. Neither did the English of this Plantation or any other in the land, till now that they had knowledge of it from the Dutch, so much as know what it was, much less that it was a commodity of that worth and value. But after it grew thus to be a commodity in these parts, these Indians fell into it also, and to learn how to make it; for the Narragansetts do gather the shells of which they make it from their shores. And it hath now continued a current commodity about this 20 years, and it may prove a drug in time.[27]

The painting of body and hair added an extra dimension to costume: Rosier reported that those at Pemaquid "paint their bodies with blacke, their faces, some with red, some with blacke, and some with blew."[28] The symbolism of these colors is not entirely clear, although of these same people another English account states that "When a Sagamo dyeth, they blacke themselues."[29] Presumably face painting relied on the same pigments as those used for leather, and these were applied directly onto the skin.

As for the head-gear, none of the savages have any, but both men and women [Souriquois and Etchemin] wear their hair loose upon their shoulder, unbound and untied, save that the men tie a knot of them upon the crown of the head, some four fingers long. . . . [T]he Armouchiquois . . . both men and women, wear their haire much longer, hanging down below the girdle. . . . [T]hey truss them up as our grooms do a horse's tail, and the men do stick in them some feathers which take their fancy, and the women a bodkin with three points. . . . In one thing the Armouchiquois differ from the Souriquois and the other savages of Newfoundland, in that they pull out their hair in front and are half bald, which the others are not.[30]

Full ceremonial dress in seventeenth-century Maine could be quite spectacular. Rosier's ship was boarded by seven men

who had beautified themselves after their manner very gallantly, though their clothing was not differing from [everyday wear] . . . yet they had newly painted their faces very deep, some all black, some red, with stripes of excellent blew over their upper lips, nose and chin. One of them wore a kinde of coronet about his head, made very cunningly, of a substance like stiffe hair coloured red, broad, and more than a handfull in depth, which we imagined to be some ensigne of superioritie; for he so esteemed it as he would not for anything exchange the same. [This would have been a roach of deer, moose, or porcupine hair, stained with red ocher.] Other[s] wore the white feathered skins of some fowle round their head, jewels in their ears, and bracelets of little white round bone, fastened together upon a leather string.[31]

The English were most impressed. Yet even as they recorded such costumery, they were contributing to its change.

Gosnold's expedition was evidently one of the earliest contacts between the English and the original peoples of Maine. As we have seen, however, trade goods had already begun to enter the region through indirect means, primarily via the Micmacs, who had been dealing with the European fishing fleets since the 1500s. The wary, unacculturated groups of the mainland were a strong contrast to the first Native groups that Gosnold encountered when he was still off the coast. These men were sailing a shallop and some wore European dress: "we came to an anker, where eight Indians, in a Baske-shallop with mast and saile, an iron grapple, and a kettle of Copper, came boldly aboord us, one of them apparelled with a wastcoat and breeches of blacke serdge, made after our sea-fashion, hose and shoes on his feet; all the rest (sauing one that had a paire of breeches of blue cloth) were all naked. . . . It seemed by some work and signes they made, that some Basks or of S. John de Luz, have fished or traded in this place."[32]

It seems more likely, however, that these bold Indians were Micmacs from the Maritimes, trading or raiding down the coast of Maine. This view is reinforced by a second account of the same meeting, which states that the Native seafarers drew a map of the coast and were familiar with Newfoundland and one of its European place-names, Placentia. "[They] came towards vs a Biscay shallop, with saile and Oares, hauing eight persons in it. . . . [T]hey came boldly aboard vs. . . . One that seemed to be their Commander wore a Wastecoate of black worke, a pair of Breeches, cloth Stockings, Shooes, Hat and Band . . . these with a piece of Chalke described the Coast thereabouts, and could name Placentia of the New-found-land; they spake divers Christian [probably Basque] words."[33]

There are numerous references to Micmacs sailing shallops around this time, whereas the peoples of Maine still used canoes. The English expedition of 1607 was accosted off Cap de La Hève, in Nova Scotia, by two "bisken" (Basque or Biscayan) shallops crewed by Micmacs.[34] That same year, Marc Lescarbot encountered another shallop of Micmac sailors 4 leagues (about 19 kilometers) out to sea off Cape Breton Island, Nova Scotia.[35] And numerous contemporary French accounts mention the use of a mixture of pidgin-Basque and broken French by the Micmacs.

Both Champlain and Lescarbot recorded the conveyance of French trade goods, usually via shallop, from Nova Scotia and New Brunswick to Maine. In 1607, for example, both described how Armouchiquois from the Saco area killed the Micmac Panoniac, "who had taken some merchandizes out of Monsier de Monts his storehouse, and went to trade with the Armouchiquois."[36]

That Micmac trading parties penetrated even farther south is suggested by Champlain, who, in recounting his 1604 visit to what is now Boston Harbor, wrote that Native people there used stone hatchets to fell trees, "for they have no others except some few which they received from the savages on the coasts of La Cadie [Acadia], who obtained them in exchange for furs."[37] Other French trade merchandise included cylindrical beads of white and blue glass, capes, bed blankets, hats, shoes, caps, woolens, shirts, and linens. Lescarbot records a Souriquois and an Etchemin chief trading gowns, short cloaks, and red waistcoats with the Almouchiquois. A third reference mentions sheets.[38]

The English were quick to follow the French example, offering brooches, bracelets, combs, mirrors, and peacock feathers. Rosier's captain gave a shirt to an Indian "who seemed neuer to have seene any before."[39] By 1629 cloth was so much in demand that the Plymouth Brethren were buying "cottons and kerseys and other such like cloth (for want of trading cloth)" to keep their traders on the Kennebec supplied.[40] The "trading cloth" referred to was probably woolen serge, which was rapidly replacing leather and furs. "[For] since they have to do with the English they purchase of them a sort of Cloth called trading Cloth of which they make Mantles, Coats with short sleeves, and caps for their heads which the women use."[41]

French trade goods in the 1680s included "blue serge caps, common Brittany linen shirts, short coarse woollen stockings . . . coloured sewing thread, pack [coarse, undyed] thread, needles, Venice beads."[42] An inventory of French goods sent to the Penobscot area in 1692 mentions blue serge again, as well as hats, stockings, shirts, and blankets.[43]

When John Gyles, an English boy captured at Pemaquid in 1689, was sold by his Maliseet master to a Frenchman in 1695, his clothing consisted of a "greasy blanket and Indian flap [loincloth]."[44] The fact that a slave of the Maliseet-Passamaquoddy had a trade blanket is an indication that wool cloth and blankets were then in common use among Native people in the Northeast.

Although the introduction of trade items into Maine was to change Native dress fairly rapidly, materials were altered faster than motifs. The basic outfit of leggings, moccasins, loincloth, and robe remained the same for a hundred years more, although shirts, caps, and coats were added, and painted and quilled leather was replaced by beaded and appliquéd cloth.

By the eighteenth and nineteenth centuries, a form of dress using cloth and European decorative materials was well established. Maliseet-Passamaquoddy and Penobscot men and women wore clothing that was fairly standardized in style and cut. It is this costume, now labeled "traditional," that Levinge described in 1847.

When they appear in full dress, [the women] wear a conical-shaped cap or headdress of blue or scarlet cloth, embroidered with white beads, and edged with ribbons; a long frock, reaching a little below the knees, with scarlet or blue cloth leggings; in finishing them, the seams are not turned in, but, on the contrary, the wider they can continue to have the surplus cloth on the outside, the more it can be bedizened with ribbons, beads, and wampum. Their mocassins [sic], made from moose leather, are beautifully embroidered with beads. The Malicete tribe use beads instead of the hair of the moose, or porcupine quills [as do] tribes in Upper and Lower Canada, and in the far West. The front of their dress is fastened with a number of circular silver buckles, the largest being placed at the top, and so diminishing as they descend; but they are more ornamental than useful. These constitute their trinkets, which they always carry about upon their persons; and, as cloth is to them expensive, the men generally appropriate that to their own use; and the poor squaws are to be most commonly seen in old chintzes and Manchester cottons; and, with a blanket, which serves in the severity of the winter as a cloak by day and as a bed by night, this completes the toilette.[45]

Levinge also comments on the Maliseet women's "magnificent long black hair . . . carefully parted down the center, and plaited behind in two long tails, through which is threaded some bright-colored ribbon." He concludes, "I have often seen their plaits reach nearly to the ground."[46]

The peaked cap of the women was worn throughout Maine and the Maritimes in varying forms. The Maliseet-Passamaquoddy type had a sharp peak and a curved lower edge. The Penobscot examples I have seen tend toward a blunter peak, while Micmac caps are straight-edged at the base.

During the mid–nineteenth century, women began to abandon the

A-11. Peaked cap with the curved bottom edge and decorative style of the Penobscots, Passamaquoddies, and Maliseets, probably made about 1870 to 1880. (Maine State Museum collection.)

peaked cap in favor of high beaver hats with a large band of trade silver around the crown, often topped with black ostrich feathers. The portrait of Sarah Nicola (Fig. E-12b), a Penobscot, shows her with this headgear around 1830.

The main item of male dress in the nineteenth century was a long wool coat modeled on, or remade from, the European army greatcoat.

The coat or hunting-frock does not reach so low as that of the [women]; it is, in general, blue, with scarlet cuffs and collar, richly worked with beads and scarlet cloth let into all the seams as in a Lancer's jacket. A broad crimson ribbon generally gives a very pretty finish to the bottom of the coat, and across the back and shoulders is a mass of embroidery. I have seen some chiefs of the Penobscot tribe with scarlet coats, almost a mass of beads. This is very magnificent....
From an embroidered [beaded] shoulder-belt or baldrick is hung the powder-horn; and their knives, tomahawks, and tobacco pouches or pitchmaugans [which are] skins (entire) upon which embroidery [beaded panels] is attached, are suspended through their belts of wampum.[47]

The men wore leggings and moccasins similar to those of the women. During the nineteenth century the loincloth gradually gave way to knee-length breeches, worn with leggings, and then to long pants.

A wood-engraving of Passamaquoddy chief John Francis, which appeared in the September 5, 1863, edition of the *Illustrated London News*, shows appliquéd leggings with a wide selvage, a military jacket with beaded borders, and a shoulder belt that may be the entire skin of a large animal such as an otter. It is possible to make out back legs and tail, which—like the entire underside of the animal—are covered with panels of beaded cloth. This was a common way of treating animal pouches. On the other hand, the object may simply be a beaded baldric with the ends cut in the shape of legs and a tail.[48]

Sometime around 1700, individual Maliseet-Passamaquoddy, Penobscot, and Micmac men began wearing an intriguing piece of headgear made of heavily beaded and appliquéd cloth. Levinge describes it as follows: "His head-dress, when in gala costume, is fashioned somewhat like that ... worn by the women, but descends much further down the back and having two pointed horns of the same material not unlike the horses' ears, on the top of the head; these are embroidered with beads; and the flap which hangs down behind is striped with ribbons of different colours."[49]

In his book *Penobscot Man*, Frank Speck claimed that this headdress was an owl's-ear decoy outfit, used in winter by deer hunters.[50] However, the

PENOBSCOT COATS ABROAD

By the mid–nineteenth century, Penobscot coats, identifiable by their elaborate and distinctive decoration, were showing up in surprising places. All six members of the Henry family (Ojibwa) wore them while on tour in Europe during the 1840s. This group portrait of the Henrys was taken in England in 1846 (Fig. A-13). How they obtained the coats is unknown, but their possession of them clearly indicates that the Maine tribes remained in touch with people and events throughout the greater Northeast.

The ambrotype in Figure A-12 shows a young Civil War soldier wearing a Penobscot coat. His hat, called a shako, bears the emblem of a New York military unit.

A-13. Daguerreotype of Maungwadas and members of his troupe who accompanied him to Europe in 1844–45, taken by George Catlin (1851?). (Courtesy of the Chicago Historical Society ICHi-08800.)

A-12. Ambrotype of militiaman wearing a Penobscot coat with Indian trappings. (Courtesy of John A. Hess.)

ears do not resemble those of any owl native to northeastern North America; nor does a man dressed as a giant owl seem a likely decoy for deer. Another more convincing explanation for the headdress is offered by Gaby Pelletier, who notes a close correspondence between its shape and the ears of the native dog, an animal much respected by Penobscots, Micmacs, and Maliseets.[51] Further evidence for the significance of dog symbolism among Native people of the Northeast can be found in John Gyles's description of a late-seventeenth-century dog feast held in preparation for war:

[The] dog's head . . . is scorched till the nose and lips have shrunk from the teeth and left them bare and grinning. This done, they fasten it on a stick, and the Indian who is proposed to be chief in the expedition, takes the head into his hand and sings a warlike song. . . . When the chief hath sung, he so places the dog's head as to grin at him who he supposeth will go [as] his second, who, if he accepts, takes the head in his hand and sings . . . and thus from one to another. . . . The Indians imagine that dog's flesh makes them bold and courageous. I have seen an Indian split a dog's head with a hatchet, take out the brains hot and eat them raw with the blood running down his jaws.[52]

Recall Levinge's statement that these caps were used for "gala" occasions, not hunting. War conferences were certainly gala occasions, with everyone quite literally "dressed to kill." Because dog brains were considered a power food and dog heads were important in a specifically male ceremony, it is not difficult to understand the transformation of the head used in the 1690s rite into a symbolic head, its potency now clothing the men rather than feeding them. The wearer of the headgear took on the tenacity and fearlessness of a dog by putting on the dog shape. Over the next two centuries, such caps became ceremonial dress for festive occasions.

During the eighteenth century, copper and brass increasingly gave way to silver, which was used to fabricate the large circular brooches and "coronets" or hatbands already mentioned, as well as gorgets, earrings, medals, wristbands, leg bands, and rings. Most of these items were made by Montreal silversmiths. By the mid–nineteenth century, both men and women took to wearing trade-silver hatbands as coronets and feathers, without the hats. These silver adornments were apparently very popular, for one Eastport resident commented that among the Passamaquoddies "The amount of silver in possession of the tribe in silver bands and circular plates [brooches] was considerable—in prosperity worn upon their persons, and when hard up a convenient pledge on which to raise funds."[53] Photographs from the period sometimes show men wearing feathers attached to elaborately beaded headbands or to silver coronets. This sort of decoration was not, however, everyday wear.

Some of the designs formerly painted on leather were continued as ribbon appliqué on cloth. These included the popular borders of parallel lines, with the upper edge often elaborated into geometric motifs. One design that seems to have been common to the Penobscot, Maliseet-Passamaquoddy, and Micmac peoples consists of the grouping of two large triangles with two or more small ones between them.

Glass beads, an important early trade item, were used in jewelry or sewn onto clothing. In the few eighteenth-century artifacts that survive, small white and blue spherical "pony beads" were used almost exclusively. In the nineteenth century, Native women began using the smaller, usually white, "seed beads" to replicate traditional painted or quilled motifs, including the double-curve design common to all three peoples. Some motifs, like the Penobscot diamond lozenge, remained specific to a single group. Around the mid–nineteenth century, colored seed beads, faceted metal beads, and sequins appeared, often worked into floral motifs, and Native work began to resemble European ladies' work of this Victorian period.

Shelter

Housing generally took the form of the wigwam. Josselyn, writing of the 1660s and early 1670s, provides a detailed account of such a structure in Maine:

Their houses, which they call *Wigwams*, are built with Poles pitcht into the ground of a round form for the most part, sometimes square, they bind down the tops of their poles, leaving a hole for smoak to go out at, the rest they cover with the bark of Trees, and line the inside of their *Wigwams* with mats made of Rushes painted with several colours, one good post they set up in the middle that reaches to the hole in the top, with a staff across before it a convenient height, they knock in a pin on which they hang their kettle, beneath that they set up a broad stone for a back which keepeth the post from burning; round by the walls they spread their mats and skins where the men sleep whilst their women dress their victuals, they have commonly two doors, one opening to South, the other to the North, and according as the wind sits, they close up one door with bark and hang a *Deare* skin or the like before the other.[54]

Josselyn seems to have been describing the dome-shaped wigwam, a style popular west of the Kennebec during the early seventeenth century; far-

A-14. Maliseet camp scene in western New Brunswick, about 1840. Watercolor over pencil by William R. Herries. (Courtesy of the National Archives of Canada.)

ther to the east, the poles of the frame were not bent down, giving the wigwam a conical shape. Though fairly simple in construction, wigwams are practical, spacious, waterproof dwellings that conserve heat remarkably well.

In conical wigwams, five or more large poles formed the main framework. These were lashed together at their tops with lengths of tough spruce root and then opened out at the other end until the desired perimeter of the wigwam's base was reached. The area inside was cleared of debris or snow and smoothed flat. The main poles were sometimes set into the ground about a foot deep. A bentwood hoop, usually of moosewood (*Viburnum cassinoides*), was then bound with more root to the insides of these poles at roughly head height to prevent any outward or inward slippage. Shorter secondary poles were then tied to this main hoop between each primary pole. The hoop thus provided stability for both frames. The gap between two of the main poles formed the wigwam's door frame. A smaller hoop was sometimes added near the top.

Next, long strips of bark from the white birch (*Betula papyrifera*) were moistened, warmed, and flattened, then laid over the wigwam frame in overlapping courses starting from the bottom. To prevent the bark from splitting or curling, the ends of each piece were whipstitched to a small split sapling—the flat side laid onto the bark surface and then oversewn with spruce root. A bone awl was used to make the necessary holes in the bark.

The long, overlapping courses were made up of sheets of bark sewn end to end, using split spruce root (its own bark removed); the sewing was done so that the flat side of the root lay against the bark or wood surface, with the rounded side giving a neat outer finish. More root tied these strips of bark to the wigwam frame. As wet birchbark quickly closes around any perforation, the awl-holes made in the wigwam cover for stitching would close around the root thread and thus keep the surface impervious to rain and drafts. The strips could be removed, rolled for transport, and reused on another wigwam. According to a Recollet missionary working among the Micmacs of Quebec's Gaspé region in 1676, "they are ornamented, as a rule, with a thousand different pictures of birds, moose, otters and beavers, which the women sketch there themselves with their paints."[55]

The bark cover reached only to the top of the secondary frame, with the apex left open for smoke to escape. (This opening was covered by a bark collar in bad weather.) Poles were laid against the construction at intervals outside, for extra stability.

Floors were made of layers of fir twigs, staked in one on top of the other, with their undersides up to point the sharp needles downward. The stems were oriented toward the central fire. This arrangement of the twigs cre-

A-15. Detail of the top of a wigwam, Penobscot, Indian Island, 1917. Photograph by Frank Speck. Note the small hoop attached to the interior of the poles. (Courtesy of the National Museum of the American Indian, Smithsonian Institution, neg. no. 12961.)

ated a springy cushion underfoot, and the interlinked stems allowed the whole mass to be picked up as a unit and discarded. A fir carpet such as this is very soft to sleep on, and it smells wonderful. Woven reed or cattail-leaf (*Typha latifolia*) mats and heaped skins provided the family with mattresses and bedding. As pointed out in Chapter 3, a wigwam at one archaeological site in Maine appears to have been "banked" with shell refuse to reduce drafts during cold weather. Gyles also mentions that wigwams had interior scaffolding for storage of household goods; one quite extensive arrangement, built inside a large wigwam and holding a butchered moose, fell on him and knocked him unconscious.[56]

A variant of the wigwam wherein one axis of the floor plan was longer than the other may simply have been a summer wigwam, described in Chapter 3. Such houses are archaeologically attested to by a post mold pattern at the Goddard site in Brooklin and appear to be depicted on a 1671 French map of the region. They may be the summerhouse form described by the Jesuit Pierre Biard, who wrote, "In Summer the shape of their houses is changed; for then they are broad and long, that they may have more air; then they nearly always cover them with bark, or mats made of tender reeds"[57] The "sometimes square" wigwam of Maine mentioned by Josselyn probably resembled the summer wigwam used throughout the region that had gables shaped like a modern A-frame. It might have a fire near each end door, and its floor plan was more rectangular than square. The basic frame consisted of two upright forked poles, spanned by a ridgepole. A variation of this form had a V-shaped floor plan, with three vertical support poles and two roof beams.

Champlain's 1607 map of present-day Saco shows not only the conical wigwam common to southern New England but also a long wigwam rather like a longhouse, a house form most often associated with the Iroquois but that was widely used by other groups throughout the Northeast. Paper birch was apparently scarce at Saco, and the houses were instead covered with oak bark.

The houses at Saco were "surrounded by palisades formed of rather large trees placed one against the other."[58] Defensive palisades are mentioned in a number of seventeenth-century accounts of the Maritime Peninsula. The village of Ouigoudi, at the site of present-day St. John, New Brunswick, for example, was described in 1606 as "a large enclosure upon raised ground enclosed with trees, great and small, fastened one to the other, and within many lodges, large and small, one of which was as big as a market-hall, wherein dwelt numerous families."[59]

While most shelters built by northeastern peoples were apparently intended to house only extended families, larger structures are also mentioned in the historical accounts. The earliest description of Etchemin wigwams, which dates to around 1610, states that they were "built with withs [withes], and covered ouer with Mats, six or seuen paces [7 to 8 meters] long."[60] Other seventeenth-century sources concerning the Micmacs mention conical structures that could hold up to thirty or thirty-five people and rectangular forms containing as many as four fires. Biard visited one building of unspecified form on the Sheepscot River that held eighty people.[61]

In addition to the wigwam, smaller structures were erected for use as sweat lodges—a form of steam bath. A late-seventeenth-century Maliseet sweat lodge involved heating a collection of small rocks and then building over them a "small hut covered with skin and mats." Water poured over the rocks created such an excess of steam that the hut had to be vented occasionally lest the occupants suffocate.[62] Various temporary shelters were also built for use on overnight journeys or at hunting camps.

Of all these house styles, however, it is the conical wigwam that has come to be recognized as the "traditional" Eastern Algonquian house form. It was portable, comfortable, and took less than a day to erect. Because of its practicality, it remained relatively unchanged in form and construction for many centuries. When Frenchmen criticized them for not building more "proper" houses, the Micmac response was, "Do we not find in ours all the conveniences and the advantages that you have in yours, such as reposing, drinking, sleeping, eating and amusing ourselves with our friends when we like?"[63] Whites continued to apply pressure, though, and one Maliseet-Passamaquoddy man is said to have complied by building a two-story house and setting up his wigwam inside it.[64]

Transportation

Canoes, snowshoes, and toboggans were invented by the Native people of North America. These prime examples of Native technology played a large role in human survival on the Maritime Peninsula. All three were rapidly adopted by European colonists and continue to be used today.

The canoe was the item of Native manufacture that most impressed the newcomers. Many Europeans would imitate Gosnold, who in 1602 appropriated one and took it back to England.[65] One such souvenir canoe was taken by Pring, who left a detailed description of it:

Canoe form varied according to group. In their classic study of Native North American watercraft, Adney and Chappelle note that "The old form of Malecite canoe used on the large rivers and along the coast appears to have had rather high peaked ends, with a marked overhang fore and aft. . . . [T]he Penobscot [also] built their canoes on the old Malecite model." Micmacs, on the other hand, built canoes with a gracefully rounded and sometimes strongly hogged shear. The small canoe of the interior Abenakis (typically around 4 meters in length) had a sharply upswept shear.

Ideal for travel in the upland streams of forested country, it was widely adopted as far west as Ontario.[66]

A Passamaquoddy coastal canoe of "old form" ranged from 5 1/2 to 6 meters in length, with a maximum beam between 60 and 110 inches and a depth amidships of 45 to 55 centimeters. It had 42 to 48 ribs that were around 8 centimeters wide and less than 2 centimeters thick. Sheathing was between 3/4 of a centimeter to 1 centimeter thick. "These canoes were still being built well into the 1880s, if not later."[67]

Their boats, whereof we brought one to Bristoll, were in proportion like a Wherrie of the Riuer Thames, seventeen foot long and foure foot broad, and made of the Barke of a Birch-tree, farre exceeding in bignesse those of England: it was sowed together with strong and tough Oziers or twigs [spruce root], and the seames covered over with Rozen . . . it was also open like a Wherrie, and sharpe at both ends, saving that the beake was a little bending roundly upward. And though it carried nine men standing vpright, yet it weighed not at the most above sixtie pounds. . . . Their Oares were flat at the end like an Oven peele [a baker's wooden shovel], made of Ash or Maple very light and strong, about two yardes long.[68]

Historically, bark canoes from the Maine-Maritimes region rarely exceeded 30 feet in length, but when they were built with rockered bottoms and hogged gunwales and had a tumble-home added to their cross sections, such vessels were capable of handling remarkably rough water.[69] The canoe's ability to navigate rough coastal waters, shallow streams, and moderate rapids made it infinitely more versatile than any European craft. In hilly wooded country where the only roads were waterways, it was the best possible means of transportation, capable of carrying great loads but light enough to be portaged from one waterway to another or around dangerous rapids. And it was fast: "This we noted as we went along, they in their Canoa with three oares, would at their will go ahead of us and about us, when we rowed with eight oars strong."[70]

The most comprehensive early account of canoe construction from the region is that given by seventeenth-century Frenchman Nicolas Denys.

A-16. Passamaquoddies Nicholas Lolu, his wife, and his child, with a canoe under construction. Houlton, Maine, July 1875. Photograph by G. John Bryson. (Courtesy of the National Anthropological Archives, Smithsonian Institution, photo no. 44743.)

A-17. Penobscot moose-hide canoe, about 1910. This canoe was probably built as a demonstration for anthropologist Frank Speck. (Courtesy of the University of Pennsylvania Museum, neg. no. NC35-13929.)

A-18. Newly constructed Micmac canoe in Digby, Nova Scotia, early twentieth century. Note that the seams have not been pitched. Photograph by Harry Cochrane. (History Collections, Nova Scotia Museum, Halifax.)

Though it refers to the making of a Micmac canoe in Nova Scotia, it applies almost as well to canoemaking in the whole of the Maritime Peninsula.

For making their canoes they sought the largest Birch trees they could find. They removed the bark of the length of the canoe, which was about two feet in the middle, and always diminished towards the two ends, falling away to nothing. The depth was such that for a man seated it came up to his armpits. The lining inside for strengthening it was of slats, of the length of the canoe and some four inches broad, lessening towards the ends in order that they might match together. On the inside the canoe was lined with them completely, as well as all along it from one end to the other. These slats were made of Cedar, which is light and which they split in as great lengths as they wished, and also as thin as they pleased. They also made from the same wood half-circles to form ribs, and gave them their form in the fire.

For sewing the canoe, they took roots of Fir [spruce] of the thickness of the little finger, and even smaller; they were very long. They split these roots into three or four parts, that is the largest ones. . . . There were also necessary two sticks of the length of the canoe, entirely round and of the thickness of a large cane, and four other shorter sticks of Beech. All these things being ready, they took their bark and bent and fixed it in the form the canoe should have; then they placed the two long pieces all along and sewed them to the rim inside with these roots. . . . The sticks being well sewed on all along, they placed also the smaller pieces of beech crosswise, one in the middle, entering at its two ends into holes made in the pieces with which the canoe is rimmed, and three others in front of it, distant a half fathom [approximately 1 meter] from one another, which lessened in length with the shape of the canoe. Three others were also placed backward at the same distances. All these pieces entered also at the ends into holes which were made in the pieces sewed all along the canoe, to which they were so firmly attached to both sides that the canoe could neither enlarge nor narrow.

Then are placed in position those big slats with which they lined all the interior of the canoe from top to bottom, and they were all made to touch one another. To hold them in place, they put over them those half-circles, the ends of which were brought to join on both sides below those pieces which were sewn all around on the top. They drove these in with force, and lined all the canoe with them from one end to the other. This made the canoe stiff to such a degree that it did not yield at any point.

There were seams in it, for in order to narrow it at the two ends they split the bark from above downwards; they then overlapped the two edges one over the other, and sewed them. But to prevent the seams from admitting water, the women and girls chewed the gum of the Fir [spruce] every day until it became a salve which they applied by aid of fire all along the seams, and this tightened them better than pitch. All this being done, the canoe was finished, and was so light that a single man could carry it on his head.[71]

Fir gum has to be emulsified by mixing with charcoal and bear fat, so that it will adhere to the bark. Otherwise, the cooling resin simply peels off.

Some Maine canoes seem to have made use of a sail, but it is not clear whether this practice was borrowed from Europeans. Adney and Chappelle note that the usual type was a dory-style spritsail, but moose hides and small trees were also used to catch the wind.[72] A story that appeared in an 1880 issue of *Scribner's Monthly* mentions a Penobscot or Passamaquoddy man, "who, for lack of a sail, put up a big bush in the bow of his canoe; all went well with him until the wind increased to a gale and he could not get forward to reef his bush. So he sat like a statue, steering with his paddle and repeating in a mournful monotone: 'Too much bush, too much bush, for little canoe.'"[73] Canoes were often ornamented, either with paint or by bark incising, in which the darker inner layer of birchbark is scraped off to show the lighter bark beneath. "The Malecite, particularly the Passamaquoddy, were especially skillful in decorating bark canoes.... Sometimes they used scraped winter bark [incising] just along the gunwales; occasionally the whole canoe was decorated in this manner above the normal load waterline.... Usually, however, the bark decoration was confined to a long panel just below the gunwales and to the ends of the canoe. The personal 'mark' of the owner-builder would usually be on the flaps near the ends."[74]

A passage in John Gyles's memoirs runs as follows: "When the spring came and the rivers broke up, we moved back to the head of St. John's River, and there made canoes of moose hides, sewing three or four together and pitching the seams with balsam mixed with charcoal. Then we went down the river . . . [to] the place where we left our birch canoes in the fall."[75] These moose-hide canoes were expedient constructions of untanned skins framed by lashed saplings and a sheathing of small poles.[76] Adney and Chappelle note, however, that the Maliseets preferred spruce-bark canoes as temporary craft; no examples of either kind have survived, except as models and in photographs.[77]

While most canoes were small craft, there was no inherent limit on length or beam, as with a dugout, for bark sheets could be sewn together to cover larger frames. The Hudson's Bay Company regularly built fur-transport canoes that were more than 11 meters long and possessed a beam of 1 3/4 meters.[78] And neither were Native peoples tradition-bound in their use of this technology, as Josselyn, writing of his 1638 visit, makes clear: "We had sight of an Indian Pinnace sailing by us made of Birch-bark, sewed together with the roots of spruce and white Cedar (drawn out into threads)

A-19. Engraving by Thomas Harriot, based on a painting by John White, showing the use of fire in dugout canoe–making in North Carolina in 1585–86. (Reproduced from Harriot 1590.)

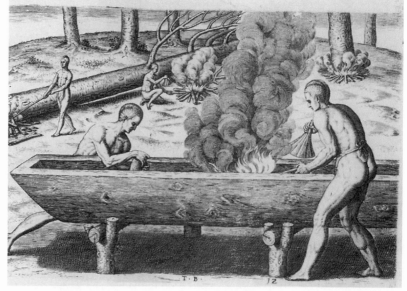

The manner of makinge their boates. XII.

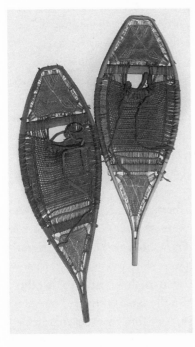

A-20. Penobscot snowshoes made about 1850 in a square-toed pattern that was said to have been adopted from the Ottawas. (Maine State Museum collection.)

with deck, and trimmed with sails top and top gallant very sumptuously."[79]

Along the coast to the west of the Kennebec, however, prime canoe birch became less abundant and boat builders there resorted to another style—the dugout. Lescarbot gives one of the first descriptions of the wooden dugouts used in western Maine: "The Armouchiquois...do make another fashion of canoes, for, having neither [metal] hatchets nor knives (except some copper ones), they burn a very straight tall tree close to the ground, and so fell it; then they take such length as they will, and use fire instead of a saw, scraping the burnt part with stones; and for hollowing out the vessel they do the same. One of those boats will hold six men and some cargo, and will make long voyages, but these kind of canoes are heavier than the others."[80]

In winter people traveled on foot, usually on the ice roads formed by frozen streams. Their household goods and butchered game could be pulled easily over the ice on toboggans. The toboggan, with its turned-up front, was manufactured from thin sheets of rock maple (*Acer saccharum*). The first slab was split from the crotch of the first branch down almost to the ground, to include the outer curve of the branch. The second slab was split from the crotch of the second branch up, and so on.[81] If whole pieces of this nature were not available, the wood was bent by pouring boiling water over it.

A sled with runners was made of maple or yellow birch (*Betula alleghaniensis*); it could carry half a moose. Two curved runners were fitted with three upright stakes each, supporting a flat bar. The runners were joined by a crosspiece running between these top bars and by two diagonally placed braces that passed either over or under the crosspiece. This bracing was covered with a platform of rough boards or stakes.[82]

According to Josselyn, "In the winter when the snow will bear them, they fasten to their feet their snowshoes which are made like a large Racket we play at *Tennis* with, lacing them with *Deers*-guts [rawhide] and the like."[83] And in 1672, Denys described the gendered division of labor used to make snowshoes: "The work of the men was to make the frame of the snowshoes, bend them, polish them, place the two bars across them, and make them all ready to be corded [by women]." He added that Micmac snowshoes were made of beech, although the term for snowshoes in most regional languages incorporates the word for ash tree [*Fraxinus sp.*; *aqm* in Micmac], and all examples I have seen from the region are of ash.[84] "Micmac *raquettes*," Denys went on, were "of the thickness [depth] of those used in playing tennis, but longer and thicker [wider] and of the same form without a handle."

The length of each was as a rule the distance from the waist to the ground. They placed there two pieces of wood which ran across, at a distance from one another equal to the length of the foot. They were corded with Moose skin, dressed to parchment; this was cut into very long cords [which were] both thick and thin. The thick were placed in the middle part of the snow-shoe, where the foot rests between the two sticks, while the thin were used at the two ends. Close against the stick in front there was left an opening in the middle of the snow-shoe to admit the end of the foot in walking. This was in order that the snow-shoe might not rise behind, and that it might do nothing but drag.[85]

Women filled in the hexagonally woven mesh using a wood or bone weaving needle. A variety of constructions and mesh sizes enabled the user to maneuver in different snow conditions. Snowshoes gave hunters a significant advantage over large animals, which were slowed down by deep snow. To run down big game in winter a more open mesh was used so that there was less snow accumulation to weigh down the shoe. Ordinary "carrying" or walking snowshoes had a closer mesh, very finely woven, that helped support and spread the weight of the wearer and his or her burdens. A good example is the Penobscot pair shown in Figure A-20. Temporary snow-shoes could be made up of withes or strips of yellow birch fiber, and in a sudden snowstorm, fir branches tied to the feet could provide a makeshift solution.

Fire

Two basic techniques were employed to make fire: percussion and friction. There is archaeological evidence for the former being used in Maine as long as four thousand years ago; it was widespread in the Northeast, although it was not encountered there by seventeenth-century Europeans.[86] However, Brereton observed it in Massachusetts as early as 1602: "They strike fire in this manner; every one carrieth about hime in a purse of tewed [fringed] leather a Minerall stone . . . and with a flat Emerie stone (wherewith Glasiers cut glasse, and cutlers glaze blades) tied to the end of a little stick, gently he striketh upon the Minerall stone, and within a stroke or two a sparke falleth upon a piece of touchwood (much like our Spunge in England) and with the least sparke he maketh a fire presently."[87] This portable firemaking kit was equivalent to the contemporary European flint, steel, and tinder. The "Minerall stone" was chalcedony, chert, or other siliceous rock; the "touchwood" rotten wood or a fungus material called punk; and the "Emerie stone" a piece of iron pyrite.

A variety of friction techniques were used to make fire. The simplest, the fire saw, is described by Josselyn: "The *Indians* will rub two sear'd sticks of any sort of wood, and kindle a fire with them presently."[88] During his captivity, Gyles observed the simple fire drill in use, apparently as a back-up option "if an Indian has lost his fire-work [flint and steel]."[89] The pump drill was the most elaborate technique used in the Northeast.[90] Joseph Nicolar, a nineteenth-century Penobscot, gave the following account:

a speed wheel made from the inner bark of the yellow birch in three or four thicknesses, fastened together so that it will have some weight, and a small soft wood spindle two or three hands long put through this wheel so that when the wheel turns it would turn the spindle. The spindle must be longer from the wheel up than below it. To the top end of this spindle some fine strips to be sufficient lengths so that when the wheel turns it carries the spindle with it and the string winds around the spindle, the other end of the string being tied to another stick which is placed in a horizontal position with one of these strings on each end, and the spindle being in an upright position so when the wheel is in motion it winds up the strings and the horizontal stick. When the operator finds the stick is well up the top of the spindle, presses the stick down, it stops the whirl of the wheel and soon begins to revolve the other way, this repeated lively, a blaze is brought at the foot of the spindle, spunk [punk] is applied and a fire is lighted.[91]

All such techniques were relatively inconvenient, and considerable effort was made to conserve fire. Nicolar also described the Penobscot method that involved carrying smoldering punk in a whole clamshell that was lined with clay, closed, and tied up tightly. The punk "burnt so slow that a very small piece lasted half a day and emitted scarcely any smoke, so that it could be carried in a pouch made for the purpose."[92]

Gear: Materials and Methods of Manufacture

A virgin who has been educated to make *monoodahs* [bags] and birch dishes, to lace snow shoes, and make indian shoes, to string wampum belts, sew birch canoes, and boil the kettle is esteemed as a lady of fine accomplishments. . . . If parents have a daughter marriageable, they seek a husband for her who is a good hunter. And if he have a gun and ammunition, a canoe, spear and hatchet, a *monoodah*, and a crooked knife, a looking-glass and paint, a pipe, tobacco, and knot-bowl to toss a kind of dice in, he is accounted a gentleman of a plentiful fortune.[93]

We shall now look at the basic equipment, furnishing, tools, and techniques of manufacture employed by Native peoples in the Northeast. The opening quote from Gyles gives us a partial inventory of Native material culture in the late 1600s, but it also provides us with a useful framework for our examination, for it draws a clear line between items made by women and items made by men.

A number of crafts were predominantly the responsibility of one sex or the other, and for the manufacture of some items these skills were combined: for snowshoes, as an example. Men did most of the woodwork, so they made snowshoe frames and weaving needles. Women were largely responsible for the treatment and working of skins, so they cut rawhide strips and wove them in as the snowshoe "filling." This integration and division of responsibilities and craft skills permitted a degree of specialization, although both men and women were probably familiar enough with all methods of manufacture to cope in emergencies.

Generally, women did the butchering, farming, and cooking, built the wigwams, and produced clothing and ornamentation. In addition they made containers of all kinds: baskets, boxes, bowls, pots. They were experts in the use of plant or animal fibers and created bags, mats, cordage, and textiles. Women also fletched arrows and made many of the smaller articles whose materials called for fine coordination and manual dexterity.

Fibers and Textiles

Native fibers and textiles were highly complex and diversified. Over the centuries, women developed weaving techniques that enabled them to make use of an enormous range of materials: the inner bark of cedar (mainly white cedar, *Thuja occidentalis*) and basswood (*Tilia americana*), rushes (mainly *Scirpus lacustris* and *Typha latifolia* [cattails]), nettle (*Labitae sp.*), Indian hemp (*Apocynum cannabinum*), sweet grass (*Hierochloë odorata*), the smaller roots of spruce (*Picea sp.*), wood fibers and splints, rawhide, tendon thread, feathers, moose hair, and porcupine quills, plus the skins of every kind of animal from moose to rabbit to eel.

Thread could be used to sew clothing and plied or braided to make strong cordage such as bowstrings. Rawhide was obtained from the untanned skins of large mammals. The entire fresh skin would be cut into a single long strip about a half centimeter wide, starting at the outer edge and cutting around the border, working in a spiral inward. The resulting length of thong was stretched and used while wet. As the skin dried, it contracted, auto-

A POSSIBLE SEVENTEENTH-CENTURY ABENAKI TWINED BAG

Oral tradition claims that this twined fiber bag (Fig. A-21) was in the possession of Mrs. Susannah Eastman Wood when she returned from two years of captivity after being taken by Indians during a raid on Haverhill in 1688. It remains unclear who the raiders were, but the captors of another woman, Hannah Dustin, traveled northward after the raid. It is therefore possible that the bag was made by a Penacook or an Abenaki. It is one of only three examples of seventeenth-century weaving provenanced to New England.[94]

A-21. Twined fiber bag from the late seventeenth century. (Courtesy of Rendall Brough.)

matically tightening any weave or binding it was used for. This made rawhide especially useful as a lashing for hafted tools or as a snowshoe filling. A third animal-derived cordage was apparently made from eel skin, which also contracts as it dries. "To make them," wrote Speck, "large eel skins in the raw state are selected and cut in strips about an inch wide, then braided in three ply."[95]

The use of moose "wool" in the Maritime Peninsula as a yarn for knitting or weaving was recorded by Speck and others. According to Speck, this "grey wool which grows thickly near the roots of the hair in the mane" was hand-rolled into yarn and then either finger-woven or woven on a small rigid-heddle loom. The latter process may have been borrowed from the Europeans, as was knitting done with wooden needles.[96]

Strips of rabbit skin, cut in the same way as rawhide but with the hair still on, were worked into textiles. The Penobscots told Speck that "one of the methods of construction was to braid together broad strips and then join these together by sewing to the width desired."[97] A second technique, used by other Eastern Algonquian people, involved twisting the strips into cords and then using them in a loop-netting technique. "The looping was done on a simple frame.... [I]t required about six days and up to two hundred skins to make a large blanket."[98] Another method was to wrap the strips around a second cord, the whole of which was woven or made into a net.

Women also made a number of vegetable-fiber "threads" and cordage. As mentioned earlier, the roots of black spruce and white cedar were used for sewing bark and for lashing together the wigwam frame. Root lashing did not have to be kept dry and could be split into a range of widths.

An even more versatile material was Indian hemp, a plant related to flax. Indian hemp was gathered in the fall. Like flax, the stalks were retted or soaked in water over a period of weeks to rot the soft tissue. The remaining fibers were softened by rolling in the hand or on the thigh, then plied into thread, twine, or rope. Quills were sometimes woven on a weft of such thread or plaited on it to make the "artificial strings" noted by Archer, in Massachusetts, who speaks more than once of "hemp" and "artificial strings coloured."[99] Beads were strung on this cordage and wampum woven on it. Indian hemp was sometimes twine-woven into bags or mats, either separately or in combination with other materials. In a twine weave, two wefts per run are passed over and under the same warp. Champlain saw Native peoples from Cape Anne (northern Massachusetts) and southward whose clothes were "made from grasses and hemp," probably twine-woven.[100]

Articles woven of Indian hemp could be patterned by dyeing warp and weft strands with vegetable dyes, a number of which are mentioned here in the section on costume. A second decorative technique, known as "false embroidery," used both dyed and undyed porcupine quills or moose hair and, later, colored yarns. False embroidery, which involves the wrapping of the decorative medium around selected outward projections of the weft strands, is done during the weaving process. The "wrong" side of the textile is not embellished and shows only the tail ends of the ornamental material, where it is carried through at the beginning and end of each wrap.

A beautiful example of this technique is the eighteenth-century fabric made by a Saco Indian named Molliocket (Marie Agathe). She presented it to Eli Twitchel of Bethel, who had it made into a wallet with a date of 1778 engraved on the silver hasp. The rectangular piece is made of tightly twine-woven vegetable fiber, probably Indian hemp. The false embroidery deco-

A-22. Twine-woven textile made by Molliocket in 1778. (Collections of the Maine Historical Society.)

A-23. Penobscot woman weaving a flexible hunting bag from the inner bark of basswood, about 1910. Photograph by Frank Speck. (Courtesy of the University of Pennsylvania Museum, neg. no. NC35-13854.)

ration is in moose hair. The weaving is apparently so fine that each projection of the double-twine weft could be covered with a single hair, wrapped only three times around each outward-facing weft strand. The moose hairs are dyed red, green, blue, and yellow, with some left the undyed white. The false embroidery covers the entire outer side of the textile in a series of geometric motifs that include a stepped figure. The inside of the woven piece is lined with green flannel, and the whole closes into a "two-fold pocketbook of European pattern," fastened with a hasp.[101]

Another intriguing Indian textile form is known only from a few fragments found in the twenty-five-hundred-year-old Micmac site at Red Bank, New Brunswick. These pieces are two-ply twine weave, with both warp and weft possibly made of sinew or the inner bark of basswood. Paired warps in this material were plaited together, using lengths of five or six moose hairs as the third element of each braid but inserted at right angles to the two other warps. Variations in the pattern were produced by alternating braided and unbraided warps in a number of different groupings. The wefts cross the weave at the end of each length of plaited-in hairs, thus tying them off.[102]

Because Indian hemp can survive a wetting, it was used in the manufacture of fishing lines and possibly for nets. "The Armouchiquois, who have hemp, make fishing lines with it."[103] The compound fishhooks that Champlain saw at Plymouth, described below, were assembled with hemp, "which in my opinion is like that of France."[104]

A second type of vegetable-fiber fishing line was basswood cordage, which was said to be stronger "diameter for diameter" than any other natural-fiber rope.[105] The fibers of the inner bark of basswood, *Tilia americana*, are gathered in the spring, when they separate more readily from the outer bark. The inner bark, which is white and free of knots, is cut into vertical strips, then pulled off. Because basswood fiber was still being used by Penobscots in the late nineteenth century, Speck was able to describe how it was harvested, processed, and manufactured into different products. "One old man with whom I traveled had the beguiling habit of singing songs to the pulling of the bark because he thought the bark came off stronger and freer on account of it. Some of the strips not more than two fingers in width and almost as thin as paper held our combined weight when we tried to swing from them. 'See what my song do, boy!' said he."[106]

Speck reports that the strips were boiled in water with wood ashes: "The lye softens the fibres and extracts the slimy juice which would otherwise make them stiff and brittle when dry." Thread and line were prepared using thin strips that were twisted and plied when wet. Speck reported that the simple dip net of basswood fiber was still used to catch fish in shallow places.

The only seventeenth-century reference to a fishing net in Maine is by Josselyn, who writes, "[T]he Alewives they take in nets like a pursenet put upon a round hoop'd stick with a handle in fresh ponds."[107] Speck noted that the Penobscot word for nets contains a reference to basswood. Such dip nets were still used for shallow-water fishing during his time but were no longer "homemade." However, the Penobscots still knew the "almost world-wide" netting knot and were able to provide him with examples of the equally widespread netting tool or bobbin.[108]

Strips of basswood bark could be woven into tumplines, the straps or slings used to carry burdens, with a central wide band crossing the forehead and narrowing at both sides to lash the load at the back. The narrower portions of tumplines were sometimes braided for greater strength, using the complex finger-weaves at which the women excelled. Bark was also plaited to make harnesses and rope, and wide strips were assembled in a checkered or twill weave to make mats and perhaps even blankets.[109]

Another bark suitable for textiles came from white cedar. A small bag made of twine-woven cedar bark was found at a sixteenth-century Micmac site near Pictou, Nova Scotia, and a contemporary site at Northport contained a twill-woven fragment of cedar bark strips.[110] The inner bark of white cedar was split and twisted and used as substitute thongs, as filling for temporary snowshoes, and for carrying bags.[111] Fibrous strips from larger logs were boiled with a small amount of fat and woven.[112]

The common bulrush grows along the edge of fresh or brackish water. It was gathered by women and girls in the fall, when it had reached its maximum height of about 2 meters. These reeds were sun-dried for several weeks, then dyed and woven into a wide variety of items: "baskets, bags and mats woven with Sparke [Indian hemp?], bark of the *Line-Tree* [probably basswood], and *Rushes* of several kindes, dyed as before, some blacke, blew, red, yellow."[113]

Women would "line the inside of their *Wigwams* with mats made of Rushes painted with several colours."[114] Lescarbot, probably referring mainly to the Micmacs, noted that such mats provided additional warmth: "[W]hen winter approaches . . . they prepare mats of rushes, wherewith they garnish their cabins, with others to sit upon, and all very skilfully; they also colour their rushes, and therewith make square patterns in their work, as our gardeners do in their garden knots, with such symmetry that nothing is found amiss therein."[115] This matting was twine-woven; fragments of woven reeds survive from the Pictou site that show at least two variations of this technique. In one, the wefts twist around a single warp. In the other, the wefts bind two warps every time, but in alternating pairs, producing a more open weave with a diamond pattern. Similar textiles were recovered from the Northport site.[116]

Lescarbot and other seventeenth-century writers noted "panniers" and "sacks" of woven reed. "They make bags of flattened rushes, which they plaited one within another."[117] New Brunswick's Red Bank site included a fragment of cattail leaves, twine-woven with an unflattened reed weft. Cattail leaves were also dried and sewn with cordage of two-ply- or three-ply grass to make mats, which were finished with braided leaves sewn along the edge.[118]

Unfortunately, there are no specimens or fragments remaining of what was probably the most beautiful Native textile, the "curious coats" woven for children with turkey feathers referred to by Josselyn.[119] Because we have no examples of this textile, it is impossible to say exactly how it was made. Josselyn mentions it three times but gives no details of its construction. In Massachusetts, Thomas Morton describes examples that were apparently "woven with twine of their own making," and John Smith saw feather cloaks or mantles made "in such a manner that nothing can be seen but feathers."[120]

Another thing that remains obscure is how and with what southern Maine Indians made their containers for cornmeal. "They beat their Corn to powder and put it up into bags," writes Josselyn.[121] These bags could have been made of hemp, bark, reed, grass, or a combination of such materials. In Massachusetts these containers were buried as subterranean silos, but there is no evidence of this practice in Maine.

In addition to making quivers and bags of vegetable fiber, women transformed animal leather and fur into pouches, knife sheaths, and cases to keep the bowstring or the musket dry. They also processed animal gut into casings for dried fruit and sausage meat. Bladders "of some animal, or a long section of the large bowel [were] commonly used as receptacles for the preservation of their Fish and Seal oil."[122]

Birchbark

Then there was birchbark, the all-purpose material that has been called "Native plastic." Women used it to make not only wigwam covers and canoes but also to make bowls, boxes, baskets, bailers, cups, dippers, hats, plates, rain gear, and torches. Rosier and his companions were offered berries in "great cups made very wittily of barke, in form almost square."[123]

And Josselyn writes: "Delicate sweet dishes too they make of *Birch-Bark* sowed with threads drawn from *Spruse* or white *Cedar-Roots* . . . these they make of all sizes from a dram cup to a dish containing a pottle, likewise Buckets to carry water or the like, large Boxes too of the same materials . . . Kettles of *Birchen-bark* which they used before they traded with the *French* for Copper Kettles."[124]

Bark peels more easily from the tree in the heat of summer. The prime time for gathering summer bark was the last week in July through the first two weeks in August, when all it took to split the bark from the trunk was slipping a finger between the two. Speck's Penobscot informants, however, indicated that the thick birchbark needed for canoes and wigwams was "best when obtained in the winter months—fire is then applied to make the tree peel. . . . The tree is felled so that it will fall upon two logs for a bed, about six inches or so from the ground. Then a slow fire is made under one side, and a lengthwise cut is made along the top of the log. The edges of the cut are loosened and, with a wooden chisel about six inches long, the bark is forced from the log little by little. Warm water poured on helps the operation."[125]

Birchbark was made into containers that could not only hold water but that could also be used to boil it. Methods included adding small red-hot stones to the water, suspending the bark vessel over the fire, or placing the vessel on two green logs over the embers. Speck writes: "I have witnessed this. On one occasion it required less than twenty minutes to bring cold water to boiling. The vessel . . . suffered no damage, although the older Indians say that such kettles did not last long."[126] To make a container, the birchbark was cut to a specific pattern, then slit, folded up, and sewn with spruce or cedar root that had been debarked and split to the required thinness. The women would dye these roots to add to the beauty of the finished bark piece.

Josselyn also noted barkwork "garnished on the out-side with flourisht works."[127] This was done using the technique of bark incising, described earlier. Such decorations were possible because, as in canoemaking, the birchbark was used inside out. According to Speck, the inner side was first darkened with dye: "A rich dark colour is given to the bark by applying a hot rag saturated with a dye made by boiling alder bark. The designs incised appear in the lighter color of the under bark."[128] The designs were actually produced by scraping away the dark innermost bark to reveal the much lighter, papery outer layers. Predyeing was not strictly necessary, as it merely enhanced the natural brown of the inner bark. Incised designs included the double-curve motif and geometric patterns, and, during more

A-24a–d. Mid-nineteenth-century
birchbark vessels, Maritime Peninsula
region. (Maine State Museum
collection.)

recent times, realistic depictions of humans, animals, and plants. Bark containers may also have been embellished, as were wigwam covers, "with a thousand different pictures of birds, moose, otters and beavers, which the women sketch there themselves with their paints."[129]

The rims of birchbark containers were reinforced with wooden hoops and oversewn with spruce root. Decoration was added in the form of porcupine quills interwoven in and out of the spruce-root stitchery around the rim. In this manner women created checkered designs of white or dyed quills. Josselyn described seeing such vessels in Maine; Denys reported seeing similar ornamentation in the Maritimes: "They made their dishes, large and small, of bark. They sewed them with the Fir [spruce] roots so well that they held water. They ornamented some of them with quills of Porcupine."[130] Quills may also have been wrapped and tied around the wooden rim of bark dishes.

Another method of ornamenting bark with porcupine quills, in which the quills were laid over the bark to form a quill mosaic, apparently originated after European contact, as a Micmac souvenir art.[131] This technique, whereby the quill ends were inserted into holes in the wet bark, seems to have been practiced well into the twentieth century by the Micmacs, although a few individuals from other tribal groups in Maine and New Brunswick may have picked it up. Quillwork mosaics on bark were made for sale to appeal to whites, and consequently took European forms: boxes, hat cases, tea cozies, panels for furniture, and the like.

A second type of ornamented, made-for-trade barkwork consisted of objects embroidered with moose hair. This technique was pioneered by the Ursuline order in Quebec and passed on to their Indian pupils, who provided them with their raw materials. The animal's mane-hairs were dyed, then threaded one at a time through steel needles and sewn directly through the birchbark or through cloth with a bark backing. Floral motifs and European embroidery stitches—such as the French knot—predominated, and the items produced ranged from card trays, glove cases, and handkerchief boxes to spectacle cases, pincushions, and watch pockets. Both the Micmacs and Maliseet-Passamaquoddies were proficient in the art of moose-hair embroidery, but Eckstorm says that in the 1870s no women at Oldtown, Maine, could be found who knew how to dye or embroider with moose hair.[132] This does not necessarily mean that the Penobscots who lived there never did fancywork of this type on bark; it may not have been as popular as with the Maliseets or as long-lasting as a moneymaking craft.

A number of other minor items were also made from birchbark, such as rain gear, for which the bark was folded and cut like a poncho, and conical moose calls (which were probably made by men). Birchbark's primary use, however, after the canoe and wigwam, was as a raw material for containers. After European contact, women redirected this craft to create birchbark canisters, hat boxes, tea caddies, and flower pots, all of which they traded or sold to the settlers.

Because of the availability of birchbark and its capacity to be transformed into lightweight, waterproof cookware that could be decorated, there was not as great an emphasis on pottery in the region as in other parts of North America. As noted in Chapter 3, although pottery was still being manufactured to the west and south of Maine until the mid–seventeenth century, there are no historic accounts of potterymaking on the Maritime Peninsula. Even the verbose Josselyn, writing of the period around 1670, does not mention it, emphasizing instead the variety of containers made of bark. At present we cannot determine when the art died out. It is probable that the early introduction of European copper pots was an important factor in its demise; if so, we would expect it to have persisted in western Maine longer than it did farther to the northeast on the Maritime Peninsula.

Basketry

Native women, the primary basketmakers, were familiar with at least four weaves. As mentioned earlier, the twine weave involves the passing of two wefts per run over and under the same warp. This weave can be used to create wickerwork, in which the warps (standards) are fairly rigid, and both they and the wefts (weavers) are circular or semicircular in cross section. Modern wicker furniture is an example. Plant shoots or branches were used from a number of species, including red-osier dogwood (*Cornus stolonifera*), alder (*Alnus crispa, rugosa*), elder (*Sambucus pubescens*), witherod (*Viburnum cassinoides*), yellow birch (*Betula alleghaniensis*), and various types of willow (*Salix sp.*). There may have also been fish and eel traps made of wicker, although the Penobscot traps described and illustrated by Speck were made of rough ash splints.[133]

The two best-known modern Native-made basket types, the rib and splint basket forms, are probably English introductions.[134] In rib baskets, a thick wooden hoop forms the rim, and another wooden hoop lashed on at right angles forms the centered handle and the midpoint of the bottom. The basket is shaped by lashing further ribs under the rim on both sides of the midpoint base and then filling in the weave with lengths of thin wood strips or with spruce root. The lashing is done with the same material.

Splint baskets, too, are apparently a European introduction, first taken up as a commercial product in the late eighteenth century.[135] While the checker, twill, and hexagonal weaves usual in splint basketry were practiced in the precontact period, there are no surviving precontact basket fragments in wood splints, and they are not mentioned in any seventeenth-century source. Although the basic construction of splint baskets is quite uniform throughout the Northeast, as the basketmakers of the Maritime Peninsula and elsewhere began to manufacture on a commercial basis they began to experiment with forms, materials, and decoration, and a large variety of new basket types emerged. Splint baskets are still produced today.

During the two hundred years that splint basketry has been made for trade, men have prepared the splints mainly from logs of black ash (*Fraxinus niger americana*), usually called brown ash by Penobscot and Passamaquoddy basketmakers, but also of poplar (*Populus*), maple (*Acer*), birch (mainly *Betula lutea*), and cedar. The preferred material for functional baskets is generally black ash, which makes tough, durable splints. Ash has another advantage: vigorous pounding of a debarked log causes the annular growth layers of this tree to separate as the soft cellular growth between them is crushed. After pounding, the layers can be easily pulled apart. Layers vary in thickness, and both sides show a rough gray brown texture—the remains of the soft tissue. This is generally scraped off. The grain is further split until the desired thickness for a particular basket type is obtained. The prepared strips are called splints. Wide splints can be cut

A-25. Writing on the bottom of this basket states that J. Bartlett Jr. bought it from "the Penobscot tribe of Indians on January 14, 1831." (Maine State Museum collection.)

A-26. Stripping splints from ash logs that have been pounded with the blunt end of a heavy axe, Old Town, 1915. Photograph by Frederick Johnson. (Courtesy of the National Museum of the American Indian, Smithsonian Institution, neg. no. 14817.)

into narrower strips using the basketry gauge, a wooden tool set with sharpened steel teeth traditionally made of watch springs. When pulled across the steel teeth, the splint is divided into a series of narrower splints of uniform width.[136]

Cedar is easily split using a mallet and wedge; the log is cut into sections, the heartwood removed, and the remaining portion split lengthwise into thin splints at right angles to the radius of the tree. Poplar sections are split along lines radiating from the center. Birch logs are so constituted that splint-sized strips can be pulled off a debarked log by hand, after starting them at one end with a knife. Small green maple saplings are split in half, then further split until several thin splints are produced. Another technique involves cutting splints from a large log with a drawknife.

A marvelous variety of baskets has been produced over the years. The utilitarian types include market baskets and baskets for apples, potatoes, fish, and eggs, backpacks, sowing and winnowing baskets, fishing creels, eel traps, laundry hampers, and wastepaper baskets. These were all made using splints, usually of unshaven ash. Fancy baskets and miniatures were often made of red or white maple (*Acer rubrum, spicatum*). Thin, narrow splints were fashioned into sewing baskets, glove cases, button baskets, and all manner of fanciful and decorative objects.

Here again there was integration of labor: men prepared the splints, while

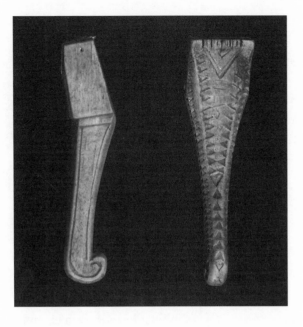

A-27. Steel-toothed gauges such as these cut splints into uniform widths for basketmaking. (Maine State Museum collection.)

women formed them into the required size using the basketry gauge. Men did the heavier weaving of functional baskets and women the finishing and the fancy baskets. It is probable, however, that men did basketwork only after it became the family's source of income.

Whether plain or fancy, the majority of splint baskets are composed of four elements: standards, weavers, hoop(s), and binding.[137] "Standards" are splints that form the entire base of square- or rectangular-bottomed baskets, the warp of round- or oval-bottomed baskets, and the warp of all basket sides. Square or rectangular bottoms are formed from checker-plaited or twill-plaited standards that serve as both warp and weft. The weft elements are placed at right angles to the warp. When the base is as large as desired, the unwoven portion of each standard is bent upward to form the vertical warp elements of the basket sides. Round or oval bases necessitate a different arrangement of standards and the use of weavers as a weft. "Weavers" are those splints that are woven horizontally through vertical standards to form the completed basket sides.

A number of methods have been perfected to construct round or oval bases. In one variation, the standards are arranged like spokes. Each standard crosses every other standard in the center of the circle or oval, and each is equidistant from the others at the perimeter of the base, where it is then bent upward to become a vertical element of the basket's sides.

A-28. Some basket styles were woven around wooden forms. Composite forms can be disassembled for removal. (Maine State Museum collection.)

A hoop is a reinforcement of carved wood that is lashed to the rim of the basket on the inside, although some baskets have a hoop on the outside of the rim as well. The side that lies against the basket is flat, but the visible part is curved. Hoop ends overlap, but they are tapered so that the rim remains an even thickness all the way around. On smaller baskets a thick piece of splint may be used instead of carved wood.

A binding is a length of narrow splint that lashes hoop to basket. Using a whipstitch, the splint is passed between the intersection of the lower edges of the top weaver and the standards. If the weave is too tight to admit the binding at this point, a small hole is punched with an awl or knife, and the binding is put on this way.

Basket lids are constructed in the same basic manner as the baskets themselves: with standards, weavers, hoops, and binding. Baskets may also possess a variety of wooden handles, wooden supports, reinforcements at the base, and feet.

The earliest known splint baskets from the Maritime Peninsula usually have a square base and a circular rim. This is the easiest form to construct. The more complex shapes were created by weaving around a removable mold or around everyday objects, such as bottles, vases, inkwells, or lamp bases.

Dyeing the wood splints was the most common method of decoration. Brown, black, and indigo blue vegetable dyes were used for many early-nineteenth-century baskets; the splints were painted with the dye on one side only, rather than being dipped entirely into the dye. After the introduction of aniline dyes in about 1865, a wide range of inexpensive colors became available to the basketmaker, and job lots of splints were dyed. Color became a primary feature.

By approximately 1850, women began incorporating a variety of decorative projecting weaves into their work. Basically, these entail the use of a second weave laid over the first, the outermost one being twisted in any of a number of ways to produce a projecting pattern that could be repeated at intervals of every second standard all around the basket or lid. Native basketmakers from the Maritime Peninsula were all familiar with the "porcupine," or "thistle" weave; the "periwinkle," or "wort" weave; and the "standard diamond" weave. Shaped splints were appliquéd onto completed weaves to form leaves and blossoms. The earliest documented decorative weave used in Maine is the porcupine style; in this case it ornaments a sewing basket made in 1863 that was given as a wedding present by Molly Molasses to Fannie Hardy Eckstorm's father.[138]

A second decorative technique used in basketry was the incorporation of sweet grass as a border along the rims of sides and lids. Lengths and braids of sweet grass were used as handles and as weavers in place of splints. This grass exudes a vanilla-like fragrance that is very pleasant to humans but offensive to moths.

A-29. A Penobscot man drying bundles of fragrant sweet grass for use in baskets, about 1910. Photograph by Frank Speck. (Courtesy of the University of Pennsylvania Museum, neg. no. NC35-13854.)

Wooden Ware

As noted above, men have done a lot of the heavy work involved in basketmaking only since around 1800. Containers made of wood, however—cups, bowls, platters, and boxes—were always made by men. An example is the bentwood box, a form that may not predate European arrival. These boxes were invariably circular or oval. The sides were formed by a single piece of wood that was steamed and bent, then treen-pegged to a wooden base. The lid, which overlapped the box sides, was made the same way. Such boxes were decorated with water-soluble paint, or mineral pigments (e.g., ocher) mixed with oil, or by burning or incising. Surviving examples all date from the late eighteenth century or after.

Large-scale wooden items such as sleds, cooking kettles, and baby carriers were also the men's responsibility. The majority of stone carving likely also fell to men. Power was added to even their humblest creations through the use of incised symbols, bas-relief decorations, and carvings in the round.

Weaponry

Men hunted, fished, waged war, and made the equipment necessary for all these activities. To bring down big game, they made spears or lances. Josselyn mentions their lances, "which formerly were no other but a staff of a yard and a half, pointed with a Fishes bone made sharp at the end, . . . but since

A-30. Bentwood box with painted decoration. Maritime Peninsula region, early to mid–nineteenth century. (Maine State Museum collection.)

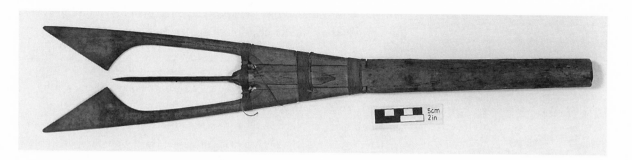

A-31. Leister for spearing salmon. The distance between the wooden side prongs is 11 millimeters. Native guides made leisters for their clients, who would often bring the business end back as a souvenir. (Maine State Museum collection)

[contact] they put on pieces of sword-blades which they purchase of the *French*, and having a strap of leather fastened to the butt end of the staff which they bring down to the midst of it."[139] The fish-bone point may have been the tail of the horseshoe crab; Lescarbot described arrowheads made by the Almouchiquois of the "tails of a certain fish . . . like to a crayfish lodged within a very hard shell, which shell is of the greatness of a dish, a long tail, likewise hard (for it is shell and sharp)."[140]

Lances were also armed with animal bones; Micmac lances, for example, were made of beech and tipped with "a large pointed bone."[141] Rosier handled an Etchemin lance that he called a dart. It was headed with a barbed bone tip, probably made from a splintered deer tibia. Rosier apparently "darted [it] among the rocks and it brake not."[142] There were also marine versions of both harpoons and lances. "Large fish, and sea mammals were harpooned, striking them with a fishgig, a kind of dart or staff, to the lower [tip] end of which they fasten a sharp jagged bone (since [contact] they make them of Iron) with a string fastened to it, as soon as the fish is struck they pull away the staff, leaving the bony head in the fishes body and fasten the other end of the string to the Canow. . . . This way they take Sturgeon. . . . The Lobsters they take with a staff two or three yardes long, made small and sharpen'd at one end, and nick'd with deep nicks to take hold."[143]

Fishing leisters had a central bone point with two wooden prongs on both sides. The prongs spread open as the bone point passed downward through the body of the fish and then closed around the fish to keep it on the point. Different point sizes were used to catch different fish, including eels, and a leister without a point was sometimes employed to catch lobsters. "Further down the New England coast, Champlain saw cod hooks made of a piece of wood, to which they attache a bone shaped like a harpoon, which they fasten very securely. . . . [T]he whole thing has the form of a little crook. The line which is attached to it is made of tree-bark [basswood bark]."[144] Such hooks may have been made in Maine as well.

For "Defense and Offense," as Josselyn put it, men relied on the bow.[145] Rosier provides a good description of archery equipment from Maine:

When we went on shore to trade with them, in one of their canoes I saw their bows and arrows, which I took up and drew an arrow in one of them, which I thought to be of strength able to carry an arrow fiue or sixe score stronglie.... Their bow is made of Witch Hazel, and some of Beech in fashion much like our bows, but they want nocks, onely a string of leather [sinew] put through a hole at one end and made fast with a knot at the other. Their arrows are made of the same wood, some of Ash, big and long, with three feathers tied on, and nocked very artificialle; headed with the long bone of a Deere, made very sharpe with two fangs in manner of a harping iron.[146]

To the northeast, Denys tells us, Micmac bows of the same period were made of unsplit maple sapling worked into shape with axes and knives, then smoothed and polished with sharp-edged shells.[147] At both ends, Micmac bows had notches around which the bowstring was knotted; the outer edge was flat, while the inner edge was left convex. A bow dating to 1660, reportedly from Sudbury, Massachusetts—to the southwest—is made of ash.[148]

In Massachusetts Pring saw bows "fiue or sixe foot long of Witch-hasel, painted blacke and yellow, the strings of three twists of sinews, bigger than our bow strings" and arrows "of a yard and a handfull long . . . of fine light wood very smooth and round with three long and deepe blacke feathers of some Eagle, Vulture, or Kite, as closely fastened with some binding matter as any Fletcher of ours can glue them on."[149] The arrows may have been of cedar, which the Micmacs used because it "splits straight," and Micmac arrows, too, had eagle-feather fletching and bone heads.[150] A type known as a "Bird" arrow consisted of a single piece of wood for both shaft and head, the larger round head having a blunt end. Although its use is not documented in Maine, the Bird arrow was widely distributed throughout the northern Algonquian range.[151] A 1602 reference to arrows from coastal Massachusetts mentions copper points, "much like our broad arrow heads, very workmanly made."[152] Similar arrowheads, in use until at least the late seventeenth century, are known throughout northeastern North America. When they were first made in Maine, however, is unclear, for in Champlain's time, a few years after Gosnold's 1602 account, European trade goods were still scarce and Almouchiquois arrows were still tipped with stone or bone.[153] Another type of masculine equipment, weaponry, included the ball-headed club—called a tomahawk—and the shield. "*Tamahawks*," wrote

A-32. Penobscot hunters at Lincoln in 1911. Photograph by Frank Speck. (Courtesy of the University of Pennsylvania Museum, neg. no. NC35-13964.)

Josselyn, "are staves two foot and a half long with a knob at the end as round as a bowl."[154] No detailed descriptions of shields are available for Maine, but to the north and east the Micmacs and the Montagnais were said to use shields made of wood that were rounded at the top and as tall as a man. In Massachusetts they were also large but made of bark.[155]

With the advent of firearms, both shields and slat armor became obsolete, as they were of little value against gunfire. The bow, the lance, the club, and the shield, together with the stone axe and knife were gradually abandoned for trade-metal implements and European guns. This process, which began with the earliest seventeenth-century contacts, accelerated so rapidly that by 1638 Josselyn remarked that "of late he is a poor *Indian* that is not master of two guns, which they purchase of the French, and powder and shot . . . likewise they have steel hatchets and knives."[156]

The French had no reservations about trading weaponry to the Native peoples of the Maritime Peninsula; it brought them enormous profit. As we have seen, however, among the English attitudes were initially divided, with Governor Bradford complaining bitterly about the renegade English who taught Indians the use of firearms during the 1620s.[157] Some European arms had reached the Maritime Peninsula by this date but, according to

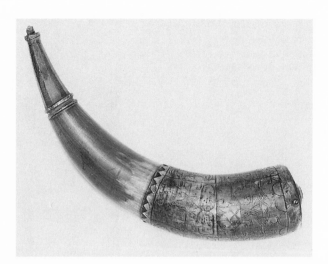

A-33. Late-eighteenth- or early-nineteenth-century powder horn, probably Penobscot. (Maine State Museum collection)

Levett, not many: "Their weapons are bows and arrows; I never saw more than two fowling pieces, one pistol, about four half-pikes, and three cutlasses amongst them."[158] This scarcity was soon remedied, by both the French and the English.

Although the bow remained in use as a weapon of war until the 1760s, by then the bow and the spear had been completely replaced by guns for hunting. In 1847 Levinge noted that though Maliseet boys were still taught how to use bows, this was "a practise entirely relinquished by the adult portion of the community," who owned "Birmingham catch-penny pieces, the vilest of guns."[159]

With the adoption of European muskets came the wearing of the powder horn. The necessary cows' horns were obtained through trade, but the Native men incised them beautifully with geometric and animal motifs. A number of examples have survived. Gunpowder canisters of incised birchbark and elaborate leather rifle cases were made by women for their male relatives.

Other Household Items

In addition to making weapons from wood, men used their woodworking skills to make household furnishings. Special care was lavished on the baby carriers, which Josselyn describes thus: "a board . . . two foot long, and a foot and half broad, bor'd full of holes on each side, having a foot beneath like a Jack that we pull Boots off with, on the top of the board a broad strap of leather which they [women] put over their forehead, the board hanging

A-34. Penobscot cradle boards.
(Courtesy of the Peabody Museum,
Harvard University.)

A-35. Miniature Maliseet lacrosse
sticks, made around 1870 by a member
of the Perley family. The game was
popular throughout the region up to
the mid–nineteenth century. (Maine
State Museum collection.)

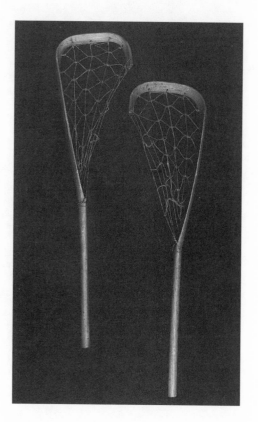

A-36. Belt cups, the personal drinking vessels of northern Indians. The example with carved double-curve motifs was probably made in the mid–nineteenth century by a Maliseet, Passamaquoddy, or Penobscot. The undecorated specimen was given to Captain John Lane by Penobscot chief Joseph Orono in the late eighteenth century. (Courtesy of the Brick Store Museum and the York Institute Museum/Dyer Library.)

A-37a–b. Early- to mid-nineteenth-century canoe model and equipment, with doll family in Maliseet/ Passamaquoddy/Penobscot dress. Equipment includes paddles, a setting pole, fish spear, a cradle board, and an ash splint basket. (Maine State Museum collection.)

at their back."[160] In one type of carrier, the baby was wrapped and laid on the board, then laced up by straps that passed through the holes on both sides. The foot at the base kept the child from sliding off. In a second type, the foot and sides were all one continuous strip of wood.

Another example of woodenware made by men is the troughlike cooking pot that was hollowed from a massive log by cutting and burning. Bowls and platters were hollowed from wood burls—the dome-shaped growths that appear on the trunks of some trees—then polished smooth. Men also made wooden cups and spoons. Almouchiquois men fashioned the agricultural implements noted by Champlain, "In place of ploughs they use an instrument of very hard wood made in the shape of a spade."[161]

Baby carriers and smaller items such as spoons and tool handles were often exquisitely carved. "Our Souriquois and Armouchiquois . . . have the art of both painting and carving, and make beasts, birds and men in stone as wood, as prettily as good workmen in these parts."[162] An extensive tool kit, with working edges of stone, shell, bone, shovel-shaped moose teeth, and the extremely sharp, tough incisors of beaver and porcupine, made this fine decorative work possible. Tools were hafted with wood, bone, and antler; lashed with natural-fiber cordage, rawhide, root, or splint; and attached with resins or animal glues. The kit would have included such tools as wooden mauls, mallets, spreaders, and spacers for canoe ribs, drill bits of bone and stone, awls, stone chisels, axes, and gouges.

Native men in Maine would later use their woodworking skills to earn livings as coopers, boatbuilders, ship's fitters, furniture makers, and general carpenters. They would still make most of their own tools, using recycled files to make metal blades. One all-purpose tool of these later trades was the so-called crooked knife. It was very likely an adaptation of a

A-38. Penobscot crooked knife with a short, straight blade made from a file, typical of the Maritime Peninsula region. Late nineteenth or early twentieth centuries. (Maine State Museum collection.)

A-39. Maliseet guide using a crooked knife to shape a setting pole for a canoe while his companion sportfishes in the background. Crooked knives are one-handed knives. Various forms were used throughout northern North America by Indians and Eskimo/Inuit peoples and were adopted by rural French Canadians as well. (Reproduced from *Picturesque Canada, vol. 2, 1882.*)

precontact implement that in its modern form spread throughout northern North America, becoming popular even among white woodsmen of Maine and the Maritimes. The blade tang is set into a hole in the handle end and wrapped with rawhide, cordage, or wire, the end of which is set into another hole and plugged. It was normally pulled toward the user, as a single-handed drawknife.

The dice used in games of chance—like the Maliseet variety mentioned by Gyles[163]—were made of bone or ivory. They were circular and flat on one side, convex on the other. The flat side was incised, usually with a modified compass-rose design. One traditional game utilizes six dice made from moose shinbone. The Micmacs call the game *waltes* and the dice *waltestaqn*. Imprecisely recorded Penobscot and Passamaquoddy terms for the same game include *werladaharmungun*; and *alltestegunuk* or *altestagen* respectively.[164] This game, in which the dice are tossed in a shallow "knot-bowl" made from a wood burl, has been played in the exact same way from before A.D. 1600 and is still played today. The score is kept with counting sticks made of wood or reed.

It was in the manufacture of tobacco pipes that men excelled as craftsmen. They used many kinds of material: wood, clay, stone, metal, bone, antler, lobster claw, and birchbark. They carved their pipes and decorated them with quills, dewclaws, teeth, feathers, and copper; after European contact, they wrapped strung beads around the stem. Within Native cultures pipes were made to be powerful, beautiful, ceremonial, functional. Here are some seventeenth-century descriptions:

their pipes, which are made of earth, very strong, blacke and short, containing a great quantity . . . [one] was then the short claw of a lobster, which will hold ten of our pipes full.[165]

They made also their pipes for holding their tobacco. They made them of wood, with a claw of Lobster. . . . They made them also of certain green stone, and of another which is red, with the stem, the whole in one piece. To hollow and pierce the stem, they made use of their bone, of which the point was a little flattened and sharpened; by dint of turning back and forth they hollowed the stone and pierced the stem. . . . As to their other kinds of pipes, they were of two pieces. The stems were made of a certain wood ["pipe-wood," or striped maple *(Acer pennsylvanicum)*]. . . . They made the stems of them of a foot or a foot and a half in length. In order to pierce them they made a ring at an inch from one end, from which they removed the wood all around as far as the middle, which they left as large as the wick of a candle; this seems like the pith, but it has none of it, or so little that it seems like none. They took this wick in their teeth which they shut tightly, and [took] all the rest of the stick in their hands, which they turned little by little and very carefully. This wick twisted so well that it detached itself inside the stick, being loosened from one end to the other of its proper thickness. It was then drawn out very carefully with a constant turning of the stick which in this manner became pierced. Then they polished it, and reduced it

A-40. Dice game with counting sticks. This specimen is Micmac. (Courtesy of the McCord Museum of Canadian History, M68.0-60.)

A-41. Penobscot man, about 1910, with a pipe typical of the region. It is made of stone and attached to a wooden stem by a leather thong. (Courtesy of the University of Pennsylvania Museum, neg. no. NC35-13871.)

to the thickness necessary to make it enter the hole of the pipe. This was sometimes of hard-wood, sometimes of Moose bone, or the claw of Lobster, or Sea-crayfish, and of other material according to the fancy of him who took it upon himself to make it.[166]

Frank Speck recorded two types of pipe in early-twentieth-century Maine—"those with a keel-based bowl set at right angles [that is, vertically] to the stem, and those with a curved flaring bowl." According to him, stone was the most common pipe material; it was cut with an axe and shaped with files and a knife.[167] The keeled-pipe style is often called a "Micmac pipe," though it was in widespread use throughout Maine and the Maritimes. It is but one of several styles of highly decorative small stone pipes used in this region from at least as early as the seventeenth century.

A common pipestone was argillite, a dark, fine-grained, slatelike stone that lends itself to carving. A number of keeled nineteenth-century argillite pipes have bowls decorated with from one to four animals carved in the round. These marvelously detailed animal figures include otters, beavers, bear, moose, frogs, turtles, and weasels. The human figure is rare, but it does occur. Secondary geometric motifs may be incised on the bowl as well.

The most impressive evidence of Native men's skill, craftsmanship, and understanding of their materials is preserved for us by Josselyn: "Instruments they had none before the *English* came amongst them, since [then] they have imitated them and will make out Kitts [gitterns, or citterns, a stringed instrument] as neatly and as Artificially as the best Fiddle-maker amongst us; and will play our plain lessons very exactly: the only Fiddler that was in the province of *Meyn*, when I was there was an *Indian* called *Scozway*, whom the Fishermen and planters when they had a mind to be merry made use of."[168] This is high praise indeed, because it is extremely difficult to make either a violin or a gittern, and to make it sound good is even harder. Making the strings and the bow and tuning and learning to play the instrument all indicate a masterly knowledge of media and techniques, a good eye for spatial relationships, and an ability to adopt and adapt, to mesh new knowledge with old. These talents, particularly as applied to woodworking, would ultimately provide the Native men of Maine with an alternative means of making a living as the coasts were settled and the forests disappeared from the riverbanks.

NOTES

Introduction

1. Adams, Van Gerven, and Levy 1978; Anthony 1990.

2. Tuck 1978a:28; Snow 1978:60; Luckenbach, Clark, and Levy 1987:25–27.

3. Jackson 1839; Chadbourne 1859.

4. Wyman 1868a:571; 1868.

5. Imamura 1996:39; Wayman 1942:256, 439–42; Wyman 1875.

6. Sanger and Sanger 1986:67.

7. Putnam 1898. The origins of the Peabody method remain unclear, but they appear to have been developed during Putnam's excavations at the Turner Mounds in Ohio (Methods of Archaeological Research 1886). Of Willoughby's work, Putnam (1898:387) said "the work was . . . admirably carried out in accordance with the Museum methods."

8. Willoughby 1898.

9. Willey and Sabloff 1993:46–49. The name was changed to the Bureau of American Ethnology in 1894.

10. Mark 1980:119–20.

11. Moorehead 1922.

12. Byers 1959, 1979; Hadlock 1939, 1941; Hadlock and Byers 1956; Hadlock and Stern 1948; Rowe 1940; Smith 1926, 1929, 1930; Snow 1968; Spiess 1985.

13. Petersen 1991; Robinson, Petersen, and Robinson 1992.

14. Taylor 1990:1–14.

15. Taylor 1990:80–95.

1. The Paleo-Indian Period

1. Smith 1985; Weddle, Lowell, and Dorian 1994.

2. Ray and Spiess 1981.

3. Shipp, Belknap, and Kelley 1989.

4. Newman, Genes, and Brewer 1985.

5. Mott, Grant, and Occhietti 1986; Bonnichsen, Keenlyside, and Turnmire 1991:25.

6. Davis et al. 1975; Mott 1977; Miller and Thompson 1979; Davis and Jacobson 1985.

7. Davis and Jacobson 1985, fig. 12.

8. Bonnichsen, Keenlyside, and Turnmire 1991:11–13; Funk and Steadman 1994:33–45, 73.

9. Speck 1935:162–63.

10. Strong 1934; Speck 1935.

11. Spiess and Wilson 1987:193–201.

12. Bonnichsen et al. 1980, 1981; Bonnichsen 1984; Bonnichsen 1988; Bonnichsen, Keenlyside, and Turnmire 1991.

13. Payne 1987.

14. Gramly 1982.

15. MacDonald 1968.

16. Gramly 1985.

17. Haynes et al. 1984.

18. Gramly 1982:54–58, 1984.

19. Caribou bone has been identified at the Whipple site in New Hampshire and at the Bull Brook site in Massachusetts. Caribou bone from the Dutchess Quarry Caves in

southeastern New York has recently been dated to around 13,000 B.P., too old for the Paleo-Indian occupation also in evidence there (Spiess, Curran, and Grimes 1985; Funk and Steadman 1994:73).

20. Gramly 1988:6.

21. Gramly 1988.

22. Bourque 1985.

23. Spiess and Wilson 1987.

24. Spiess and Wilson 1987:121–22.

25. Stephen Pollock, University of Southern Maine, personal communication, 1996 and 1997. The rhyolite called Neponset rhyolite has now been identified to a source at Mount Jasper in Berlin NH. Pollock also believes that the chert originally attributed to Vermont and common in both the Michaud and Vail collections may actually be a variety of Munsungan chert.

26. Spiess and Wilson 1987:125–27.

27. Spiess and Wilson 1987:144; Wilson and Spiess 1990:23.

28. Doyle et al. 1985.

29. Cox and Petersen 1997. See Chapdelaine 1994 for a slightly later date from the late Paleo-Indian Rimouski site in Quebec.

30. Ellis and Deller 1990:59; Mason 1981; Chapdelaine and Bourget 1994; Doyle et al. 1985.

31. Wilson and Spiess 1990. See also Bonnichsen, Keenlyside, and Turnmire 1991:25–31.

32. Grimes et al. 1984:171.

33. Oldale, Whitmore, and Grimes 1987.

34. Frison 1989.

35. Nathan Hamilton, University of Southern Maine, personal communication.

2. The Archaic Period

1. Davis and Jacobson 1985; Jacobson, Webb and Grimm 1987; Anderson et al. 1992; Meltzer and Mead 1986; Pielou 1991:254–57.

2. B. Smith 1986:6–18.

3. Bonnichsen, Keenlyside, and Turnmire 1991:6–7, 22–23; Moira McCaffrey, McCord Museum, personal communication, 1989; Pintal 1998:35–75.

4. Ritchie 1932; 1936:18.

5. Funk 1978:19–20.

6. LaSalle and Chapdelaine 1990:13–15; Sanger, Belcher, and Kellogg 1992:156; Chapdelaine and Bourget 1992; Funk and Wellman 1984; Robinson 1992:76–79.

7. Petersen 1991; Sanger, Belcher, and Kellogg 1992.

8. Hamilton et al 1997.

9. Fitting 1968:442; Funk 1978:19–21; Sanger 1979:23–34; Ritchie 1971a:3; Ritchie 1980:16–19; Ritchie and Funk 1971.

10. Crock, Petersen, and Anderson 1993; Sanger 1988:86–88; Willoughby 1973:215 (fig. 120g).

11. Barnhardt, Belknap, and Kelley 1997.

12. Belknap et al. 1994; Zielinski et al. 1994; Michael Retelle, Bates College, personal communication, and Arthur Spiess, Maine Historic Preservation Commission, personal communication, 1996.

13. Jacobson, Webb, and Grimm 1987; Petersen and Putnam 1992:14–42; Sanger, Belcher, and Kellogg 1992:150–51.

14. Robinson 1992:96; Broyles 1966.

15. Spiess 1992:183; Will 1996:14.

16. Curran and Thomas 1979; Spiess 1992:175, 183.

17. Spiess, Bourque, and Gramly 1983:237–38; Basley 1986.

18. Sanger 1975:70; Spiess, Bourque, and Cox 1983:101–3; Bourque 1994.

19. Bourque 1991; Cole-Will and Will 1996; Robinson 1996:99–106.

20. For a conservative view on Middle Archaic population size, see Sanger 1975. A more liberal view is taken by Petersen and Putnam 1992:15–25 and Robinson and Petersen 1993. See also Dincauze 1976:118–25; Robinson 1992; Robinson and Petersen 1992; Sanger, Belcher, and Kellogg 1992.

21. Murphy 1997; Sanger 1991b:81; Spiess, Bourque, and Gramly 1983:238–44.

22. Broyles 1966:38–40; Dincauze 1976:26–37.

23. Petersen 1991:108–9; Robinson 1992:95.

24. Spiess, Bourque, and Gramly 1983:232–34.

25. Spiess 1992:174–83.

26. Bourque 1980, 1981.

27. Little 1786:18; Petersen et al. 1994.

28. Bourque 1995:243–44.

29. Bourque 1992:23, 119,175; 1995a:33–34.

30. Cox 1991:154–55; Spiess, Bourque, and Cox 1983:93; Barnhardt et al. 1995.

31. Robinson 1996:102–6; Cole-Will and Will 1996; Leveillee 1997.

32. Petersen et al. 1994:222.

33. Funk 1976:235–38; Ritchie 1980:84–89.

34. Cox 1991; Sanger 1975; Tuck 1991:48–50.

35. Ritchie 1971b:40–41

36. Bradstreet and Davis 1975:16–17; Jacobson, Webb, and Grimm 1987; Sanger 1975:67–68; Sanger et al. 1977:460–62; Tuck 1982:207.

37. Cox 1991.

38. Cox 1991:151; Ritchie 1979.

39. See, for example, Cox 1991:155–59; Robinson 1992:72–73.

40. Plumet et al. 1993:40, 57–69, 81–84, 89–97.

41. Funk 1978:26.

42. Ritchie 1969:218; Dincauze 1975:24; Bourque 1995:33–39, 223–37.

43. Dincauze 1976:123–25.

44. Dincauze 1975:24–25.

45. Bourque 1976:22; 1983:60–61.

46. Bourque 1995:39, 234.

47. Robinson 1985:40–41, 103–5.

48. Dincauze 1974:49.

49. Bourque 1992:34–39; 1994.

50. Moorehead 1922:129–30.

51. Smith 1948.

52. Bourque and Krueger 1994.

53. Modified from Bourque 1995:140.

54. Sanger 1973; Bourque 1991.

55. Rowe 1940:7, viii; Byers 1979:35, 40, 52; Bourque 1994.

56. Sanger 1975:62; Sanger et al. 1977.

57. Sanger 1975:62; Bourque 1994.

58. Bourque and Cox 1981.

59. Dincauze 1974:47–48; 1975:31–32; Ritchie 1969:231.

60. Robinson 1985:86–89; Willoughby 1973:43–45, 50, 63; Staples and Athearn 1969; Robbins 1980:45–46.

61. Sanger 1991a; Sanger and Davis 1991:72–77.

62. Bourque 1992:25–28; Ritchie 1971b:37–38; 90–91.

63. Tuck 1976:25–79; Byers 1979:24–71; Bourque 1992:23–39; Bourque 1994.

64. Tuck 1976.

65. Tuck 1976:25–39, 205–22; Bourque and Krueger 1994; Bourque 1995:140; Jelsma 1997.

66. Tuck 1971:350–57; 1976:98–112, 1978b; Fitzhugh 1972:129–30.

67. Hulme 1994:74

68. Bourque, Belknap, and Schnitker 1997; Webb et al. 1993.

69. Bourque 1994; Robinson 1996:139; Jelsma 1997.

70. Davenport, Davenport, and Timbrook 1993; Munro and Seligman 1996:114–15; Strauss 1987:127–28; Watanabe 1972:146–47

71. Robinson 1996:115; Clermont and Chapdelaine 1998:97–103; Penman 1977. For forms found to the west of New England, see Beauchamp 1902.

72. Bourque 1975:43–44; Tuck 1976:162–67; Jelsma 1997.

73. Bourque 1992:93–95; 1976:29; Dincauze 1968, 1972, 1974:49–50, 1975:29–30; Sanger 1973:132; 1975:71.

74. Witthoft 1949:10–11; 1953:14–15; Sanger 1973:123; Dumais 1978:69–71; Kenyon 1980.

75. Will 1981; Bourque 1995:100–138.

76. Bourque 1995:138–45.

77. Bourque and Krueger 1994.

78. Bradstreet and Davis 1975:17.

79. Bourque 1995:149, 157–58, 164, 266–69; Dincauze 1974:56, 66 Leveillee 1997:72; Pfeiffer 1980:131; Regensberg 1975:49, 51, 118, 124–25; 1976:108; Whittall 1984:17–20.

80. Hedden 1994:30–33, 60–61. Charcoal from this feature produced a date of 3520±90 B.P. Dincauze 1968:plates 7, 9, 15, 17; Driver and Massey 1957:233–37; Josselyn 1860:179–82. Looking farther afield, it has recently been suggested that the steatite bowls of more southerly Susquehanna sites may have used in nut processing (Truncer 1997).

81. Ritchie 1969:153–54; Dincauze 1968; 1975:29–30; Dumais 1978:69–71; Pfeiffer 1980; Smith 1922; Bourque 1992:94; Bourque 1976:29; Byers 1979:70; Borstel 1982:58–65; Pfeiffer 1992:79.

82. Bourque 1995:266–69.

83. Bourque 1995:162–65; Dincauze 1975:30–31; Pfeiffer 1980:131; Robinson 1997:39.

84. Bourque 1995:165–67.

85. Turnbaugh 1975; Cook 1976; Dincauze 1974:27; Tuck 1978a:37–39; Bourque 1995:244–53.

86. Bourque 1995:121–32.

87. Turnbaugh 1975:59–60.

88. Witthoft 1953:14–15; Ritchie 1980:151–54; Snow 1980:240–42, 249–50.

89. Ritchie 1969:165; Dincauze 1968:87–88.

90. Bradstreet and Davis 1975:17; Jacobson, Webb, and Grimm 1987.

91. Bourque 1994

92. See, for example, Dincauze 1968:19–23, 66–70; 85–90; 1975:29; Ritchie 1980:156–78.

93. Bourque 1995:253–54.

94. Bourque 1983

3. The Ceramic Period

1. Siebert 1967; Luckenbach, Clark, and Levy 1987; Fiedel 1991:21–23.

2. Brown 1986:600; B. Smith 1986:30.

3. Garland 1986:47–71; Harn 1986:256–68; Kraft 1970:138; Mason 1981:216; Spence, Pihl, and Murphy 1990:125–37.

4. Ritchie 1980:190.

5. Hulton 1984:121.

6. Belcher 1989:179–81; Petersen and Sanger 1991:118–23; Rutherford 1991:105.

7. Petersen and Sanger 1991:111–70; Bourque 1992:91–118; 1995a:192–93.

8. Petersen and Sanger 1991:123; Nash, Stewart, and Deal 1991:216.

9. Petersen and Sanger 1991:123–32; Bourque 1992:93–97; 1995:200–206.

10. Petersen and Sanger 1991:132–48; Bourque 1992:97–98; 1995:206–9.

11. Gookin 1792:151; Petersen and Sanger 1991:148–59; Bourque 1995:209–14; Champlain 1922, 1:357–58; Clermont, Chapdelaine, and Barré 1983:66–110; Pendergast and Trigger 1972:114–19, 166–249; Thomas 1992:369–72; Willoughby 1909:fig. 13–14; 1973:fig. 116.

12. Bourque and Whitehead 1994.

13. Clermont, Chapdelaine, and Barré 1983:116–28; Pendergast and Trigger 1972:119–31, 252–57; Weber 1970.

14. Clermont, Chapdelaine, and Barré, 1983:111; Willoughby 1978:15.

15. Willoughby 1924.

16. Sanger 1979:99.

17. Spiess 1987:18.

18. Bradstreet and Davis 1975:10.

19. Benson and Dodds 1977:75–76.

20. Spiess 1987:17–18.

21. Sanger 1987; 1988:90–91.

22. Spiess, Bourque, and Cox 1983; Bourque 1995:243–44; Sanger 1988:91.

23. Sanger 1988:91; Bourque 1995:220–21.

24. Sanger and Sanger 1986.

25. Bourque 1995:220–21; Spiess and Lewis forthcoming.

26. Bourque 1995:190, 193.

27. Bourque and Krueger 1994.

28. Palmer 1949.

29. Wyman 1875; Fairbridge 1976; Spiess 1985:103–4.

30. Sanger and Sanger 1986:67–68.

31. Sanger and Sanger 1986:73–74.

32. Sanger and Sanger 1986:75–76.

33. Levermore 1912:386.

34. Hart and Sidell 1997:524.

35. Smith 1997; Petersen and Sidell 1996; Hart and Sidell 1977:525, 531–32.

36. Riley et al. 1994.

37. Bendermer and Dewar 1994:379–87; Bendermer, Kellogg, and Largy 1991; Crawford, Smith, and Bower 1997; Fritz 1990:405–7, 410–11; 1994; Heckenberger, Petersen, and Sidell 1992:131, 140; Petersen and Sidell 1996; B. Smith 1986:66–69; 1997; Will 1996, ch. 3:16–17.

38. Champlain 1922, 1:321.

39. Prins 1992.

40. Demeritt 1991:195; Hulme 1994:74.

41. See, e.g., Ritchie 1980:72–77.

42. See, e.g., Belcher 1989:175–78; Sanger 1976:6–15.

43. Cowie, Petersen, and Sidell 1992:3.

44. Bourque 1992:296–97.

45. Ritchie 1971b.

46. Cox forthcoming; Nassaney and Pyle 1999:243–45.

47. Pastore 1992:11–12; Fitzhugh 1972:89–90, 286.

48. Adney and Chapelle 1964:3–173.

49. Cox forthcoming.

50. Bourque and Cox 1981:12–16.

51. Williams 1994:219–20.

52. McGhee 1984.

53. Skaare 1979:13.

54. Cox forthcoming.

55. Bourque and Whitehead 1994:135.

56. Cox forthcoming.

57. Turnbull 1976:50–62.

58. Tooker 1978:6–7.

59. Willey and Sabloff 1993:47–48.

60. Ritchie 1980:201–5; Ritchie and Dragoo 1959; Dragoo 1963; Dragoo 1976:1–9; Griffin 1961.

61. Bourque 1994:29–34.

62. Turnbull 1986.

63. Bourque 1994:30, 33–37; Davis 1991:109.

64. Hedden 1996:13–19.

65. Vastokas and Vastokas 1973:76–91, 121–29.

66. Hedden 1996:14; Day 1978:157–58; Eckstorm 1980:35–38; Spindler 1978:715–16.

67. B. Smith 1986:50–53; Emerson 1986:624.

68. This estimate is somewhat revised from Hedden 1996, fig. 3, on the basis of recent sea-level data from Machias presented in Gehrels, Belknap, and Kelley 1996:fig. 11.

69. Hedden 1996:19.

70. Bourque 1994:37–39.

71. Siatta 1998.

4. Introduction to the Historic Past

1. For the English, see Hubbard 1971; Penhallow 1973. For the French, see Charlevoix 1900; Bacqueville 1753; JR.

2. Williamson 1991; Parkman 1983.

3. YD, 10, fol. 237–38, 257–58, BM, 8:11–15; 23:10–12.

4. Webster 1934:57–66.

5. MacBeath 1979; Ryder 1979, 1979a; Campeau 1979.

6. Champlain 1922. Historic documents present us with many various spellings of group names. According to University of Nebraska Press policy, the spellings used here are generally those used in Trigger 1978, which also lists variant spellings.

7. Bakker 1988:12; Bourque and Whitehead 1994; Bourque 1989:262.

8. Champlain 1922, 1:269.

9. Champlain 1922, 1:292–97; 3:348–62; Bourque 1989:262, 267–71.

10. Bourque 1989:262–63; Champlain 1922, 1:325; J. Smith 1986, 1:328, 2:407; JR, 3:209. Champlain uses Almouchiquois instead of Lescarbot's Armouchiquois.

11. Champlain 1922, 1:326–28, 337–39; Lescarbot 1907–14, 2:308n. 9, 325, 3:144.

12. Champlain 1922, 5:313–17; 6:43–44.

13. Bourque 1989:271–72.

14. Day 1981:32–37; JR, 36:101–5; NYCD, 9:5; Penhallow 1973:2.

15. For a recent, concise discussion of bands, tribes, and more complex categories of society, see Diamond 1997:265–81.

5. Early European and Native Contacts

1. Gurvich 1988.

2. McGhee 1984.

3. Crosby 1986:19–28, 197–98; Ramenofsky 1987:137–76.

4. Morison 1971:112–27; Wolf 1982:101–25.

5. Cumming, Skelton, and Quinn 1972:147–48; 213–30.

6. Meinig 1986:24–31, 56–58; Innis 1940:23–26, 31–51.

7. Goddard and Bragdon 1988:2. This discussion of political leadership owes much to the work of Alvin Morrison (1976, 1991).

8. Levett 1988:53

9. Bourque 1989:262; Champlain 1922, 1:316, 319, 364–65; Morrison 1976:506–8; 1991:230–32; Quinn and Quinn 1983:421, 433.

10. JR, 2:73; 3:87–91; Fried 1960; Morrison 1976:502–10.

11. Bourque and Whitehead 1994:132–35; Lescarbot 1907–14:362–63.

12. Innis 1930:11–12, 14; Bailey 1937:8–10.

13. Lescarbot 1907–14, 2:24; Bakker 1988, 1992; Barkham 1978.

14. Quinn 1940, 2:282.

15. Quinn 1962:333, 341.

16. Rowse 1955, chs. 7–9, 11; Trudel 1966:27.

17. Quinn and Quinn 1983:112–203, 212–30, 231–311; J. Smith 1986, 1:323–61.

18. Strachey 1983:406–15.

19. Champlain 1922, 1:367–70; Eccles 1990:15–18; MacBeath 1979; MacDonald 1983:11–23.

20. Juet 1906.

21. Gorges 1890, 2:19

22. JR, 3:105.

23. Salisbury 1982:101–2, 267–68.

24. Davies 1983:413; Purchas 1983:347–48; Quinn and Quinn 1983:470–76; Rosier 1983:311; J. Smith 1986, 1:328–29, 407, 3:279; Gorges 1890, 2:14, 19. Bessabez is the French version of the name; English sources use "Bashabas."

25. Bourque and Whitehead 1994.

26. Gorges 1890, 2:74–76.

27. Baxter 1906:377; Bourque and Whitehead 1994:138, 339.

28. Winslow 1974:58; Bradford 1991:89; HCEI, 4:225–26; Johnson 1910:78; White 1968:25; Winthrop 1853, 1:71–72; Higginson, Sept. 1629, in Emerson 1976:37.

29. Spiess and Spiess 1987; Dermer 1841:350.

30. Levett 1988:39

31. BM, 3:28.

32. BM, 3:47; Bradford 1991:260; Young 1846:385–86.

33. Moody 1978:2, 3, 51.

34. Denys 1908:97–98; MacBeath 1979d, 1979e; Ryder 1979, 1979a; Squires 1979. Claude LaTour also operated a trading post on the Penobscot River, which was destroyed by the English adventurer David Kirke in 1629 (Report of the Canadian Archivist 1894:ix).

35. Bradford 1991:193–96, 200–202, 232–33, 237–38; Brymner 1894; Burrage 1914:189, 267; Churchill 1995a:52–57; MAHSP, 45:493–98.

36. Harvey 1979; Mahaffie 1995:50–58; Moir 1979.

37. MacBeath 1979d:593; Mahaffie 1995:59–61.

38. Baudry 1979b:503; Bradford 1991:275–79; Faulkner and Faulkner 1987:16; MacBeath 1979d:592–93; Winthrop 1853, 1:198; Mahaffie 1995:59–62.

39. MacDonald 1983, chs. 7–14; MacBeath 1979b,c,d,e:502; Rawlyk 1973:2–21.

40. Churchill 1979, chs. 5–6; 1995a:57–59, 62–65; 1994:374–75; Clark 1970:65–66; Moody 1933, chs. 3–5; Reid 1977:Introduction and chs. 1 and 3.

41. Baker 1985:78–85, 97, 107–12; Churchill 1995a:65–66; Burrage 1904:123–24, 128–32; 1914:185–86, 241–44.

42. Levett 1988:50. Samoset was an important sagamore from the Pemaquid area who had learned some English from fishermen (Bradford 1991:79–80).

43. Couillard–Després 1932:68, 73; LeBlant and Baudry 1967:381, 383; MacBeath 1979d; Ryder 1979:99–102.

44. Bradford 1991:89; Perley 1924, 1:47. Morison, editor of the 1991 edition of Bradford, repeats a common error by identifying the Tarrentines as Abenakis. The submission is reprinted in Bradford 1912:227.

45. Bradford 1810:57.

46. Bradford 1991:207.

47. BM, 3:102.

48. MacBeath 1979c; 1979d; 1979f.

49. Denys 1908:446, 448.

50. MAHSC, 4th ser., vol. 6:570–71; Reid 1981:70; MacDonald 1983:77.

51. Winthrop 1853, 1:156.

52. BM, 3:25–26, 28–29. It is difficult for several reasons to evaluate the volume of the early seventeenth-century fur trade on the Maritime Peninsula. Chief among them are the incompleteness of records from the many different traders—the French of Acadia and Quebec, the English of New England and the Dutch on the Hudson River, as well as ship-born traders of all three nationalities; the measurement of fur volumes in various noncomparable units—numbers of pelts, their monetary value and their weight; and the frequent fluctuations in the price. A few statistics for the 1610s through the 1640s clearly indicate that the trade was of major economic consequence. In 1614 traders in Acadia were able to ship 25,000 beaver pelts to France. On the Hudson River during the 1620s and 1630s the Dutch shipped around 7,000 beaver pelts and 800-850 otter pelts annually. The most productive year at the Plymouth Colony's Kennebec River trading post was 1634, when 3,366 pounds of beaver and 346 otter pelts were shipped (Phillips 1961:69, 121, 152).

53. Banks 1884; Bradford 1991:206–9, 232–33; Churchill 1979:29–30; Hubbard 1815:145; James 1963:16; MAHSP, 45:493–98; Shurtleff 1853–54, 1:100; Winthrop 1853, 1:62–63; Wood 1865:79.

54. Baker 1984:96–97; Burrage 1914:241–44; 1904, 1:123–30; Churchill 1975:x; Faulkner and Faulkner 1987:16–18.

55. NYCD, 9:6; Calloway 1990:65–69. Champlain 1922, 1:98–109, 295; Sagard 1866, 1:149–50; JR, 15:223–31; 28:203–5.

6. The Second Half of the Seventeenth Century

1. Baker 1984:100–105; Ranlet 1980:4, 282–90; James 1963:17; Bradford 1991:262–63; Morton 1883:282–85; Morison 1933, 29:135–36; Noyes, Libby, and Davis 1972:378, 400, 547.

2. JR, 24:61.

3. Sewall 1847:194–95.

4. JR, 38:35.

5. Moody 1978:120–21; Winthrop 1853, 2:83.

6. Shurtleff 1853–54, 2:24; Trigger 1976:631.

7. Winthrop 1853, 2:101.

8. Bourque 1994:13.

9. Eccles 1990:33–34, 64; Innis 1940:91; Trigger 1976:459, 467, 471, 476.

10. Peña 1990:21–36, 83; Bradford 1991:203–4; Jennings 1984:78–79; Morrison 1984:77.

11. Peña 1990:29–30; Bachman 1969:93–94.

12. Bailey 1969:27; Dunbabin 1979; Maverick 1885:232; JR, 12:187–89; 16:101, 18:235–39; 21:67–69; 34:57.

13. Jennings 1984:90; JR, 34:57; 38:39–41; Leger 1929:40; Morrison 1984:77–82.

14. Marshall 1967:86; Morrison 1984:79; JR, 24:59–63.

15. JR, 28:203–5; 215, 29:67–9; Day 1984:39–40; Morrison 1984:79–80; Thomas 1990:240–41.

16. Jennings 1984:90, 95–96, 112.

17. Dennis 1993:76–115.

18. White 1991:1–49; Trigger 1976:622–26, 663–64, 735–36.

19. Jennings 1984:49–50, 92–96, 102–30; NYCD, 1:150; JR, 31:85. For more on firearms, see Hunt 1940:167–72.

20. Campeau 1979a:281–82; Morrison 1984:84; JR, 28:229, 29:71, 31:183–207.

21. Jennings 1984:98–99; Trigger 1976:724–88.

22. BM, 4:443–36; Day 1984:40–41; Druillettes 1857; NYCD, 9:5–6; Salisbury 1982:63–64; JR, 35:55; 36:53, 83–139; 37:95, 257–59; NYCD, 9:5.

23. De Nant 1927; Dumas 1979:234; JR 30:185; 36:227.

24. Rawlyk 1973:24–25; Faulkner and Faulkner 1987:20; Roberts 1979; Fergusson 1979.

25. Reid 1981:136, 245; Letter of Ignatius, 337–38, 341.

26. JR 60:263.

27. Rawlyk 1973:25–32; Ryder 1979c, 1979b; MacBeath 1979d.

28. Rawlyk 1973:25–32; Ryder 1979b, 1979c; MacBeath 1979d.

29. Rawlyk 1973:32–34; Clark 1968:107–8, 121; Faulkner and Faulkner 1987:28; Macbeath 1979a; Ryder 1979c; Baudry 1979a.

30. Roberts 1979.

31. Rawlyk 1973:37–39; Faulkner and Faulkner 1987:29; Tuttle 1889:127–59; Baudry 1979; Mahaffie 1995:98–99; Roberts 1979, 1979a.

32. Shurtleff 1853–54, 4:165, pt. 1.

33. JR 47:107, 141–44; Day 1984:41; Maverick 1885:232.

34. NYCD, 13:224–27; Shurtleff and Pulsifer, 10:282; MAHSP, 1st ser., vol. 1:232; JR, 47:279.

35. NYCD, 13:224–28; Thomas 1990:243.

36. Van Laer 1932:332; O'Callaghan 1850–51, 4:41; NYCD 13:308–9; Day 1984:42; Thomas 1990.

37. Van Laer 1932:358; MAHSC, 1st ser., vol. 1:164–65; Day 1984:43.

38. Eccles 1990:69–70; Jennings 1984:128–29, 131–32; Lamontagne 1979:556; Richter 1992:103–4; Verney 1991:3, 78–80.

39. Day 1984:44.

40. Gookin 1792:163; Richter 1992:117–18.

41. MA, 30:3; NHPP, 1:174; Shurtleff 1853–54, 2:55; Winthrop 1853, 2:185, 203, 263.

42. Churchill 1994:241; 1995:66–67; DRHA 1988, 1:39.

43. YD, 10:156:Baker 1989:239–42.

44. LCRD, 1:18–19; YD, 2:13; 9:254; 18:235.

45. Baker 1989:245–46; Jennings 1976:144–45. I am indebted to Edwin Churchill for this detailed information regarding Indian deeds.

46. Willis 1972:113, 885; YD, 1:74 (pt. 1), 122; 2:191; 10:261; 16:113; 18:82.

47. YD, 1:6 (pt. 1).

48. Hubbard 1971, 2:263–64.

49. Grumet 1979;1989; Jennings 1976:144.

50. Baker 1989:244–46; YD, 2:13, 191; 18:82.

51. JR 3:111

52. Laval in Leger 1929:149–55.

53. JR, 37:257; Maine Indian Deeds file, MSM; YD, 1:6 (pt. 1), 2:113–14.

54. Baker 1989:249–51; Drake 1851:284; LCRD 1:16–19; Prins 1996; MHGR, 7:21–22; "Deed: Robin Hood to George Davis, January 9, 1668/9," MSL; Johnson, 1847:233–36; YD, 2:32; 3:23; 10:82, 261; 11:139; 15:224; 18:82; "Necodehant, Obias and Dick Swash to George Davie, January 9, 1666/7."

55. Day 1984:44; Shurtleff 1853–54, 4:361 (pt. 2).

56. Hubbard 1971, 2:99; Prins 1996:102–9.

57. Edwin Churchill, MSM, personal communication.

58. YD, 2:191; 4:5; 9:254; 18:82.

59. BM, 5:139, 165, 315; 6:123–25; 9:25,66; Church 1867:42–65; Hubbard 1971, 2:129, 178, 183, 186–87, 209.

60. Druillettes 1857:310; Prins and Bourque 1987; Statement of the Kennebec Claims:5.

61. Laval 1929:153–54; JR, 60:263–65.

62. Faulkner and Faulkner 1987:26–27.

63. Bourque 1989:263.

64. Church 1867:50–54; Mather 1952:225–26.

65. Haefeli and Sweeney 1997; Penhallow 1973:2, 8–9, 48, 61, 75, 112, 116.

66. Bourque 1989:264.

67. Druillettes 1857:310.

68. Hubbard 1971, 2:149.

69. BM 23:204–6; BMADD, 154–88; YD 9:229; PR, 7:9, 105; LCRD 1:9–11, 22–24; Bourque 1989:266; Hubbard 1971, 2:154–55, 189.

70. Bourque 1989:266–71. The ethnic labeling of Native groups on the Maritime Peninsula remains confused because of the continuing invocation of putative geographically based "tribes" referred to in English sources. French ethnic terminology is generally much more accurate because it reflects information derived from their Native informants.

71. Faulkner and Faulkner 1987:29.

72. Baudry 1979:63; Reid 1981:138, 246; JR, 60:263.

7. The War Years

1. Calloway 1996; Farrell 1996; Horton 1996; Jennings 1976:298–326; Leamon 1996; Muttersbaugh 1996; Purvis 1996.

2. Wigglesworth 1871.

3. Quin 1994:329.

4. Leach 1958:30–49.

5. Drake 1851:197; Jennings 1976:294–95.

6. Jennings 1976:297; Easton 1952:8–12.

7. Muttersbaugh 1996.

8. NYCD, 3:263.

9. Jennings 1976:322–24; 1984:43.

10. Shurtleff 1853–54, 5:299–300; Jennings 1976:322–24.

11. Dwight 1969, 1:160; Churchill 1975:xi; 1994:241–42; Hubbard 1971, 2:133, 135, 148–49.

12. Day 1981:16; 60, 233, 251; JR, 35, 259–63; PRCC, 2:495; Melvoin 1989:120–21. The complex movements of Indians of the Maritime Peninsula to and from mission villages located in French territory near or on the St. Lawrence River is beyond the scope of this book. See Day 1981 for a detailed history.

13. BM, 6:118–19; Hubbard 1971, 2:95–99, 103–4, 113, 134, 220–23; MA, 67:253; 69:141–42; Vinton 1864:115.

14. BM, 6:89–90 Hubbard 1971, 2:50, 100–128, 153–54; Coll. de Ms. 1:272.

15. Hubbard 1971, 2:148–49, 176. Madockawando's followers included veterans well known from earlier fighting in southern New England, e.g., Megunaway and Simon (Hubbard 1971, 2:223).

16. BM, 6:137–39, 151; Day 1981:16; JR. 40:233; Hubbard 1971, 2:53, 138–46, 159–202; Vinton 1864:115; Williamson 1991, 1:534–37; Hutchinson 1936, 1:294; MA, 69:84. Among the settlements attacked, from east to west, were those located in present-day New Harbor, Pemaquid, Boothbay, Damariscove; Bath, Casco Bay, Scarborough, Wells, and York.

17. Hubbard 1971, 2:149–51; Churchill 1975:xi, xviii.

18. BM, 8:118–20; Hubbard 1971, 2:136–37, 151; MEHSMC, 77, box 2/32; Murdoch 1865–67, 1:214; Siebert 1982:139–40.

19. Hubbard 1971, 2:136; 152.

20. Hubbard 1971, 2:152–56.

21. BM, 6:118–19; Hubbard 1971, 2:157–59, 198–204, 219; JR, 60:263–65.

22. Baker 1988; BM, 6:149–51; Rawlyk 1973:36; Salagnac 1969a:5; MA, 69:84; MEHSMC, Captain Joshua Scottow to Governor John Leverett; Summers and Chartrand 1981:8–9.

23. Hubbard 1971, 2:131–32; NHPP, 1:357.

24. Hubbard 1971, 2:179–81; BM, 6:130–31.

25. BM, 6:153–55.

26. Hubbard 1971:221–22.

27. Melvoin 1989:120–21; Belknap 1831:80–81; BM, 6:166–67; Hubbard 1971, 2:227–29; Hutchinson 1936, 1:295; MAHSP, 2nd ser., vol. 7:171; NYCD, 13:504.

28. Hough 1856:6–8; Belknap 1831:82–83; BM, 6:179–80, 189–93; Bradley and Camp, 1994:7–8; Harris 1690:229; Hubbard 1971, 2:238–39; MAHSP, 2nd ser., vol. 7:144–72.

29. BM, 6:153–55; 166–67; NYCD, 3:144–49, 248–49, 9:144–49, 13:519–26; Belknap 1831:81; Hubbard, 1:217–18, 3:248–49.

2:226–27, 239; Richter 1982:56; 1992:136–37, MA, 30:182, 69:165.

30. Greene and Harrington 1932:3; Heidenreich 1987; Daigle 1987; MAHS, 3rd ser., vol. 1:82–83; NAC, C11, vol. 1:399–400; Saint-Castin to Bradstreet, Prince Collection, MAHS; Salagnac 1969a:6; Webster 1934:203–4. Morse 1935:148–49; Coll. de Ms., 1:272–73, 309; Day 1981:30; Michelson 1977:4.

31. Bourque 1989:267–71; Webster 1934:212–13.

32. Belknap 1831:83; Raimo 1980:132; Mather 1952:186–87.

33. CSP, 11:633–35, 679, 686–88, 740, 12:89; NHHSC, 8:251–56.

34. White 1991.

35. Coll. de Ms, 1:348, our translation; NYCD 9:194, 14:768; White 1991:29–49.

36. Roy 1921:66; JR, 63:61–67; NAC, C11D, 1:399–400; CSP, 11:634.

37. Eccles 1969:101–2.

38. Leamon 1996.

39. BM, 6:266, 395; Coll. de Ms., 1:369, 399, 403, 411–13, 430–31; NYCD, 9:355, 380, 919; Rawlyk 1973:55–57; NAC, C11D, 1:399–400, 2:47; Parkman Manuscripts, 27:519; 29:512; Baudry 1979:649; Bourque 1989:269; Charland 1969; Lord, Sexton, and Harrington 1944, 1:26–28, 34; JR, 1:15; Prins 1992.

40. Coll. de Ms, 1:410–13; 445–46; MEHSC, 1st ser., vol. 6:281.

41. BM, 6:421–22.

42. CSP, 13:46; BM, 5:142; 6:421–22; MAHSC 3rd ser., vol. 1:101–4; Baxter 1894:14; Coll. de Ms., 1:410–13, 445–46; NYCD, 3:482, 555, 557, 561–62, 661; 9:392; MEHSMC, 1st ser., vol. 6:281; CSP, 12:430; Burnet 1727:Aug. 7, 1686; Mather 1952:190–91; Day 1981:24.

43. PRCC, 2:19 (pt. 1–2); 3:451; Coll. de Ms, 1:435, our translation; CSP, 13:46; BM, 5:51; 6:440–48; MA, Inter Charter, 34:96; Mather 1952:268–69; 3:451; Sewall 1973:176.

44. CSP, 13:46; Hutchinson Papers 2:314–17.

45. CSP, 13:46.

46. CSP, 13:116; Coll. de Ms., 1:477–78; BM, 5:2, 51, 55–56; 6:499–501; 9:4–8, 22–23; Lord, Sexton, and Harrington 1944:42.

47. BM, 4:459–64; 9:37–38,56–58; CSP, 13:82; Gyles 1981:98; MA, 107:311; New England Historical Genealogical Society, 18:161–63; Church 1867:8–32; Coll. de Ms., 1:478–80.

48. BM, 6:452–54.

49. CSP, 13:116–17, 149; Richter 1982:81–82.

50. Eccles 1990:101–3; Richter 1992:159–60; BM, 6:452–54.

51. BM, 5:55–56, 132–33, 144, 237; Coll. de Ms., 1:455–61, 497, 503–4, 2:4–5, 29; Douville 1969:285; Eccles 1979:138–39; MAHSP, 2nd ser., vol. 7:153; New England Historical Genealogical Society, 2:150; NYCD, 9:9, 472–73; O'Callaghan 1850–51, 2:146–7; Quinn 1994:319–20; Salagnac 1969a:6; Sewall 1973: 254, 259.

52. White 1991:x–iv, 30–40; Coll. De Ms., 1:469–71; Day 1981:31; NAC MG1, C11A, 10:191–91v; 11:129–30v; 12:159–62.

53. Rawlyk 1973:60–61.

54. Rawlyk 1973:60–61; CSP, 13:264–65; O'Callaghan 1850–51, 2:147; Leamon 1996:345–46; Stacey 1979:544–45; Webster 1934:24; Eccles 1990:102.

55. Church 1867:42–65; Mather 1952:225–7; MA, 30:317, 447; BM, 5:164–66; 231–35, 243–74, 280–81, 288.

56. BM, 5:310–21; CSP, 13:580–81; Webster 1934:36.

57. DRHA 1988, 2:54; LeBlanc 1979:576; Webster 1934:9–10, 32–37.

58. BM, 5:343–44; Mather 1952:232–38; Webster 1934:41–42; Brown 1998:71–72.

59. Church 1867:85, 90–92; Coll. de Ms., 2:89–90; Hutchinson 1936, 2:83.

60. Bradley and Camp 1994:37–60; Coll. de Ms, 2:98–100.

61. NAC, C11D, 2:442; Webster 1934:48.

62. BM, 10:7–11; Coll. de Ms., 2:127; Brown 1998:72–74.

63. AR, 7:377, 457; BM 8:11–15; NAC, C11D, 2:452; MA, 30:333–35; NYCD, 9:571; Webster 1934:48, 62; YD, 10:258.

64. Coll. de Ms., 2:111, 129–30; MPCR, 33:48.

65. Webster 1934:71.

66. Coll. De Ms., 2:164; Bourque 1989:269; Webster 1934: 53–62.

67. MA, 8:39–40; Shurtleff 1853–54, 2:273 ; Sewall 1973:319; Webster 1934:57, 64–65; Brown 1998:79–85.

68. Eames manuscript, A–2.

69. DePaoli 1994:256.

70. BM, 10:252; Mather 1952:259; NYCD, 9:642–43; Webster 1934:16, 145–46.

71. BM, 828–32; Leamon 1996:349–50; Baudoin 1900:72–77; CSP, 15:142–44; Pothier 1969:394; MA, 2:422; 30:441–42; MAHSP, 1st ser., vol. 1:132; Parkman Manuscripts, 74:21; Coll. de Ms., 2:239; Webster 1934:111; NHPP, 2:299–300; Mather 1952:263–66.

72. CSP, 17:558.

73. Baudry 1979:649; LeBlanc 1979:577; Lee 1896, 236–37; Salagnac 1969a:7; Stacey 1979:545–46; Webster 1934:16–17, 20.

8. The Era of the Mission

1. Webster 1934:68.

2. JR, 67:161, 177; Lord, Sexton, and Harrington 1944:41–42; Prins and Bourque 1987:144–49; White 1991:49.

3. BNL, no. 47; Hutchinson 1936, 2:83.

4. Eckstorm 1980:78; Lapomarda 1978; Prins 1988. Louis-Pierre Thury, missionary on the Penobscot, had abandoned the downriver mission at Pentagoet prior to his death in 1699. (Baudry 1979c; Webster 1934:199).

5. Webster 1934:69, 78; Prins 1992:63–64.

6. MA, 30:468, 473; 119:185, 190.

7. Leger 1929:55–57; Day 1981:16–17; Marshall 1967:86.

8. Leger 1929:57–58; Day 1981:5.

9. Leger 1929:58–62; Day 1981:5, 12ff.

10. Leger 1929:62–64; Day 1981:33.

11. Day 1981:39–45.

12. Jennings 1984:176; Surtees 1985:68; Richter 1992:119–20.

13. Lord, Sexton, and Harrington 1944, 1:68–72.

14. CSP, 18:187.

15. CSP, 18:96.

16. CSP, 18:599; NYCD, 4:758–59. The five castles, or villages, are not identified, but they are likely to have included Penacook on the Merrimack River, Naracamigook on the Androscoggin, Amaseconti on the Sandy (a tributary of the Kennebec), Norridgewock on the Kennebec, and Pentagoet on the Penobscot. If Naracamigook was not an important village at that time, Meductic, on the St. John, may also have been included.

17. CSP, 18:270; Jennings 1984:176; Richter 1992:196–97.

18. NYCD, 4:898–99; Richter 1992:203–13; Havard 1992:189–96; Sawaya 1998:23–31.

19. Richter 1992:214, 362–63; NYCD, 4:759; Aquilla 1983:55–57; Zoltvany 1969:114–15.

20. White 1991:49; Eccles 1990:106.

21. Havard 1992:193; Richter 1992:207, 211; Brandão and Starna 1996.

22. Zoltvany 1974:74; Coll. de Ms., 2:237, 391.

23. BM, 23:29–37; CSP, 20:570; NYCD, 9:756; New England Historical Genealogical Society, 34:91–93; Gay n.d.:136–37; MEHSL, 1st ser., vol. 3:344–46.

24. Coll. de Ms., 2:405–6; BM, 9:151–53; Gay n.d.:151–52; Hitchings 1980:55; Penhallow 1973:5.

25. AR, 8:300; Coll de Ms, 2:405–6; CSP, 21:385, 542–43; MAHSC, 6th ser., vol. 3:172; Day 1981:33; LaChasse 1708; New England Historical Genealogical Society, Jan 1880:91; NYCD, 9:756–82; Prins and Bourque 1987:149.

26. BM, 9:179; Penhallow 1973:3–11; Haefeli and Sweeney 1997:18–19.

27. BM, 9:140–42, 189–90; MAHSC, 6th ser., vol. 3:150–52, 172 Penhallow 1973:9–23; Haefeli and Sweeney 1997:49.

28. BM, 9:189–90; BNL 47, 58, 62, 116, 129, 171, 175, 211, 233, 362; Lanctot 1964, 2:159.

29. Coll. De Ms., 2:414–16; BNL 47, 56; Rosenfeld 1969:287; MPHS:312. The massing of population on the Penobscot is reflected in a census supplied by La Chasse in 1708. It lists warriors only on the Kennebec (28) and St. John (52), but on the Penobscot, 126 warriors are listed along with 262 women and children (La Chasse 1708).

30. NAC, C11D, 6:260–63, our translation; Coll. De Ms., 2:456–59; MPHS, 417; Zoltvany 1974:77–79; BM, 9:279–80; NAC, C11D, 6:28; Morrison 1984, 160–61; Penhallow 1973:47.

31. Barron 1975:112; Blasingham 1956; Champlain 1922, 1:103; Cox 1905:58; Grace 1764; CSP, 11:634; Nasatir 1990:357; 439, 696; NAC, C11D, 1:399–400; RAPQ, 1926–27:358, 374–88, 395, 403; 1927–28:365, 375; Steele 1990:152–53; White 1991:188, 220.

32. Mather 1879:49; BM, 23:5; Mather 1952:276; Webster 1934:115

33. BM, 10:379–81; 23:58–60; BNL no. 56; Charland 1969; MAHS, 6th ser., vol. 3:369; *New England Weekly Journal* 13; PAC, C11A, 45:146–54; White 1991:161–65; JR, 67:129.

34. Zoltvany 1974:77–80; BM, 9:262–63; Douville 1969:285; Penhallow 1973:48–49.

35. BM, 9:252, 308–9, 336–37.

36. Penhallow 1973:60–61.

37. BM, 9:302–3; NYCD, 9:850–51.

38. Baudry 1969:38–39; BNL 342; Reid 1994:91; Mahaffie 1995:138; CSP, 26:200; Lanctot 1964, 2:160–61; Penhallow 1973:62–67.

39. CSP, 25:550–54; Salagnac 1969; Mahaffie 1995:140–41; Zoltvany 1974:106–7; Dickason 1971:73.

40. CSP, 26:89, 149.

41. CSP, 26:307, 27:181–82.

42. BM 8:32–36; 9:340–42; 23:38–39, 51–57; Childress 1996; DRHA, 4:86; Penhallow 1973:80–82; Dickason 1976:64–72; Salagnac 1969b:512.

43. Coll. de Ms., 3:5; DRHA, 3:80; NYCD, 9:932; JR. 67:133–229; Day 1981:34.

44. BM, 23:84–85.

45. PR, 1:38–39; HJ, 1:62–63.

46. MEHSC, 1st ser., vol. 3:361–74; BM 23:82–83; Coll. de Ms., 3:22–24, 44; BNL 695, 696; Dickason 1976:83; Eckstorm, 1939:210; NF 1893:145–49.

47. Coll. de Ms., 3:31–32, 54; BM, 9:443–49, 457–59; PRCC, 3:182–85; HJ, 2:270–73; Lord, Sexton, and Harrington 1944, 1:124–26; MA, 52:77–84.

48. Baxter 1894:281–94; Whitehead 1991:94; Coll. de Ms., 3:57, 68; HJ, 3:29; JR, 67:103; NYCD, 9:903–4; Penhallow 1973:84; Zoltvany 1974:180.

49. Baxter 1894:109–18; BM, 9:463–64; Coll. de Ms., 3:58, 69, 85; DRHA 1988, 3:82; JR, 67:103–5, 111; Parkman Manuscripts, 31:291; NYCD, 9:904; Penhallow 1973:85; PRCC, 3:86, 182; Salagnac 1974.

50. Coll. de Ms., 3:61, 79, 83; HJ, 3:117, 194; 4:40; JR, 67:114–15; Sewall 1973:983; Zoltvany 1974:182.

51. Penhallow 1973:91–92; Baxter 1894:120–23; HJ, 3:152–52, 159; JR, 67:113–15; Trask 1901:45–46; Williamson 1991, 2:97.

52. BM, 10:154–55; BNL 964; Coll de Ms., 3:86–87; CCWR 3:187, 190, 190a, 9:911, 937; HJ, 10:339; NYCD, 9:911; Parkman Manuscripts, 31:294; Penhallow 1973:85–86.

53. BNL 967, 968; HJ, 4:96; Penhallow 1973:91; Dickason 1976:73–77.

54. HJ, 4:79–81; BNL 965, 969; Raimo 1980:137–38; Dickason 1976:87; Sutherland 1974:516; NYCD, 9:991; MAHSC, 2nd ser., vol. 8:266–67; Penhallow 1973:97–98; Zoltvany 1974:181; BM, 10:154; BNL 965, 969, 970, 973, 974.

55. Baxter 1894:333; BNL 1001; Penhallow 1973:88–91, 95–96, 99; NYCD, 9:933–38; Parkman Manuscripts, 31:319–20.

56. BNL 1025, 1026; BM, 10:152–53; 23:110–28; Richter 1992:375.

57. BM, 23:119–20.

58. Richter 1992:256; BNL 1062.

59. BM, 23:128–48, 153–57, 168–86 (quote is on p. 182); Richter 1992:244–45.

60. BNL 1028.

61. BM, 10:207–8; BNL 1067–70, 1072, 1075, 1076; Baxter 1894:383–84; DRHA 1988, 3:82; NYCD, 9:937; Penhallow 1973:103–4.

62. Baxter 1894:383; BNL 1074, 1112–15; Coll. De Ms., 3:108–9; Eckstorm 1939:204–5; Penhallow 1973:107, 110, 112–14; BM, 10:121–13.

63. BM, 10:238–55, 305; 23:186–202; *Boston Gazette*, Nov. 1–8, 1725; BNL 1159; NYCD, 9:947–55; Penhallow 1973:119–20; Smith 1849:44; Calloway 1990:121–22; MEHSC, 1st ser., vol. 3:377–405; BNL 1177, 1178; NYCD, 9:966–67.

64. AR, 11:238; Lord, Sexton, and Harrington 1944, 1:140; Liste 1929:69; MEHSC, 1st ser., vol. 3:411–46; NYCD, 9:1002–3; Eckstorm 1980:78; BM, 23:257–61, 299–301; 25:17; Day 1981:37. Dummer's treaty was ratified by Maliseets and Micmacs at Annapolis Royal in May 1728 (Hamilton and Spray 1977: 24–25).

65. BM, 23:217–31; 29:267; HJ, 11:109.

66. MAHS, Belcher Letter Book, 4:83.

67. BM, 10:337, 358–59, 364, 371–72, 374, 378, 381; Calloway 1990:126–29; Day 1981:39; Raimo 1980:138–39.

68. BM, 23:236–98; MAHS, Belcher Letter Book, 4:256.

69. Lord, Sexton, and Harrington 1944, 1:148–51; BM, 23:245–46.

70. BM, 23:237–43, 251; MAHS, Waldo Papers, April 10, 1736; Lord, Sexton, and Harrington 1944, 1:153; Raimo 1980:141; Taylor 1990:32.

71. *Bulletin des Recherches Historique* 1911; BM, 23:290–302; Lord, Sexton, and Harrington 1944, 1:166–67; NAC, C11A; 78:2–13, 40–46, 81:251–54, 114:98–134, 327–15, 115:14–20; Pritchard 1995:15, 28; Rawlyk 1994:124; NYCD, 6:542.

72. BM, 23:296–98; Rawlyk 1994:121–22; Mahaffie 1995:201–5; Akins 1869, 1:149; Krugler 1983:260; Pote 1894:1–5; Sutherland 1974a:438.

73. Mahaffie 1995:206–14; Lincoln 1912, 1:247–48, 256–58; Pote 1894:65–66.

74. Calloway 1990:148–59; NYCD, 10:32–34; NAC, C11A, 81:12–37; 87:2–14.

75. Coleman 1925, 2:235–36; Whitehead 1991:106; Smith 1849:124–30.

76. BM, 23:303–4; Ghere 1988:186; NYCD, 9:548; NAC, C11A, 83:74, 173; 115, 207–8.

77. BM, 8:50–55; Coll. de Ms., 3:155; Lord, Sexton, and

Harrington 1994, 2:140; MEHSC, 1st ser., vol. 4:157–58; NAC, C11A, 93:171–73, Patterson 1994:129–33; Upton 1979:51.

78. BM, 23:325–54; Ghere and Morrison 1996; Hutchinson 1936, 3:4; Smith 1849:143; Thayer 1899.

79. BM, 23:387, 395–96, 409–10, 441–43; PNAC, C11A, 87:365–86; 95:361–63; NYCD, 10:218–19; Raimo 1980:143; Thayer 1899:187–92.

80. BM, 23:415–19, 449; Lord, Sexton, and Harrington 1944, 1:185; MA 32:353,364.

81. BM, 23:435; Akins 1869:682–86.

82. Purvis 1996:687; Eccles 1990:191–92.

83. BM, 23:445–55.

84. Lord, Sexton, and Harrington 1944, 1:192.

85. Lincoln 1912, 2:12–13, 23, 32.

86. BM, 12:246–54.

87. Bartlett 1853:83–84; BM, 23:455; 24:18–20, 67–68; Lincoln 1912, 2:78; HCEI, 4:90; Johnson 1921–65, 2:123; MA, 6:180, 32:353, 565. For Abenaki involvement in the Seven Years War, see Steele 1990.

88. BM, 24:30.

89. BM, 24:22–23, 86–87.

90. BM, 24:35–36.

91. Whitehead 1991:140; BM, 23:425–26; 24:24–26; Coll. de Ms, 3:515–16; NAC, C11A, 100:7, 24, cf. Ghere 1988:241.

92. BM, 24:36–37, 41–44; 63–64, 67–68; Ghere and Morrison 1997; Ghere 1988:248–54. Phips took over the duties of governor when Shirley, promoted to major general in February 1755, assumed the command of British forces in North America soon thereafter. (Raimo 1980:142–43)

93. Dussieux 1883:238–45.

94. Steele 1990:124–25, 144, 151–53; Patterson 1994:144–48; Col. de Ms., 4:114–17; JR, 70:195–99; NYCD, 10:607, 616, 618–19.

95. Ghere 1988:259–67; Coll. De Ms., 4:154, 173–74; NYCD, 10:683–84; Knox 1914, 2:169–70; MA, Bundle on Indians, IR 1796, ch. 86.

96. Calloway 1990:175–81; Day 1981:43–45.

97. BPRO, War Office 34, vol. 25 (pt. 2); BM, 13:168; BPRO, War Office 34, vol. 25 (pt. 3).

98. Eccles 1990:214–22; PANS, RG1, vol. 36; Murchie 1945:108–9; BM, 24:114–30.

99. De Vorsey 1996; PANS, RG1, vols. 430–32; Jacobs 1988:10; BM, 8:55–59.

100. Murchie 1945:179–82; Dickason 1976:123; Bumstead 1994:178.

101. HJ 1764–65:31; Raymond 1943:130–46.

102. HJ 1764, 65:31.

103. BM, 24:118.

104. BM, 24:123–33, 145–47, 153–56; Ghere and Morrison 1996; Williamson 1991:370–71.

105. MA, Trade Records, 120:443.

106. Chadwick 1889:144–48. On the St. John River would-be settlers were less numerous, but in 1762 Maliseets confronted one party of New Englanders hoping to settle on abandoned Acadian farms at St. Anne (present-day Fredericton NB) and convinced them to retreat downriver (Raymond 1943:142).

107. Whiting 1947:170; BM, 24:75–76.

108. BM 24:157–59.

Epilogue

1. Continental Congress 3:401.

2. Ford 1889, 3:375, 391, 4:207, 231, 237; American Archives, 4th ser., vol. 2:cols. 621–22, 1734, 1735; vol. 3:cols. 301, 339, 348, 1275–76.

3. Ghere 1993:199, 202; Bartlett 1853:83–84; Roberts 1940:251; Drake 1851:340; Walker, Conkling, and Buesing 1980:59; True 1994:50–74; McBride and Prins 1996:338–39. Higgins was of English ancestry, captured at Berwick as a boy.

4. Wroth 1975:2294; BM, 16:241–42; Walker, Conkling, and Buesing 1980:58. Orono was of mixed European and Indian ancestry.

5. Kidder 1867:53; BM, 15:164, 333, 380, 408, 425.

6. Kidder 1867:54–59; Walker, Conkling, and Buesing 1980:59–62. Saint-Aubin was of mixed French and Indian ancestry (La Chasse 1708).

7. BM, 24:158–93.

8. Kidder 1867:13; Raymond 1943:217–20.

9. Kidder 1867:247, 311; BM, 24:174–93; Hunt 1973:120, 124–25; Prins 1985:10; Raymond 1943:219–27; Leamon 1993:96; Walker, Conkling, and Buesing 1980:62–63. Late in 1779 the Maliseet chief Pierre Toma renounced his allegiance to the British, telling Allan's secretary that he had acted in fear but had never actually harmed the American's interests (Hamilton and Spray 1977:53–54).

10. Ford 1889, 3:375, 391, 4:207, 231, 237.

11. Kidder 1867:284–85.

12. Whitehead 1939:221–23. Italics are my translation from the French. The Colonel Louis mentioned in Du Ponceau's account is also known as Louis Cook (Graymont 1983:39–40).

13. Bumstead 1994:170; Hunt 1973:134–35, 141; Kidder 1867:78, 88, 300–1; Calloway 1995:68–80; Williamson 1991, 2:478.

14. Tufts 1930:61–67; McBride and Prins 1996; Leamon 1993:192–93; Day 1981:59–60; Eckstorm 1980:19; Ghere 1993:202; True 1936:27.

15. BM, 21:235–47; MA, Maine Attorney General 1977:27–55; Horsman 1988:32.

16. Chadwick 1889:144–48; MA, Maine Attorney General 1977:48; HJ 1764–65:29; Allis 1954, 36:212–14.

17. Maine Attorney General 1977:54–60.

18. Maine Attorney General 1977:64.

19. BM, 8:127–32, 204–8; Maine Attorney General 1977:67–71.

20. Eckstorm 1980:175; Walker, Conkling, and Buesing 1980:69; Treat 1820:16–34; Peale 1830:20. Here is Treat's description of Attean's farm: "Mattawamkee Point, North of the Stream, the present residence of John Attean, the Indian Governor, is a very pleasant situation—there are three very good Wigwams here, and they have raised this season 60 bushels of potatoes—beans and peas etc—The corn is of a small yellow kind and ripened early and is good" (33).

21. Erickson 1982:88.

22. Condon and Barry 1994:580–82; Maine Laws 1835:258–60; Bradley 1835; Walker, Conkling, and Buesing 1980:77–78; Wabanakis of Maine and the Maritimes 1989.

23. Maine Laws 1839:560–62; Eckstorm 1980:13, 19, 138, 145–47, 159, 178–80, 194–97.

24. Holmes 1839:7; Thoreau 1987:9, 12–13.

25. Penobscot Indians 1863:209; Thoreau 1987:399–400; Erickson 1978:125.

26. Penobscot Indians 1863:209; Thoreau 1987:6, 215, 401–2.

27. Shaw 1910:58; Maine Laws 1852:282–83; 1853:24.

28. Penobscot Indians 1863:210.

29. Thoreau 1987:237.

30. Henry 1829–37:4; Lester 1987; Smith 1989; Sabine 1852:110–11; Bausseron, 1991:95–96.

31. IR; Indian Population in the United States and Canada 1915:18–19, 262–64; Lester 1987; Proctor 1942:10.

32. Chamberlain 1899:1–2.

33. Proctor 1942:6–7, 10–11, 64.

34. BM, 24:1–24; Bradley 1835; Eckstorm 1980:66, 201; Snow 1978:144–45; Treat 1820:33; Malinowski and Sheets 1998:237.

35. Kidder 1867:250, 271, 307–8; American Archives, 2:cols.; Davis 1974:12–13; Raymond 1943:218–19.

36. Kidder 1867:81; BM, 8:98–102; Davis 1974:14–16; Allis 1954:215; Lord, Sexton, and Harrington 1944, 1:591; Erickson 1985:88; Sabine 1852:110.

37. Smith 1988; Erickson 1978:125; Sabine 1852:103–4; Maine Laws 1849:141, 1852:429; Fewkes 1890.

38. Sabine 1852:110–11. A herring stick resembles a narrow, long-bladed oar. When held underwater, fishermen can feel the impact of herring schools as they pass by. Herring are traditionally pursued at night by torchlight.

39. Lincoln County News, Waldoboro ME, Jan. 2, 1885; Erickson 1982:91; Leighton 1937; Sabine 1852:111; Smith 1993:317–72. Some Penobscots and Micmacs also hunted porpoise.

40. Portland Sunday Telegram, Feb. 29, 1920.

41. Proctor 1942:6–7, 10–11, 64.

42. Lapomarda 1978; Gyles 1736:14; Prins 1992:61, Raymond 1943:83–84; Lord, Sexton, and Harrington 1944:96; NF 1893:145–49.

43. Morse 1822:64; Prins 1992:61–67; Raymond 1943:16, 49, 84, 203, 232; Ganong 1899:291; MAHS, 2nd ser., vol. 9:263.

44. Erickson 1978:125; Raymond 1943:86, 265–66; Vetromile 1866:122; Smith 1988.

45. Indian Population in the United States and Alaska 1915:18–19, 262–64; Erickson 1978; Johnson 1995:79, 111, 121–22.

46. Bock 1976:117; Rawlyk 1973:230–40.

47. MA, Trade Records, vol. 120; Elder 1871:4; Prins 1996a:177–83; Whitehead 1991:206, 226; Ruth H. Whitehead, Nova Scotia Museum, personal communication, 1995; Indian Population in the United States and Alaska 1915:18–19, 262–64.

48. Maine Laws 1871; Bock 1976:117–20; Martijn 1989.

49. Speck 1915:505; Walker, Conkling and Buesing 1980:51; Tucker 1839:45. In 1835 a contemporary observer, R. G. A. Levinge confirmed the Confederacy chiefs visits at three-year intervals (1846:102).

50. Speck 1915:495.

51. Speck 1919; 1940:240–45; Leavitt and Francis 1990; Walker 1990:29.

52. JR, 63:179; NYDC, 14:898–99.

53. Havard 1992:138; Sawaya 1998:56–57, 145–49.

54. Sawaya 1998:35–36, 53–54; 91–92, 144–56; 161–62; Jennings 1984:35; Tooker 1978:434–35; MAHSC, 3rd ser., vol. 5:78, 93–94.

55. Walker, Conkling, and Buesing 1980:68–69.

56. *Royal Gazette*, July 17, 1839; WC, Letter of Slyvanus Leland, Aug. 25, 1848; Sawaya 1998:57, 147. See also Letters of David Dunn, August 1825; Thomas Wyerite, J. Match, and C. R. Hathweay, July 16, 1847: J. Sylvanus Leland and Jacob Kimball, [1848?]; Sylvanus Leland, J. O'Donnell and Peter Gilligan, 1849; C. R. Hathaway et al., July 31, 1860; John Francis, Oct. 3, 1860; Maine Attorney General, July 1, 1864; W. B. Nutt, Joseph Gunnison, G. W. Shadbourne, W. Long, and C. B. Pains, July 22, 1865.

57. WC, Letter of the Grand Chiefs at Caughnawaga, Aug. 19, 1839.

58. Eckstorm 1980:140–47; Walker, Conkling, and Buesing 1980:74–76.

59. WC, Letter of the Grand Chiefs at Caughnawaga, Dec. 18, 1854.

60. Speck 1915:498.

61. Nicolar 1893:137–39.

62. WC, Letter of the Grand Chiefs at Caughnawaga, July 31, 1865.

63. Murchie 1945:65–66.

64. Speck 1915:498; Tucker 1839:45.

65. Morse 1822:66; IR; Sabine 1852:100–101.

66. 1955 Maine Public Law Chapter 405, sec. 1; O'Toole and Tureen 1971:2; Proctor 1942:8.

67. 1955 Maine Public Law Chapter 405, sec. 1; O'Toole and Tureen:12; Proctor 1942:8, 13–14; Nash 1988:270–72; Malinowski and Sheets 1998:235; Kelly 1988:75–76.

68. *Wabanakis of Maine* 1989: C95–C102; O'Toole and Tureen 1971:12–13; Malinowski and Sheets 1998, 1:107; Bausseron 1991:47–51; Kelly 1988:77–80.

69. O'Toole and Tureen 1971; Walker, Conkling, and Buesing 1980:77–79; Bausseron 1991:51–60; *Wabanakis of Maine* 1989:B–158–160; Tiller 1996:353–9; 25 CSCA, sec. 1721 et seq.; Federal Public Law 102–71, Nov. 26, 1991.

70. *Wabanakis of Maine* 1989: C99–C102; Tiller 1996:355–59; Malinowski and Sheets 1998:227–37; Bausseron 1991: 61–69.

Appendix

1. Quinn 1962:340–41.

2. Quinn 1962:341.

3. Levinge 1846:116.

4. Champlain 1922, 1:298, 308; 3:363, 371.

5. Rosier 1983:276–77.

6. Lescarbot 1907–14, 3:132–33.

7. Josselyn 1988:92–93.

8. Whitehead 1980:11.

9. Whitehead 1980:11.

10. Rosier 1983:303.

11. Josselyn 1988:101.

12. Josselyn 1988:102.

13. Quinn 1962:334.

14. Rosier 1983:277.

15. Lescarbot 1907–14, 3:159.

16. Pring 1983:220.

17. Archer 1983:122.

18. Brereton 1983:150.

19. Brereton 1983:155–56.

20. Champlain 1922, 1:180–83, 260–64. Isle Haute is not to be confused with Isle au Haut on the central Maine coast.

21. Bourque and Cox 1981:13–15.

22. Salwen 1978:166; Quinn and Quinn 1983:108–9; Bourque and Whitehead 1994; Bourque 1994:37–40.

23. Lescarbot 1907–14, 3:157.

24. Lescarbot 1907–14, 3:158.

25. Josselyn 1988:101.

26. Ceci 1980; Peña 1990.

27. Bradford 1991:203.

28. Rosier 1983:268.

29. Purchas 1983:150.

30. Lescarbot 1907–14, 3:133–35.

31. Rosier 1983:287.

32. Brereton 1983:145–46.

33. Archer 1983:117.

34. Davies 1983.

35. Lescarbot 1907–14, 2:548. See Bourque and Whitehead 1994 for a discussion of these native traders.

36. Lescarbot 1907–14, 2:143, 317, 324–25; Champlain 1922, 1:338, 442, 458.

37. Champlain 1922, 1:338–39.

38. Champlain 1922, 1:212; Bailey 1969:48–50; Lescarbot 1907–14, 2:323; JR, 4:207.

39. Rosier 1983:272.

40. Bradford 1991:220.

41. Josselyn 1988:92–93.

42. Bailey 1969:49–50.

43. Bailey 1969:50.

44. Gyles 1981:125.

45. Levinge 1846:111–12.

46. Levinge 1846:109.

47. Levinge 1846:113–14.

48. *Illustrated London News*, Sept. 5, 1863, 249.

49. Levinge 1846:112–13.

50. Speck 1970:45.

51. Pelletier 1977:10.

52. Gyles 1981:120.

53. Kilby 1888:487.

54. Josselyn 1988:91.

55. LeClercq 1910:100.

56. Gyles 1981:110–11.

57. JR, 3:77.

58. Champlain 1922, 1:329.

59. Lescarbot 1907–14, 2:356.

60. Lescarbot 1907–14, 2:356; Purchas 1905–7:939.

61. JR, 3:41.

62. Gyles 1981:114.

63. LeClercq 1910:103.

64. Levinge 1846:123.

65. Archer 1983:130.

66. Adney and Chappelle 1964:59, 70–74, 113–22.

67. Adney and Chappelle 1964:74–75.

68. Pring 1983:223.

69. Adney and Chapelle 1964:58–98.

70. Rosier 1983:281–82.

71. Denys 1908:420–22.

72. Adney and Chappelle 1964:75.

73. Porpoise-Shooting 1880:802.

74. Adney and Chapelle 1964:82.

75. Gyles 1981:104.

76. Adney and Chapelle 1964:217–18; Mike Martin, personal communication, July 1981.

77. Adney and Chapelle 1964:220.

78. Adney and Chapelle 1964:138.

79. Josselyn 1988:23.

80. Lescarbot 1907–14, 3:194.

81. Whitehead 1980:45.

82. Whitehead 1980:45.

83. Josselyn 1988:92.

84. See, e.g., Rale 1833:518.

85. Denys 1908:420.

86. Willoughby 1898; Flannery 1939:34–35; Hough 1926: 111–14.

87. Brereton 1983:156–57.

88. Josselyn 1988:50.

89. Gyles 1981:123.

90. Hough 1926:97–99.

91. Nicolar 1893:143–44.

92. Nicolar 1893:142.

93. Gyles 1981:121.

95. Speck 1970:137.

94. Mather 1952:265; George R. Hamell, New York State Museum, Albany, personal communication to Bruce Bourque.

96. Speck 1970:134; Wallis and Wallis 1955:87; Whitehead 1980:53.

97. Speck 1970:134.

98. Burnham 1981:3.

99. Archer 1983:131.

100. Champlain 1922, 1:355.

101. Willoughby 1905:91–92; 1973:256–58.

102. Whitehead 1980:53.

103. Lescarbot 1907–14, 3:192.

104. Champlain 1922, 1:344.

105. Schneider 1972:198–99.

106. Speck 1970:135.

107. Josselyn 1988:100.

108. Speck 1970:86.

109. Speck 1970:22, 84, 127–28, 136.

110. Whitehead 1980:52; Gordon 1993.

111. Whitehead 1980:52.

112. Wallis and Wallis 1955:78.

113. Josselyn 1988:102.

114. Josselyn 1988:91.

115. Lescarbot 1907–14, 3:201.

116. Gordon 1997:62–63; Harper 1957:27; Whitehead 1980:51.

117. Denys 1908:423.

118. Gordon 1997:58–59; Whitehead n.d.:37.

119. Josselyn 1988:70, 93, 102.

120. Morton 1883:142; J. Smith 1986, 1:160, 2:115.

121. Josselyn 1988:93.

122. Dièreville 1933:180.

123. Rosier 1983:280.

124. Josselyn 1988:102–3.

125. Speck 1970:122–23. See also Levinge 1846:116–17.

126. Speck 1970:116.

127. Josselyn 1988:101.

128. Speck 1940:163.

129. LeClercq 1910:100.

130. Denys 1908:423.

131. Whitehead 1982:27.

132. Eckstorm 1932:38.

133. Speck 1940:88.

134. Brasser 1975:20–22; Gordon 1997:38.

135. Smith 1977:54; Coffin 1856:325.

136. Whitehead 1980:61–62.

137. Whitehead 1980:62–63.

138. Eckstorm 1932:plate 4.

139. Josselyn 1988:99.

140. Lescarbot 1907–14, 3:191.

141. Denys 1908:428.

142. Rosier 1983:275.

143. Josselyn 1988:100.

144. Champlain 1922, 1:344.

145. Josselyn 1988:103–4.

146. Rosier 1983:274–75.

147. Denys 1908:419.

148. Hamilton 1972:30–32.

149. Pring 1983:220–21.

150. Denys 1908:419.

151. Flannery 1939:71.

152. Brereton 1983:155.

153. Rosier 1983:275; Lescarbot 1907–14, 3:191; Stone 1974:276; Beauchamp 1902:15, 19, 25–36; Bourque and Whitehead 1994:144. One such arrowhead found on Nautilus Island in Penobscot Bay is in the collection of the Wilson Museum, Castine ME, catalog number EW-ME-LW.

154. Josselyn 1988:104.

155. Champlain 1922, plate 81; Gookin 1792:152; Lescarbot 1907–14, 3:503, 504; de Peiresc 1967:106; JR, 2:41.

156. Josselyn 1988:103–4.

157. Bradford 1991:207.

158. Levett 1988:54.

159. Levinge 1846:115.

160. Josselyn 1988:92.

161. Champlain 1922, 1:327.

162. Lescarbot 1907–14, 3:98–99.

163. Gyles 1981:121.

164. Culin 1907:84.

165. Rosier 1983:279–80.

166. Denys 1908:424.

167. Speck 1970:196.

168. Josselyn 1988:97.

BIBLIOGRAPHY

Adams, William Y., Dennis P. Van Gerven, and Richard Levy. 1978. The Retreat from Migrationism. *Annual Review of Anthropology* 7:483–532.

Adney, A. Tappan, and Howard I. Chapelle. 1964. *The Bark Canoes and Skin Boats of North America*. Washington DC: Smithsonian Institution.

Akins, Thomas B. 1869. *Selections from the Public Documents of the Province of Nova Scotia*. Halifax: Charles Annand.

Allis, Frederick S., Jr., ed. 1954. *William Bingham's Maine Lands, 1790–1820*. Publications of the Colonial Society of Massachusetts, vols. 36–37. Boston.

American Archives. 1837–1853. *American Archives: consisting of a Collection of Authentick Records . . . Compiled and edited by Peter Force*. Prepared and published under authority of an act of Congress. Washington DC.

Anderson, R. Scott, George L. Jacobson Jr., Ronald B. Davis, and Robert Stuckenrath. 1992. Gould Pond, Maine: Late-Glacial Transitions from Marine to Upland Environments. *Boreas* 21:359–71.

Anthony, David W. 1990. Migration in Archaeology: The Baby and the Bathwater. *American Anthropologist* 92(4):895–914.

Aquilla, Richard. 1983. *The Iroquois Restoration: Iroquois Diplomacy on the Colonial Frontier, 1701–1754*. Detroit: Wayne State University Press.

AR *(Acts and Resolves, Public and Private, of the Province of Massachusetts Bay.)* 1903–72. 55 vols. Boston.

Archer, Gabriel. [1625] 1983. The Relation of Captaine Gosnols Voyage to the North part of Virginia, begunne the sixe and twentieth of March, Anno 42. Elizabethe Reginae 1602. And deliured by Gabriel Archer, A Gentleman of the said Voyage. In *The English New England Voyages*, edited by David B. Quinn and Allison M. Quinn, 112–38. London: Hakluyt Society.

Bachman, Van Cleaf. 1969. *Peltries or Plantations: The Economic Policies of the Dutch West India Company in New Netherlands, 1623–1639*. Studies in History and Political Science, 87th ser., no. 2. Baltimore: Johns Hopkins University Press.

Bacqueville de la Potherie, Claude-Charles. 1753. *Histoire del'Amerique Septentrionale*. Paris: Brocas.

Bailey, Alfred G. 1969. *The Conflict of European and Eastern Algonkian Cultures, 1504–1700: A Study in Canadian Civilization*. 2nd ed. Toronto: University of Toronto Press.

Baker, Emerson W. 1984. Trouble to the Eastward: The Failure of Anglo-Indian Relations in Early Maine. Ph.D. diss. College of William and Mary, Williamsburg VA.

———. 1985. *The Clark and Lake Company: The Historical Archaeology of a Seventeenth-Century Maine Settlement*. Occasional Publications in Maine Archaeology no. 4. Augusta: Maine Archaeological Society and Historic Preservation Commission.

———. 1988. New Evidence on the French Involvement in

King Philip's War. *Maine Historical Society Quarterly* 26(2):85–91.

———. 1989. "A Scratch with a Bear's Paw": Anglo-Indian Land Deeds in Early Maine. *Ethnohistory* 36(3): 235–56.

Bakker, Peter. 1988. Basque Pidgin Vocabulary in European-Algonquian Trade Contacts. In *Papers of the Nineteenth Algonquian Conference*, edited by William Cowan, 7–15. Ottawa: Carleton University.

———. 1992. A Basque Etymology for the Amerindian Tribal Name *Iroquois. Memoriae L. Mitxelena Magistri Sacrum*. Annuario del Seminario del Filolgía Vasca "Julio de Urquijo." Gehigarriak, XIV.

Banks, Charles E. 1884. Walter Bagnall. *Maine Historical and Genealogical Recorder* 1(2):61–64.

Barkham, Selma. 1978. The Basques: Filling a Gap in Our History between Jacques Cartier and Champlain. *Canadian Geographic Journal* 96:8–19.

Barnhardt, Walter A., Daniel F. Belknap, and Joseph T. Kelley. 1997. Stratigraphic Evolution of the Inner Continental Shelf in Response to Late Quaternary Relative Sea-Level Change, Northwestern Gulf of Maine. *Geological Society of America Bulletin* 109(5): 317–20.

Barnhardt, Walter A., W. Roland Gehrels, Daniel F. Belknap, and Joseph T. Kelley. 1995. Late Quaternary Relative Sea-Level Change in the Western Gulf of Maine: Evidence for a Migrating Glacial Forebulge. *Geology* 23(4):317–20.

Barron, Bill. 1975. *The Vaudreuil Papers*. New Orleans: Polyanthos.

Bartlett, William S. 1853. *The Frontier Missionary: A Memoir of the Life of the Rev. Jacob Bailey, Missionary at Pownalborough, Maine; Cornwallis and Annapolis, Nova Scotia*. Boston: Ide and Dutton.

Basley, David J. 1986. Lake Whitefish Management Plan. In *Planning for Maine's Inland Fish and Wildlife, October 1, 1986 through September 30, 1991*, vol. 2, pt. 1. Maine Department of Inland Fish and Wildlife.

Baudoin, Abbé. 1900. Journal du voyage que j'ay fait avec M. D'Iberville, captaine de frigate, de France en l'Acadie en l'Isle de Terreneuve. Du 26 Juin Jusq'en Mai 1697. In Gosselin, Abbé Auguste, *Les Normands au Canada: Journal d'une expédition de D'Ibreville*, Evreux. 31–86.

Baudry, René. 1969. Auger de Subercasse, Daniel d'. *Canadian Dictionary of Biography*, vol. 2. Toronto: University of Toronto Press.

———. 1979. Chambly, Jacques de. *Canadian Dictionary of Biography*, vol. 1. Toronto: University of Toronto Press.

———. 1979a. Andigné de Grandfontaine, Hector. *Canadian Dictionary of Biography*, vol. 1. Toronto: University of Toronto Press.

———. 1979b. Menou d'Aulnay, Charles de. *Canadian Dictionary of Biography*, vol. 1. Toronto: University of Toronto Press.

———. 1979c. Thury, Louis-Pierre. *Canadian Dictionary of Biography*, vol. 1. Toronto: University of Toronto Press.

Bausseron, Sylvie. 1991. *Passamaquoddy Indians and Their Survival as a Distinct Community*. Mémoire de Maîtrise, Départment des Lettres et Sciences Humaines, Départment d'Anglais, Université de Metz, France.

Baxter, James P., ed. 1894. *Pioneers of New France in New England*. Albany NY: Munsell's Sons.

———. 1906. *A Memoir of Jacques Cartier*. New York: Dodd and Mead.

BB (*Broadsides and Ballads*). 1927. Boston: Massachusetts Historical Society.

Beauchamp, William M. 1902. *Metallic Implements of the New York Indians. New York State Archaeological Bulletin*, no. 55. Albany.

Belcher, William R. 1989. Prehistoric Fish Exploitation in East Penobscot Bay. *Archaeology of Eastern North America* 17 (fall):175–91.

Belknap, Daniel F., Douglas C. Kellogg, Bruce J. Bourque, and Steven L. Cox. 1994. Geological Stratigraphy at the Sebasticook Lake Fish Weir from Core Samples. Maine State Museum.

Belknap, Jeremy. 1831. *The History of New Hampshire*. Dover NH: S. C. Stevens and Ela and Wadleigh.

Bendermer, Jeffrey C. M., and Robert E. Dewar. 1994. The Advent of Prehistoric Maize in New England. In *Corn and Culture in the New World*, edited by Sissel

Johannessen and Christine A. Hastorf, 369–93. University of Minnesota Publications in Anthropology no. 5, Minneapolis.

Bendermer, Jeffrey C. M., Elizabeth A. Kellogg, and Tonya Baroody Largy. 1991. A Grass-Lined Maize Storage Pit and Early Maize Horticulture in Central Connecticut. *North American Archaeologist* 12(4):325–49.

Benson, Denis A., and Donald G. Dodds. 1977. *The Deer of Nova Scotia*. Halifax: Department of Lands and Forests, Province of Nova Scotia.

Blasingham, Emily J. 1956. The "New England Indians" in the Western Great Lakes Region. *Proceedings of the Indiana Academy of Sciences*, vol. 66:47–49. Indianapolis: Indiana Academy.

BM. 1869–1916. *Documentary History of the State of Maine*, edited by James P. Baxter. 24 vols. Portland: Maine Historical Society.

BMADD (British Museum Manuscript Collection. Additional Documents). n.d.

BNL (Boston News Letter).

Bock, Philip K. 1976. Micmac. In *Northeast*. Vol. 15 of *Handbook of North American Indians*, edited by Bruce G. Trigger, 109–12. Washington DC: Smithsonian Institution.

Bonnichsen, Robson. 1984. Paleoindian Sites in the Munsungan Lake Region, Northern Maine. *Current Research* 1:3–4. Center for the Study of Early Man, University of Maine, Orono.

———. 1988. The Coming of the Fluted Point People. *Habitat: Journal of the Maine Audubon Society*, January, 34–36.

Bonnichsen, Robson, David Keenlyside, and Karen Turnmire. 1991. Paleoindian Patterns in Maine and the Maritimes. In *Prehistoric Archaeology in the Maritime Provinces: Past and Present Research*, edited by Michael Deal and Susan Blair, 1–36. Reports in Archaeology no. 8. Fredericton: New Brunswick Archaeological Services, Cultural Affairs, Department of Municipalities, Culture and Housing.

Bonnichsen, Robson, V. Konrad, V. Clay, T. Gibson, and D. Schnurrenberger. 1980. Archaeological Research at Munsungan Lake: 1980 Preliminary Technical Report of Activities. Munsungan Lake Paper no. 1.

Orono: Institute for Quaternary Studies, University of Maine.

Bonnichsen, Robson, E. Lahti, B. Lepper, R. Low, J. McMahon, and S. Oliver. 1981. Archaeological Research at the Thoroughfare. In Archaeological Research at Munsungan Lake: 1981 Technical Report of Activities. Munsungan Lake Paper no. 7. Orono: Institute for Quaternary Studies and the Center for the Study of Early Man, University of Maine.

Borstel, Christopher L. 1982. *Archaeological Investigations at the Young Site, Alton, Maine*. Occasional Publications in Maine Archaeology no. 2. Augusta: Maine Archaeological Society and Historic Preservation Commission.

Boston Gazette.

Bourque, Bruce J. 1975. Comments on the Late Archaic Populations of Central Maine: The View from the Turner Farm. *Arctic Anthropology* 12(2):35–45.

———. 1976. The Turner Farm Site: A Preliminary Report. *Man in the Northeast*, no. 11:21–30.

———. 1980. Field notes. Maine State Museum.

———. 1981. Field notes. Maine State Museum.

———. 1983. The Turner Farm Archaeological Project. *National Geographic Society Reports* 15:59–65.

———. 1985. Paleo-Indian "Meat Cache" Moved. *Broadside* 7(2).

———. 1989. Ethnicity on the Maritime Peninsula, 1600–1759. *Ethnohistory* 36(3):257–84.

———. 1991. Field notes. Maine State Museum.

———. [1971] 1992. *Prehistory of the Central Maine Coast*. New York: Garland.

———. 1994. Evidence for Prehistoric Exchange on the Maritime Peninsula. In *Prehistoric Exchange Systems in North America*, edited by J. E. Ericson and T. G. Baugh, 23–46. New York: Plenum.

———. 1995. *Diversity and Complexity in Prehistoric Maritime Societies: A Gulf of Maine Perspective*. New York: Plenum.

Bourque, Bruce J., Daniel F. Belknap, and Detmar Schnitker. 1997. "Prehistoric Cultural Responses to Changes in the Gulf of Maine," with oceanographers D. F. Belknap and D. Schnitker. In *Proceedings of the Gulf of Maine Ecosystem Dynamics Scientific Symposium* and Workshop, edited by Gordon T. Wallace and Eugenia F. Braasch, 279–80. RARGOM Report 7–1. Hanover NH: Regional Association for Research on the Gulf of Maine.

Bourque, Bruce J., and Steven L. Cox. 1981. Excavations at the Goddard Site, Brooklin, Maine: A Preliminary Report. *Man in the Northeast*, no. 22:3–28.

Bourque, Bruce J., and Harold W. Krueger. 1994. Dietary Reconstruction from Human Bone Isotopes for Five New England Coastal Populations. In *Paleonutrition: The Diet and Health of Prehistoric Americans*, edited by Kristin D. Sobolik, 195–209. Southern Illinois University Center for Archaeological Investigations. Occasional paper no. 22. Carbondale.

Bourque, Bruce J., and Ruth H. Whitehead. 1994. Trade and Alliances in the Contact Period. In *American Beginnings: Exploration, Culture, and Cartography in the Land of Norumbega*, edited by E. W. Baker, E. A. Churchill, R. S. D'Abate, K. Jones, V. A. Konrad, and H. E. Prins, 131–47. Lincoln: University of Nebraska Press. (Reprint of Tarrentines and the Introduction of European Trade Goods in the Gulf of Maine. *Ethnohistory* 32[4]:327–41.)

BPRO (British Public Record Office, Kew, England).

Bradford, William. 1810. Governor Bradford's Letter Book. *Massachusetts Historical Society Collections*, 1st ser., vol. 3:27–76. Boston.

———. 1912. *History of Plymouth Plantation 1620–1647*. 2 vols. Boston: Massachusetts Historical Society.

———. [1952] 1991. *Of Plymouth Plantation*, edited by Samuel E. Morison. New York: Alfred A. Knopf.

Bradley, Robert L., and Helen B. Camp. 1994. *The Forts of Pemaquid, Maine*. Occasional Publications in Maine Archaeology no. 10. Augusta: Maine Archaeological Society and Historic Preservation Commission.

Bradley, Zebulon. 1835. Survey of the Islands in the Penobscot River above Indian Island, Oldtown, 1835. Oldtown ME: Sewall Company.

Bradstreet, Theodore E., and Ronald B. Davis. 1975. Mid-Postglacial Environments in New England with Emphasis on Maine. *Arctic Anthropology* 8(2):7–22.

Brandão, J. A., and William A. Starna. 1996. The Treaties of 1701: A Triumph of Iroquois Diplomacy. *Ethnohistory* 43(2):209–44.

Brasser, Ted J. 1975. *A Basketful of Indian Culture Change*. National Museum of Man Mercury Series. Canadian Ethnology Service Paper no. 22. Ottawa: National Museums of Canada.

Brereton, John. [1602] 1983. A Briefe and Trve Relation of the Discoverie of the North Part of Virginia; . . . In *The English New England Voyages*, edited by David B. Quinn and Allison M. Quinn, 143–203. London: Hakluyt Society.

Brown, Craig J. 1998. "The Great Massacre of 1694": Understanding the Destruction of Oyster River Plantation. *Historical New Hampshire* 33(3/4):69–89.

Brown, James A. 1986. Early Ceramics and Culture: A Review of Interpretations. In *Early Woodland Archaeology*. Vol. 2 of Kampsville Seminars in Archaeology, edited by Kenneth B. Farnsworth and Thomas E. Emerson. 596–608. Kampsville IL: Center for American Archaeology Press.

Broyles, Bettye J. 1966. Preliminary Report: The St. Albans Site (46 Ka 27). Kanawah County WV. *West Virginia Archaeologist*, no. 19: 1–43.

Brymner, Douglas. 1894. Report Concerning the Canadian Archives for the Year 1904, viii–ix. Ottawa.

Bulletin des Recherches Historique. 1911. 37(7):411.

Bumstead, J. M. 1994. 1763–1783: Resettlement and Rebellion. In *The Atlantic Region to Confederation: A History*, edited by Phillip A. Buckner and John G. Reid, 156–83. Toronto: University of Toronto Press.

Burnet, William. 1727. Folio volume assembled between 1703 and 1707. Worcester MA: American Antiquarian Society.

Burnham, Dorothy. 1981. *The Comfortable Arts: Traditional Spinning and Weaving in Canada*. Ottawa: National Gallery of Canada.

Burrage, Henry S. 1904. The Plymouth Colonists in Maine. *Maine Historical Society Collections*, 3rd ser., vol. 1. Portland.

Burrage, Henry S., ed. 1914. *The Beginnings of Colonial Maine*. Portland: State of Maine.

Byers, Douglas S. 1959. The Eastern Archaic: Some Problems and Hypotheses. *American Antiquity* 24:233–56.

———. 1979. *The Nevin Shellheap: Burials and Observations.* Papers of the R. S. Peabody Foundation for Archaeology no. 9. Andover MA.

Calloway, Collin G. 1990. *The Western Abenakis of Vermont, 1600–1800.* Norman: University of Oklahoma Press.

———. 1995. *The American Revolution in Indian Country.* New York: Cambridge University Press.

———. 1996. Dummer's War (1722–1727). *Colonial Wars of North America, 1512–1763, an Encyclopedia,* edited by Alan Gallay. New York: Garland.

Campeau, Lucien. 1979. Biard, Pierre. *Dictionary of Canadian Biography,* vol. 1. Toronto: University of Toronto Press.

———. 1979a. Druillettes, Gabriel. *Dictionary of Canadian Biography,* vol. 1. Toronto: University of Toronto Press.

CCWR (Connecticut Colonial War Records). Public Records of the Colony of Connecticut, 1636–1776, edited by James Hammond Trumbull. Lockwood and Brainerd, 1850–90.

Ceci, Lynn. 1980. The First Fiscal Crisis in New York. *Economic Development and Cultural Change* 28(4):839–47.

Chadbourne, Paul A. 1859. Oyster Shell Deposit in Damariscotta. *Maine Historic Society Collections,* 1st ser., vol. 6:350–51. Portland.

Chadwick, Joseph. [1764] 1889. Account of a Journey from Fort Pownal—Now Fort Point—Up the Penobscot River to Quebec, in 1764, by Joseph Chadwick. *Bangor Historical Magazine* (later the *Maine Historical Magazine*) 4:141–48.

Chamberlain, Montague. 1899. *The Penobscot Indians.* (Reprinted from the *Cambridge Tribune* of February 4, 1899.)

Champlain, Samuel de. 1922. *The Works of Samuel de Champlain,* edited by H. H. Langton and W. F. Ganong. 6 vols. Toronto: Champlain Society.

Chapdelaine, Claude, and Steve Bourget. 1992. Un Site Paléoindien Récent à Rimouski. *Recherches Amérindiennes au Québec* 22(1):17–32.

———. 1994. *Il y a 8000 Ans à Rimouski: Paléoécologie et Archéologie d'un Site de la Culture Plano.* Pàléo-Quebec 22. Montréal: Recherches Amérindiennes au Québec.

Charland, Thomas. 1969. Bigot, Jacques. *Dictionary of Canadian Biography,* vol. 2. Toronto: University of Toronto Press.

Charlevoix, Pierre F.-X. [1744] 1900. *History and General Description of New France.* 6 vols. New York: F. P. Harper.

Childress, Boyd. 1996. Utrecht, Treaty of (1713). In *Colonial Wars of North America, 1512–1763, an Encyclopedia,* edited by Alan Gallay. New York: Garland.

Church, Benjamin. 1867. *The History of the Eastern Expeditions of 1689, 1690, 1692, 1696, and 1704 against the Indians and French.* Boston: B. K. Wiggin and W. P. Lunt.

Churchill, Edwin. 1975. Introduction to *Archaeological Excavations at Pemaquid,* by Helen Camp, ix–xvi. Augusta: Maine State Museum.

———. 1979. Too Great the Challenge: The Birth and Death of Falmouth, Maine. Ph.D. diss., University of Maine, Orono.

———. 1994. Mid-Seventeenth-Century Maine: A World on the Edge. In *Norumbega: American Beginnings,* edited by Emerson W. Baker, Edwin A. Churchill, Richard S. D'Abate, Kristine L. Jones, Victor A. Konrad, and Harald E. L. Prins, 241–60. Lincoln: University of Nebraska Press.

———. 1995. The European Discovery of Maine. In *Maine: The Pine Tree State from Prehistory to the Present,* edited by Richard W. Judd, Edwin A. Churchill, and Joel W. Eastman, 31–50. Orono: University of Maine Press.

———. 1995a. English Beachheads. In *Maine: The Pine Tree State from Prehistory to the Present,* edited by Richard W. Judd, Edwin A. Churchill, and Joel W. Eastman, 51–75. Orono: University of Maine Press.

Clark, Andrew Hill. 1968. *Acadia: The Geography of Early Nova Scotia to 1760.* Madison: University of Wisconsin Press.

Clark, Charles E. 1970. *The Eastern Frontier: The Settlement of Northern New England, 1610–1763.* New York: Alfred A. Knopf.

Clarke, Noah T. 1931. *The Wampun Collection of the New York State Museum.* New York State Museum Bulletin no. 288. The Twentieth Report of the Director of the Division of Science and the State Museum. Albany.

Clermont, Norman, and Claude Chapdelaine. 1998. *Île Morrison: Lieu sacré et atelier de l'Archaïque dans l'Outaouais.* Recherches Amérindiennes au Québec, Montréal, no. 28.

Clermont, Norman, Claude Chapdelaine, and Georges Barré. 1983. *Le Site Iroquoien de Lanoraie: Témoinage d'une Maison-Longue.* Recherches Amérindiennes au Québec, Montréal, no. 3.

Coffin, Paul. 1856. Missionary Tour in Maine. *Collections of the Maine Historical Society,* 1st ser., vol. 4.:301–36.

Cole-Will, Rebecca, and Richard Will. 1996. A Probable Middle Archaic Cemetery: The Richmond-Castle Site in Surry, Maine. *Archaeology of Eastern North America* 24:149–58.

Coleman, Emma Lewis. 1925. *New England Captives Carried to Canada Between 1677 and 1760 during the French and Indian Wars.* 2 vols. Portland ME: Southworth Press.

Coll. de Ms. 1883. *Collection de Manuscrits, contenant Lettres, Memoirs, et Autres Documents Historiques Relatifs à la Nouvelle France.* Quebec: A. Coté et Cie.

Condon, Richard H., and William D. Barry. 1994. The Tides of Change. In *Maine: The Pine Tree State from Prehistory to the Present,* edited by R. W. Judd, E. A. Churchill, and J. W. Eastman, 554–85. Orono: University of Maine Press.

Continental Congress. 1774–1789. *Journals of the Continental Congress, 1774–1789.* Edited by Worthington C. Ford et al. 34 vols. Washington DC: Government Printing Office. 1904–37.

Cook, Thomas G. 1976. Broadpoint: Culture, Phase, Horizon, or Knife. *Journal of Anthropological Research* 32(4):337–57.

Couillard-Després, Azarie. 1932. *Charles de Saint-Etienne de le Tour, Gouverneur, Lieutenant-Général en Acadie, et son Temps, 1593–1666, au Tribunal de l'Histoire.* Saint-Hyacinthe, Imp.

Cowie, Ellen R., James B. Petersen, and Nancy Asch Sidell. 1992. "Contact Period in Central Maine: Archaeological Investigations at Ethnohistoric Norridgewock."

Paper presented at the 32nd annual meeting of the Northeastern Anthropological Association, Bridgewater State College, Bridgewater MA, March 1992.

Cox, Belinda J., and James B. Petersen. 1997. The Varney Farm (36–57 ME): A Late Paleoindian Encampment in Western Maine. *Maine Archaeological Society Bulletin* 37(2):25–49.

Cox, Isaac J. 1905. *The Journeys of Robert Cavelier de LaSalle.* 2 vols. New York: A. S. Barnes.

Cox, Steven L. 1991. Site 95.20 and the Vergennes Phase in Maine. *Archaeology of Eastern North America* 19: 135–61.

———. Forthcoming. *Goddard: A Prehistoric Village Site on Blue Hill Bay, Maine.*

Crawford, Gary W., David G. Smith, and Vandy E. Bowyer. 1997. Dating the Entry of Corn (*Zea mays*) into the Lower Great Lakes Region. *American Antiquity* 62(1):112–29.

Crock, John G., James B. Petersen, and Ross M. Anderson. 1993. Scalloping for Artifacts: A Biface and Plummet from Eastern Blue Hill Bay, Maine. *Archaeology of Eastern North America* 21:179–92.

Crosby, Alfred W., Jr. 1986. *Ecological Imperialism: The Biological Expansion of Europe, 900–1900.* New York: Cambridge University Press.

CSP (*Calendar of State Papers, Colonial Series, America and the West Indies . . . Preserved in Her Majesty's Public Record Office*). 1860. 46 vols. Edited by W. Noel Sainsbury, et al. London: various publishers.

Culin, Stewart. 1907. Games of the North American Indians. Bureau of American Ethnology, *24th Annual Report.* Washington DC: Government Printing Office.

Cumming, William P., Raleigh A. Skelton and David B. Quinn. 1972. *The Discovery of North America.* New York: American Heritage Press.

Curran, Mary Lou, and Peter A. Thomas. 1979. Phase III-Data Recovery: Wastewater Treatment System in the Riverside Archaeological District, Gill, Massachusetts. Department of Anthropology, University of Vermont, Burlington.

Daigle, Jean. 1987. Acadian Marshland Settlement. In *Historical Atlas of Canada,* edited by Cole R. Harris, R.

Cole, and Geoffrey Matthews, plate 29. Toronto: University of Toronto Press.

Davenport, Demarest, John R. Davenport, and Jan Timbrook. 1993. The Chumash and the Swordfish. *Antiquity* 67:257–72.

Davies, Robert. 1983. The Narrative of the North Virginia Voyage and Colony (compiled by William Strachey). In *The English New England Voyages*, edited by David B. Quinn and Allison M. Quinn, 397–441. London: Hakluyt Society.

Davis, Harold A. 1974. *An International Community on the St. Croix (1604–1930)*. Maine Studies no. 64. Orono: University of Maine.

Davis, Ronald B., T. Bradstreet, R. Stuckenrath Jr., and H. Borns. 1975. Vegetation and Associated Environments during the Past 14,000 Years Near Moulton Pond, Maine. *Quaternary Research* 5:435–65.

Davis, Ronald B., and George L. Jacobson, Jr. 1985. Late Glacial and Early Holocene Landscapes in Northern New England and Adjacent Areas of Canada. *Quaternary Research* 23:341–68.

Davis, Stephen A. 1991. The Ceramic Period of Nova Scotia. In *Prehistoric Archaeology in the Maritime Provinces: Past and Present Research*, edited by Michael Deal and Susan Blair, 93–108. Reports in Archaeology no. 8. Fredericton: New Brunswick Archaeological Services, Cultural Affairs, Department of Municipalities, Culture and Housing.

Day, Gordon M. 1978. Western Abenaki. In *Northeast*. Vol. 15 of *Handbook of North American Indians*, edited by Bruce G. Trigger, 148–59. Washington DC: Smithsonian Institution.

———. 1981. *The Identity of the Saint Francis Indians*. National Museum of Man Mercury Series. Canadian Ethnology Service Paper no. 71. Ottawa: National Museums of Canada.

———. 1984. The Ourage War. In *Extending the Rafters: Interdisciplinary Approaches to Iroquoian Studies*, edited by Michael K. Foster, Jack Campisi and Marianne Mithun, 35–50. Albany: State University of New York Press.

Day, Gordon M. and Bruce G. Trigger. 1978. Algonquin. In *Northeast*. Vol. 15 of *Handbook of North American*

Indians, edited by Bruce G. Trigger, 798–804. Washington DC: Smithsonian Institution.

Demeritt, David. 1991. Agriculture, Climate, and Cultural Adaptation in the Prehistoric Northeast. *Archaeology of Eastern North America* 19:183–202.

De Nant, Candide. 1927. *Pages Glorieuses de L'Épopé Canadienne: Une Mission Capuchine en Acadie*. Montréal: Éditions Le Devoir.

Dennis, Matthew. 1993. *Cultivating a Landscape of Peace*. Ithaca NY: Cornell University Press.

Denys, Nicholas. [1672] 1908. *The Description and Natural History of the Coasts of North America (Acadia)*. Translated and edited by William F. Ganong. Toronto: Champlain Society.

De Paoli, Neill. 1994. Anglo Trade at Pemaquid. In Robert L. Bradley and Helen B. Camp, *The Forts of Pemaquid, Maine*, 253–65. Occasional Publications in Maine Archaeology no. 10. Augusta: Maine Archaeological Society and Historic Preservation Commission.

de Peiresc, Nicholas-Claude de Fabri. 1967. Observations de Peiresc sur curiosites rapportes d'Acadie par Pierre du Gua/ sieur de Mons (1606). In *Nouveaux documents sur Champlain et Son Epoque*. Publications des Archives Publiques du Canada, no. 15, vol. 1, 102–6. Ottawa: Archives Publiques du Canada.

Dermer, Thomas. 1841. Thomas Dermer to Samuel Purchase, December 27, 1619. *New York Historical Society Collection*, 2nd ser., vol. 1:350.

De Vorsey, Louis, Jr. 1996. Proclamation Line of 1763. *Colonial Wars of North America, 1512–1763, an Encyclopedia*, edited by Alan Gallay. New York: Garland.

Diamond, Jared. 1997. *Guns, Germs and Steel: The Fates of Human Societies*. New York: W. W. Norton and Company.

Dickason, Olive P. 1976. *Louisbourg and the Indians: A Study in Imperial Race Relations, 1713–1760*. History and Archaeology, vol. 6:1–200. Ottawa: Ministry of Supply and Services Canada.

Dièreville, N. de. [1708] 1933. *Relation of the Voyage to Port Royale in Acadia*, edited by John C. Webster. Toronto: Champlain Society.

Dincauze, Dena F. 1968. *Cremation Cemeteries in Eastern*

Massachusetts. Papers of the Peabody Museum of Archaeology and Ethnology, vol. 59, no. 2. Cambridge MA.

————. 1972. The Atlantic Phase: A Late Archaic Culture in Massachusetts. *Man in the Northeast,* no. 4:40–61.

————. 1974. An Introduction to Archaeology in the Greater Boston Area. *Archaeology of Eastern North America* 2(1):39–66.

————. 1975. The Late Archaic Period in Southern New England. *Arctic Anthropology* 12(2):23–34.

————. 1976. *The Neville Site: Eight Thousand Years at Amoskeag, Manchester, New Hampshire.* Peabody Museum Monographs, no. 4. Cambridge MA.

Douville, Raymond. 1969. Hertel de Rouville, Jean-Baptiste. *Dictionary of Canadian Biography,* vol. 2. Toronto: University of Toronto Press.

Doyle, Richard, Nathan Hamilton, James Petersen, and David Sanger. 1985. Late Paleo-Indian Remains from Maine and Their Correlations in Northeastern Prehistory. *Archaeology of Eastern North America* 13:1–34.

Dragoo, Don W. 1963. *Mounds for the Dead.* Annals of the Carnegie Museum, vol. 7. Pittsburgh: Carnegie Museum.

————. 1976. Adena and the Eastern Burial Cult. *Archaeology of Eastern North America* 4 (winter):1–9.

Drake, Samuel G. 1851. *Biography and History of the Indians of North America, from Its First Discovery.* 11th ed. Boston: Benjamin B. Mussey and Co.

DRHA (*Documents Relatifs a l'Histoire Acadienne, Inventaire Analytique des 25 Premiers Volumes de RG1 aux Archives Publiques de la Nouvelle-Écosse*). 1988. Groupe de Recherche sur les Sources Archivistiques Acadiennes. Fredericton: Archives Provinciales du Nouveau-Brunswick.

Driver, Harold E., and William C. Massey. 1957. Comparative Studies of North American Indians. *Transactions of the American Philosophical Society* 47, pt. 2. Philadelphia.

Druillettes, Gabriel. 1857. Narrative of a Voyage, Made for the Abenaquiois Mission, and Information Acquired of New England and Dispositions of the Magistrates of That Republic for Assistance against the Iroquois. The Whole by me, Gabriel Druillettes, of the Society of Jesus, translated and edited by John Gilmary Shea, 309–20. *Collections of the New York Historical Society,* 2nd ser., vol. 3, pt. 2.

Dumais, Pierre. 1978. Le Bas Saint-Laurent, in *Images de la Préhistoire du Québec,* edited by Claude Chapdelaine, 63–74. Recherches Amérindiennes au Québec, Montréal.

Dumas, G.-M. 1979. Côme de Mantes. *Dictionary of Canadian Biography,* vol. 1. Toronto: University of Toronto Press.

Dunbabin, Thomas. 1979. Young, Thomas. *Dictionary of Canadian Biography,* vol. 1. Toronto: University of Toronto Press.

Dussieux, Louis. 1883. *La Canada Sous la Domination Française.* L[i]brarie Victor LeCoffre, Paris.

Dwight, Timothy. 1969. *Travels in New England and New York.* Cambridge MA: Belknap Press of Harvard University Press.

Eames, Wilberforce. Eames Manuscripts, New York Public Library.

Easton, John. [1675] 1952. A Relation of the Indyan Warre, by Mr. Easton, of Roade Isld., 1675. In *Narratives of the Indian Wars, 1675–1699,* edited by C. H. Lincoln, 7–17. New York: Charles Scribner's Sons.

Eccles, William J. 1969. Brisay de Denonville, Jacques-René de. *Dictionary of Canadian Biography,* vol. 2. Toronto: University of Toronto Press.

————. 1979. Buade de Frontenac et de Palluau, Louis de. *Dictionary of Canadian Biography,* vol. 1. Toronto: University of Toronto Press.

————. 1990. *France in America.* East Lansing: Michigan State University.

Eckstorm, Fannie H. 1932. *The Handicrafts of the Modern Indians of Maine.* Lafayette National Park Museum Bulletin no. 3. Bar Harbor ME: Robert Abbe Museum.

————. 1939. Who Was Paugus? *New England Historical Quarterly* 12:203–26.

————. 1980. *Old John Neptune and other Maine Indian Shamans,* 2nd. ed. Orono: University of Maine Press.

EIHC (*Essex Institute Historical Collections*). 1869–. Salem MA: Essex Institute Press.

Ellis, Chris J., and D. Brian Deller. 1990. Paleo-Indians. In *The Archaeology of Southern Ontario to A.D. 1650*

edited by Chris Ellis and Neal Ferris, 37–63. Occasional Publications no. 5. London: Ontario Archaeological Society.

Emerson, Everett, ed. 1976. *Letters from New England: The
Massachusetts Bay Colony, 1629–1638.* Amherst: University of Massachusetts Press.

Emerson, Thomas E. 1986. A Retrospective Look at the Earli-
est Woodland Cultures in the American Heartland.
In *Early Woodland Archaeology.* Vol. 2 of Kampsville
Seminars in Archaeology, edited by Kenneth B.
Farnsworth and Thomas E. Emerson, 621–31.
Kampsville IL: Center for American Archaeology Press.

Erickson, Vincent O. 1978. Maliseet-Passamaquoddy. *Northeast.* Vol. 15 of *Handbook of North American Indians,* 123–36, edited by Bruce G. Trigger. Washington
DC: Smithsonian Institution.

———. 1982. Economic Factors and the Development of
Factionalism among the Passamaquoddy in the
Early Nineteenth Century. *Papers of the Thirteenth
Algonquian Conference,* edited by William Cowan,
169–78. Ottawa: Carleton University.

Fairbridge, Rhodes W. 1976. Shellfish-Eating Preceramic
Indians in coastal Brasil. *Science* 192:353.

Farrell, David R. 1996. Queen Anne's War (1702–1713). *Colonial Wars of North America, 1512–1763, an Encyclopedia,* edited by Alan Gallay, 613–17. New York:Garland.

Faulkner, Alaric, and Gretchen Faulkner. 1987. *The French
at Pentagoet: An Archaeological Portrait of the
Acadian Frontier.* Occasional Publications in Maine
Archaeology no. 5. Special Publications of the New
Brunswick Museum, St. John. Augusta: Maine His-
toric Preservation Commission.

Fergusson, C. Bruce. 1979. Leverett, John. *Dictionary of Canadian Biography,* vol. 1. Toronto: University of
Toronto Press.

Ferrari, Filipo. 1823. *Costumi Civili e Militari della Corte di
Roma.* Rome: Presse Luigi Nicoletti.

Fewkes, J. Walter. 1890. A Contribution to Passamaquoddy
Folk-Lore. *The Journal of American Folk-Lore,*
3(11):257–81.

Fiedel, Stuart J. 1991. Correlating Archaeology and Linguistics: The Algonquian Case. *Man in the Northeast,*
no. 41:9–32.

Fitting, James. 1968. Environmental Potential and the Post-
glacial readaptation in Eastern North America.
American Antiquity 33(4):441–45.

Fitzhugh, William W. 1972. Environmental Archaeology and
Cultural Systems in Hamilton Inlet, Labrador.
Smithsonian Contributions to Anthropology no. 16.
Washington DC: Smithsonian Institution.

Flannery, Regina. 1939. *An Analysis of Coastal Algonquian
Culture.* Anthropological Series, no. 7. Washington
DC: Catholic University of America.

Ford, Chauncey, ed. 1889. *The Writings of George Washington.* New York: G. P. Putnam's Sons.

Fried, Morton H. 1960. On the Evolution of Social Stratifi-
cation and the State. In *Culture in History: Essays in
Honor of Paul Radin,* edited by Stanley Diamond,
713–31. New York: Columbia University Press.

Frison, George C. 1989. Experimental Use of Clovis Weaponry and Tools on African Elephants. *American
Antiquity* 54(4):766–84.

Fritz, Gayle J. 1990. Multiple Pathways to Farming in
Precontact Eastern North America. *Journal of World
Prehistory* 4(4):387–435.

———. 1994. Are the First American Farmers Getting
Younger? *Current Anthropology* 35:305–8.

Funk, Robert. 1976. *Recent Contributions to Hudson Valley
Prehistory.* New York State Museum Memoir 22.
Albany.

———. 1978. Post-Pleistocene Adaptations. In *Northeast.*
Vol. 15 of *Handbook of North American Indians,* ed-
ited by Bruce G. Trigger, 16–27. Washington DC:
Smithsonian Institution.

Funk, Robert E., and David W. Steadman. 1994. *Archaeo-
logical and Paleoenvironmental Investigations in the
Dutchess Quarry Caves, Orange County, New York.*
Buffalo NY: Persimmon Press.

Funk, Robert, and Beth Wellman. 1984. Evidence of Early
Holocene Occupations in the Upper Susquehanna
Valley, New York State. *New York State Archaeologi-
cal Bulletin* no. 34.

Ganong, William F. 1898. Relics of the Acadian Period. *New
Brunswick Magazine* 2(6):289–95.

Garland, Elizabeth B. 1986. Early Woodland Occupations
in Michigan: A Lower St. Joseph Valley Perspective.

In *Early Woodland Archaeology.* Vol. 2 of Kampsville Seminars in Archaeology, edited by Kenneth B. Farnsworth and Thomas E. Emerson, 47–83. Kampsville IL: Center for American Archaeology Press.

Gay, F. L. n.d. Notes on Cyprian Southack. Bound transcripts, hand copied. New York Public Library.

Gehrels, W. Roland, Daniel F. Belknap, and Joseph T. Kelley. 1996. Integrated High-Precision Analyses of Holocene Relative Sea-Level Changes: Lessons from the Coast of Maine. Geological Society of America Bulletin, vol. 108, no. 9.

Ghere, David L. 1988. Abenaki Factionalism, Emigration, and Social Continuity: Indian Society in Northern New England, 1725 to 1765. Ph.D. diss., University of Maine, Orono.

———. 1993. The "Disappearance" of the Abenaki in Western Maine: Political Organization and Ethnocentric Assumptions. *American Indian Quarterly* 17(2):193–207.

Ghere, David L., and Alvin H. Morrison. 1996. Sanctions for Slaughter: Peacetime Violence on the Maine Frontier, 1749–1772. In *Papers of the 27th Algonquian Conference,* edited by David H. Pentland, 105–16. Winnipeg: University of Manitoba.

Goddard, Ives, and Katheleen J. Bragdon. 1988. *Native Writings in Massachusetts,* vol. 1. Philadelphia: American Philosophical Society.

Gookin, Daniel. 1792. Historical Collections of the Indians in New England. *Collections of the Massachusetts Historical Society,* 1st ser., vol. 1:141–226. Boston.

Gordon, Joleen. 1993. *Construction and Reconstruction of a Mi'kmaq Sixteenth-Century Cedar-Bark Bag.* Curatorial Report no. 76. Halifax: Nova Scotia Museum.

———. 1997. *Mi'kmaq Textiles, Twining: Rush and Other Fibres, BkCp-1 Site, Pictou, Nova Scotia.* Curatorial Report no. 82. Halifax: Nova Scotia Museum.

Gorges, Ferdinando. 1890. *Sir Ferdinando Gorges and His Province of Maine,* edited by James P. Baxter. 3 vols. Boston: Prince Society.

Grace, Henry. 1764. *The History of the Life and Sufferings of Henry Grace: Being a Narrative of the Hardships He Underwent during Several Years Captivity among the Savages of North America . . . .* Reading, Eng.: privately printed.

Gramly, R. Michael. 1982. *The Vail Site: A Paleo-Indian Encampment in Maine.* Buffalo Society of Natural Sciences Bulletin, vol. 30. Buffalo NY.

———. 1984. Kill Sites, Killing Ground and Fluted Points at the Vail Site. *Archaeology of Eastern North America* 12:184–91.

———. 1985. Recherches Archéologiques au Site Paléoindien de Vail, dans le Nord-ouest du Maine, 1980–1983. *Recherches Amérindiennes au Québec* 15(1–2):57–118.

———. 1988. *The Adkins Site: A Paleo-Indian Habitation and Associated Stone Structure.* Buffalo NY: Persimmon Press.

Grant, George Monro, ed. 1882. *Picturesque Canada: The Country As It Was and Is.* Toronto: Belden Brothers.

Graymont, Barbara. 1983. Atiatoharongwen. *Canadian Dictionary of Biography,* vol. 6. Toronto: University of Toronto Press.

Greene, Evarts B., and Virginia D. Harrington. 1932. *American Population before the Federal Census of 1790.* New York: Columbia University Press.

Griffin, James B. 1961. (Review of) The Eastern Dispersal of Adena, by William A. Ritchie and Don W. Dragoo. *American Antiquity* 26(4):572–73.

Grimes, J., W. Eldridge, B. G. Grimes, A. Vaccaro, F. Vaccaro, J. Vaccaro, N. Vaccaro, and A. Orsini. 1984. Bull Brook II. *Archaeology of Eastern North America* 12:159–83.

Grumet, Robert. 1979. "We Are Not So Great Fools": Changes in Upper Delawaran Socio-Political Life, 1630–1758. Ph.D. diss., Rutgers University.

———. 1989. The Selling of Lenapehoking. Archaeological Society of New Jersey Bulletin no. 44:1–6.

Gurvich, I. S. 1988. Ethnic Connections Across Bering Strait. In *Crossroads of Continents: Cultures of Siberia and Alaska,* edited by William W. Fitzhugh and Aron Crowell, 17–21. Washington DC: Smithsonian Institution Press.

Gyles, John. [1736] 1981. Memoirs of Odd Adventures, Strange Deliverances, Etc. In *Puritans among the Indians,* edited by Alden T. Vaughan and Edward

W. Clark, 93–131. Cambridge MA: Belknap Press of Harvard University Press.

Hadlock, Wendel S. 1939. *The Taft's Point Shellmound at West Gouldsboro, Maine.* Lafayette National Park Museum Bulletin no. 5. Bar Harbor ME: Robert Abbe Museum.

———. 1941. *Three Shellheaps on Frenchman's Bay.* Lafayette National Park Museum Bulletin no. 6. Bar Harbor ME: Robert Abbe Museum.

Hadlock, Wendel S., and Douglas S. Byers. 1956. Radiocarbon Dates from Ellsworth Falls, Maine. *American Antiquity* 21:419–20.

Hadlock, Wendel S., and Theodore Stern. 1948. Passadumkeag, A Red Paint Cemetery, 35 Years after Moorehead. *American Antiquity* 14:98–103.

Haefeli, Evan, and Kevin Sweeney. 1997. Revisiting The Redeemed Captive. In *After King Philip's War*, edited by Colin Calloway, 29–71. Hanover NH: University of New England Press.

Hamilton, Nathan, John P. Mosher, Diana C. Crader, and Nancy Asch Sidell. 1997. Early Holocene Adaptation in the Appalachian Uplands of Northwestern Maine. Paper presented at the 62nd annual meeting of the Society for American Archaeology, April 2–6, 1997, Nashville TN.

Hamilton, T. M. 1972. *Native American Bows.* York PA: George Shumway.

Hamilton, Willis D., and W. A. Spray. 1977. *Source Materials Relating to the New Brunswick Indian.* Fredericton NB: Hamray Books.

Hanson, John W. 1849. *The History of the Old Towns, Norridgewock and Canaan, Starks, Skowhegan and Bloomfield. . . .* Boston: privately printed.

Harn, Alan D. 1986. The Marion Phase Occupation of the Larson Site in the Central Illinois River Valley. In *Early Woodland Archaeology.* Vol. 2 of Kampsville Seminars in Archaeology, edited by Kenneth B. Farnsworth and Thomas E. Emerson, 244–79. Kampsville IL: Center for American Archaeology Press.

Harper, J. Russell. 1957. Two Seventeenth-Century Copper-Kettle Burials. *Anthropologica*, no. 4:11–36.

Harriot, Thomas. 1590. *A Brief and True Report of the New Found Land of Virginia.* Frankfort am Main: Theodore de Bry.

Harris, Benjamin. 1690. Publick Occurrences Both Forreign and Domestick, no. 1. *Historical Magazine and Notes and Queries Concerning the Antiquities, History, and Biography of America* 1:228–31.

Hart, John P., and Nancy Asch Sidell. 1997. Additional Evidence for Early Curcurbit Use in the Northern Eastern Woodlands of the Allegheny Front. *American Antiquity* 62(3):523–37.

Harvey, D. C. 1979. Alexander, Sir William. *Dictionary of Canadian Biography*, vol. 1. Toronto: University of Toronto Press.

Havard, Giles. 1992. *La Grande Paix de Montréal: Les voies de la diplomatie franco-amérindienne.* Recherches Amérindienne au Québec, Montréal.

Haynes, C. Vance, D. J. Donahue, A. J. T. Jull, and T. H. Zabel. 1984. Application of Accelerator Dating to Fluted Point Paleoindian Sites. *Archaeology of Eastern North America* 12:184–91.

HCEI (Historical Collections of the Essex Institute). 1859–66. Salem MA: Essex Institute.

Heckenberger, Michael J., James B. Petersen, and Nancy A. Sidell. 1992. Early Evidence of Maize Agriculture in the Connecticut River Valley of Vermont. *Archaeology of Eastern North America* 20:125–49.

Hedden, Mark. 1994. Site 53.38 Waterville Bridge Ramp Approach: Archaeological Data Recovery. File Report. Augusta: Maine Historic Preservation Commission.

———. 1996. Thirty-Five Hundred Years of Shamanism in Maine Rock Art. Proceedings from the Eastern States Rock Art Conference. In *Rock Art of the Eastern Woodlands, Proceedings from the Eastern States Rock Art Conference,* edited by Charles H. Faulkner. American Rock Art Research Association Occasional Paper no. 2. San Miguel CA.

Heidenreich, Conrad. 1987 Expansion of French Trade, 1667–1696. In *Historic Atlas of Canada,* edited by Cole R. Harris, R. Cole, and Geoffrey Matthews, plate 38. Toronto: University of Toronto Press.

Henry, George. (1829–1837). *The Emmigrant's Guide, or Canada As It Is*. Quebec: William Gray.

Hitchings, Sinclair. 1980. Guarding the New England Coast: The Naval Career of Cyprian Southack. In *Seafaring in Colonial Massachusetts*, 43–65. Charlottesville: University Press of Virginia.

HJ (House Journal). 1715–77. *Journals of the House of Representatives of Massachusetts*. 55 vols. Boston: Massachusetts Historical Society, 1919–90.

Holmes, Ezekiel. 1839. *Report of an Expedition and Survey of the Territory on the Aroostook River, during the Spring and Autumn of 1838*. Augusta ME: Smith and Robinson.

Horsman, Reginald. 1988. British Indian Policies, 1776–1815. In *History of Indian—White Relations*. Vol. 4 of *Handbook of North American Indians*, edited by Wilcomb E. Washburn, 29–39. Washington DC: Smithsonian Institution.

Horton, Donald J. 1996. King George's War (1744–1748). In *Colonial Wars of North America, 1512–1763, an Encyclopedia*, edited by Alan Gallay, 333–38. New York: Garland.

Hough, Franklin Benjamin. 1856. Papers Relating to Pemaquid and Parts Adjacent in the Present State of Maine, known as Cornwall County, when under the Colony of New York. Compiled from Official Records in the Office of the Secretary of State at Albany N.Y. Albany: Weed and Parson.

Hubbard, William. [ca. 1680] 1815. *A General History of New England, From the Discovery to MDCLXXX*. Cambridge: Hilliard and Metcalfe, for the Massachusetts Historical Society.

———. [1865] 1971. *The History of the Indian Wars in New England from the First Settlement to the Termination of the War with King Philip, in 1677*, edited by Samuel G. Drake. New York: Burt Franklin.

Hulme, Mike. 1994. Historic Records and Recent Climatic Change. In *The Changing Global Environment*, edited by Neil Roberts, 69–97. Cambridge MA: Blackwell.

Hulton, Paul. 1984. *America 1585: The Complete Drawings of John White*. Chapel Hill: University of North Carolina Press.

Hunt, George T. 1940. *The Wars of the Iroquois: A Study in Intertribal Relations*. Madison: University of Wisconsin Press.

Hunt, Richard I. 1973. British-American Rivalry for the Support of the Indians of Maine and Nova Scotia, 1775–1783. Masters thesis, University of Maine, Orono.

Hutchinson, Thomas. 1936. *History of the Colony of Massachusetts Bay*. 3 vols. Cambridge MA: Harvard University Press.

Hutchinson Papers. 1865. Publications of the Prince Society. Vols. 2–3. Albany NY.

Imamura, Keiji. 1996. *Prehistoric Japan: New Perspectives on Insular East Asia*. Honolulu: University of Hawaii Press.

Indian Population in the United States and Alaska, 1910. 1915. Washington DC: Government Printing Office.

Innis, Harold A. 1930. *The Fur Trade in Canada: An Introduction to Canadian Economic History*. Toronto: University of Toronto Press.

———. 1940. *The Cod Fisheries, The History of an International Economy*. New Haven CT: Yale University Press.

IR (Index of Resolves). Maine Law Library, Augusta.

Jackson, Charles T. 1839. *Third Annual Report on the Geology of the State of Maine*. Augusta ME: Smith and Robinson.

Jacobs, Wilbur R. 1988. British Indian Policies to 1763. In *History of Indian-White Relations*. Vol. 4 of *Handbook of North American Indians*, edited by Wilcomb E. Washburn, 5–12. Washington DC: Smithsonian Institution.

Jacobson, George L., Jr., Thomas Webb III, and E. C. Grimm. 1987. Patterns and Rates of Vegetation Change during the Deglaciation of Eastern North America. In *North America and Adjacent Oceans During the Last Deglaciation*, edited by W. F. Ruddiman and H. E. Wright Jr., 277–88. Geology of North America, vol. K–3. Boulder: Geological Society of America.

James, Sidney V. 1963. *Three Visitors to Early Plymouth*. Plymouth MA: Plimoth Plantation.

Jelsma, Johan. 1997. A Bed of Ochre: Mortuary Practices and Social Structure of a Maritime Archaic Indian Society at Port au Choix, Newfoundland. Ph.D. diss., Rijksuniversiteit Groningen, The Netherlands.

Jennings, Francis. 1976. *The Invasion of America: Indians, Colonialism, and the Cant of Conquest*. Chapel Hill: University of North Carolina Press, 1975. Reprint, New York: W. W. Norton.

———. 1984. *The Ambiguous Iroquois Empire: The Covenant Chain Confederation of Indian Tribes with English Colonies*. New York: W. W. Norton.

Johnson, Edward. [1654] 1910. *Wonder-Working Providence, 1628–1651*, edited by J. Franklin Jameson. New York: Charles Scribner's Sons.

Johnson, Laurence. 1995. *Le réserve malécite de Viger, une project-pilote du "programme de civilisation" du gouvernement canadien*. Mémoire présenté à la Faculté des études supérieurs en vue de l'obtention du grade de Maître ès sciences en anthropologie, Université de Montréal.

Johnson, Samuel. 1847. Account of an Ancient Settlement on Sheepscot River. In *Collections of the Maine Historical Society*, 1st ser., vol. 2:229–37. Portland.

Johnson, Sir William. 1921–65. *The Papers of Sir William Johnson*. Albany: Division of Archives and History, State University of New York.

Josselyn, John. [1672] 1860. New-England's Rarities Discovered. *Archaeologica Americana*: Transactions and Collections of the American Antiquarian Society, vol. 4.:105–238.

———. [1674] 1988. *John Josselyn, Colonial Traveler*: A Critical Edition of *Two Voyages to New-England*, edited by Paul J. Lindholdt. Hanover NH: University Press of New England.

JR (*The Jesuit Relations and Other Allied Documents*). 1896–1901. 73 vols. Edited by Reuben G. Thwaites. Cleveland: Borrows Brothers.

Juet, R. [1610] 1906. The third Voyage of Master Henrie Hudson toward Nova Zambia, and his returne, his passing from Farre Islands, to New-found Land and along to forty foure degrees and ten minutes, and thence to Cape Cod, and so to thirtie three; and along the Coast to the Northward, to fortie two degrees and a half, and up the River neere to fortie three degrees. In *Hakluytus Posthumus or Purchas His Pilgrimes*, vol. 13, edited by Samuel Purchas, 333–74. Glasgow: James MacLehose and Sons.

Kelly, Lawrence C. 1988. United States Indian Policy, 1900–1980. In *History of Indian—White Relations*. Vol. 4 of *Handbook of North American Indians*, edited by Wilcomb E. Washburn, 66–80. Washington DC: Smithsonian Institution.

Kent, Barry, Ira F. Smith III, and Catherine McCann. 1976. Archaic and Transitional Periods. In *Foundations of Pennsylvania Prehistory*, edited by Barry C. Kent, Ira F. Smith III, and Catherine McCann, 85–96.

Kenyon, Ian T. 1980. The George Davidson Site: An Archaic "Broadpoint" Component in Southwestern Ontario. *Archaeology of Eastern North America* 8:11–28.

Kidder, Frederick. 1867. *Military Operations in Eastern Maine and Nova Scotia during the Revolution, Chiefly Compiled from the Journals of Colonel John Allan, with Notes and a Memoir of Col. John Allan*. Albany NY: Joel Munsell. (Reprinted in 1971 by Krauss Reprint, Millwood NY.)

Kilby, William H. 1888. *Eastport and Passamaquoddy: A Collection of Historical and Biographical Sketches*. Eastport ME: Edward E. Shead.

Knox, John. 1914. *The Journal of Captain John Knox: An Historical Journal of the Campaigns in North America*, edited by A. G. Doughty. Toronto: Champlain Society.

Kraft, Herbert C. 1970. *The Miller Field Site, Part 1*. South Orange NJ: Seton Hall University Press.

Krugler, John D. 1983. Gorham, John. *Canadian Dictionary of Biography*, vol. 5. Toronto: University of Toronto Press.

La Chasse, Pierre de. 1708. Manuscript census of Acadia. Newberry Library, Chicago.

Lamontagne, Léopold. 1979. Prouville de Tracy. *Canadian Dictionary of Biography*, vol. 1. Toronto: University of Toronto Press.

Lanctot, Gustave. 1963–1965. *A History of Canada*. 3 vols. Cambridge MA: Harvard University Press.

Lapomarda, Vincent A. 1977. *The Jesuit Heritage in New England*. Worcester MA: Jesuits of Holy Cross College.

———. 1978. The Jesuit Missions of Western Maine: A Forgotten Chapter in American Religious History. *Maine History News* 14(3):6–8 and 14(4):7.

LaSalle, Pierre, and Claude Chapdelaine. 1990. Review of

Late-Glacial and Holocene Events in the Champlain and Goldthwait Seas Areas and Arrival of Man in Eastern Canada. Archaeological Geology of North America, edited by Norman P. Lasca and Jack Donahue. Centennial special vol. 4, ch 1: 1–19. Geological Society of America.

Laval, Francois de. 1929. Circa Statum Ecclesiae Nascentis Inter Algonquinos. In *The Catholic Missions of Maine, 1611–1820*, by Mary C. Legere, 149–55. Studies in American Church History no. 8. Washington DC: Catholic University of America.

LCRD (Lincoln County Registry of Deeds). Wiscassett ME.

Leach, Douglas E. 1958. *Flintlock and Tomahawk*. New York: Macmillan.

Leamon, James. 1993. *Revolution Downeast: The War for American Independence in Maine*. Amherst: University of Massachusetts Press.

———. 1996. King William's War (1689–1697) In *Colonial Wars of North America, 1512–1763, an Encyclopedia*, edited by Alan Gallay, 341–54. New York: Garland.

Leavitt, Robert M., and David A. Francis, eds. 1990. *Wapapi Akonutomakonol: The Wampum Records, Wabanaki Traditional Laws*. Micmac-Maliseet Institute. Fredericton: University of New Brunswick.

LeBlanc, Émery. 1979. Robinau de Villebon, Joseph. *Dictionary of Canadian Biography*, vol. 1. Toronto: University of Toronto Press.

LeBlant, Robert, and René Baudry. 1967. Nouveaux Documents sur Champlain et son Epoque, vol. 1. Ottawa: Archives Publique du Canada.

LeClercq, Chrestien. 1910. *New Relation of Gaspesia (Nouvelle relation de la Gaspésie, 1691)*. Translated and edited by W. F. Ganong. Toronto: Champlain Society.

Lee, Sidney. 1896. *Dictionary of National Biography*, vol. 15. New York: Macmillan.

Leger, Mary C. 1929. *The Catholic Indian Missions in Maine, 1611–1820*. Studies in American Church History no. 8. Washington DC: Catholic University of America.

Leighton, Alexander H. 1937. Twilight of the Indian Porpoise Hunters. *Natural History*, June, 410–58.

Lescarbot, Marc. [1618] 1907–14. *The History of New France*. 3 vols. Toronto: Champlain Society.

Lester, Joan. 1987. "We Didn't Make Fancy Baskets Until We Were Discovered": Fancy-Basket Making in Maine. In *A Key into the Language of Woodsplint Baskets*, edited by Ann McMullen and Russell G. Handsman, 39–60. Washington CT: American Indian Archaeological Institute.

Letter of Ignatius. 1905. (Letter of the Capuchin Ignatius of Paris) *Report Concerning Canadian Archives for the Year 1904*, 333–41. Ottawa.

Leveillee, Alan. 1997. *A Program of Archaeological Data Recovery: The Millbury III Cremation Complex, Millbury, Massachusetts*. (January 1997 draft) Public Archaeology Laboratory Report no. 396. The Public Archaeology Laboratory, Pawtucket RI.

Levermore, Charles H. 1912. *Forerunners and Competitors of the Pilgrims and Puritans*. New York: New England Society of Brooklyn.

Levett, Christopher. [1628] 1988. A Voyage into New England, Begun in 1623 and Ended in 1624. In *Maine in the Age of Discovery: Christopher Levett's Voyage, 1623–1624 and A Guide to Sources*, edited by Roger Howell Jr. and Emerson W. Baker, 33–68. Portland: Maine Historical Society.

Levinge, R. G. A. 1846. *Echoes From the Backwoods*. 2 vols. London: H. Colburn.

Lincoln, Charles H., ed. 1912. *Correspondence of William Sherley*. 2 vols. New York: Macmillan.

Liste. 1929. *Liste des Missionaires—Jesuites: Nouvelle-France at Louisiane, 1611–1800*. Montréal: Collège de Sainte-Marie.

Little, Daniel. 1786. Journal of a Tour to Penobscot. Maine State Museum, Augusta. Microfilm.

Lord, Robert H., John E. Sexton, and Edward T. Harrington. 1944. *History of the Archdiocese of Boston In Various Stages of Its Development, 1604 to 1943*. 3 vols. New York: Sheed and Ward.

Luckenbach, Alvin H., Wayne E. Clark, and Richard S. Levy. 1987. Rethinking Cultural Stability in Eastern North American Prehistory: Linguistic Evidence from Eastern North America. *Journal of Middle Atlantic Archaeology* 3:1–29.

MA (Massachusetts Archives, Boston).

MacBeath, George. 1979. Du Gua de Monts, Pierre. *Dictionary of Canadian Biography, vol. 1. Toronto: University of Toronto Press.

———. 1979a. Joybert (Joibert) De Soulanges et de Marson, Pierre de. Canadian Dictionary of Biography, vol. 1. Toronto: University of Toronto Press.

———. 1979b. Motin, Jeanne. Canadian Dictionary of Biography, vol. 1. Toronto: University of Toronto Press.

———. 1979c. Razilly, Isaac de. Canadian Dictionary of Biography, vol. 1. Toronto: University of Toronto Press.

———. 1979d. Saint-Étienne de La Tour, Charles de. Canadian Dictionary of Biography, vol. 1. Toronto: University of Toronto Press.

———. 1979e. Saint-Etienne de La Tour, Claude de. Canadian Dictionary of Biography, vol. 1. Toronto: University of Toronto Press.

———. 1979f. Thomas, Jean. Canadian Dictionary of Biography, vol. 1. Toronto: University of Toronto Press.

MacDonald, George F. 1968. Debert: A Paleo-Indian Site in Central Nova Scotia. National Museum of Man, Anthropology Paper no. 16. Ottawa.

MacDonald, M. A. 1983. Fortune and LaTour: The Civil War in Acadia. New York: Methuen.

Mahaffie, Charles D., Jr. 1995. A Land of Discord Always: Acadia from Its Beginnings to the Expulsion of Its People, 1604–1775. Camden ME: Downeast.

MAGCR (Massachusetts General Court Records).

MAHS (Massachusetts Historical Society, Boston).

MAHSC (Collections of the Massachusetts Historical Society). 1792–. 88 vols. Boston.

MAHSP (Proceedings of the Massachusetts Historical Society). 1791–. 107 vols. Boston.

Maine Laws. 1821–. Augusta ME: various publishers.

Maine Attorney General. 1977. Summary of Massachusetts/Penobscot Relations—Update, August 20. Maine State Museum.

Malinowski, Sharon, and Anna Sheets, eds. 1998. Northeast, Southeast, Caribbean. Vol. 1 of The Gale Encyclopedia of Native American Tribes. New York: Gale.

Mark, Joan. 1980. Four Anthropologists: An American Science in Its Early Years. New York: Science History Publications.

Marshall, Joyce, ed. and trans. 1967. Word from New France:

The Selected Letters of Marie de l'Incarnation. Toronto: Oxford University Press.

Martijn, Charles A. 1989. An Eastern Micmac Domain of Islands. Actes du Vingtième Congrès des Algonquinistes, 208–31. Ottawa: Carleton University.

Mason, Ronald J. 1981. Great Lakes Archaeology. New York: Academic Press.

Mather, Cotton. [1707] 1879. A Memorial of the Present Deplorable State of New England. Collections of the Massachusetts Historical Society, 5th ser., vol. 6.:35–64. Boston.

———. [1699] 1952. Decennium Luctuosum: A History of Remarkable Occurrences in the Long War, Which New-England Hath Had with the Indian Savages, from the Year 1688 to the Year 1698. In Narratives of the Indian Wars, 1675–1699, edited by C. H. Lincoln, 169–300. New York: Charles Scribner's Sons.

Maverick, Samuel. 1885. A Briefe Description of New England and the Several Townes Therein. New England Historical and Genealogical Register 39:34–49.

McBride, Bunny, and Harald E. L. Prins. 1996. Molly Ocket, A Pigwacket Doctor. In Northeast Indian Lives, 1632–1816, edited by Robert S. Grumet, 321–47. Amherst: University of Massachusetts Press.

McGhee, Robert. 1984. Contact Between Native North Americans and the Medieval Norse: A Review of the Evidence. American Antiquity 49(1):4–26.

MEHSC (Collections of the Maine Historical Society).

MEHSMC (Maine Historical Society Manuscript Collection).

Meinig, Donald W. 1986. The Shaping of America: A Geographical Perspective on 500 Years of History. New Haven CT: Yale University Press.

Meltzer, David J., and James I. Mead. 1986. Dating Late Pleistocene Extinctions: Theoretical issues, Analytical Biases, and Substantive Results. In Environments and Extinctions in Late Glacial North America, edited by James I. Mead and David J. Meltzer, 3–31. Orono: Center for the Study of Early Man, University of Maine.

Melvoin, Richard L. 1989. New England Outpost: War and Society in Colonial New Deerfield. New York: W. W. Norton.

On Methods of Archaeological Research in America. 1886. Johns Hopkins University Circulars 5(49).

MHGR *(Maine Historical and Genealogical Recorder)*. 1884–97. Portland.

Michelson, Gunther. 1977. Iroquoian Population Statistics. *Man in the Northeast*, no. 14:3–17.

Miller, N. G., and G. Thompson. 1979. Boreal and Western North American Plants in the Late Pleistocene of Vermont. *Journal of the Arnold Arboretum* 60(2):167–218.

Moir, John S. 1979. Kirke, Sir David. *Canadian Dictionary of Biography*, vol. 1. Toronto: University of Toronto Press.

Moody, Robert E. 1933. *The Maine Frontier, 1607–1763*. Ph.D. diss., Yale University, New Haven CT.

Moody Robert E., ed. 1978. *The Letters of Thomas Gorges, Deputy Governor of the Province of Maine, 1640–1643*. Portland: Maine Historical Society.

Moorehead, Warren K. 1922. *A Report on the Archaeology of Maine*. Andover MA: Andover Press.

Morison, Samuel E., ed. 1933. *Suffolk Court Files*. Publications of the Colonial Society of Massachusetts, vols. 29–30. Boston.

Morison, Samuel E. 1971. *The European Discovery of America: The Northern Voyages*. New York: Oxford University Press.

Morrison, Alvin H. 1976. Dawnland Directors: Status and Role of Seventeenth Century Wabanaki Sagamores. In *Papers of the Seventh Algonquian Conference, 1976*, edited by William Cowan, 495 ff. Ottawa: Carleton University.

————. 1991. Dawnland Directors' Decisions: Seventeenth-Century Encounter Dynamics on the Wabanaki Frontier. *Papers of the Twenty-Second Algonquian Conference*, 225–45. Ottawa: Carleton University.

Morrison, Kenneth M. 1984. *The Embattled Northeast: The Elusive Ideal of Alliance in Abenaki-Euroamerican Relations*. Berkeley: University of California Press.

Morse, Jedidiah. 1822. *Report to the Secretary of War of the United States on Indian Affairs*. New Haven CT: S. Converse.

Morse, William I. 1935. *Acadiensia Nova (1598–1779)*. London: Bernard Quatritch.

Morton, Thomas. [1637] 1883. *The New English Canan, or New Canaan: Containing an Abstract of New England Composed in Three Books*. Boston: Prince Society.

Mott, R. J. 1977. Late-Pleistocene and Holocene Palynology in Southeastern Quebec. *Géographie Physique et Quaternaire* 31(1–2):139–49.

Mott, R. J., Douglas R. Grant, and S. Occhietti. 1986. Late Glacial Climatic Oscillation in Atlantic Canada Equivalent to the Allerod/Younger Dryas Event. *Nature* 323:247–50.

MPCR (*Province and Court Records of Maine*, vol. 33). 1928. Portland: Maine Historic Society.

MPHS (*Historical Collections: Collections and Researches made by the Michigan Pioneer and Historical Society*, vol. 33). 1904. Lansing MI: Robert Smith Printing, printers and binders for the state.

MSL (Maine State Library, Augusta). Manuscript.

MSM (Maine State Museum, Augusta). Research File.

Munro, Neal G., and B. Z. Seligman. 1996. *Ainu Creed and Cult*. The Kegan Paul Japan Library, vol. 4. New York: Kegan Paul International.

Murchie, Guy. 1945. *Glimpses of the Past*, copies from the *Saint Croix Courier*, January 1892–July 1895.

Murdoch, Beamish. 1865–67. *History of Nova Scotia or Acadie*. 3 vols. Halifax: J. Barnes.

Murphy, Brent. 1997. Researching the Early Holocene of the Maritime Provinces. Paper presented to the Canadian Archaeology Association 30th annual conference, Saskatoon, Saskatchewan.

Muttersbaugh, Bert M. 1996. King Philip's War (1675–1676). In *Colonial Wars of North America, 1512–1763, an Encyclopedia*, edited by Alan Gallay, 339–41. New York: Garland.

NAC (National Archives of Canada, Ottawa).

Nasatir, Abraham P. 1990. *Before Lewis and Clark: Documents Illustrating the History of the Missouri, 1785–1804*. Lincoln: University of Nebraska Press.

Nash, Philleo. 1988. Twentieth-Century United States Government Agencies. In *History of Indian-White Relations*. Vol. 4 of *Handbook of North American Indians*, edited by Wilcomb E. Washburn, 26–275. Washington DC: Smithsonian Institution.

Nash, Ronald J., Frances L. Stewart, and Michael Deal. 1991. Melanson, a Central Place in Southwestern Nova Scotia. In *Prehistoric Archaeology in the Maritime Provinces: Past and Present Research* edited by

Michael Deal and Susan Blair, 221–33. Reports in Archaeology no. 8. Fredericton: New Brunswick Archaeological Services, Cultural Affairs, Department of Municipalities, Culture and Housing.

Nassaney, Michael S., and Kendra Pyle. 1999. The Adoption of the Bow and Arrow in Eastern North America: A View from Central Arkansas. *American Antiquity* 64(2):243–63.

Newell, Catherine S-C. 1981. *Molly Ockett*. Bethel ME: Bethel Historical Society.

New England Historical Genealogical Society. 1847–. *New England Historical and Genealogical Register*. Boston.

New England Weekly Journal. Boston.

Newman, William A., Andrew N. Genes, and Thomas Brewer. 1985. Pleistocene Geology of Northeastern Maine. In *Late Pleistocene History of Northeastern New England and Adjacent Quebec*, edited by H. W. Borns Jr., P. LaSalle, and W. B. Thompson. Special Paper no. 197. Boulder: Geological Society of America.

NF (*Nouvelle France: Documents Historiques, Correspondence Échangé entre Les Authorités Françaises et les Gouverneurs et Intendants, Publiés par Order de la Législature de la Province De Québec*). 1893. 3 vols. Québec: L.-J. Demers and Frère.

NHHSC (*Collections of the New Hampshire Historical Society*, vol. 8). 1824–. Concord NH:Jacob B. Moore.

NHPP (*Provincial Papers of New Hampshire*). 1867–1941. 39 vols. Concord.

Nicolar, Joseph. 1893. *Life and Traditions of the Red Man*. Bangor ME: C. H. Glass. (Reprinted in 1979 by Saint Anne's Point Press, Fredericton, NB).

Noyes, Sybil, Charles Libby, and Walter Davis. [First published in five parts, 1928–39] 1972. *Genealogical Dictionary of Maine and New Hampshire*. Baltimore: Genealogical Publishing.

NYCD 1853–57. *Documents Relative to the Colonial History of the State of New York . . . .*, edited by Edmund B. O'Callaghan and Berthold Fenrow. 15 vols. Albany NY: Weed, Parsons and Company.

O'Callaghan, Edmund B., ed. 1850–51. *The Documentary History of the State of New York*. Albany: Weed, Parsons and Company.

Oldale, Robert N., Frank C. Whitmore, and John R. Grimes. 1987. Elephant Teeth from the Western Gulf of Maine, and Their Implications. *National Geographic Research* 3(4):439–46.

O'Toole, Francis J., and Thomas N. Tureen. 1971. State Power the Passamaquoddy Tribe: "A Gross National Hypocracy"? *Maine Law Review* 32(1):1–39.

Palmer, Ralph. 1949. *Maine Birds*. Bulletin of the Museum of Comparative Zoology, no. 102. Cambridge MA: Museum of Comparative Zoology, Harvard University.

PANS (Public Archives of Nova Scotia, Halifax).

Parkman, Francis. [1865] 1983. *France and England in North America*. New York: Viking Press.

Parkman, Francis. Parkman Manuscripts. Massachusetts Historical Society, Boston.

Pastore, Ralph T. 1992. *Shanawdithit's People: The Archaeology of the Beothuks*. St. John's NF: Atlantic Archaeology.

Patterson, Stephen E. 1994. 1744–1763: Colonial Wars and Aboriginal Peoples. In *The Atlantic Region to Confederation: A History*, edited by Phillip A. Buckner and John G. Reid, 125–55. Toronto: University of Toronto Press.

Payne, James H. 1987. Windy City (154–16): A Paleoindian Lithic Workshop in Northern Maine. Master's thesis, University of Maine, Orono.

Peale, Titian R. 1830. Hunting Recollections. *The Cabinet of Natural History and American Rural Sports*.

Pelletier, Gaby. 1977. *Micmac and Maliseet Decorative Traditions*. St. John: New Brunswick Museum.

Peña, Elizabeth Shapiro. 1990. Wampum Production in New Netherland and Colonial New York: The Historical and Archaeological Context. Ph.D. diss., Boston University.

Pendergast, James F., and Bruce G. Trigger. 1972. *Cartier's Hochelaga and the Dawson Site*. Montreal: McGill-Queen's University Press.

Penhallow, Samuel. [1726] 1973. *The History of the Wars of New-England, with the Eastern Indians. . . .* Facsimile reprint in *Penhallow's Indian Wars*. Williamstown MA: Corner House.

Penman, J. T. 1977. The Old Copper Culture: An Analysis of

Old Copper Artifacts. *The Wisconsin Archaeologist* 58(1):3–23.

The Penobscot Indians. 1863. *The Maine Teacher* 5(7):209–10.

Perley, Sidney. 1924. *History of Salem, Massachusetts*. 3 vols. Salem: privately printed.

Petersen, James B. 1991. *Archaeological Testing at the Sharrow Site: A Deeply Stratified Early to Late Holocene Cultural Sequence in Central Maine*. Occasional Publications in Maine Archaeology no. 8. Augusta: Maine Archaeological Society and Historic Preservation Commission.

Petersen, James B., and David E. Putnam. 1992. Early Holocene Occupation in the Central Gulf of Maine Region. In *Early Holocene Occupation in Northern New England*, edited by Brian S. Robinson, James B. Petersen, and Ann K. Robinson, 13–61. Occasional Publications in Maine Archaeology no. 9. Augusta: Maine Archaeological Society and Historic Preservation Commission.

Petersen, James B., Brian S. Robinson, Daniel F. Belknap, James Stark, and Lawrence K. Kaplan. 1994. An Archaic and Woodland Period Fish Weir Complex in Central Maine. *Archaeology of Eastern North America* 22:197–222.

Petersen, James B., and David Sanger. 1991. An Aboriginal Sequence for the Maine and the Maritime Provinces. In *Prehistoric Archaeology in the Maritime Provinces: Past and Present Research*, edited by Michael Deal and Susan Blair, 121–78. Reports in Archaeology no. 8. Fredericton: New Brunswick Archaeological Services, Cultural Affairs, Department of Municipalities, Culture and Housing.

Petersen, James B., and Nancy Asch Sidell. 1996. Mid-Holocene Evidence of *Curcubita* Sp. From Central Maine. *American Antiquity* 61(4):685–98.

Phillips, Paul C. 1961. *The Fur Trade*. Norman: University of Oklahoma Press.

Pielou, E. C. 1991. *After the Ice Age: The Return of Life to North America*. Chicago: University of Chicago Press.

Pintal, Jean-Yves. 1998. *Aux frontièr de la mer: La Préhistoire de Blanc-Sablon*. Ministière de la Culture et des Communications, Gouvernement du Québec, Collection Patrimoines Dosier 102.

Pfeiffer, John. 1980. The Site: A Susquehanna Cremation Burial in Southern Connecticut. *Man in the Northeast*, no. 19:129–33.

———. 1992. Late and Terminal Archaic Cultural Adaptations of the Lowest Connecticut Valley. Ph.D. diss., State University of New York at Albany.

Plumet, Patrick, Jean-François Moreau, Hélène Gauvin, Marie-France Archambault and Virginia Elliot. 1993. *Le Site Lavoie (DbEj–11: L'Archaïque aux Grandes Bergeronnes, Haute Côte-Nord du Saint-Laurent, Québec*. Recherches Amérindiennes au Québec, Montréal.

Porpoise-Shooting. 1880. *Scribners' Monthly* 22 (October):801–11.

Pote, William, Jr. 1894. The Journal of Captain William Pote, Jr., during His Captivity in the French and Indian War. New York: Dodd Mead and Company.

Pothier, Bernard. 1969. Le Moyne d'Iberville et d'Ardillières, Pierre. *Canadian Dictionary of Biography*, vol. 2. Toronto: University of Toronto Press.

PR (Pejepscot Records). Maine Historical Society, Portland.

PRCC (*Public Records of the Colony of Connecticut, 1636–1776*). 1850–90. 15 vols. Hartford CT: Lockwood and Brainard.

Pring, Martin. [1625] 1983. A Voyage Set Out from the Citie of Bristoll, 1603. In *The English New England Voyages*, edited by David B. Quinn and Allison M. Quinn, 214–28. London: Hakluyt Society.

Prins, Harald, E. L. 1985. Two George Washington Medals: Missing Links in the Chain of Friendship between the United States and the Wabanaki Confederacy. *The Medal*, no. 7 (winter):9–12.

———. 1988. Amesocontee: Abortive Tribe Formation on the Colonial Frontier. Paper presented at the Annual Conference of the American Society for Ethnohistory, Williamsburg VA.

———. 1992. Cornfields at Meductic: Ethnic and Territorial Reconfigurations in Colonial Acadia. *Man in the Northeast*, no. 44:55–72.

———. 1996. Chief Rawandagon Alias Robin Hood: Native 'Lord of Misrule' in the Maine Wilderness. In *Northeastern Indian Lives*, edited by Robert S. Grumet, 93–115. Amherst: University of Massachusetts.

———. 1996a. *The Mi'kmaq: Resistance, Accomodation and Cultural Survival.* New York: Harcourt Brace College Publishers.

Prins, Harald, E. L., and Bruce J. Bourque. 1987. Norridgewock: Village Translocation on the New England—Acadian Frontier. *Man in the Northeast*, no. 33:137–58. (Reprinted in the *Kennebec Proprietor* 4[4]:4–12.)

Pritchard, James. 1995. *Anatomy of a Naval Disaster: The 1746 French Naval Expedition to North America.* Montreal: McGill-Queens University Press.

Proctor, Ralph W. 1942. Maine Legislative Research Committee Report on Maine Indians. Maine State Library.

Purchas, Samuel. [1617, 1619] 1905–70. *Hakluytus Posthumus or Purchas His Pilgrimes,* 20 vols. Glascow: James MacLehose and Sons, 1905–7.

———. 1983. Pilgrimage. In *The English New England Voyages,* edited by David B. Quinn and Allison M. Quinn, 347–51. London: Hakluyt Society.

Purvis, Thomas L. 1996. Seven Years War (1754–1763). In *Colonial Wars of North America, 1512–1763, an Encyclopedia,* edited by Alan Gallay. New York: Garland.

Putnam, Frederick W. 1898. Editor's note to *Prehistoric Burial Places in Maine,* by Charles C. Willoughby. Archaeological and Ethnological Papers of the Peabody Museum, vol. 1, no. 6:387–88. Cambridge MA.

Quin, Arthur. 1994. *The New World: An Epic of Colonial America from the Founding of Jamestown to the Fall of Quebec.* New York: Faber and Faber.

Quinn, David B. 1940. *The Voyages and Colonizing Enterprises of Sir Humphrey Gilbert.* 2 vols. 2nd ser., nos. 83–84. London: Hakluyt Society.

———. 1962. The Voyage of Etienne Bellenger to the Maritimes in 1583: A New Document. *Canadian Historical Review* 43:328–43.

Quinn, David B., and Alison M. Quinn. 1983. *The English New England Voyages: 1602–1608.* London: Hakluyt Society.

Raimo, John W. 1980. *Biographical Directory of American Colonial and Revolutionary Governors, 1607–1798.* Westport CT: Meckler Books.

Rale, Sébastien. 1833. A Dictionary of the Abenaki Language in North America [1691–1722], edited by John Pickering. *Memoirs of the American Academy of Arts and Sciences,* n.s. 1:375–565.

Ramenofsky, Ann F. 1987. *Vectors of Death: The Archaeology of European Contact.* Albuquerque: University of New Mexico Press.

Ranlet, Philip. 1980. Lord of Misrule: Thomas Morton of Merry Mount. *New England Historical and Genealogical Register* 134(4): 282–90.

RAPQ (Rapport de L'archiviste de la Province De Québec). 1922–60. Quebec: various printers.

Rawlyk, George A. 1973. *Nova Scotia's Massachusetts: A Study of Massachusetts-Nova Scotia Relations, 1630 to 1784.* Montreal: McGill-Queen's University Press.

———. 1994. 1720–44: Cod, Louisbourg, and the Acadians. In *The Atlantic Region to Confederation: A History,* edited by Phillip A. Buckner and John G. Reid, 107–24. Toronto: University of Toronto Press.

Ray, Clayton E., and Arthur Spiess. 1981. The Bearded Seal, *Erignathus barbatus,* in the Pleistocene of Maine. *Journal of Mammology* 62(2):423–27.

Raymond, William O. 1943. *The River St. John: Its Physical Features, Legends and History from 1604 to 1784.* Sackville NB: Tribune Press.

Regensberg, Richard A. 1975. Burial Complex: Savich Farm Site. Seton Hall University, South Orange NJ.

———. 1976. The Late Archaic Period—The Savich Farm Site. In *History, Culture and Archaeology of the Pine Barrens: Essays from the Third Pine Barrens Conference,* edited by John W. Swinton, 101–15. Pomona NJ: Stockton State College, Center for Environmental Research.

Reid, John G. 1977. *Maine, Charles II and Massachusetts: Governmental Relationships in Early Northern New England.* Portland: Maine Historical Society.

———. 1981. *Acadia, Maine and New Scotland: Marginal Colonies in the Seventeenth Century.* Toronto: University of Toronto Press.

———. 1994. 1686–1720: Imperial Intrusions. In *The Atlantic Region to Confederation: A History,* edited by Phillip A. Buckner and John G. Reid, 78–103. Toronto: University of Toronto Press.

Richter, Daniel K. 1982. Rediscovered Links in the Covenant Chain: Previously Unpublished Transcripts of New

York Indian Treaty Minutes, 1677–91. *Proceedings of the American Antiquarian Society* 92(1):45–85. Worcester MA.

———. 1992. *The Ordeal of the Longhouse: The Peoples of the Iroquois League in the Era of European Colonization.* Chapel Hill: University of North Carolina Press.

Riley, T. J., G. R. Waltz, C. J. Barreis, A. C. Fortier, and K. E. Parker. 1994. Accelerator Mass Spectroscopy (AMS) Dates Confirm Early *Zea mays* in the Mississippi River Valley. *American Antiquity* 59(3):490–98.

Ritchie, William A. 1932. *The Lamoka Lake Site.* Researches and Transactions of the New York State Archaeological Association, vol. 7, no. 2. Rochester.

———. 1936. *New Evidence Relating to the Archaic Occupation of New York.* Researches and Transactions of the New York State Archaeological Association, vol. 8, no. 1. Rochester.

———. 1969. *The Archaeology of Martha's Vineyard.* Garden City NY: Natural History Press.

———. 1971a. The Archaic in New York. *New York State Archaeological Association Bulletin* 52:2–12.

———. 1971b. *A Typology and Nomenclature for New York Projectile Points.* New York State Museum and Science Service Bulletin 384.

———. 1979. The Otter Creek no. 2 Site in Redline County, Vermont. *New York State Archaeological Bulletin* 76:1–21.

———. 1980. *The Archaeology of New York State.* 3rd. ed. Harrison NY: Harbor Hill Books.

Ritchie, William A., and Don W. Dragoo. 1959. The Eastern Dispersal of Adena. *American Antiquity* 25(1):43–50.

Ritchie, William A., and Robert E. Funk. 1971. Evidence of Early Archaic Period Occupation on Staten Island. *Pennsylvania Archaeologist* 41:45–60.

Robbins, Maurice. 1980. *Wapanucket: An Archaeological Report.* Attleboro: Massachusetts Archaeological Society.

Roberts, Kenneth. 1940. *March to Quebec.* Camden ME: Downeast.

Roberts, William I. III. 1979. Aernoutsz, Juriaen. *Dictionary of Canadian Biography,* vol. 1. Toronto: University of Toronto Press.

———. 1979a. Rhoades, John. *Dictionary of Canadian Biography,* vol. 1. Toronto: University of Toronto Press.

Robinson, Brian S. 1985. *The Nelson Island and Seabrook Marsh Sites: Late Archaic, Maritime Oriented People on the Central New England Coast.* Occasional Publications in Northeastern Anthropology no. 9, edited by James B. Petersen, 1–107. Rindge NH: Franklin Pierce College.

———. 1992. Early and Middle Archaic Period Occupation in the Gulf of Maine Region: Mortuary and Technological Patterning. In *Early Holocene Occupation in Northern New England,* edited by Brian S. Robinson, James B. Petersen, and Ann K. Robinson, 63–116. Occasional Publications in Maine Archaeology no. 9. Augusta: Maine Archaeological Society and Historic Preservation Commission.

———. 1996. A Regional Analysis of the Moorehead Burial Tradition: 8500–3700 B.P. *Archaeology of Eastern North America* 24:95–148.

———. 1997. Archaic Period Burial Patterning in Northeastern North America. *The Review of Archaeology* 17(1):33–44.

Robinson, Brian S., and James B. Petersen. 1992. Introduction: Archaeological Visibility and Patterning in Northern New England. In *Early Holocene Occupation in Northern New England,* edited by Brian S. Robinson, James B. Petersen, and Ann K. Robinson, 1–11. Occasional Publications in Maine Archaeology no. 9. Augusta: Maine Archaeological Society and Historic Preservation Commission.

———. 1993. Perceptions of Marginality: The Case of the Early Holocene in Northern New England. *Northeast Anthropology,* no. 46:61–75.

Robinson, Brian S., James B. Petersen, and Ann K. Robinson. 1992. *Early Holocene Occupation in Northern New England.* Occasional Publications in Maine Archaeology no. 9. Augusta: Maine Archaeological Society and Historic Preservation Commission.

Rosenfeld, M. C. 1969. Hilton, Winthrop. *Dictionary of Canadian Biography,* vol. 2. Toronto: University of Toronto Press.

Rosier, James. [1605] 1983. A True relation of the most prosperous voyage made this present yeere 1605, by Captaine George Weymouth, in the discovery of the land of Virginia . . . . Written by Iames Rosier, a Gentleman employed in the voyage. In *The English New England Voyages,* edited by David B. Quinn and Allison M. Quinn, 251–311. London: Hakluyt Society.

Rowe, John H. 1940. *Excavations in the Waterside Shell Heap, Frenchman's Bay, Maine.* Excavators Club Papers 1(3). Cambridge MA: Harvard University.

Rowse, Alfred L. 1955. *The Expansion of Elizabethan England.* New York: St. Martin's Press.

Roy, Pierre-Georges. 1921. *Inventaire des Insinuations du Conseil Souverain de la Nouvelle-France.* "Eclaireur" Limitée, Beauceville, Québec.

Royal Gazette. Frederickton NB.

Rutherford, Douglas E. 1991. The Ceramic Period of New Brunswick. In *Prehistoric Archaeology in the Maritime Provinces: Past and Present Research,* edited by Michael Deal and Susan Blair, 109–19. Reports in Archaeology no. 8. Fredericton: New Brunswick Archaeological Services, Cultural Affairs, Department of Municipalities, Culture and Housing.

Ryder, Huia. 1979. Biencourt de Poutrincourt et de Saint-Just, Jean de. *Canadian Dictionary of Biography,* vol. 1. Toronto: University of Toronto Press.

———. 1979a. Biencourt de Saint-Just, Charles. *Canadian Dictionary of Biography,* vol. 1. Toronto: University of Toronto Press.

———. 1979b. Crowne, William. *Canadian Dictionary of Biography,* vol. 1. Toronto: University of Toronto Press.

———. 1979c. Temple, Thomas. *Canadian Dictionary of Biography,* vol. 1. Toronto: University of Toronto Press.

Sabine, Lorenzo. 1852. Remnants of New England Tribes. *Christian Examiner,* vol. 52:97–117.

Sagard, Gabriel. [1636] 1866. *Histoire du Canada et Voyages Que Les Freres Mineurs Recollets Y Ont Faicts Pour La Conversion DDS Infidels . . . ,* 4 vols. Paris: E. Tross.

Salagnac, George C. 1969. Abbadie de Saint-Castin, Bernard-Anselm d'. *Dictionary of Canadian Biography,* 2. Toronto: University of Toronto Press.

———. 1969a. Abbadie de Saint-Castin, Jean Vincent d'. *Dictionary of Canadian Biography,* vol. 2. Toronto: University of Toronto Press.

———. 1969b. Pastour de Costabelle, Phillipe. *Dictionary of Canadian Biography,* vol. 2. Toronto: University of Toronto Press.

———. 1974. Abbadie de Saint-Castin, Joseph d'. *Dictionary of Canadian Biography,* vol. 3. Toronto: University of Toronto Press.

Salisbury, Neal. 1982. *Manitou and Providence.* New York: Oxford University Press.

Salwen, Burt. 1978. Indians of Southern New England and Long Island: Early Period. In *Northeast.* Vol. 15 of *Handbook of North American Indians,* edited by Bruce G. Trigger, 160–76. Washington DC: Smithsonian Institution.

Sanger, David. 1973. *Cow Point: An Archaic Cemetery in New Brunswick.* National Museums of Canada Mercury Series. Canadian Ethnology Service Paper no. 12. Ottawa.

———. 1975. Culture Change as an Adaptive Process in the Maine-Maritimes Region. *Arctic Anthropology* 12(2):60–75.

———. 1976. The Earliest Settlements. In *Maine Forms of American Architecture,* edited by Deborah Thompson, 3–14. Camden ME: *Downeast Magazine.*

———. 1979. *Discovering Maine's Archaeological Heritage.* Augusta: Maine Historic Preservation Commission.

———. 1987. *The Carson Site and the Late Ceramic Period in Passamaquoddy Bay, New Brunswick.* Canadian Museum of Civilization, Mercury Series, Paper no. 135.

———. 1988. Maritime Adaptations in the Gulf of Maine. *Archaeology of Eastern North America* 16:81–99.

———. 1991a. Five Thousand Years of Contact between Maine and Nova Scotia. *Maine Archaeological Society Bulletin* 32(2):55–61.

———. 1991b. Cow Point Revisited. In *Prehistoric Archaeology in the Maritime Provinces: Past and Present Research,* edited by Michael Deal and Susan Blair, 81–91. Reports in Archaeology no. 8. Fredericton: New Brunswick Archaeological Services, Cultural Affairs, Department of Municipalities, Culture and Housing.

Sanger, David, Ronald B. Davis, Robert G. McKay, and Harold W. Borns. 1977. The Hirundo Archaeological Project—An Interdisciplinary Approach to Central Maine History. In *Amerinds and Their Paleoenvironments in Eastern North America*, edited by Walter S. Newman and Bert Salwen, 457–71. *Annals of the New York Academy of Sciences*, vol. 288. New York.

Sanger, David, William R. Belcher, and Douglas C. Kellogg. 1992. Early Holocene Occupation at the Blackman Stream Site, Central Maine. In *Early Holocene Occupation in Northern New England*, edited by Brian S. Robinson, James B. Petersen, and Ann K. Robinson, 149–61. Occasional Publications in Maine Archaeology no. 9. Augusta: Maine Archaeological Society and Historic Preservation Commission.

Sanger, David, and Stephen A. Davis. 1991. Preliminary Report on the Bain site and the Chegoggin Archaeological Project. In *Prehistoric Archaeology in the Maritime Provinces: Past and Present Research*, edited by Michael Deal and Susan Blair, 67–79. Reports in Archaeology no. 8. Fredericton: New Brunswick Archaeological Services, Cultural Affairs, Department of Municipalities, Culture and Housing.

Sanger, David, and Mary Jo Sanger. 1986. Boom and Bust on the River: The Story of the Damariscotta Oyster Shell Heaps. *Archaeology of Eastern North America* 14:65–78.

Sawaya, Jean-Pierre. 1998. *La Fédération des Sept Feux de la Valeé du Saint-Laurent, XXVIIe–XIXe Siècle*. Quebec: Septentrion.

Schmidt, Elisabeth W. 1990. *Minority Military Service in Maine, 1775–1783*. National Society Daughters of the American Revolution.

Schneider, Richard. 1972. *Crafts of the North American Indians*. New York: Van Nostrand Reinhold.

Sewall, Joseph. 1847. The History of Bath. *Collections of the Maine Historical Society*, 1st ser., vol. 2:189–228. Portland.

Sewall, Samuel. 1973. *The Diary of Samuel Sewall*. 2 vols. New York: Farrar, Straus and Giroux.

Shaw, Charles D. 1910. Some Facts Relating to the Early History of Greenville and Moosehead Lake. Historical Collections of Piscataquis County, Maine. Dover ME: Observer Press.

Shea, John G. 1886. *The Catholic Church in Colonial Days: 1521–1753*. New York: John G. Shea.

Shipp, R. Craig, Daniel F. Belknap, and Joseph T. Kelley. 1989. A Submerged Shoreline on the Inner Continental Shelf of the Western Gulf of Maine. *Studies in Maine Geology* 5:11–28. Maine Geological Survey, Augusta.

Shurtleff, Nathaniel B., ed. 1853–54. *Records of the Governor and Company of the Massachusetts Bay*. 5 vols. in 6. Boston: William White.

Shurtleff, Nathaniel B. and David Pulsifer, eds. 1855–61. *Records of the Colony of New Plymouth, in New England*. 12 vols. in 9. Boston: William White.

Siatta, Dean J. 1998. Review of *Cahokia and Ideology in the Mississippian World*, edited by Timothy R. Pauketat and Thomas E. Emerson. *American Anthropologist* 100(1):224–25.

Siebert, Frank T. 1967. The Original Home of the Proto-Algonquian People. Contributions to Anthropology: Linguistics I (Algonquian). Anthropological Series 78, National Museum of Canada Bulletin no. 214, 13–47. Ottawa.

———. 1982. Frank Speck, Personal Reminiscences. *Papers of the Thirteenth Algonquian Conference*, 91–142. Ottawa: Carleton University.

Skaare, Kolbjørn. 1979. An Eleventh Century Norwegian Penny Found on the Coast of Maine. *Meddelelser fra Norsk Numismatisk Forening*, no. 2 (May):4–17.

Smith, Benjamin L. 1948. *An Analysis of the Maine Cemetery Complex*. Attleboro: Massachusetts Archaeological Society.

Smith, Bruce D. 1986. The Archaeology of the Southeastern United States: From Dalton to deSoto, 10, 5000–500 B.P. *Advances in World Archaeology*, vol. 5., 1–91.

———. 1997. Initial Domestication of *Crucurbita pepo* in the Americas 10,000 Years Ago. *Science* 276:932–34.

Smith, Geoffrey W. 1985. Chronology of Late Wisconsinan Deglaciation of Coastal Maine. In *Late Pleistocene History of Northeastern New England and Adjacent Quebec*, edited by H. W. Borns Jr., P. LaSalle, and W. B. Thompson. Geological Society of America Special Paper 197.

Smith, John. 1986. *The Complete Works of Captain John Smith (1580–1631)*, edited by Philip L. Barbour. 3 vols.

Chapel Hill: University of North Carolina Press.

Smith, Nicholas N. 1988. From Beads to Paper: Passamaquoddy Problems and the Dissolution of a Caughnawaga Grand Council Tradition. *Papers of the Nineteenth Algonquian Conference*, edited by William Cowan, 191–99. Ottawa: Carleton University.

———. 1989. The Economics of the Wabanaki Basket Industry. *Actes du Vingtième Congrès des Algonquiniste*, 306–16. Ottawa: Carleton University.

———. 1992. Fort La Presentation: The Abenaki. *Papers of the Twenty-Third Algonquian Conference*, 344–53. Ottawa: Carleton University.

———. 1993. The Wabanaki as Mariners. *Papers of the Twenty-Fourth Algonquian Conference*, 364–80. Ottawa: Carleton University.

Smith, Raoul N. 1977. A Description of the Penobscot and Passamaquoddy Indians in 1808. *Man in the Northeast*, no. 14:52–56.

Smith, Thomas. 1849. Extracts from Smith's Journal. In *Journals of the Rev. Thomas Smith and the Rev. Samuel Deane, Pastors of the First Church in Portland*, edited by William Willis. Portland ME: Joseph S. Bailey.

Smith, Walter B. 1922. Indian Village Site Near Bangor. In *Archaeology of Maine*, by Warren K. Moorehead, 134–45. Andover MA: Andover Press.

———. 1926. *Indian Remains of the Penobscot Valley and Their Significance.* University of Maine Studies, 2nd. ser., no. 7. Orono.

———. 1929. *The Jones Cove Shell-Heap at West Gouldsboro, Maine.* Lafayette National Park Museum Bulletin no. 1.

———. 1930. *The Lost Red Paint People of Maine.* Lafayette National Park Museum Bulletin no. 2.

Snow, Dear R. 1968. A Century of Maine Archaeology. *Maine Archaeological Society Bulletin* 8:8–25.

———. 1978. Late Prehistory of the Atlantic Coast. In *Northeast*. Vol. 15 of *Handbook of North American Indians*, edited by Bruce G. Trigger, 58–69. Washington DC: Smithsonian Institution.

———. 1980. *The Archaeology of New England.* New York: Academic Press.

Southhack, Cyprian. 1720. New England Coasting Pilot. A long roll map covering New York to Cape Canso entered at the Public Record Office, Kew, in 1720.

Speck, Frank G. 1915. Eastern Algonquian Wabanaki Confederacy. *American Anthropologist*, n.s. 17:492–508.

———. 1919. *The Functions of Wampum among the Eastern Algonquian.* Memoir of the American Anthropological Association, vol. 4. Lancaster PA.

———. 1935. Mammoth or "Stiff-Legged Bear." *American Anthropologist* 37:159–63.

———. [1940] 1970. *Penobscot Man: Life History of a Forest Tribe in Maine.* New York: Octagon Books.

Spence, Michael W., Robert H. Pihl, and Carl Murphy. 1990. Cultural Complexes of the Early and Middle Woodland Periods. In *The Archaeology of Southern Ontario to A.D. 1650*, edited by Chris J. Ellis and Neal Ferris. Occasional Publications no. 5. London: Ontario Archaeological Society.

Spiess, Arthur E. 1985. Wild Maine and the Rustication Scientist: A History of Anthropological Archaeology in Maine. *Man in the Northeast*, no. 30:101–29.

———. 1987. Faunal Remains: They May Hold Enough Information to be Called Archaeological Guidebooks. *Northern Raven*, winter 1987–88, 14–23. Woodstock VT: Center for Northern Studies.

———. 1992. Archaic Period Subsistence in New England and the Atlantic Provinces. In *Early Holocene Occupation in Northern New England*, edited by Brian S. Robinson, James B. Petersen, and Ann K. Robinson, 163–85. Occasional Publications in Maine Archaeology no. 9. Augusta: Maine Archaeological Society and Historic Preservation Commission.

Spiess, Arthur E., Bruce J. Bourque, and Steven L. Cox. 1983. Cultural Complexity in Maritime Cultures: Evidence from Penobscot Bay, Maine. In *The Evolution of Maritime Cultures on the Northeast and Northwest Coasts of America*, edited by Ronald J. Nash, 91–108. Publication no. 11. Burnaby BC: Department of Archaeology. Simon Fraser University.

Spiess, Arthur E., Bruce J. Bourque, and R. Michael Gramly. 1983. Early and Middle Archaic Site Distribution in Western Maine. *North American Archaeologist* 4(3):225–44.

Spiess, Arthur E., Mary Lou Curran, and John R. Grimes. 1985. Caribou (*Rangifer tarandus* L.) Bones from

New England Paleoindian Sites. *North American Archaeologist* 6:145–59.

Spiess, Arthur E., and Robert A. Lewis. Forthcoming. *The Turner Farm Fauna: Five Thousand Years of Hunting and Fishing in Penobscot Bay, Maine.* Occasional Publications in Maine Archaeology. Augusta: Maine Archaeological Society and Historic Preservation Commission.

Spiess, Arthur E., and Bruce D. Spiess. 1987. New England Pandemic of 1616–1622: Cause and Archaeological Implications. *Man in the Northeast*, no. 34:71–83.

Spiess, Arthur E., and Deborah B. Wilson. 1987. *Michaud: A Paleoindian Site in the New England-Maritimes Region.* Occasional Publications in Maine Archaeology no. 6. Augusta: Maine Archaeological Society and Historic Preservation Commission.

Spindler, Louise S. 1978. Menominee. In *Northeast.* Vol. 15 of *Handbook of North American Indians*, edited by Bruce G. Trigger, 708–24. Washington DC: Smithsonian Institution.

Squires, W. Austin. 1979. Argall, Sir Samuel. *Dictionary of Canadian Biography*, vol. 1. Toronto: University of Toronto Press.

Stacey, C. P. 1979. Phipps, Sir William. *Canadian Dictionary of Biography*, vol. 1. Toronto: University of Toronto Press.

Staples, Arthur C., and Roy C. Athearn. 1969. The Bear Swamp Site. *Bulletin of the Massachusetts Archaeological Society* 30(3–4):1–9.

Statement of the Kennebec Claims by the Committee Appointed by a Resolve of the General Court of the 28th of October, A.D. 1783. 1893. Pamphlet at the Maine State Library, Augusta.

Steele, Ian K. 1990. *Betrayals: Fort William Henry and the Massacre.* New York: Oxford University Press.

Stone, Lyle M. 1974. *Fort Michilimackinac: 1715–1781.* East Lansing: Michigan State University Museum.

Strachey, William. [1612] 1983. The Narrative of the North Virginia Voyage and Colony. In *The English New England Voyages*, edited by David B. Quinn and Allison M. Quinn, 397–415. London: Hakluyt Society.

Strauss, Alan E. 1987. Magic and Ritual on the Open Ocean. *Archaeology of Eastern North America* 15 (fall):125–36.

Strong, W. D. 1934. North American Indian Traditions Suggesting a Knowledge of the Mammoth. *American Anthropologist* 36:81–88.

Summers, Jack L., and René Chartrand. 1981. *Military Uniforms in Canada.* Canadian War Museum Historical Publication no. 16. Ottawa: National Museum of Man, National Museums of Canada.

Surtees, Robert J. 1985. The Iroquois in Canada. In *The History and Culture of Iroquois Diplomacy*, edited by Francis Jennings and William N. Fenton, 67–83. Syracuse: Syracuse University Press.

Sutherland, Maxwell. 1974. Philipps, Richard. *Canadian Dictionary of Biography*, vol. 3. Toronto: University of Toronto Press.

———. 1974a. Mascarene, Paul. *Canadian Dictionary of Biography*, vol. 3. Toronto: University of Toronto Press.

Taylor, Alan. 1990. *Liberty Men and Great Proprietors: Revolutionary Settlement on the Maine Frontier, 1760–1820.* Chapel Hill: University of North Carolina Press.

Taylor, Royal E. 1987 *Radiocarbon Dating: An Archaeological Perspective.* Orlando FL: Academic Press.

Thayer, Henry O. 1899. A Page of Indian History. *Collections of the Maine Historical Society*, 2nd ser., vol. 10:81–103. Portland.

Thomas, Peter A. [1979] 1990. *In the Maelstrom of Change: The Indian Trade and Cultural Process in the Middle Connecticut River Valley, 1635–1665.* New York: Garland.

———. 1992. Early and Middle Archaic Periods as Represented in Western Vermont. In *Early Holocene Occupation in Northern New England*, edited by Brian S. Robinson, James B. Petersen, and Ann K. Robinson, 187–202. Occasional Publications in Maine Archaeology no. 9. Augusta: Maine Archaeological Society and Historic Preservation Commission.

Thoreau, Henry David. 1987. *The Maine Woods.* New York: Harper and Row.

Tiller, Veronica E. V. 1996. *American Indian Reservations and Trust Areas.* Washington DC: Economic Development Administration, U.S. Department of Commerce.

Tooker, Elisabeth. 1978. History of Research. In *Northeast.* Vol. 15 of *Handbook of North American Indians*, edited by Bruce G. Trigger, 6–13. Washington DC: Smithsonian Institution.

Trask, William B. 1901. *Letters of Colonel Thomas Westbrook and Others Relative to Indian Affairs in Maine, 1722–1726.* Boston: Littlefield.

Treat, Joseph. 1820. Diary. Maine State Archives, Augusta.

Trigger, Bruce G. 1976. *Children of Aataensic: A History of the Huron People.* Montreal: McGill-Queen's University Press.

———. 1978. *Handbook of North American Indians.* Vol. 15, *Northeast.* Washington DC: Smithsonian Institution.

Trudel, Marcel. 1966. New France, 1524–1713. *Dictionary of Canadian Biography*, vol. 1. Toronto: University of Toronto Press.

True, Emma J. 1936. *History of Greenville, 1836–1936.* Augusta ME: Augusta Press.

True, Nathaniel T. [1859] 1994. *The History of Bethel, Maine.* Bowie MD: Heritage Books.

Truncer, James. 1997. Steatite Vessel Function. *Abstracts of the 62nd Annual Meeting of the Society for American Archaeology, April 2–6, 1997,* 221.

Tuck, James A. 1971. An Archaic Cemetery in Port au Choix, Newfoundland. *American Antiquity* 36(3):343–58.

———. 1976. *Ancient People of Port au Choix: The Excavation of an Archaic Indian Cemetery in Newfoundland.* Newfoundland Social and Economic Studies no. 17. St. John's: Memorial University of Newfoundland.

———. 1978a. Regional Cultural Development. In *Northeast.* Vol. 15 of *Handbook of North American Indians*, edited by Bruce G. Trigger, 28–43. Washington DC: Smithsonian Institution.

———. 1978b. Archaic Burial Ceremonialism in the "Far Northeast." *Essays in Northeastern Anthropology in Memory of Marian E. White*, edited by William E. Englebrecht and Donald Grayson, 67–77. Occasional Publications in Northeastern Anthropology, no. 5. Rindge NH: Franklin Pierce College.

———. 1982. Prehistoric Archaeology in Atlantic Canada since 1975. *Canadian Journal of Archaeology* 6:201–18.

———. 1991. The Archaic Period in the Maritime Provinces. In *Prehistoric Archaeology in the Maritime Provinces: Past and Present Research*, edited by Michael Deal and Susan Blair, 29–66. Reports in

Archaeology no. 8. Fredericton NB: New Brunswick Archaeological Services, Cultural Affairs, Department of Municipalities, Culture and Housing.

Tucker, Ephriam. 1839. *Five Months in Labrador and Newfoundland, During the Summer of 1838.* Concord NH: I. S. Boyd and W. White.

Tufts, Henry. 1930. *The Autobiography of a Criminal.* New York: Duffield and Company.

Turnbaugh, William A. 1975. Toward an Explanation of the Broadpoint Dispersal in Eastern North American Prehistory. *Journal of Anthropological Research* 31(1):51–68.

Turnbull, Christopher J. 1976. The Augustine Site: A Mound from the Maritimes. *Archaeology of Eastern North America* 4:50–62.

———. 1986. *The McKinley Collection: Another Middlesex Tradition Component from Red Bank, Northumberland County, New Brunswick.* Manuscript in Archaeology no. 17E. Fredericton NB: Department of Tourism, Recreation and Heritage.

Tuttle, Charles W. 1889. *Captain Francis Champernowne, the Dutch conquest of Acadia, and Other Historical Papers.* Boston: John Wilson and Son.

Upton, L. F. S. 1979. *Micmacs and Colonists: Indian-White Relations in the Maritimes, 1713–1867.* Vancouver: University of British Columbia Press.

Van Laer, Arnold J. F. 1932. *Correspondence of Jeremias van Rensselaer, 1651–1674.* Albany: University of the State of New York.

Vastokas, Joan M. and Romas Vastokas. 1973. *Sacred Art of the Algonquians.* Peterborough ON: Mansard Press.

Verney, Jack. 1991. *The Good Regiment: The Carignan-Salières Regiment in Canada, 1665–1668.* Toronto: McGill-Queen's University Press.

Vetromile, Rev. Eugene. 1866. *The Abenakis and their History. . .* New York: James B. Kirker. (Reprinted in 1984 by New York: AMsPress.)

Vinton, John A. 1864. *The Giles Memorial: Genealogical Memoirs of the Families Bearing the names of Giles, Gould, Holmes, Jennison, Leonard, Lindall, Curwen, Marshall, Robinson, Sampson, and Webb.* Boston: Henry W. Dutton and Son.

The Wabanakis of Maine and the Maritimes: A Resource Book

about Penobscot, Passamaquoddy, Maliseet, Micmac, and Abenaki Indians. 1989. Bath ME: American Friends Service Committee.

Walker, Willard. 1990. Wabanaki Wampum Protocol. In *Wapapi Akomutomakonol: The Wampum Records, Wabanaki Traditional Laws*, edited by Robert M. Leavitt and David A. Francis, 25–35. Micmac-Maliseet Institute. Fredericton: University of New Brunswick.

Walker, Willard, Robert Conkling, and Gregory Buesing. 1980. A Chronological Account of the Wabanaki Confederacy. In *Political Organization of Native North Americans*, edited by Ernest L. Schusky, 41–84. Washington DC: University Press of America.

Wallis, W. D., and Wallis, R. S. 1955. *The Micmac Indians of Eastern Canada*. Minneapolis: University of Minnesota Press.

Watanabe, H. 1972. *The Ainu Ecosystem*. Seattle: University of Washington Press.

Wayman, Dorothy G. 1942. *Edward Sylvester Morse, a Biography*. Cambridge: MA: Harvard University Press.

WC (Wabanaki Collection). Museum of the American Indian. Huntington Free Library, Bronx NY.

Webb, Thomas, III, Bartlein, P. J., Harrison, S. P., and Anderson, K. H. 1993. Vegetation, Lake Levels, and Climate in Eastern North America for the Past 18,000 Years. In *Global Climates since the Last Glacial Maximum*, edited by H. E. Wright, J. E. Kutzbach, T. Webb III, W. F. Ruddiman, F. A. Street-Perrot, and P. J. Bartlein, 415–67. Minneapolis: University of Minnesota Press.

Weber, J. Cynthia. 1970. Types and Attributes in the Study of Iroquois Pipes. Ph.D. diss., Harvard University, Cambridge.

Webster, John C. 1934. *Acadia at the Turn of the Seventeenth Century*. New Brunswick Museum Monograph Series, no. 1. St. John.

Weddle, Thomas K., Thomas V. Lowell, and Christopher C. Dorian. 1994. Glacial Geology of the Penobscot River Basin between Millinocket and Norway. In *Guidebook to Field Trips in North-Central Maine, New England Intercollegiate Geological Conference, 85th Annual Meeting*, edited by L. S. Hanson and D. W.

Caldwell, 193–212. Augusta: Maine Geological Survey.

Wheeler, George A. 1875. History of Castine, Penobscot and Brooksville. Bangor ME: Burr and Robinson.

Whittall, James P., II. 1984. An Archaic Cremational Burial: Eagle Bridge, Hoosick Falls, New York. *Archaeological Quarterly* 6(1).

White, John. [1630] 1968. *The Planter's Plea*. Amsterdam: Theatrum Orbis Terrarum; New York: Da Capo Press.

White, Richard. 1991. *The Middle Ground: Indians, Empires and Republics in the Great Lakes Region, 1650–1815*. New York: Cambridge University Press.

Whitehead, James L. 1939. Notes and Documents: The Autobiography of Peter Stephen Du Ponceau. *Pennsylvania Magazine of History and Biography* 61(1):189–227.

Whitehead, Ruth H. n.d. *Plant Fibre Textiles from the Hopps Site: BkCp–1*. Curatorial Report no. 59. Halifax: Nova Scotia Museum.

———. 1980. *Elitekey: Micmac Material Culture from 1600 A.D., to the Present*. Halifax: Nova Scotia Museum.

———. 1982. *Micmac Quillwork*. Halifax: Nova Scotia Museum.

———. 1991. *The Old Man Told Us*. Halifax: Nimbus Publishing.

Whiting, B. J. 1947. Incident at Quantabacook, 1764. *New England Quarterly* 20(1):169–98.

Wigglesworth, Edward. 1871. God's Controversy with New England. *Massachusetts Historical Society Proceedings*, vol. 12:89.

Will, Richard. 1981. Study of Prehistoric Bone Tools from the Turner Farm Site, North Haven, Maine. Master's thesis, University of Maine, Orono.

———. 1996. *Phase III Archaeological Date Recovery at the Little Ossippee North Site (7.7), Bonny Eagle Project (FERC #2529), Cumberland County, Maine*. Draft report prepared for Central Maine Power Company, Augusta.

Willey, Gordon, and Jeremy Sabloff. 1993. *A History of American Archaeology*. New York: W. H. Freeman and Company.

Williams, Stephen. 1994. *Fantastic Archaeology: The Wild Side of American Archaeology*. Philadelphia: University of Pennsylvania Press.

Williamson, William D. [1832] 1991. *The History of the State of Maine: From Its First Discovery, A.D. 1602, to the Separation, A.D. 1820, Inclusive*. Bowie MD: Heritage Books.

Willis, William. 1972. *The History of Portland*. Somerswoath NH: New Hampshire Publishing.

Willoughby, Charles C. 1898. *Prehistoric Burial Places in Maine*. Archaeological and Ethnological Papers of the Peabody Museum, vol. 1, no. 6. Cambridge MA.

———. 1905. Textile fabrics of the New England Indians. *American Anthropologist*, n.s. 7:85–93.

———. 1909. Pottery of the New England Indians. *Putnam Anniversary Volume*, pp. 83–101. Cambridge MA: Peabody Museum.

———. 1924. *Indian Burial Place in Winthrop, Massachusetts*. Papers of the Peabody Museum of American Archaeology and Ethnology, vol. 11, no. 1. Cambridge MA.

———. [1935] 1973. *Antiquities of the New England Indians*. New York: AMS Press.

———. [1924] 1978. *Indian Burial Place at Winthrop, Massachusetts*. Millwood NY: Krauss Reprint.

Wilson, Deborah, and Arthur Spiess. 1990. Study Unit I: Fluted Point Paleoindian. *Maine Archaeological Society Bulletin* 30(1):15–32.

Winslow, Edward. [1622] 1974. *Relation . . . of the Beginnings and Proceedings of the English Plantation Settled at Plimouth in New England* (Mourt's Relation). Norwood NJ: Walter J. Johnson.

Winthrop, John. 1853. *Winthrop's Journal, "History of New England," 1630 to 1649*, edited by James K. Hosmer. New York: Charles Scribner's Sons.

Winthrop Papers. 1929. Massachusetts Historical Society, Boston.

Witthoft, John. 1949. An Outline of Pennsylvania Indian History. *Pennsylvania Archaeologist* 16(3):3–15.

———. 1953. Broad Spearpoints and the Transitional Period Cultures. *Pennsylvania Archaeologist* 23(1):4–31.

Wolf, Eric. 1982. *Europe and the People Without History*. Berkeley: University of California Press.

Wood, William. [1634] 1865. *New England's Prospect*. Boston: Prince Society.

Wroth, L. Kinvin. 1975. *Province in Rebellion: A Documentary History of the Founding of the Commonwealth of Massachusetts, 1773–1785*. Cambridge MA: Harvard University Press.

Wyman, Jeffries. 1868. A Recent Examination of Shell Heaps on Goose Island in Casco Bay, Maine. *Boston Society of Natural History Proceedings*, vol. 11.:288–89.

———. 1868a. An Account of Some Kjoekkenmoeddings, or Shell Heaps, in Maine and Massachusetts. *American Naturalist* 1(11)561–65.

———. 1875. Fresh-Water Shell Mounds of the St. Johns River, Florida. *Peabody Academy of Science Memoirs*, vol. 1, no. 4. Salem MA.

YD (*York Deeds*), various editors. 1897–1910. 18 vols. Portland and Bethel ME: various publishers.

Young, Alexander. 1846. Early Records of Charlestown. In *Chronicles of the First Planters of the Colony of Massachusetts Bay, 1623–1636*. Boston: C. C. Little and J. Brown.

Zielinski, G. A., P. A. Mayewski, L. D. Meeker, S. Whitlow, M. S. Twicker, M. Morrison, D. A. Meese, A. J. Crow, and R. B. Alley. 1994. Record of Volcanism since 7000 B.C. from DISP2 Greenland Ice Core and Implications for the Volcano-Climate System. *Science* 264:948–52.

Zoltvany, Yves F. 1969. Callière, Louis-Hector de. *Dictionary of Canadian Biography*, vol. 2. Toronto: University of Toronto Press.

———. 1974. *Phillipe de Rigaud de Vaudreuil: Governor of New France 1703–1725*. Toronto: McClelland and Stewart.

INDEX

Illustrations are indicated by page references followed by an *i*. Photographs are indicated by *p* and maps are indicated by *m*.

Maine Department of Transportation, 27

Maine Geological Survey, 18

Maine Historic Preservation Commission, 27, 30

Maine Indian Claims Settlement Act (1980), 232, 247

Maine Law Review, 247

Maine Paleo-Indians: animal species hunted by, 36, 37–38; decline of, 37–38; early evidence of, 20; summary of occupation by, 33–36

Maine Paleo-Indian sites: Adkins, 25–27, 26*p*, 28*i*; Dam, 30–31*p*, 34*p*; Lamoreau, 29*p*; of late Paleo-Indian period, 31–33; Michaud, 27–30, 29*p*; Munsungan Lake, 20–21*p*; Vail site/Magalloway Valley complex, 22–27

Maine, selected localities map, 8*m*

Maine Native Americans. *See* Eastern Indians

Maine State Museum, xv, 7, 30, 45

maize-bean-squash trinity, 86–87

maize horticulture: during Ceramic period, 86–87; impact on Maine Native Americans by, 108

Maliseet camp scene (1840) [Herries watercolor over pencil], 270*i*

Maliseets (Etchemins): Annapolis Royal raids (1724) by, 194, 198; break with Caughnawaga by, 244; conditions of modern, 247–48; Dover raid (1689) by, 162; economic activities/employment of, 230, 232; European description of women, 265–66; formerly western Etchemin group, 144; guides preparing for night fishing, 236*i*; guides on St. John River (1882), 234*i*; medal (1778) given to, 213*p*; moose-hair embroidery by, 291; response to Wiscasset incident by, 200; spearfishing for salmon, 236*i*; support during Revolutionary War by, 212, 213–14, 225–26; treaty (1776) between Massachusetts and, 212. *See also* Passamaquoddies (Maliseets)

mammoth species, 17*p*, 17–19

"Map of the Province of New Hampshire" (Blanchard and Langdon), 206*p*

maps: Aubery (1715), 182*m*; *Carte pour servir Eclaircissement du Papier Terrier de la Nouvelle France*, 134*m*; Dummer's War (1721–26), 192*m*; English 1688, 161*m*; Fort Brunswick, 183*m*; French claims/settlements (1604–1763) in Maine, 211*m*; French and Indian Wars (1745–63), 198*m*; Gulf of Maine watershed, 6*m*; Indian tribes, trading posts, settlements (1620–76), 130*m*; King Philip's War (1675–78), 149*m*; King William's War (1688–99), 150*m*; Lescarbot (1609), 114*m*; Maine coastal explorations (1524–1614), 112*m*; plan of St. George Fort, 117*m*; Queen Anne's War (1703–13), 176*m*; of Saco by Champlain (1613), 116*m*; selected localities of Maine, 8*m*; Vail site (Paleo-Indian), 23*m*

Maquas (Mohawks), 165

marine conditions: Ceramic period, 84–86; Late Archaic period, 50; Middle Archaic period, 45–46; Moorehead phase, 53–55, 56–57. *See also* animal species; diet

Maritime Archaic tradition, 57, 61

Maritime Peninsula: Early Archaic sites at, 39*p*; historical record of, 104–5; late Paleo-Indian points on, 31–33; mortuary practices during Early Archaic period of, 42–43; Natives of the, 105–8, 318 n.70; rocker stamping pottery of, 76, 79; role in Maine's cultural dynamism by, xvi–xvii

Massachusetts: declaration of war against Eastern Indians, 201–2; fortification proposal (King William's War), 165*p*; military commission of, 184*p*; Passamaquoddies cede land (1794) to, 226, 240–41; Penobscots cede land (1818, 1833) to, 217–18; proclamation of day of thanksgiving (1675), 151*p*; response to Native complaints (1764) by, 207–8; treaty (1776) between Maliseets and, 212. *See also* New England

Mather, Cotton, 157, 180

Mattawamkeag, 216, 217

Meductic (Maliseet mission village), 229–30

Meiaskwat, Charles, 133

Membertou, 115

Meneer, Philip, 176

Meneval, Governor, 164

Menneville, Ange de, Marquis Duquesne, 202

Michaud site artifacts, 29*p*

Michaud site (Paleo-Indian), 27–30

Micmac canoe, 276*p*

Micmac pipe, 308

Micmacs (Souriquois): description of trading parties, 263; economic activities/employment (19th century) of, 232–35; during King George's War, 197, 198, 199; moose-hair embroidery by, 291; naming of, 144; raids during Dummer's War by, 186, 192–93, 194; state of modern, 247, 248; support during Revolutionary War by, 212, 213

Middle Archaic period, 43–46

"Minerall stone," 280

mission era. *See* eighteenth century

mission villages: establishment of interior, 171–72; Meductic (Maliseet), 229–30

Mitchell, Alice, 230*p*

Mitchell, Peter, 230*p*

moccasins, 253*p*, 254

Mohawks: Abenakis fear of, 133, 134–35; assistance during Dummer's War by, 193–94; conflict with other tribes by, 127; Covenant Chain alliance and, 174–75, 239; fur trade by, 132; Iroquois League strategy regarding, 134–35; Jesuit conversions among, 174; during King William's

War, 162–63; role in King Philip's War by, 156; surge in warfare by, 138–40; Wabanaki Confederacy and, 235, 239. *See also* Iroquois

Mohegans, 139

Mohotoworomet (Robin Hood), 139, 143

Molliocket (Marie Agathe), 284, 285

Montagnais, 127

Montcalm, Marquis de, 202, 204

Moorehead, Warren K., 5, 51, 52

Moorehead phase (Late Archaic period): artifacts of, 52*p*, 56*p*, 58*p*, 59*p*, 60*p*; disappearance of, 61; marine hunting during, 53; Red Paint cemeteries of, 4, 5, 51–54; relations between contemporaneous cultures and, 55–61; similarities of Maritime Archaic tradition to, 57, 61; Susquehanna tradition compared to, 62–64, 65–66

Moose Brook, 27, 30

moose-hair embroidery, 291

moose population (Ceramic period), 84

moose "wool," 283

Morain, Jean, 138

Morse, Sylvester S., 3, 4

mortuary practices: of Early Archaic period populations, 42–43; of Moorehead phase/Maritime Archaic tradition, 61; of Susquehanna tradition, 65–66. *See also* burial mounds

Muddy River, 65

Munsungan Lake, 20, 26

Munsungan Lake site (Paleo-Indian), 20–21*p*

Muscongus Company, 184–85, 186

musket with matchlock, 135*p*

narrow hexagonal bayonets (Cow Point cemetery), 59*p*

narrow slate bayonets (Moorehead-phase cemeteries), 59*p*

Narrows site (Late Archaic period), 48–49

Native accommodation strategy (late 17th century), 172–74. *See also* Covenant Chain alliance

Native Americans, 9. *See also* Native North Americans

Native basket industry. *See* basketry

Native baskets (20th century), 239*p*

Native basket sellers (19th century), 235*p*, 237*p*

Native clothing: basic, 252; brooches/coronets (18th century), 268–69; decoration/variations of, 254–56; European description of, 262–66; headdresses, 266, 268; of males (19th century), 266–68; materials of personal ornaments used in, 256–58; moccasins, 253*p*, 254; painting of body/hair to enhance, 261–62; Passamaquoddy female's costume, 260*i*; pre-European, 251, 254–56; shell beads used on, 259–60; women's body robes, 254

Native cultural education, 247–48

Native fibers/textiles, 282–88

Native gear manufacturing: basketry, 292–97; birchbark material used in, 288–92; fibers and textiles used in weaving, 282–84, 286–88; gender roles in, 281–82; household items, 302–9; weaponry, 298–302; wooden ware, 298*p*

Native land deeds, 140–42

Native languages, 105

Native Maine culture: clothing, accessories, decorative techniques of, 251–69; fire technology of, 280–81; materials/manufacturing gear, 281–309; promoting education on, 247–48; shelter/housing of, 218, 219*p*, 225, 269–73; transportation of, 273–80

Native music recording (1890), 227

Native North American-European contacts: Bellenger's comments on, 249–50; Columbus's voyages as, 111, 113–14; during European trade/settlement, 120–21; evolution from friendly to conflict, 121, 123–27; first encounters of, 113–14; in fur trade, 115, 117–18; significance of, 111–13; virgin-soil epidemics through, 113, 118–20

Native North Americans: accommodation strategy by, 172–73; bands, tribes, clans of, 107–8; Covenant Chain alliance of, 150, 159, 160*i*, 173–75, 239; cultural education promoted by, 248; definitions/terms referring to, 9–11; description of 19th century Maine village of, 218; following the King Philip's War, 156–57; governmental relations with, 244–46; images used as decorative elements, 206*p*; map showing settlements (1688) of, 161*m*; map showing settlements (1715) of, 182*m*; map showing tribes (1620–76) of, 130*m*; of the Maritime Peninsula, 105–8, 318 n.70; political reemergence in 20th century of, 246–48; population/ethnicity (17th century) of, 142–44; recording of music (1890) by, 227; response to American Revolution by, 209–10, 212–15; response to King Philip's War by, 152; sagamore authority among early, 115; "virgin-soil epidemics" suffered by, 113, 118–20; weakening resolve during King William's War of, 165–68. *See also* Eastern Indians; Native Maine culture

Native transportation: canoe styles, 274; construction of canoes for, 274–80; description of canoes, 273–74; snowshoes, 252*p*, 279*p*, 279–80

Native village (19th century), 218

Native women: basketry labor role of, 294–95; body robes of, 254; craft roles of, 280–81; Penobscot woman weaving, 285*p*; portraits (19th century) of, 224*p*; weaving techniques used by, 282–88

Nelson, Philomene, 241

Neptune, Francis Joseph, 226

Penobscot river driver (ambrotype), 227*p*

Penobscot River Valley, 14

Penobscots (Etchemins): Abenaki "moose slaughter" (1850) protested by, 222–23; Bar Harbor camp (19th century), 238*p*; basketmakers, 235*p*; breaks with Caughnawaga council by, 243; during/following Dummer's War, 192, 194, 197; economic activities/employment of, 223, 224; encroachment of English settlement and, 204, 206, 207; government protection of region for, 207–8; Old Party/New Party rivalry of, 218–19, 226–27; response to Wiscassett incident by, 199–200, 207; after the Revolution, 215–18, 220, 222–23, 225; during St. George's War, 199; Seven Years' War and, 201–4; state of modern, 247–48; state-run trust fund for, 218; support of Revolutionary War by, 212, 213–14

Penobscot silver brooches, 222*p*

Penobscot snowshoes, 279*p*

Penobscot woman weaving (1910), 285*p*

percussion fire technique, 280

pestle (stone) [Ceramic period], 100*p*

Petersen, James, 32

petroglyphs (rock art) [early Ceramic period], 96–97

pewter vessels (Old Point), 190*p*

Phélypeaux de Pontchartrain, Louis, 179

Philip (Pokanoket chief sachem), 148–49, 153

Phillips, Richard, 192

Phillips Academy, 5

Phips, Spencer, 200, 202, 203

Phips, William, 104, 164, 166, 167, 169

pictographs (Western Maine), 97

pièces esquillées (stone wedges), 22

Plan of a New Cleared American Farm (1791–92), 216*p*

Pleistocene epoch: animal species of late, 16–17, 19–20; deglaciation of Maine during, 14–17, 15*i*; glacial period of, 13; retreat of glaciers during end of, 14

plummets (Moorehead-phase cemeteries), 58*p*

Plymouth Colony: Native liquor trade at, 129; Native welcome to Pilgrims of, 121; small pox epidemic (1633) in, 119–20

Polis, Joe, 222

Ponchartrain, 181

Popham Colony, 120

porcupine quills decoration, 255–56*p*, 291

Portneuf (Indian chief), 165, 166

Port Royal (Nova Scotia): captured by English (1654), 137; captured by English (1690), 164; de Monts expedition moved to, 118; returned to France (1667), 138; sacking of (1631), 120; view of de Monts's habitation at, 116*i*

pot (North Carolina, 1585) [White watercolor], 83*i*

pottery: Ceramic period artifacts, 77*p*, 78*p*, 79*p*, 80*p*, 81*p*, 82*p*; Ceramic period innovations for, 75–76, 79–80, 82–83

pouches (19th century), 257*p*

powder horn (18th or 19th century), 302*p*

Powell, John Wesley, 4, 5

Preble, Jedediah, 204

Preble, John, 214

Pre-Dorset (or Paleo-Eskimo) culture, 61

Presumpscot formation, 14, 17

Pring, Martin, 118, 257, 273, 300

projectile points (Early Archaic period), 40*p*

projectile points/scrapers (Ceramic period), 90*p*

pseudo-scallop shell stamping pottery (Ceramic period), 77*p*, 79

Purchase, Thomas, 121, 152

Putnam, Frederick Ward, 4

quahog (*Mercenaria mercenaria*) [Damariscotta heaps], 86

Quebec, 163–64

Queen Anne's War (1703–13): handbill on fur prices during, 177*i*; King's presents during, 175, 184; map of, 176*m*; origins/events of, 175–81; Treaty of Utrecht and aftermath of, 182–86

rabbit skin/textile, 283–84

radiocarbon dating, 10

Rale, Sébastien, 171, 177–78, 184–85, 186, 187, 194; writing box of, 187*p*

Rale monument, 191*p*

Ramah chert points (Moorehead phase), 56*p*

Randolph, Edward, 160, 161–62

Razilly, Isaac de, 120–21, 136

Red Paint cemeteries (Moorehead phase), 4, 5, 51–54

religious ceremonialism: during early Ceramic period, 94–97, 100; rock art and shaminism, 96. *See also* Catholic missionary activities

Revolutionary War: Abenaki at Valley Forge during, 214; Abenakis following the, 215; continued settlement following the, 217; Native responses during, 209–10, 212–15; Penobscots following the, 215–18, 220, 222–23, 225

rib basket forms, 292

Rigaud, Philippe de, Marquis de Vaudreuil, 176

Ritchie, William A., 38, 66

Robert Abbe Museum of Stone Age Antiquities, 5

Robinau de Portneuf, René, 164

Robin Hood (Mohotoworomet), 139, 143

Robinson, Hans, 207, 208